MW01120502

Baking and Pastry Formulas

Baking

and Pastry

Formulas

Educational Task Force

JOHNSON & WALES UNIVERSITY College of Culinary Arts *Volume* II

Harborside Press
Providence, Rhode Island

© Johnson & Wales University College of Culinary Arts,
1985, 1988, 1992, 1996, and 1997.

Published by: Harborside Press
765 Allens Avenue
Providence, Rhode Island 02905

All rights reserved. No part of this publication may be
reproduced, stored in a retrieval system, or transmitted,
in any form or by any means, electronic, mechanical,
photocopying, recording, or otherwise, without the prior
written permission of the publisher.

Senior developmental editors: Johnson & Wales Food/
    Educational Task Force & Firebrand LLC
Cover design: Firebrand LLC
Interior design: Firebrand LLC
Production & Coordination: Firebrand LLC
Photography: YUM and Others
Photographer: Ronald Manville, YUM
Food stylist: James E. Griffin

ISBN: 1-890724-05-x

Printed in the United States of America

Contents

Message From the President

The College of Culinary Arts of Johnson & Wales is committed to your success as a future foodservice professional. The revised curriculum of the College of Culinary Arts, presented in these textbooks, is a reflection of this commitment. This carefully designed yet flexible curriculum provides you with an exciting challenge to learn and to excel in your foodservice career.

Our unique *upside-down* curriculum ensures your immediate, hands-on involvement with your chosen profession. Your laboratory and related classroom studies provide valuable experiences to build confidence in your skills.

Clearly, your formal education in the baking and pastry arts is only the beginning of your lifelong study. This education, however, is the foundation on which your success will be built, a foundation established by *Volume 1— Fundamentals* and *Volume 2—Formulas*. In these books

you will learn the behind-the-scenes facts and theories of preparation and presentation. These fundamentals will prepare you to explore, discover, and create your own food frontiers.

The faculty and staff of the College of Culinary Arts have spent thousands of hours and dedicated years of their own knowledge and experience to the development of this curriculum. I urge you to use these books as a tool, a resource, a guide. I invite you to learn from them and to enjoy the learning.

The success of the Johnson & Wales vision for the College of Culinary Arts can only be judged by your success as a culinarian. We are proud of you, our student, of the graduate you will become, and of these volumes of knowledge that you will take with you throughout your baking and pastry career.

John A. Yena
President

Message From the Director

I am very happy to welcome you to Johnson & Wales University's International Baking & Pastry Institute.

More than once, I'm sure, you have eaten a dessert or pastry that tasted so delicious and looked so beautiful that you preserved its image in your mind hoping that someday you would be able to recreate its taste, aroma, and beauty.

There are young chefs today who can create an incredible plated dessert of chocolate mousse but don't know the basics of poaching a pear or making a simple pie crust: This is wrong. I believe you have to master the basics before you can start thinking and creating with your head.

The great news is that both are possible with proper instruction and discipline. Soon you will be able to recapture the memories of that spectacular dessert and begin to design your own desserts and pastries as quickly and easily as opening a jar. But first, you must pay attention, discipline yourself, and learn all the basics and techniques.

Savor the knowledge you learn here; don't rush things. Knowledge is a wonderful thing, especially in the pastry profession. In order to succeed you must embrace and possess knowledge—a vital factor in achievement.

I truly believe that you *will* achieve. How do I know that? Because you chose to educate yourself at Johnson & Wales University. Welcome. And good luck.

Lars Johansson
Director
International Baking and Pastry Institute

Acknowledgments

The International Baking and Pastry Institute textbooks have been written by people who truly love baking. I wish to thank all the faculty, administration, and friends of the university for their support and participation in this tremendous undertaking. Their collective work represents their dedication to educating students who will keep the flame of culinary inspiration alive for fuuture generations.

Thomas L. Wright

Vice President
Culinary Education

Special thanks to the following individuals for their tireless efforts and dedication in producing these textbooks:

Pauline Allsworth	James Griffin	Paul J. McVety	Christine Stamm
Linda Beaulieu	Karl Guggenmos	Robert Nograd	Michel Vienne
Dr. Barbara Bennett	Edward Korry	Pamela Peters	Bradley Ware
Lynn Dieterich	Victoria A. McCrae	Jacquelyn B. Scott	

Educational Task Force

Carolyn Buster	Jean-Jacques Dietrich	Edward Korry	Christine Stamm
Martha Crawford	Meridith Ford	Robert Nograd	Frank Terranova
Elaine Cwynar	Karl Guggenmos	Pamela Peters	William Travis
Mary Ann DeAngelis	Frederick Haddad	Patrick Reed	Bradley Ware
John Dion	Lars Johannson	Janet Rouslin	

Providence Administration, Faculty and Support Staff

Thomas L. Wright, M.S., Vice President of Culinary Education

Jean-Michel Vienne, C.C.P., C.E.P., C.A.P., Dean, College of Culinary Arts

Dorothy Jeanne Allen, M.S., Associate Professor; A.S., B.S., M.S., Johnson & Wales University

Pauline Allsworth, Office Manager

Frank Andreozzi, B.S., Assistant Professor; B.S., Providence College

Charles Armstrong, A.O.S., Instructor; A.O.S., Culinary Institute of America

Soren Arnoldi, Danish Master Chef, Associate Instructor; Falke Hotel, Tivoli Gardens Wivex, Palace Hotel, Copenhagen, Apprenticeship

John Aukstolis, A.S., Instructor; A.S., Johnson & Wales University

Adrian Barber, A.O.S., Associate Instructor; A.O.S., Culinary Institute of America

Claudia Berube, A.S., Instructor; A.S., Johnson & Wales University

Steven Browchuk, M.A., Certified T.I.P.S. Trainer, Associate Professor; B.A., Roger Williams College; M.A., University of Sorbonne; M.A., Middlebury College

Victor Calise, Associate Instructor

Carl Calvert, B.S., Instructor; A.O.S., B.S., Johnson & Wales University

Gerianne Chapman, M.B.A., Associate Professor; A.O.S., B.S., Johnson & Wales University; B.A., George Washington University; M.B.A., University of Rhode Island

John S. Chiaro, M.S., C.E.C., C.C.E., Associate Professor; B.A., Rhode Island College; M.S., Johnson & Wales University

Cynthia Coston, A.S., Instructor; A.S., Schoolcraft College

Laurie Coughlin, Administrative Assistant

Martha Crawford, B.S., C.W.P.C., Instructor; A.O.S., Culinary Institute of America; B.S., University of Michigan

Elaine R. Cwynar, B.A., Associate Instructor; A.S., Johnson & Wales University; B.A., University of Connecticut

William J. Day, M.S., C.F.E., Associate Professor and Director of Continuing Education; B.S., Bryant College; M.S., Johnson & Wales University

Mary Ann DeAngelis, M.S., Assistant Professor; B.S., M.S., University of Rhode Island

Richard DeMaria, B.S., Instructor; B.S., University of Rhode Island

Jean-Luc Derron, Associate Instructor; Hotel Schwanen Switzerland; steinli Trade School, Switzerland, Apprenticeship; Certification, Department of Labor and Trade, Switzerland; Confiserie Bachmann, Switzerland, Apprenticeship

Lynn Dieterich, Coordinator Faculty Support Services

Jean Jacques Dietrich, M.A., Senior Instructor; A.S., New York City Technological College; B.A., Hunter College; M.A., Johnson & Wales University

John R. Dion, B.S.,., C.E.C., C.C.E., Associate Instructor; A.O.S., Culinary Institute of America; B.S., Johnson & Wales University

Rene R. Dionne, Director of Corporate Relations/ Purchasing

Reginald B. Dow, A.O.S., Storeroom Manager; A.O.S., Culinary Institute of America

Kevin Duffy, B.S., Instructor; B.S., Johnson & Wales University

Thomas Dunn, B.S., Instructor; A.O.S., B.S., Johnson & Wales University

Roger Dwyer, B.A., Instructor; B.A., George Washington University

Neil Fernandes, B.S., Storeroom Office Manager; B.S. Johnson & Wales University

Paula Figoni, M.B.A., Instructor; B.S., University of Massachusetts; M.S., University of California; M.B.A., Simmons College Graduate School of Management

Ernest Fleury, M.S., Associate Professor, A.O.S., Johnson & Wales University; A.S., Community College of Rhode Island; B.S., M.S., Johnson & Wales University

Meridith Ford, B.S., Instructor; A.O.S., B.S., Johnson & Wales University

James Fuchs, A.O.S., Instructor; A.O.S., Johnson & Wales University

Nancy Garnett-Thomas, M.S., R.D., L.D.N., Associate Professor; A.O.S., Culinary Institute of America; B.A., Colby College; M.S., University of Rhode Island

William Gormley, B.S., Instructor; A.O.S., B.S., Johnson & Wales University

James Griffin, M.S., C.W.C., C.C.E., Associate Dean & Associate Professor; A.O.S., B.S., M.S., Johnson & Wales University

Frederick Haddad, A.O.S., C.E.C., C.C.E., Associate Instructor; A.O.S., Culinary Institute of America

Rainer Hienerwadel, B.S., Instructor; A.O.S., B.S., Johnson & Wales University

J. Jeffrey Howard, B.A., Instructor; B.A., University of Massachusetts

Lars E. Johansson, C.P.C., C.C.E., Director, International Baking & Pastry Institute

Steven Kalble, A.S., Instructor; A.S., Johnson & Wales University

Linda Kender, B.S., Associate Instructor; A.S., B.S., Johnson & Wales University

Edward Korry, M.A., Assistant Professor; B.A., University of Chicago; M.A., University of Cairo

C. Arthur Lander, B.S.; Instructor; B.S., Johnson & Wales University

Kelly Lawton, Administrative Assistant

Hector Lipa, B.S., C.E.C., C.C.E., Associate Instructor; B.S., University of St. Augustine, the Philippines

Laird Livingston, A.O.S., C.E.C., C.C.E., Associate Instructor; A.O.S., Culinary Institute of America

Michael D. Marra, M.Ed., Associate Professor; B.A., M.Ed., Providence College

Susan Desmond-Marshall, M.S., Associate Professor; B.S., University of Maine; M.S., Johnson & Wales University

Victoria A. McCrae, Assistant to the Vice President

Diane McGarvey, B.S., Instructor; A.O.S., B.S., Johnson & Wales University

Jack McKenna, B.S., C.E.C., C.C.E., C.C.P., Director of Special Projects

Paul J. McVety, M.Ed., Assistant Dean and Associate Professor; A.S., B.S., Johnson & Wales University; M.Ed., Providence College

Michael Moskwa, M.Ed., Assistant Professor; B.A.,

University of Rhode Island; M.Ed., Northeastern University

Sean O'Hara, M.S., Certified T.I.P.S. Trainer, Instructor; A.O.S., B.S., M.S., Johnson & Wales University

George O'Palenick, M.S., C.E.C., C.C.E., Associate Professor; A.O.S., Culinary Institute of America; A.S., Jamestown Community College; B.S., M.S., Johnson & Wales University

Robert Pekar, B.S., Associate Instructor; A.O.S., Culinary Institute of America; A.S., Manchester Community College; B.S., Johnson & Wales University

Pamela Peters, A.O.S.,C.E.C., C.C.E., Director of Culinary Education; A.O.S., Culinary Institute of America

David Petrone, B.S., Associate Instructor; A.O.S., B.S., Johnson & Wales University

Felicia Pritchett, M.S., Associate Professor; A.O.S., B.S., M.S., Johnson & Wales University

Thomas J. Provost, Instructor

Ronda Robotham, B.S., Instructor; B.S., Johnson & Wales University

Robert Ross, B.S., Associate Instructor; A.S., B.S., Johnson & Wales University

Janet Rouslin, B.S., Instructor; B.S., University of Maine

Cynthia Salvato, A.S., C.E.P.C., Instructor; A.S., Johnson & Wales University

Stephen Scaife, B.S., C.E.C., C.C.E., Associate Instructor; A.O.S., Culinary Institute of America, B.S., Johnson & Wales University

Gerhard Schmid, Associate Instructor; European Apprenticeship, Germany

Louis Serra, B.S., C.E.C., Instructor; A.O.S., B.S, Johnson & Wales University

Christine Stamm, M.S., C.W.C., Associate Professor; A.O.S., B.S., M.S., Johnson & Wales University

Laura Schwenk, Administrative Assistant

Adela Tancayo-Sannella, Certified T.I.P.S. Trainer, Associate Instructor

Mary Ellen Tanzi, B.A., Instructor; B.A., Rhode Island College

Frank Terranova, B.S., C.E.C., C.C.E., Associate Instructor; B.S., Johnson & Wales University

Segundo Torres, B.S., Associate Instructor; B.S., Johnson & Wales University

Helene Houde-Trzcinski, M.S., Instructor; B.S., M.S., Johnson & Wales University

Peter Vaillancourt, B.S., Instructor; B.S., Roger Williams College

Paul VanLandingham, Ed.D, C.E.C., IMP, CFBE, C.C.E., Professor; A.O.S, Culinary Institute of America; B.S., Roger Williams College; M.A., Anna Maria College; Ed.D., Nova University

Suzanne Vieira, M.S., R.D., L.D.N., Department Chair, Foodservice Academic Studies; Associate Professor; B.S., Framingham State College; M.S., University of Rhode Island

Bradley Ware, M.Ed., C.C.C., C.C.E., Associate Professor; A.S., Johnson & Wales University; B.S., Michigan State University; M.Ed., Providence College; C.A.G.S., Salve Regina University

Gary Welling, A.O.S., Instructor; A.O.S., Johnson & Wales University

Robin Wheeler, Receptionist

Ed Wilroy, B.A., Continuing Education Coordinator; A.O.S., Johnson Wales University; B.A., Auburn University

Kenneth Wollenberg, B.S., Associate Instructor; A.O.S., B.S., Johnson & Wales University

Robert Zielinski, A.S., Instructor; A.S., Johnson & Wales University

Branch Campuses Administration and Faculty

CHARLESTON
Karl Guggenmos, B.S., C.E.C., G.C.M.C., Director of Culinary Education

Diane Aghapour, B.S., Instructor

Patricia Agnew, M.E., Assistant Professor

Donna Blanchard, B.A., Instructor

Robert Bradham, Instructor

Matthew Broussard, C.W.C., Instructor

Jan Holly Callaway, Instructor

Wanda Crooper, B.S., C.C.E., C.W.P.C., Associate Instructor

James Dom, M.S., Associate Professor

Armin Gronert, G.C.M.P.C., Associate Instructor

Kathy Hawkins, Instructor

David Hendrieksen, B.S., C.C.E., C.C.C., Associate Instructor

Andrew Hoxie, M.A., Assistant Professor

John Kacaia, C.E.C., Instructor

Michael Koons, A.O.S., C.E.C., C.C.E., Associate Instructor

Audrey McKnight, A.O.S., Instructor

Mary McLellan, M.S., Adjunct

Marcel Massenet, C.E.P.C., Associate Instructor

Stephen Nogle, A.A.S., C.E.C., C.C.E., Associate Instructor

Daniel Polasek, Instructor

Frances Ponsford, B.S., Instructor

Lloyd Regier, Ph.D., Adjunct

Victor Smurro, B.S., C.C.C., Associate Instructor

Susan Wigley M.Ed., C.C.E., C.W.C., Associate Professor

NORFOLK
Robert Nograd, Acting Director

Fran Adams, M.S., Instructor; B.S., M.S., Old Dominion University

Guy Allstock, III, M.S., Storeroom Instructor; B.S., M.S., Johnson & Wales University

Christian Barney, B.A., Associate Instructor; B.A., Old Dominion University

Ed Batten, A.O.S., Instructor; A.O.S., Johnson & Wales University

Susan Batten, C.E.C., C.C.E., Culinary Technology Degree, Associate Instructor; Culinary Technology Degree, Asheville Buncombe Technical Institute

Bettina Blank, M.S., Instructor; B.S., Grand Valley State University; M.S., Boston University

Dedra Butts, B.S., Instructor; B.S., Johnson & Wales University

Tim Cameron, M.A., C.E.C., Associate Professor; B.A., Milligan College; M.A., Old Dominion

Donna Curtis, B.A., Instructor; B.A., Northern Michigan University; Reading Specialist Degree, Memphis State University.

Art M. Elvins, A.A.S., C.E.C., Associate Instructor; A.A.S., Johnson & Wales University

Kristen Fletcher, R.D., M.S., Instructor; B.S., M.S., Virginia Polytechnic Institute

Scarlett Holmes-Paul, M.A., Instructor; B.S. Western Michigan University; M.A. Eastern Michigan University

Joan Hysell, M.Ed., Instructor; B.P.S., SUNY Institute of Technology at Utica/Rome; M.Ed., Ohio University

John Keating, M.S., Oenology Instructor; B.S., Georgetown University; M.S., George Washington University

Lisa Kendall, M.A., Instructor; B.A., State University of New York; M.A., Old Dominion University

Greg Kopanski, M.S., Instructor; B.S., New York University; M.S., Old Dominion University.

Jerry Lanuzza, B.S., Instructor; B.S., Johnson & Wales University

Peter Lehmuller, B.A., Instructor; A.O.S., Culinary Institute of America; B.A., State University of New York, Albany

Alex Leuzzi, M.S., Associate Instructor; B.S., Pikesville College; M.S., Fairleigh Dickinson University

Melanie Loney, M.S., Associate Instructor; B.S., M.S., Old Dominion University

Mary Matthews, M.S., Instructor; B.S., M.S., Old Dominion University

Carrie Moranha, A.A.S., Dining Room /Beverage Instructor; A.A.S. Johnson & Wales University

Maureen Nixon, M.A., Instructor; B.A., North Carolina State University; M.A., Norfolk State University.

Shelly Owens, B.A., Baking & Pastry Instructor; B.A., Townson State University

Patrick Reed, A.O.S, C.C.C., C.C.E., Associate Instructor; A.O.S., Culinary Institute of America

Gregory Retz, B.S., Instructor; A.A.S., Johnson & Wales University; B.S., Virginia Polytechnic

Steven Sadowski, C.E.C., A.O.S., Associate Instructor; A.O.S., Johnson & Wales University

Bonita Startt, M.S ., Instructor; B.S., M. S., Old Dominion University

Fred Tiess, A.A.S., Instructor; A.A.S., State University of New York, Poughkeepsie; A.O.S., Culinary Institute of America

NORTH MIAMI

Donato Becce, Instructor; Diploma di Qualifica, Instituto Professionale, Alberghiero di Stato, Italy

Kenneth Beyer, B.B.A., Instructor; A.B.A., Nichols College; B.B.A., University of Miami

Drue Brandenburg, B.S., C.C.E., C.E.C., Instructor; A.O.S., Culinary Institute of America; B.S., Oklahoma State University

Dennis Daugherty, M.Ed., Instructor; B.S., University of Maryland; M.Ed., Pennsylvania State University

Melvin Davis, B.A., Instructor; B.A. University of Maryland

Alberto Diaz, English Master Pastry Chef, Instructor

Claus Esrstling, C.E.C., Instructor

John Goldfarb, B.S., Instructor; A.O.S., Culinary Institute of America; B.S., Florida International University

John Harrison, B.S., Instructor; A.O.S., Culinary Institute of America; B.S., University of New Haven

James Hensley, Instructor

Giles Hezard, Instructor; Certification of Professional Aptitude - College D'Enseignement Technique Masculin, Audincourt, France

Alan Lazar, B.A., Instructor; B.A. Monmouth College

Lucille Ligas, M.Ed., Assistant Professor, Indiana University of Pennsylvania; B.S. Ed. Indiana University of Pennsylvania

Charles Miltenberger, C.E.P.C., Instructor

Betty Murphy, M.S.Ed. Instructor; B.S.Ed. Eastern Illinois University; M.S.Ed., University of Guam

Larry Rice, M.S., Instructor; A.S., Johnson & Wales University; B.S., Florida International University; M.S., Florida International University

Mark Testa, Ph.D., Associate Professor; A.A.S., State University of New York at Farmingdale; B.P.S., New York Institute of Technology; M.A.L.S. State University of New York at Stony Brook; Ph.D., Barry University

Todd Tonova, M. S., Instructor; A.O.S., Culinary Institute of America; B.S., Florida International University; M.S., Florida International University

Karen Woolley, B.S., Instructor; A.O.S., Culinary Institute of America; B.S., Florida State University

VAIL

Todd M. Rymer, M.S., Director; B.A., New College; M.S., Florida International University

Paul Ferzacca, A.O.S., Instructor; A.O.S. Kendall College

David Hite, A.S., Instructor; A.S. Johnson & Wales University

Robert Kuster, Instructor; Diploma, Swiss Hotel School, Lucerne; Diploma, Trade School, Cook's Apprenticeship, Lucerne; Diploma, Institute Stavia, Estavater Le-Lac

Katie Mazzia; B.S. R.D., Instructor; R.D., Saint Joseph's Health Center; B.S., Ohio State

Paul Reeves, B.S., Instructor; B.S., Saint Cloud State University

David B. Sanchez, A.O.S., Instructor; A.O.S., Johnson & Wales University

Culinary Advisory Council

Scott Armendinger, Editor, Journal Publications, Rockland, ME

Michael P. Berry, Vice President of Food Operations and Concept Development, Walt Disney World, Orlando, FL

Edward Bracebridge, Chef Instructor, Blackstone Valley Tech, Upton, MA

Gerry Fernandez, Technical Service Specialist, General Mills, Inc., Minneapolis, MN

John D. Folse, C.E.C., A.A.C., Owner, Executive Chef, Chef John Folse & Company, Donaldsonville, LA

Ira L. Kaplan, President, Servolift/Eastern Corp., Boston, MA

Gustav Mauler, VP, Food & Beverage, Treasure Island Hotel, Las Vegas, NV

Franz Meier, President, MW Associates, Columbia, SC

Roland Mesnier, Executive Pastry Chef, The White House, Washington, DC

Stanley Nicas, Chef/Owner, Castle Restaurant, Leicester, MA

Robert J. Nyman, President, The Nyman Group, Livingston, NJ

Johnny Rivers, Food & Beverage Manager/Executive Chef, Thyme & Associates,

Joseph Schmidt, Owner, Joseph Schmidt Confections, San Francisco, CA

Martin Yan, President, Yan Can Cook, Inc., Foster City, CA

Johnson & Wales University *Distinguished Visiting Chefs 1979–1997*

1 Dr. Jean Joaquin
2 Garry Reich
3 Dr. Hans J. Bueschkens
4 Michael Bourdin
5 Christian Inden
6 Casey Sinkeldam
7 John Kempf
8 Bernard S. Urban
9 Marcel Paniel
10 Lutz Olkiewicz
11 Dr. Joel Robuchon
12 Ray Marshall
13 Francis Hinault
14 Wally Uhl
15 Gunther Heiland
16 Dr. Pierre Franey
17 Jean-Jacques Dietrich
18 Uri Guttmann
19 William Spry
20 Dr. Stanley Nicas
21 Dr. Paul Elbling
22 Angelo Paracucchi
23 Albert Kellner
24 Hans K. Roth
25 Gerhard Daniel
26 Jacques Noe
27 Andre Rene
28 Dr. Anton Mosimann
29 Dr. Roger Verge
30 Gerhard Schmid
31 Karl Ronaszeki

32 Jacques Pepin
33 Klauss Friedenreich
34 Arno Schmidt
35 Lucien Vannier 🏺
36 Dr. Wolfgang Bierer
37 Dr. John L. Bandera
38 Albert Marty
39 Dr. Siegfried
    Schaber
40 Dr. Michael Minor
41 Raimund Hofmeister
42 Henry Haller
43 Dr. Noel Cullen
44 Dr. Carolyn Buster
45 Dr. Madeleine
    Kamman
46 Udo Nechutnys
47 Andrea Hellrigl 🏺
48 George Karousos
49 Warren LeRuth
50 Rene Mettler
51 Dr. Johnny Rivers

52 Milos Cihelka
53 Dr. Louis
    Szathmary 🏺
54 Philippe Laurier
55 Dr. Hans J. Schadler
56 Franz Klampfer
57 Jean-Pierre Dubray
58 Neil Connolly
59 Joachim Caula
60 Dr. Emeril LaGasset†
61 Dr. Roland Mesnier
62 Bernard Dance
63 Hartmut Handke
64 James Hughes†
65 Paul Bocuse
66 Dr. Martin Yan
67 Marcel Desaulniers
68 Heinz H. Veith
69 Benno Eigenmann
70 Johanne Killeen &
    George Germon
71 Dr. John D. Folse

72 Dr. Christian
    Rassinoux
73 Dr. Gustav E. Mauler
74 Dr. Keith Keogh
75 Clayton Folkners
76 Kenneth Wade
77 Dr. Roland E.
    Schaeffer
78 Dr. William Gallagher
79 Van P. Atkins
80 Hiroshi Noguchi
81 Jasper White
82 Albert Kumin
83 Alfonso Contriscianit
84 Dr. Victor Gielisse
85 Reimund D. Pitz
86 Daniel Brucet
87 Antoine Schaefers
88 Michael Ty
89 Phil Learned
90 Joseph Schmidt
91 John Halligan

92 Willy O. Rossel
93 John J. Vyhnanek
94 Roberto Gerometta
95 Robert A. Trainor†
96 Ewald & Susan Notter
97 Joseph Amendola
98 David Paul Johnson
99 Thomas Pedersen
100 André Soltner
101 Christian Clayton†
102 Konstantinos
     Exarchos
103 Christian Chemin
104 Lars Johansson
105 Paul O'Connell†

SPECIAL FRIENDS
John J. Bowen
Joseph P. Delaney
Socrates Inonog
Franz K. Lemoine

† Alumni
🏺 Deceased

Partial List of Companies Associated with Johnson & Wales University

Adam's Mark Hotels and
  Resorts
Allied Domecq Retailing
American General
  Hospitality, Inc.
AmeriClean Systems, Inc.
Angelica Uniform Group
Antigua Hotel Association
Aramark Services, Inc.
Automatic Sales, Inc.
AVTECH Industries
Bacardi & Company,
  Ltd.

Bacon Construction
  Company
Balfour Foundation
Banfi Vintners
Basic American Frozen
  Foods
Bertoill, USA, Inc.
Boston Chicken, Inc.
Boston Park Plaza
  Hotel
Braman Motors
Brinker International
Bristol Hotel Company

Bugaboo Creek
  Steakhouse
Bushiri Hotel Aruba
Campbell Food Service
  Company
Carlson Companies, Inc.
Carnival Cruise Lines
Cartier, Inc.
Celebrity Cruise Lines
Choice Hotels
Citizens Financial
  Group
Cleveland Range, Inc.

Club Corporation
  International
Comstock-Castle Stove
  Company
Concord Hospitality
Cookshack
Cookson America, Inc.
Coors Brewing Company
Crabtree McGrath
  Associates
Daka Restaurants, Inc.
Darden Restaurants
Deer Valley Resort

Denny's Restaurants

Dial Corporation

Digital Equipment Corporation

DiLeonardo International

Doral Arrowwood

E.A. Tosi & Sons Company, Inc.

E-H Enterprises

Ecolab, Inc.

Edison Electric Institute

Edwards Super Food Store

EGR International

Electric Cooking Council

Eurest Dining Service

F. Dick

Felchlin, Inc.

Feinstein Foundation

Flik International Corporation

Forbes

Friendly Ice Cream Corporation

Frymaster

G.S. Distributors

Garland Commercial Industries

Gavin Sales Company

General Mills

Godfather's Pizza, Inc.

The Golden Corral Corporation

Grand Western Brands, Inc.

Grisanti, Inc.

Groen, a Dover Industries Co.

Hallsmith-Sysco Food Services

Harman Management Corporation

Harris-Teeter, Inc.

Harvard University

Hasbro, Inc.

Hatch-Jennings, Inc.

HERO

Hiram Walker & Sons, Inc.

Hilton Hotels

Hobart Corporation

Houlihan's Restaurant Group

Houston's Restaurants

Hyatt Hotels Corporation

Ice-O-Matic

Ikon

Intercontinental Hotels

International Metro Industries

Interstate Hotels

Keating of Chicago, Inc.

Kiawah Island Resorts

Kraft Foods, Inc.

Lackman Food Service

Le Meridien Hotel Boston

L.J. Minor Corporation

Legal Sea Foods, Inc.

Loews Hotels

Longhorn Steaks, Inc.

Lyford Cay Foundation, Inc.

Manor Care Health Services

Market Forge Company

Marriott International, Inc.

Max Felchlin, Inc.

Massachusetts Electric Company

McCormick & Company, Inc.

Moet & Chandon

Morris Nathanson Design

Motel 6

MTS Seating

Nabisco Brands, Inc.

Narragansett Electric Company

National Votech Educators

National Banner Company, Inc.

National Prepared Foods Assoc.

National Student Organization

Nestle USA, Inc.

New England Electric System

New World Development Company

Norwegian Seafood Council

Opryland Hotel

Paramount Restaurant Supply

PepsiCo, Inc.

Pillsbury Corp.

The Proctor & Gamble Co.

Providence Beverage

Prudential Insurance Company

Quadlux

The Quaker Oats Company

Radisson Hospitality Worldwide

Ralph Calise Fruit & Produce

Red Lion Hotels

Renaissance Hotels & Resorts

Restaurant Data Concepts

Rhode Island Distributing Company

Rhode Island Foundation

Rich Products Corporation

The Ritz-Carlton Hotel

Robert Mondavi Winery

Robot Coupe

Ruth's Chris Steak House

Saunders Hotel Group

Joseph Schmidt Confections

Schott Corporation

Select Restaurants, Inc.

Servolift/Eastern Corp.

Sharp Electronic Corporation

Somat Corporation

Southern Foods

State of Rhode Island, Department of Education

Stonehard

Sun International

Sunrise Assisted Living

Swiss American Imports, Ltd.

Swiss Chalet Fine Foods

Sysco Corporation

TACO, Inc.

Taco Bell

Tasca Ford Sales, Inc.

Tekmatex, Inc.

The Delfield Company

The Waldorf-Astoria

Thermodyne Foodservice Products

Toastmaster

Tufts University

Tyson Foods, Inc.

U.S.D.A./Bell Associates

United States Army

United States Navy

University of Connecticut

Vail Associates

Vulcan Hart Corporation

Walt Disney World

Wells Manufacturing Company

Wyatt Corporation

Wyndham Hotels & Resorts

The Techniques

Assembling:

1. Collect and prepare all of the ingredients to the formula.
2. Clear the area for assembly.
3. Fit the pieces together according to formula instructions or instructor's guidelines.

Baking:

1. Preheat the oven.
2. Position the item appropriately in the oven.
3. Check for appropriate firmness and/or color.

Blending:

1. Combine the dry ingredients on low speed.
2. Add the softened fat(s) and liquid(s).
3. Mix the ingredients on low speed.
4. Increase the speed gradually.

Blooming:

Gelatin sheets or leaves:
1. Fan the sheets out.
2. Cover the sheets in liquid.
3. Sheets are bloomed when softened.

Granular gelatin:
1. Sprinkle the gelatin.
2. Gelatin is ready when it is cream of wheat consistency.

Brushing:

1. Use a pastry brush.
2. Lightly apply the glaze.

Caramelizing:

Wet method:
1. Use an extremely clean pot.
2. Place the sugar and water on high heat.
3. Never stir the mixture once the sugar begins to dissolve.
4. Once caramelized, shock in ice water.

Chopping:

1. Use a sharp knife.
2. Hold the food product properly.
3. Cut with a quick downward motion.

Coating:

❶ Use a coating screen, with a sheet pan underneath.

❷ Ensure that the product is the correct temperature.

❸ Coat the product using an appropriately-sized utensil.

Combing:

❶ Prepare the item with the appropriate amount of icing.

❷ Drag a clean comb across the surface.

Combining:

❶ Prepare the components to be combined.

❷ Add one to the other, using the appropriate mixing method (if needed).

Cooking:

❶ Choose the appropriate heat application: baking, boiling, simmering, etc.

❷ Prepare the formula according to instructions.

❸ Cook according to instructions.

Covering:

❶ Prepare the product to be covered with a sticky layer of buttercream, food gel, or other medium that is called for in the formula.

❷ Roll out the covering material.

❸ Cover the product with the covering material.

❹ Smooth the covered product with a bowl scraper to remove wrinkles and air bubbles.

Creaming:

❶ Soften the fats on low speed.

❷ Add the sugar(s) and cream; increase the speed slowly.

❸ Add the eggs one at a time; scrape the bowl frequently.

❹ Add the dry ingredients in stages.

Crystallizing:

❶ Boil the product for 30 seconds to 2 minutes.

❷ Drain the water; cook until tender and translucent.

❸ Strain the sugar syrup.

❹ Dredge the product; dry on a screen.

Cutting:

❶ Use a sharp knife to cut to the directed size.

Decorating:

❶ Follow the formula's instructions or the instructor's guidelines to appropriately decorate each cake or pastry.

Dipping:

❶ Prepare the product to the proper dipping temperature.

❷ Carefully submerge the product.

❸ Dry on parchment paper or a screen.

Dredging:

❶ Coat the food product.

❷ Sprinkle or toss the product in an appropriate dredging application.

Filling:

❶ Cut open the food product.

❷ Carefully spread the filling using an icing spatula.

❸ Carefully pipe the filling using a pastry bag.

Flambéing:

❶ Heat the food product and liqueur in a shallow pan.

❷ The pan needs to be very hot.

❸ Carefully tilt the pan into the open flame; ignite the liqueur.

Folding:

Do steps 1, 2, and 3 in one continuous motion.

❶ Run a bowl scraper under the mixture, across the bottom of the bowl.

❷ Turn the bowl counterclockwise.

❸ Bring the bottom mixture to the top.

Freezing:

❶ Prepare the product.

❷ Place the product in the freezing cabinet for the appropriate length of time.

Frying:

❶ Heat the frying liquid to the appropriate temperature.

❷ Place the food product into the hot liquid.

❸ Cook the product, turning frequently, until golden brown and tender.

Heating:

❶ Prepare the food product according to the formula's instructions.

❷ Choose the appropriate method of heating (on the range or stove top, in the oven, etc.)

❸ Apply the product to the heat.

Icing:

❶ Use a clean icing spatula.

❷ Work quickly and neatly.

Kneading:

❶ Prepare the kneading surface with the appropriate medium (flour, cornstarch, etc.).

❷ Press and form the dough into a mass using soft, determined strokes.

❸ Continue kneading until appropriate consistency and/or temperature is achieved.

Laminating:

❶ Allow a proper time to rest dough.

❷ Roll the dough out to a ½-inch to ¾-inch thickness.

❸ Evenly spread the fat.

❹ Allow a proper time for the dough to rest.

❺ Refrigerate for several hours.

Melting:

❶ Prepare the food product to be melted.

❷ Place the food product in an appropriately sized pot over direct heat or over a double boiler.

❸ Stir frequently or occasionally, depending on the delicacy of the product, until melted.

OR

❶ Place the product on a sheet pan or in a bowl, and place in a low oven until melted.

Mixing:

❶ Follow the proper mixing procedure: creaming, blending, whipping, or combination.

Molding:

❶ Wash your hands.
❷ Clear the work area.
❸ Carefully shape the substance.

Napper:

❶ Stir the sauce frequently.
❷ Frequently check the consistency of the sauce.

Peeling:

❶ Use a clean paring knife or peeler.
❷ Do not peel over an unsanitary surface.

Piping:

With bag:
❶ Use a bag with a disposable tip; cut the bag at 45-degree angle.
❷ Fill to no more than half full.
❸ Burp the bag.

With cone:
❶ Cut and fold the piping cone to the appropriate size.
❷ Fill the cone with a small amount.
❸ Fold the ends to form a triangle.
❹ Pipe the desired designs.

Poaching:

❶ Bring the liquid to a boil; then reduce to a simmer.
❷ Submerge and anchor the product.
❸ Do not overcook the product.

Portioning:

❶ Mark the product for portioning, using a ruler, if necessary.
❸ Cut, spoon, or scoop the product with the appropriate-sized utensil.

Pouring:

❶ Place the product in an appropriate container for pouring: a pitcher or large ladle.

❷ Pour the product into desired containers or over another product.

Proofing:

❶ Set a proof box to the proper temperature.

❷ Do not over- or underproof the dough.

Pulling:

❶ Pay attention; do not get distracted.

❷ Sugar must be at an even temperature.

❸ Work with clean equipment and hands.

Puréeing:

❶ Do not overfill the food processor.

❷ First pulse the food processor.

❸ Turn food processor to maximum speed to puree food.

Reducing:

❶ Bring the sauce to a boil; then reduce to a simmer.

❷ Stir often; reduce to the desired consistency.

Ribboning:

❶ Use a high speed on the mixer.

❷ Do not overwhip the egg yolks.

Rolling:

❶ Prepare the rolling surface by dusting with the appropriate medium (flour, cornstarch, etc.).

❷ Use the appropriate style pin (stick pin or ball bearing pin) to roll the dough to desired thickness; rotate the dough during rolling to prevent sticking.

Rubbing:

❶ Use a pastry cutter to keep the fat in large pieces.
❷ Add the liquid in stages.

Scalding:

❶ Heat the liquid on high heat.
❷ Do not boil the liquid.

Shaping:

❶ Prepare the medium to be shaped.
❷ Prepare the surface area for shaping.
❸ Mold medium into desired shapes according to the instructor's directions.

Simmering:

❶ Place the prepared product in an appropriate-sized pot.
❸ Bring the product to a boil, then reduce the heat to allow the product to barely boil.
❹ Cook until desired doneness is achieved.

Slicing:

❶ Prepare the product for cutting; clean and clear the work area.
❷ Slice the product using the "claw" grasp or the rocking motion.

Slow Baking:

❶ Use an appropriate baking dish.
❷ Use hot water in the pan.
❸ Replenish the water when needed.

Soaking:

❶ Place the item(s) to be soaked in a large bowl or appropriate container.
❷ Pour water or other liquid over the items to be soaked.
❸ Allow to sit until desired saturation or softening is achieved.

Spiking:

❶ Use chocolate that is appropriately tempered.

❷ Drag the truffles across a screen.

❸ Use three to four clean swift strokes.

Spreading:

❶ Using an icing spatula or off-set spatula, smooth the icing or other spreading medium over the surface area.

Stretching:

❶ Cover the surface area with a clean pastry cloth.

❷ First roll the dough with pin.

❸ Use the back of your hands to stretch the dough.

Stuffing:

❶ Place the stuffing inside the cavity of the food product using a gloved hand or a piping bag.

❷ Be sure to fill the cavity completely.

Tempering:

❶ Whisk the eggs vigorously while ladling hot liquid.

Thickening:

❶ Mix a small amount of sugar with the starches.

❷ Create a slurry.

❸ Whisk vigorously until thickened and translucent.

Washing:

❶ Brush or spray the product to the desired saturation.

❷ Do not under- or oversaturate.

Whipping:

❶ Hold the whip at a 55-degree angle.

❷ Create circles, using a circular motion.

❸ The circular motion needs to be perpendicular to the bowl.

1

Cakes: Bases

Cakes: Bases

PASTRY TECHNIQUES:

Creaming, Whipping, Folding

Creaming:

1. Soften the fats on low speed.
2. Add the sugar(s) and cream; increase the speed slowly.
3. Add the eggs one at a time; scrape the bowl frequently.
4. Add the dry ingredients in stages.

Whipping:

1. Hold the whip at a 55-degree angle.
2. Create circles, using a circular motion.
3. The circular motion needs to be perpendicular to the bowl.

Folding:

Do steps 1, 2, and 3 in one continuous motion.
1. Run a bowl scraper under the mixture, across the bottom of the bowl.
2. Turn the bowl counterclockwise.
3. Bring the bottom mixture to the top.

HACCP:

Store at 40° F for 1 day. After 1 day, store at 0° F.

HAZARDOUS FOODS:

Eggs
Egg whites

CHEF NOTE:

This formula is a special sponge cake of low volume for use with combed stencils to fill in spaces.

Almond Sponge Cake

Use with silpat and combed stencils

YIELD:		1 pound, 3 ounces.	2 pounds, 6 ounces.

INGREDIENTS:

Almond meal		4 ounces	8 ounces
Flour, cake		1 ounce	2 ounces
Sugar, confectionery		4 ounces	8 ounces
Eggs, whole		5 ounces	10 ounces
Butter, unsalted, melted		1 ounce	2 ounces
Egg whites, at room temperature		3½ ounces	7 ounces
Cream of tartar		Pinch	Pinch
Sugar, granulated		½ ounce	1 ounce

METHOD OF PREPARATION:

1. Gather the equipment and ingredients.
2. Sift together the almond meal, cake flour, and confectionery sugar.
3. Whisk the whole eggs lightly, and add to the dry ingredients.
4. Add the melted butter to the mixture, and combine well.
5. Whip the egg whites on high speed; add the cream of tartar when the whites foam up; add the sugar gradually as the whites increase in volume. Reduce the speed as the meringue thickens, to avoid overmixing.
6. Fold the whipped egg whites into the mixture in three stages.
7. Ready for use.

How to Use Almond Sponge Cake:

1. Spread the batter uniformly over the silpat mat.
2. Comb in the desired decoration.
3. Freeze until completely set.
4. Spread the sponge cake batter for the silpat on top evenly.
5. Bake at 400° F, but *do not overbake*.
6. Once cool, place the sheet on top, and invert the mat.
7. Remove the silpat mat.
8. Cut the cake to the desired shape and sizes.
9. Utilize, as directed, for siding and garnishes.

Angel Food Cake

Whipping:
1. Hold the whip at a 55-degree angle.
2. Create circles, using a circular motion.
3. The circular motion needs to be perpendicular to the bowl.

HACCP:
Store at 40° F for 1 day. After 1 day, store at 0° F.

HAZARDOUS FOOD:
Egg whites

YIELD:	4 pounds, 12¾ ounces.	9 pounds, 9½ ounces.
	5, 8-inch Cakes	10, 8-inch Cakes

INGREDIENTS:

Egg whites	2 pounds	4 pounds
Flour, cake	12 ounces	1 pound, 8 ounces
Sugar, confectionery	12 ounces	1 pound, 8 ounces
Cream of tartar	¼ ounce	½ ounce
Sugar, granulated	1 pound, 4 ounces	2 pounds, 8 ounces
Salt	⅛ ounce	¼ ounce
Extract, vanilla	¼ ounce	½ ounce
Extract, almond	⅛ ounce	¼ ounce

METHOD OF PREPARATION:

1. Gather the equipment and ingredients.
2. Bring the egg whites to room temperature; it may be necessary to warm them over a double boiler.
3. Sift together the cake flour and confectionery sugar.
4. Place the egg whites in a bowl, and whip on high speed; add the cream of tartar when the egg whites foam up; add the sugar gradually as the whites increase in volume. Reduce the speed as the meringue thickens, to avoid overmixing. After the meringue is mixed, add the salt, vanilla extract, and almond extract.
5. Whip to soft, moist peaks; *do not overmix*. Turn the mixer speed to medium during the process of whipping, to prevent overmixing.
6. Remove from the mixer, and fold in the sifted cake–confectionery sugar mixture.
7. Fill 8-inch angel food cake pans with 14 ounces of batter.
8. Bake at 375° F for 25 minutes, or until light golden brown on top and sides and set in center.
9. Remove from the oven, and invert to assist unmolding.

CHEF NOTE:
Chocolate angel food cake can be made by replacing 25% of the cake flour with cocoa powder.

ICINGS

CAKES: FINISHED

CREAMS

FILLINGS

PIES

SLOW BAKING

BATTER

DOUGHS

SAUCES

Baumkuchen

YIELD: 4 pounds, 12¼ ounces.

Creaming, Whipping, Folding

Creaming:
1. Soften the fats on low speed.
2. Add the sugar(s) and cream; increase the speed slowly.
3. Add the eggs one at a time; scrape the bowl frequently.
4. Add the dry ingredients in stages.

Whipping:
1. Hold the whip at a 55-degree angle.
2. Create circles, using a circular motion.
3. The circular motion needs to be perpendicular to the bowl.

Folding:
Do steps 1, 2, and 3 in one continuous motion.
1. Run a bowl scraper under the mixture, across the bottom of the bowl.
2. Turn the bowl counterclockwise.
3. Bring the bottom mixture to the top.

HACCP:
Store at 40° F for 1 day. After 1 day, store at 0° F.

HAZARDOUS FOODS:
Egg yolks
Egg whites

CHEF NOTES:
1. Flavorings could be rum, kahlua, or any fruit compound.
2. Baumkuchen can be baked in layers on a sheet pan and used for making petit fours.
3. This version of baumkuchen is very moist and suitable for eating, unlike others, which are intended for centerpieces.
4. For safety reasons (for all production), sugar may be added to the egg whites just before whipping.

INGREDIENTS:

Almond paste	3½ ounces
Flavorings	As needed
Butter, unsalted, room temperature	12 ounces
Egg yolks, room temperature	14 ounces
Egg whites	1 pound, 5 ounces
Sugar, granulated	14 ounces
Cornstarch	7 ounces
Flour, pastry, sifted	4¾ ounces
Preserves, apricot	As needed

METHOD OF PREPARATION:

1. Gather the equipment and ingredients.
2. Place the almond paste and flavorings in a bowl with a paddle, and cream until smooth.
3. Change the paddle to a whip.
4. Add the room-temperature butter; whip to a pale color.
5. Slowly add the egg yolks into the butter mixture; whip to full volume.
6. In another bowl, whip the egg whites, granulated sugar, and cornstarch to a medium peak.
7. Add the meringue to the butter mixture.
8. Fold in the sifted pastry flour.

Baking Options:

1. Bake in a baumkuchen machine; see instructions according to the machine.
2. Bake in the oven on a half sheet pan.

Baking Instructions:

1. Prepare a half sheet pan with parchment paper.
2. Spread the batter about ¹⁄₁₂-inch thick.
3. Bake at 550° F, top heat only.

4. Take out of the oven.
5. Brush with thinned down apricot preserves on top (ratio of preserves to water, 1:1).
6. Add more batter, $\frac{1}{12}$-inch thick.
7. At this point, bake with a double sheet pan.
8. Repeat until all of the batter is used.
9. Cool.

CAKES: BASES

ICINGS

CAKES: FINISHED

CREAMS

FILLINGS

PIES

SLOW BAKING

BATTER

DOUGHS

SAUCES

PASTRY TECHNIQUES:
Whipping, Folding

Whipping:
1. Hold the whip at a 55-degree angle.
2. Create circles, using a circular motion.
3. The circular motion needs to be perpendicular to the bowl.

Folding:
Do steps 1, 2, and 3 in one continuous motion.
1. Run a bowl scraper under the mixture, across the bottom of the bowl.
2. Turn the bowl counterclockwise.
3. Bring the bottom mixture to the top.

HACCP:
Store at 40° F for 1 day. After 1 day, store at 0° F.

HAZARDOUS FOODS:
Egg yolks
Egg whites

Baumkuchen for Centerpieces

YIELD: 6 pounds, 15 ounces.

INGREDIENTS:

Butter, unsalted, softened	1 pound, 4 ounces
Sugar, granulated	1 pound, 2 ounces
Almond paste	2½ ounces
Egg yolks	1 pound, 5 ounces
Extract, lemon	To taste
Egg whites	2 pounds
Salt	To taste
Cornstarch	9 ounces
Flour, cake, sifted	9 ounces

METHOD OF PREPARATION:

1. Gather the equipment and ingredients.
2. Place the butter, half of the granulated sugar, and the almond paste into bowl.
3. Paddle until light, fluffy, and lump-free.
4. Add the egg yolks and lemon extract to the butter mixture.
5. Place the egg whites in a bowl, and whip to a medium peak; slowly add the salt and remaining granulated sugar to make a meringue.
6. Sift together the cornstarch and cake flour.
7. Fold one third of the meringue into the butter mixture.
8. Then fold in the sifted dry ingredients.
9. Fold in the remaining two thirds of the meringue.
10. Bake on a baumkuchen machine, layer after layer, until all of the batter is used.

CHEF NOTE:
Lemon extract can be replaced by other flavorings, such as brandy or compounds.

Caracas Sponge Cake

PASTRY TECHNIQUES:
Combining, Whipping, Folding

Combining:
Bringing together two or more components.
1. Prepare the components to be combined.
2. Add one to the other, using the appropriate mixing method (if needed).

Whipping:
1. Hold the whip at a 55-degree angle.
2. Create circles, using a circular motion.
3. The circular motion needs to be perpendicular to the bowl.

Folding:
Do steps 1, 2, and 3 in one continuous motion.
1. Run a bowl scraper under the mixture, across the bottom of the bowl.
2. Turn the bowl counterclockwise.
3. Bring the bottom mixture to the top.

HACCP:
Store at 40° F. for 1 day. After 1 day, store at 0° F.

HAZARDOUS FOODS:
Egg yolks
Egg whites

YIELD:	8 pounds, ¾ ounce 5½, 9-inch Cakes	16 pounds, 1½ ounces 11, 9-inch Cakes

INGREDIENTS:		
Almond paste	8½ ounces	1 pound, 1 ounce
Sugar, confectionery	5 ounces	10 ounces
Egg yolks	1 pound, 10¼ ounces	3 pounds, 4½ ounces
Extract, vanilla	½ ounce	1 ounce
Egg whites	2 pounds, 3 ounces	4 pounds, 6 ounces
Sugar, granulated	1 pound, 5 ounces	2 pounds, 10 ounces
Nougat, ground	8½ ounces	1 pound, 1 ounce
Crumbs, cake	9 ounces	1 pound, 2 ounces
Flour, bread, sifted	6½ ounces	13 ounces
Butter, unsalted, melted	8½ ounces	1 pound, 1 ounce

METHOD OF PREPARATION:

1. Gather the equipment and ingredients.
2. Grease the 9-inch cake pans.
3. Place the almond paste and confectionery sugar in a bowl, and combine with a paddle until crumbly.
4. Slowly add the egg yolks into the mixture, and combine until it is a smooth paste.
5. Add the vanilla extract, and continue whipping until the mixture is at full volume.
6. In another mixing bowl, place the egg whites, and whip them to a medium-stiff peak, slowly adding the granulated sugar.
7. Remove from the mixer, and fold, by hand, the whipped egg whites into the almond paste mixture.
8. Combine the ground nougat, cake crumbs, and sifted cake flour.
9. Fold the ingredients carefully into the egg mixture.
10. Fold in the melted butter.
11. Fill the pans with 1 pound, 8 ounces of batter.
12. Bake at 350° F until golden brown.

CAKES: BASES
ICINGS
CAKES: FINISHED
CREAMS
FILLINGS
PIES
SLOW BAKING
BATTER
DOUGHS
SAUCES

Carrot Cake

PASTRY TECHNIQUE:
Combining

Combining:
Bringing together two or more components.
1. Prepare the components to be combined.
2. Add one to the other, using the appropriate mixing method (if needed).

HACCP:
Store at 40° F for 1 day. After 1 day, store at 0° F.

HAZARDOUS FOOD:
Eggs

YIELD:	11 pounds, 4 ounces.	22 pounds, 8 ounces.
	5, 9-inch Cakes	10, 9-inch Cakes

INGREDIENTS:

Flour, bread	2 pounds, 2 ounces	4 pounds, 4 ounces
Baking powder	1¼ ounces	2½ ounces
Baking soda	¾ ounce	1½ ounces
Cinnamon, ground	¾ ounce	1½ ounces
Salt	½ ounce	1 ounce
Nutmeg, ground	¼ ounce	½ ounce
Sugar, granulated	2 pounds, 7 ounces	4 pounds, 14 ounces
Oil, vegetable	2 pounds	4 pounds
Eggs, whole	1 pound, 8 ounces	3 pounds
Raisins, seedless	12 ounces	1 pound, 8 ounces
Carrots, grated	2 pounds, 4 ounces	4 pounds, 8 ounces

METHOD OF PREPARATION:

1. Gather the equipment and ingredients.
2. Grease the cake pans thoroughly.
3. Sift together the bread flour, baking powder, baking soda, cinnamon, salt, and nutmeg.
4. Place the granulated sugar and oil in a bowl, and combine using a paddle.
5. Add the eggs slowly in stages to the sugar-oil mixture, and combine.
6. Add the sifted ingredients into sugar-oil mixture; combine thoroughly.
7. Fold in the raisins and grated carrots.
8. Fill 9-inch by 3-inch cake pans with 2 pounds, 3 ounces of batter.
9. Bake at 350° F for 45 minutes, or until light golden brown.

Chocolate Applesauce Cake

PASTRY TECHNIQUE:
Combining

Combining:
Bringing together two or more components.
1. Prepare the components to be combined.
2. Add one to the other, using the appropriate mixing method (if needed).

HACCP:
Store at 40° F. for 1 day. After 1 day, store at 0° F.

HAZARDOUS FOODS:
Eggs
Buttermilk

YIELD:	8 pounds, 9½ ounces.	17 pounds, 3 ounces.
	6, 9-inch Cakes	12, 9-inch Cakes
	1 Sheet Cake	2 Sheet Cakes

INGREDIENTS:

Flour, cake, sifted	1 pound, 11 ounces	3 pounds, 6 ounces
Cocoa powder, sifted	1½ ounces	3 ounces
Baking soda, sifted	¾ ounce	1½ ounces
Baking powder, sifted	¾ ounce	1½ ounces
Salt	¾ ounce	1½ ounces
Cinnamon, ground	¾ ounce	1½ ounces
Sugar, brown	2 pounds, 4 ounces	4 pounds, 8 ounces
Oil, vegetable	1 pound, 5 ounces	2 pounds, 10 ounces
Eggs, whole	13 ounces	1 pound, 10 ounces
Applesauce	12 ounces	1 pound, 8 ounces
Buttermilk	1 pound, 8 ounces	3 pounds

METHOD OF PREPARATION:

1. Gather the equipment and ingredients.
2. Sift together the cake flour, cocoa powder, baking soda, baking powder, salt, and cinnamon.
3. Place all of the sifted ingredients and the brown sugar in bowl. Blend together using a paddle.
4. Slowly add the oil, to avoid lumps from forming, and mix into a paste.
5. Add the eggs in stages, scraping in between.
6. Add the applesauce slowly, scraping regularly.
7. Add the buttermilk, and mix until smooth.
8. Fill 9-inch cake pans with 1 pound, 7 ounces of batter, or fill 1 sheet pan with 8 pounds, 9½ ounces of batter.
9. Bake at 360° F until firm.

CAKES: BASES

ICINGS

CAKES: FINISHED

CREAMS

FILLINGS

PIES

SLOW BAKING

BATTER

DOUGHS

SAUCES

PASTRY TECHNIQUES:
Whipping, Melting, Folding

Whipping:
1. Hold the whip at a 55-degree angle.
2. Create circles, using a circular motion.
3. The circular motion needs to be perpendicular to the bowl.

Melting:
1. Prepare the food product to be melted.
2. Place the food product in an appropriate-sized pot over direct heat or over a double boiler.
3. Stir frequently or occasionally, depending on the delicacy of the product, until melted.

OR
1. Place the product on a sheet pan or in a bowl, and place in a low-temperature oven until melted.

Folding:
Do steps 1, 2, and 3 in one continuous motion.
1. Run a bowl scraper under the mixture, across the bottom of the bowl.
2. Turn the bowl counterclockwise.
3. Bring the bottom mixture to the top.

HACCP:
Store at 40° F for 1 day. After 1 day, store at 0° F.

HAZARDOUS FOODS:
Egg yolks
Egg whites

Chocolate Chiffon Genoise

YIELD:	4 pounds, 3 ounces.	12 pounds, 9½ ounces.
	3, 9-inch Cakes	9, 9-inch Cakes

INGREDIENTS:

Egg yolks	1 pound	3 pounds
Sugar, granulated	9⅓ ounces	1 pound, 12 ounces
Flour, cake	10⅔ ounces	2 pounds
Baking soda	Pinch	½ ounce
Baking powder	⅓ ounce	1 ounce
Salt	To taste	To taste
Butter, unsalted	4 ounces	12 ounces
Chocolate, dark, semisweet	9⅓ ounces	1 pound, 12 ounces
Egg whites	10⅔ ounces	2 pounds
Sugar, granulated	6⅔ ounces	1 pound, 4 ounces

METHOD OF PREPARATION:

1. Gather the equipment and ingredients.
2. Place the egg yolks and 1 pound, 12 ounces of the granulated sugar in a bowl, and place over a double boiler.
3. Stir continuously until it reaches 120° F.
4. Remove from the heat, and place on a mixer.
5. Whip on the highest speed to full volume.
6. Sift together the cake flour, baking soda, baking powder, and salt.
7. Melt the butter. Keep it on the cool side.
8. Melt the chocolate; do not heat it higher than 122° F.
9. Add the melted butter to the melted chocolate, and combine well.
10. Add the sifted dry ingredients into the whipped egg yolks.
11. Fold the combined butter-chocolate mixture into the egg yolk mixture.
12. In another bowl, whip the egg whites to medium peak; slowly add 1 pound, 4 ounces of granulated sugar to make a meringue.
13. Carefully fold the meringue into the batter.
14. Scale 1 pound, 6 ounces of batter into lightly greased, 9-inch cake pans.
15. Bake at 375° F until firm and dry in the center.

Chocolate Genoise

PASTRY TECHNIQUES:
Whipping, Melting, Folding

Whipping:
1. Hold the whip at a 55-degree angle.
2. Create circles, using a circular motion.
3. The circular motion needs to be perpendicular to the bowl.

Melting:
1. Prepare the food product to be melted.
2. Place the food product in an appropriate sized pot over direct heat or over a double boiler.
3. Stir frequently or occasionally, depending on the delicacy of the product, until melted.

OR
1. Place the product on a sheet pan or in a bowl, and place in a low-temperature oven until melted.

Folding:
Do steps 1, 2, and 3 in one continuous motion.
1. Run a bowl scraper under the mixture, across the bottom of the bowl.
2. Turn the bowl counterclockwise.
3. Bring the bottom mixture to the top.

HACCP:
Store at 40° F for 1 day. After 1 day, store at 0° F.

HAZARDOUS FOOD:
Eggs

YIELD:		3 pounds, 10⅞ ounces.	7 pounds, 5¾ ounces.
		2, 9-inch by 3-inch Pans	4, 9-inch by 3-inch Pans

INGREDIENTS:			
Flour, cake		6 ounces	12 ounces
Cornstarch		6 ounces	12 ounces
Cocoa powder		4 ounces	8 ounces
Baking soda		1/16 ounce	⅛ ounce
Water		½ ounce	1 ounce
Butter, unsalted		4 ounces	8 ounces
Eggs, whole		1 pound, 8 ounces	3 pounds
Salt		⅛ ounce	¼ ounce
Extract, vanilla		¼ ounce	½ ounce
Sugar, granulated		14 ounces	1 pound, 12 ounces

METHOD OF PREPARATION:

1. Gather the equipment and ingredients.
2. Properly grease the 9-inch by 3-inch cake pans.
3. Sift together the cake flour, cornstarch, and cocoa powder; set aside.
4. Dissolve the baking soda in water, and set aside.
5. Melt the butter, and set aside. (Butter should be only lukewarm.)
6. Place the whole eggs, salt, vanilla extract, granulated sugar, and baking soda–water mixture in a bowl; immediately whisk over a warm water bath. (Never scale ingredients together in advance, or lumping will occur when the dry sugar comes in contact with the eggs.)
7. Heat the mixture to 110° F, constantly mixing. *Do not cook* the mixture.
8. Remove the bowl from the warm bath, and place on the mixer; whip on high speed to full volume. (Full volume can be determined by the "5-second track method." See chef note 3.)
9. When full volume is reached, remove the bowl from the mixer, and immediately fold the dry ingredients into the whipped egg mixture. Use your hand along with a plastic scraper to distribute the sifted dry ingredients evenly. This is a combination of the folding technique (turning the bowl counterclockwise with the left hand and scraping up from the bottom with the right hand in a clockwise rotation; finish out on top of the batter with your right hand and scraper palm up and shaking vigorously to distribute the flour and starch). Work quickly. Continue mixing until all of the ingredients are completely incorporated. (The longer it takes to combine the ingredients, the greater the chance that lumps will be trapped in the batter.)
10. Place a small amount of batter in another small bowl.

CHEF NOTES:

1. The following methods test for doneness:
   (a) Check for color; a golden brown is good.
   (b) Check to see if the cake is pulling away from the sides of the pan.
   (c) Touch the center of cake, and it should spring back.
2. Sponge cake is a very delicate cake; do not slam the door or knock the pans together.
3. The following is the "5-second track method":
   Put ½ inch of your fingertip through the batter. If it holds a track for 5 seconds before closing, it is done. If it fails to hold a track, whip more. Check several times during mixing. Stay with the machine to monitor its progress. Keep track of mixing times and speeds. As the batter thickens, reduce the speed to medium, and check more frequently. *Do not overmix;* this will result in loss of volume or total collapse. Eggs should be cool at the end of this process.

11. Using your fingers, quickly whisk the melted butter into this batter until completely incorporated.
12. Fold this butter mixture, gently, back into the remaining batter.
13. Scale the batter at 1 pound, 11 ounces per 9-inch by 3-inch pan, approximately two thirds full.
14. Bake at 350° F for approximately 35 to 40 minutes. Test for doneness. (See chef note 1.)
15. When done, remove from the oven, and place on a cooling rack.

CAKES: BASES

ICINGS

CAKES: FINISHED

CREAMS

FILLINGS

PIES

SLOW BAKING

BATTER

DOUGHS

SAUCES

PASTRY TECHNIQUES:
Whipping, Folding, Spreading

Whipping:
1. Hold the whip at a 55-degree angle.
2. Create circles, using a circular motion.
3. The circular motion needs to be perpendicular to the bowl.

Folding:
Do steps 1, 2, and 3 in one continuous motion.
1. Run a bowl scraper under the mixture, across the bottom of the bowl.
2. Turn the bowl counterclockwise.
3. Bring the bottom mixture to the top.

Spreading:
1. Using an icing spatula or off-set spatula, smooth the icing or other spreading medium over the surface area.

HACCP:
Store at 40° F for 1 day. After 1 day, store at 0° F.

HAZARDOUS FOOD:
Eggs

Chocolate Jelly Roll Sponge Cake

YIELD:		4 pounds, 6¾ ounces	8 pounds, 13½ ounces
		2 Sheets	4 Sheets

INGREDIENTS:

Potato starch		12 ounces	1 pound, 8 ounces
Flour, cake		2 ounces	4 ounces
Cocoa powder		3 ounces	6 ounces
Baking powder		¾ ounce	1½ ounces
Eggs, whole		2 pounds	4 pounds
Sugar, granulated		1 pound, 5 ounces	2 pounds, 10 ounces

METHOD OF PREPARATION:

1. Gather the equipment and ingredients.
2. Sift together the potato starch, cake flour, cocoa powder, and baking powder.
3. Place the eggs and granulated sugar in a bowl; whip to full volume.
4. When the eggs reach full volume, remove from the mixer, and fold in sifted dry ingredients carefully by hand.
5. Scale 2 pounds, 3 ounces of batter per pan into straight, parchment-lined sheet pans.
6. Spread evenly in each pan.
7. Bake at 410° F for approximately 10 to 15 minutes; test for doneness (see chef notes).
8. Remove from the oven.
9. Roll up each jelly roll while still hot.
10. Cool in the rolled position.
11. Unroll to fill, and reroll.

CHEF NOTES:
Use the following methods to test for doneness:
1. Check for color; golden brown is good.
2. Check for firmness; the cake should spring back when touched.

CAKES: BASES
ICINGS
CAKES: FINISHED
CREAMS
FILLINGS
PIES
SLOW BAKING
BATTER
DOUGHS
SAUCES

PASTRY TECHNIQUES:
Combining

Combining:
Bringing together two or more components.
1. Prepare the components to be combined.
2. Add one to the other, using the appropriate mixing method (if needed).

HACCP:
Store at 40° F for 1 day. After 1 day, store at 0° F.

HAZARDOUS FOODS:
Egg whites
Eggs
Milk

Chocolate Layer Cake

(High-Ratio)

YIELD: 4 pounds, 5 ounces. 12 pounds, 15 ounces.
3, 9-inch Cakes 9, 9-inch Cakes

INGREDIENTS:

Flour, cake, sifted	13⅓ ounces	2 pounds, 8 ounces
Cocoa powder, sifted	2⅔ ounces	8 ounces
Baking soda, sifted	¼ ounce	¾ ounce
Baking powder, sifted	⅓ ounce	1 ounce
Salt	⅓ ounce	1 ounce
Sugar, granulated	1 pound, 4 ounces	3 pounds, 12 ounces
Shortening, high-ratio	6¾ ounces	1 pound, 4¼ ounces
Egg whites	5⅓ ounces	1 pound
Eggs, whole	2⅔ ounces	8 ounces
Milk, whole	1 pound, 1⅓ ounces	3 pounds, 4 ounces

METHOD OF PREPARATION:
1. Gather the equipment and ingredients.
2. Sift together the cake flour, cocoa powder, baking soda, baking powder, and salt.
3. Place the sifted dry ingredients, granulated sugar, shortening, egg whites, whole eggs, and one third of the milk into a bowl.
4. Mix together, using a paddle, on medium speed for 5 minutes.
5. Add the remaining milk in three parts; scrape the bowl between additions, and mix until smooth. Mix for 3 minutes.
6. Fill 9-inch cake pans with 1 pound, 7 ounces of batter.
7. Bake at 375° F for 25 to 30 minutes or until done.
8. Remove, and turn onto sugar-flour–dusted, paper-lined pans to cool.

Decorating Paste

PASTRY TECHNIQUES:
Combing, Spreading

Combing:
1. Prepare the item with the appropriate amount of icing.
2. Drag a clean comb across the surface.

Spreading:
1. Using an icing spatula or off-set spatula, smooth the icing or other spreading medium over the surface area.

HACCP:
Store at 40° F for 1 day. After 1 day, store at 0° F.

HAZARDOUS FOOD:
Egg whites

YIELD:	14 ounces.	1 pound, 12 ounces.
INGREDIENTS:		
Sugar, confectionery, sifted	3½ ounces	7 ounces
Butter, unsalted, soft	3½ ounces	7 ounces
Egg whites	3½ ounces	7 ounces
Flour, pastry, sifted	3½ ounces	7 ounces
Coloring, food (optional)	As needed	As needed

METHOD OF PREPARATION:

1. Gather the equipment and ingredients.
2. Place the sugar, butter, and egg whites in a bowl; combine until smooth.
3. Add the pastry flour; blend until smooth and well incorporated.
4. *Optional:* Mix coloring, as desired.
5. Rest for 1 hour.

How to Use Decorating Paste:

1. Spread the paste uniformly over the silpat mat.
2. Comb in the desired decoration.
3. Freeze until completely set.
4. Spread the sponge cake batter for the silpat on top evenly.
5. Bake at 400° F, but *do not overbake*.
6. Once cool, place a sheet on top, and invert the mat.
7. Remove the silpat mat.
8. Cut the cake to the desired shape and sizes.
9. Utilize, as directed, for siding and garnishes.

CHEF NOTES:
1. Prior to use, decorating paste should rest for about 1 hour to allow for absorption of the flour.
2. Consistency can be adjusted by adding either more flour to thicken or oil to thin.
3. Cocoa butter can be sprayed over the cake surface to prevent drying when used for siding and garnishes.
4. Decorating paste can be frozen until needed.

CAKES: BASES

ICINGS

CAKES: FINISHED

CREAMS

FILLINGS

PIES

SLOW BAKING

BATTER

DOUGHS

SAUCES

PASTRY TECHNIQUES:
Combing, Spreading

Combing:
1. Prepare the item with the appropriate amount of icing.
2. Drag a clean comb across the surface.

Spreading:
1. Using an icing spatula or off-set spatula, smooth the icing or other spreading medium over the surface area.

HACCP:
Store at 40° F for 1 day. After 1 day, store at 0° F.

HAZARDOUS FOOD:
Egg whites

Decorating Paste, Chocolate

YIELD:	11¼ ounces.	1 pound, 6½ ounces.

INGREDIENTS:

Sugar, confectionery, sifted	2¾ ounces	5½ ounces
Butter, soft	2¾ ounces	5½ ounces
Egg whites	2¾ ounces	5½ ounces
Flour, pastry, sifted	2 ounces	4 ounces
Cocoa powder, sifted	1 ounce	2 ounces
Almond sponge cake batter (see page 3)	As needed	As needed

METHOD OF PREPARATION:
1. Gather the equipment and ingredients.
2. Place the sugar, butter, and egg whites in a bowl; combine until smooth.
3. Sift together the pastry flour and cocoa powder.
4. Add the sifted mixture into the butter mixture, and blend until smooth and well incorporated.

How to Use Decorating Paste:
1. Spread the paste uniformly over the silpat mat.
2. Comb in the desired decoration.
3. Freeze until completely set.
4. Spread the almond sponge for the silpat on top evenly.
5. Bake at 400° F, but *do not overbake*.
6. Once cool, place the sheet on top, and invert the mat.
7. Remove the silpat mat.
8. Cut the cake to the desired shape and sizes.
9. Utilize, as directed, for siding and garnishes.

CHEF NOTES:
1. Prior to use, decorating paste should rest for about 1 hour to allow for absorption of the flour.
2. Consistency can be adjusted by adding either more flour to thicken or oil to thin.
3. Cocoa butter can be sprayed over the cake surface to prevent drying when used for siding and garnishes.
4. Decorating paste can be frozen until needed.

PASTRY TECHNIQUES:
Whipping, Combining, Spreading

Whipping:
1. Hold the whip at a 55-degree angle.
2. Create circles, using a circular motion.
3. The circular motion needs to be perpendicular to the bowl.

Combining:
Bringing together two or more components.
1. Prepare the components to be combined.
2. Add one to the other, using the appropriate mixing method (if needed).

Spreading:
1. Using an icing spatula or off-set spatula, smooth the icing or other spreading medium over the surface area.

HACCP:
Store in a cool, dry area.

HAZARDOUS FOOD:
Eggs

Dobos Layers

Production Basis

YIELD:		1 pound, 15⅔ ounces	5 pounds, 15 ounces
		7, 9-inch Layers	21, 9-inch Layers

INGREDIENTS:

Butter, unsalted, warm		8 ounces	1 pound, 8 ounces
Extract, vanilla		To taste	To taste
Salt		To taste	To taste
Sugar, granulated		8 ounces	1 pound, 8 ounces
Eggs, whole		7⅔ ounces	1 pound, 7 ounces
Flour, pastry, sifted		4 ounces	12 ounces
Flour, cake, sifted		4 ounces	12 ounces

METHOD OF PREPARATION:

1. Gather the equipment and ingredients.
2. Place the butter, vanilla extract, salt, and sugar in a bowl.
3. Whip to a light consistency.
4. Slowly add the eggs, and mix at medium speed until incorporated.
5. At low speed, add the sifted flours, and mix until incorporated.
6. Spread the batter ⅛-inch thick to fill 8⁷⁄₁₆-inch circles on lightly greased, parchment-lined sheet pans.
7. Bake at 380° F until golden.
8. After the disks are baked, trim while they are still hot.
9. Cool before use or storage.
10. Wrap airtight to store.

CAKES: BASES

ICINGS

CAKES: FINISHED

CREAMS

FILLINGS

PIES

SLOW BAKING

BATTER

DOUGHS

SAUCES

Frangipane No. 1

YIELD:	4 pounds, 8½ ounces.	9 pounds, 1 ounce.
	½ Sheet Pan	1 Sheet Pan

INGREDIENTS:

Almond paste	2 pounds, 3 ounces	4 pounds, 6 ounces
Eggs, whole	1 pound, 1½ ounces	2 pounds, 3 ounces
Butter, unsalted, room temperature	1 pound, 1½ ounces	2 pounds, 3 ounces
Flour, cake	2½ ounces	5 ounces

METHOD OF PREPARATION:

1. Gather the equipment and ingredients.
2. Place the almond paste in a bowl with a paddle; soften by adding a small amount of eggs a little at a time until smooth.
3. In another bowl, soften the butter; scrape well.
4. Add the softened almond paste to the softened butter; scrape well.
5. Cream the butter and almond paste until light in color.
6. Fold in the sifted flour by hand.
7. Place 4 pounds, 8½ ounces of batter into a greased, paper-lined half sheet pan.
8. Bake at 325° F for 20 minutes, or until firm.

PASTRY TECHNIQUES:
Creaming, Combining, Folding

Creaming:
1. Soften the fats on low speed.
2. Add the sugar(s) and cream; increase the speed slowly.
3. Add the eggs one at a time; scrape the bowl frequently.
4. Add the dry ingredients in stages.

Combining:
Bringing together two or more components.
1. Prepare the components to be combined.
2. Add one to the other, using the appropriate mixing method (if needed).

Folding:
Do steps 1, 2, and 3 in one continuous motion.
1. Run a bowl scraper under the mixture, across the bottom of the bowl.
2. Turn the bowl counterclockwise.
3. Bring the bottom mixture to the top.

HACCP:
Store at 40° F, for 1 day. After 1 day, store at 0° F.

HAZARDOUS FOOD:
Eggs

Frangipane No. 2

PASTRY TECHNIQUES:
Creaming, Combining, Folding

Creaming:
1. Soften the fats on low speed.
2. Add the sugar(s) and cream; increase the speed slowly.
3. Add the eggs one at a time; scrape the bowl frequently.
4. Add the dry ingredients in stages.

Combining:
Bringing together two or more components.
1. Prepare the components to be combined.
2. Add one to the other, using the appropriate mixing method (if needed).

Folding:
Do steps 1, 2, and 3 in one continuous motion.
1. Run a bowl scraper under the mixture, across the bottom of the bowl.
2. Turn the bowl counterclockwise.
3. Bring the bottom mixture to the top.

HACCP:
Store at 40° F for 1 day. After 1 day, store at 0° F.

HAZARDOUS FOOD:
Eggs

YIELD:	7 pounds, 5 ounces.	14 pounds, 10 ounces.

INGREDIENTS:		
Butter, unsalted	2 pounds	4 pounds
Almond paste	3 pounds	6 pounds
Eggs, whole	2 pounds	4 pounds
Flour, cake, sifted	5 ounces	10 ounces

METHOD OF PREPARATION:

1. Gather the equipment and ingredients.
2. Place the butter in a bowl, and soften with a paddle; then remove.
3. Place the almond paste in another bowl, and mix on low speed, with paddle, to soften. Add one or two eggs to further soften the paste; scrape well.
4. When the almond paste and butter are the same consistency, add the butter into the almond paste, and incorporate well.
5. Mix on medium speed to aerate.
6. Add the remaining eggs in stages, and scrape well.
7. Fold in the sifted flour, by hand, and incorporate well.

Scale:

1. 7 pounds, 5 ounces for full, 1-inch sheet pan; bake at 325° F.
2. 2 pounds, 7 ounces for full, thin sheet pan; bake at 400° F.
3. 3 pounds, 10½ ounces for full, 1-inch half sheet pan; bake at 325° F.

CAKES: BASES

ICINGS

CAKES: FINISHED

CREAMS

FILLINGS

PIES

SLOW BAKING

BATTER

DOUGHS

SAUCES

German Chocolate Cake

PASTRY TECHNIQUES:
Creaming, Combining, Whipping, Folding

Creaming:
1. Soften the fats on low speed.
2. Add the sugar(s) and cream; increase the speed slowly.
3. Add the eggs one at a time; scrape the bowl frequently.
4. Add the dry ingredients in stages.

Combining:
Bringing together two or more components.
1. Prepare the components to be combined.
2. Add one to the other, using the appropriate mixing method (if needed).

Whipping:
1. Hold the whip at a 55-degree angle.
2. Create circles, using a circular motion.
3. The circular motion needs to be perpendicular to the bowl.

Folding:
Do steps 1, 2, and 3 in one continuous motion.
1. Run a bowl scraper under the mixture, across the bottom of the bowl.
2. Turn the bowl counterclockwise.
3. Bring the bottom mixture to the top.

HACCP:
Store at 40° F for 1 day. After 1 day, store at 0° F.

HAZARDOUS FOODS:
Eggs
Egg whites
Buttermilk

YIELD:	10 pounds. 7, 9-inch Cakes	20 pounds. 14, 9-inch Cakes.
INGREDIENTS:		
Cocoa powder, sifted	3 ounces	6 ounces
Extract, vanilla	1 ounce	2 ounces
Salt	¼ ounce	½ ounce
Water, cold	12 ounces	1 pound, 8 ounces
Sugar, granulated	3 pounds	6 pounds
Butter, unsalted, or margarine	12 ounces	1 pound, 8 ounces
Shortening, high-ratio	11 ounces	1 pound, 5 ounces
Baking soda, sifted	¾ ounce	1½ ounces
Eggs, whole	12 ounces	1 pound, 8 ounces
Egg whites	12 ounces	1 pound, 8 ounces
Flour, cake, sifted	1 pound, 8 ounces	3 pounds
Buttermilk	1 pound, 8 ounces	3 pounds
German chocolate cake icing (see page 112)	As needed	As needed

METHOD OF PREPARATION:
1. Gather the equipment and ingredients.
2. Place the sifted cocoa powder, vanilla extract, salt, cold water, and one eighth of the granulated sugar in mixing bowl; blend together, and set aside.
3. Place the remaining granulated sugar, butter, shortening, and baking soda in a bowl, and cream together, using a paddle, at medium speed for 5 minutes.
4. Slowly add the whole eggs; continue mixing, and scrape the bowl as needed; mix for an additional 5 minutes.
5. Place the egg whites in a bowl, and whip to a stiff peak.
6. Add the sifted cake flour, cocoa-water mixture, and buttermilk to the creaming mixture. Scrape the bowl and mix for 5 minutes.
7. Gently fold the beaten egg whites, by hand, into the creamed mixture; incorporate well.
8. Fill 9-inch cake pans with 1 pound, 7 ounces of batter.
9. Bake at 360° F until set in the center and firm in texture.
10. Turn out onto paper-lined sheet pans to cool, or cool in pans on wire racks.
11. Cover the cake with German chocolate cake icing.

Hazelnut Cake

PASTRY TECHNIQUES:
Whipping, Folding

Whipping:
1. Hold the whip at a 55-degree angle.
2. Create circles, using a circular motion.
3. The circular motion needs to be perpendicular to the bowl.

Folding:
Do steps 1, 2, and 3 in one continuous motion.
1. Run a bowl scraper under the mixture, across the bottom of the bowl.
2. Turn the bowl counterclockwise.
3. Bring the bottom mixture to the top.

HACCP:
Store at 40° F for 1 day. After 1 day, store at 0° F.

HAZARDOUS FOODS:
Egg yolks
Egg whites

YIELD:	7 pounds, 4½ ounces 4, 9-inch Cakes	14 pounds, 9 ounces 8, 9-inch Cakes

INGREDIENTS:		
Egg yolks	1 pound	2 pounds
Sugar, granulated	1 pound, 6 ounces	2 pounds, 12 ounces
Egg whites	1 pound, 10 ounces	3 pounds, 4 ounces
Salt	½ ounce	1 ounce
Extract, vanilla	To taste	To taste
Lemon juice	To taste	To taste
Flour, hazelnut	3 pounds, 4 ounces	6 pounds, 8 ounces

METHOD OF PREPARATION:

1. Gather the equipment and ingredients.
2. Place the egg yolks and one third of the granulated sugar in bowl; whip to full volume.
3. Place the egg whites and remaining granulated sugar in a bowl; whip to a medium peak to make a meringue.
4. Fold the meringue into the egg yolk mixture by hand.
5. Add the salt, vanilla extract, and lemon juice; incorporate well.
6. Gently incorporate the hazelnut flour.
7. Scale 1 pound, 12 ounces of batter into each of the lightly greased, paper-lined, 9-inch cake pans.
8. Bake at 350° F until firm in the center.

CAKES: BASES

ICINGS

CAKES: FINISHED

CREAMS

FILLINGS

PIES

SLOW BAKING

BATTER

DOUGHS

SAUCES

Jelly Roll Sponge Cake

PASTRY TECHNIQUES:
Whipping, Folding, Spreading

Whipping:
1. Hold the whip at a 55-degree angle.
2. Create circles, using a circular motion.
3. The circular motion needs to be perpendicular to the bowl.

Folding:
Do steps 1, 2, and 3 in one continuous motion.
1. Run a bowl scraper under the mixture, across the bottom of the bowl.
2. Turn the bowl counterclockwise.
3. Bring the bottom mixture to the top.

Spreading:
1. Using an icing spatula or off-set spatula, smooth the icing or other spreading medium over the surface area.

HACCP:
Store at 40° F for 1 day. After 1 day, store at 0° F.

HAZARDOUS FOODS:
Egg yolks
Egg whites

YIELD:	2 pounds, 1 ounce.	6 pounds, 3 ounces.
	1 Sheet Pan	3 Sheet Pans

INGREDIENTS:

Flour, bread, sifted	4 ounces	12 ounces
Flour, cake, sifted	1⅓ ounces	4 ounces
Baking powder, sifted	Pinch	½ ounce
Salt	Pinch	¼ ounce
Simple syrup, warm (see page 415)	2⅔ ounces	8 ounces
Egg yolks	7 ounces	1 pound, 5 ounces
Honey	1⅔ ounces	5 ounces
Oil, vegetable	1⅔ ounces	5 ounces
Extract, vanilla	⅓ ounce	1 ounce
Extract, lemon	⅛ ounce	¼ ounce
Egg whites	10 ounces	1 pound, 14 ounces
Sugar, granulated	4⅔ ounces	14 ounces

METHOD OF PREPARATION:

1. Gather the equipment and ingredients.
2. Sift together the bread and cake flours, baking powder, and salt; set aside.
3. Prepare the simple syrup; after it is warm, set it aside.
4. Place the egg yolks, honey, oil, vanilla extract, and lemon extract in a bowl; whip to full volume.
5. When the egg yolk mixture just about reaches full volume, turn down the mixer to medium speed, and slowly add the warm simple syrup in a slow, steady stream.
6. In another bowl, place the egg whites, and whip to a medium peak, slowly adding the granulated sugar to make a meringue. (This procedure should be started when the egg yolks are about half whipped.)
7. When the egg yolks and egg whites are both done, remove the bowls from the mixers, and fold the meringue into the egg yolk mixture by hand. *Do not overmix.* (This process should be done very carefully.)
8. Fold in the dry ingredients carefully by hand.
9. Scale 2 pounds, 1 ounce of batter per pan into straight, parchment-lined sheet pans.

CHEF NOTES:
Use the following methods to test for doneness:
1. Check for color; golden brown is good.
2. Check for firmness; the cake should spring back.

10. Spread evenly in the pan.
11. Bake at 420° F for approximately 10 to 15 minutes. Test for doneness. (See chef notes.)
12. Remove from the oven.
13. Roll up each jelly roll while still hot.
14. Cool in the roll position.
15. Unroll to fill and reroll.

Liquid Shortening Sponge Cake, Chocolate

PASTRY TECHNIQUE:
Blending

Blending:
1. Combine the dry ingredients on low speed.
2. Add the softened fat(s) and liquid(s).
3. Mix the ingredients on low speed.
4. Increase the speed gradually.

HACCP:
Store at 40° F for 1 day. After 1 day, store at 0° F.

HAZARDOUS FOODS:
Eggs
Milk

YIELD:	10 pounds, 13¾ ounces.	21 pounds, 11½ ounces.
	7, 9-inch Cakes	14, 9-inch Cakes

INGREDIENTS:

Eggs, whole	3 pounds, 5 ounces	6 pounds, 10 ounces
Shortening, liquid, high-ratio	1 pound, 4 ounces	2 pounds, 8 ounces
Milk, whole	1 pound, 4 ounces	2 pounds, 8 ounces
Extract, vanilla	1 ounce	2 ounces
Sugar, granulated	2 pounds, 12 ounces	5 pounds, 8 ounces
Flour, cake	1 pound, 10 ounces	3 pounds, 4 ounces
Baking powder	2 ounces	4 ounces
Salt	1 ounce	2 ounces
Baking soda	¾ ounce	1½ ounces
Cocoa powder	6 ounces	12 ounces

METHOD OF PREPARATION:

1. Gather the equipment and ingredients.
2. Grease the cake pans thoroughly.
3. Place all of the liquid ingredients in a mixing bowl.
4. Sift all of the dry ingredients together.
5. Place all of the sifted dry ingredients on top of the liquid ingredients in bowl.
6. Using a whip, whip on first speed until all of the ingredients are blended slightly, approximately 30 seconds.
7. Whip for 4 minutes on high speed; scrape the bowl well.
8. Whip for 3 minutes on medium speed; scrape the bowl well.
9. Fill 9-inch cake pans with 1 pound, 9 ounces of batter.
10. Bake at 350°F, until the cake is golden brown.
11. Cool in the pans for 5 to 10 minutes.
12. Turn out onto paper-lined sheet pans, and remove the pans.

Liquid Shortening Sponge Cake: Vanilla

PASTRY TECHNIQUE:

Blending

Blending:

1. Combine the dry ingredients on low speed.
2. Add the softened fat(s) and liquid(s).
3. Mix the ingredients on low speed.
4. Increase the speed gradually.

HACCP:

Store at 40° F for 1 day. After 1 day, store at 0° F.

HAZARDOUS FOODS:

Eggs
Milk

YIELD:	10 pounds, 6 ounces.	20 pounds, 12 ounces.
	7, 9-inch Cakes	14, 9-inch Cakes

INGREDIENTS:		
Eggs, whole	3 pounds, 5 ounces	6 pounds, 10 ounces
Shortening, liquid, high-ratio	1 pound, 4 ounces	2 pounds, 8 ounces
Milk, whole	1 pound	2 pounds
Extract, vanilla	2 ounces	4 ounces
Sugar, granulated	2 pounds, 8 ounces	5 pounds
Flour, cake	2 pounds	4 pounds
Baking powder	2¼ ounces	4½ ounces
Salt	¾ ounce	1½ ounces

METHOD OF PREPARATION:

1. Gather the equipment and ingredients.
2. Grease the cake pans thoroughly.
3. Place all of the liquid ingredients in a mixing bowl.
4. Sift all of the dry ingredients together.
5. Place all of the sifted ingredients on top of the liquid ingredients in bowl.
6. Using a whip, whip on first speed until the ingredients are blended slightly, approximately 30 seconds.
7. Whip for 4 minutes on high speed; scrape the bowl well.
8. Whip for 3 minutes on medium speed; scrape the bowl well.
9. Fill 9-inch cake pans with 1 pound, 7 ounces of batter.
10. Bake at 350° F, until the cake is golden brown.
11. Cool in the pans for 5 to 10 minutes.
12. Turn out onto paper-lined sheet pans, and remove the pans.

Luisenroulade

CAKES: BASES

ICINGS

CAKES: FINISHED

CREAMS

FILLINGS

PIES

SLOW BAKING

BATTER

DOUGHS

SAUCES

PASTRY TECHNIQUES:

Whipping, Folding, Spreading

Whipping:
1. Hold the whip at a 55-degree angle.
2. Create circles, using a circular motion.
3. The circular motion needs to be perpendicular to the bowl.

Folding:

Do steps 1, 2, and 3 in one continuous motion.
1. Run a bowl scraper under the mixture, across the bottom of the bowl.
2. Turn the bowl counterclockwise.
3. Bring the bottom mixture to the top.

Spreading:
1. Using an icing spatula or off-set spatula, smooth the icing or other spreading medium over the surface area.

HACCP:

Store at 40° F for 1 day. After 1 day, store at 0° F.

HAZARDOUS FOOD:

Egg yolks
Egg whites

YIELD:	1 pound, 10⅓ ounces 1 Sheet Cake 1-inch by 25-inch	4 pounds, 15 ounces 3 Sheet Cakes 17-inch by 25-inch

INGREDIENTS:

Egg yolks	5½ ounces	1 pound, ½ ounce
Sugar, granulated	1⅔ ounces	5 ounces
Egg whites	7⅓ ounces	1 pound, 6 ounces
Sugar, granulated	2¾ ounces	8½ ounces
Flour, cake, sifted	3 ounces	9 ounces
Crumbs, cake, yellow	3 ounces	9 ounces
Nougat, crushed	3 ounces	9 ounces
Salt	To taste	To taste
Extract, vanilla	To taste	To taste
Extract, lemon	To taste	To taste

METHOD OF PREPARATION:

1. Gather the equipment and ingredients.
2. Place the egg yolks in a bowl with 5 ounces of granulated sugar, and whip to a stiff peak.
3. Place the egg whites in another bowl, and whip to a medium-stiff peak; slowly add 8½ ounces of granulated sugar to make a meringue.
4. Incorporate the meringue into the egg yolk mixture by hand.
5. Combine all of the dry ingredients: cake flour, cake crumbs, nougat, and salt.
6. Fold into the egg mixture.
7. Fold in the flavorings.
8. Fill one parchment-lined sheet pan with 1 pound, 10⅓ ounces of batter.
9. Bake at 380° F until golden but firm in the center and dry to the touch on the top.

Pound Cake No. 1

PASTRY TECHNIQUE:
Combining

Combining:
Bringing together two or more components.
1. Prepare the components to be combined.
2. Add one to the other, using the appropriate mixing method (if needed).

HACCP:
Store at 40° F for 1 day. After 1 day, store at 0° F.

HAZARDOUS FOOD:
Eggs

YIELD:	6 pounds, 6 ounces.	12 pounds, 12 ounces.
	6 Loaves	12 Loaves

INGREDIENTS:		
Flour, cake, sifted	1 pound, 9¾ ounces	3 pounds, 3½ ounces
Shortening, high-ratio	8 ounces	1 pound
Butter, unsalted, softened	8 ounces	1 pound
Sugar, granulated	1 pound, 12½ ounces	3 pounds, 9 ounces
Dry milk solids (DMS), sifted	2½ ounces	5 ounces
Salt	½ ounce	1 ounce
Baking powder, sifted	¼ ounce	½ ounce
Water	12½ ounces	1 pound, 9 ounces
Eggs, whole	1 pound	2 pounds

METHOD OF PREPARATION:

1. Gather the equipment and ingredients.
2. Place the cake flour, shortening, butter, granulated sugar, DMS, salt, and baking powder in a bowl.
3. Using a paddle, mix on low speed to blend all of the ingredients together until smooth.
4. Gradually add water to the mixture.
5. Add the whole eggs in stages; continue to mix until smooth, scraping the bowl as needed throughout. When all of the eggs have been added, continue mixing until the batter is smooth and creamy.
6. Fill each greased, aluminum loaf pan with 1 pound, 1 ounce of batter. Place the loaf pans on sheet pans for baking.
7. Bake at 375° F for 30 minutes, or until golden brown and the center splits. The center split must be dry before removing the cakes from the oven.

CAKES: BASES

ICINGS

CAKES: FINISHED

CREAMS

FILLINGS

PIES

SLOW BAKING

BATTER

DOUGHS

SAUCES

PASTRY TECHNIQUES:
Creaming

Creaming:
1. Soften the fats on low speed.
2. Add the sugar(s) and cream; increase the speed slowly.
3. Add the eggs one at a time; scrape the bowl frequently.
4. Add the dry ingredients in stages.

HACCP:
Store at 40° F for 1 day. After 1 day, store at 0° F.

HAZARDOUS FOOD:
Eggs

Pound Cake No. 2
(Sandkuchen)

YIELD:	4 pounds, 11½ ounces	9 pounds, 7 ounces

INGREDIENTS:		
Butter, unsalted (70° F)	1 pound, 1½ ounces	2 pounds, 3 ounces
Sugar, granulated	1 pound, 1½ ounces	2 pounds, 3 ounces
Eggs, whole (70° F)	1 pound, 1½ ounces	2 pounds, 3 ounces
Extract, vanilla	½ ounce	1 ounce
Extract, lemon	½ ounce	1 ounce
Salt	½ ounce	1 ounce
Flour, cake, sifted	10½ ounces	1 pound, 5 ounces
Cornstarch	10½ ounces	1 pound, 5 ounces
Baking powder	½ ounce	1 ounce

METHOD OF PREPARATION:

1. Gather the equipment and ingredients.
2. Place the butter in a bowl with a paddle, and cream until smooth.
3. Add the granulated sugar, and cream on medium speed until light, approximately 10 minutes.
4. Add the eggs, vanilla extract, and lemon extract in stages. Scrape the bowl well between additions.
5. Mix until light and fluffy, approximately 6 minutes.
6. Sift together the salt, cake flour, cornstarch, and baking powder.
7. Remove the butter mixture from the machine, and fold in the sifted dry ingredients; incorporate well.

Scale into Grease Pans:

1. 2 pounds, 8 ounces for a 9-inch by 3-inch cake round; bake at 350° F for 25 to 30 minutes.
2. 1 pound, 5 ounces for a 6-inch by 3-inch cake round; bake at 375° F for approximately 35 minutes.
3. 1 pound for a standard, rectangular loaf pan; bake at 375° F for approximately 35 minutes, or until golden brown.

Sacher Cake: Classical

Chopping, Melting, Whipping, Folding

Chopping:

1. Use a sharp knife.
2. Hold the food product properly.
3. Cut with a quick downward motion.

Melting:

1. Prepare the food product to be melted.
2. Place the food product an appropriate sized pot over direct heat or over a double boiler.
3. Stir frequently or occasionally, depending on the delicacy of the product, until melted.

OR

1. Place the product on a sheet pan or in a bowl, and place in a low oven until melted.

Whipping:

1. Hold the whip at a 55-degree angle.
2. Create circles, using a circular motion.
3. The circular motion needs to be perpendicular to the bowl.

Folding:

Do steps 1, 2, and 3 in one continuous motion.
1. Run a bowl scraper under the mixture, across the bottom of the bowl.
2. Turn the bowl counterclockwise.
3. Bring the bottom mixture to the top.

HACCP:

Store at 40° F for 1 day. After 1 day, store at 0° F.

HAZARDOUS FOODS:

Egg yolks
Egg whites

YIELD:		5 pounds.	10 pounds.
		2, 9-inch Cakes	4, 9-inch Cakes

INGREDIENTS:			
Butter, unsalted, softened	1 pound	2 pounds
Extract, vanilla	To taste	To taste
Sugar, granulated	1 pound	2 pounds
Chocolate, dark, semi-sweet	1 pound	2 pounds
Egg yolks	6½ ounces	13 ounces
Egg whites	9½ ounces	1 pound, 3 ounces
Flour, cake	1 pound	2 pounds

METHOD OF PREPARATION:

1. Gather the equipment and ingredients.
2. Place the butter, vanilla extract, and sugar in a bowl; whip until light and fluffy.
3. Chop the chocolate, and melt using a double boiler.
4. Once the butter mixture has been whipped light and fluffy, add the melted chocolate.
5. Blend until smooth.
6. Gradually add the egg yolks into the chocolate-butter mixture, and combine until smooth.
7. In another bowl, whip the egg whites to a medium peak.
8. Sift the cake flour.
9. Alternately fold in the sifted flour and egg whites into the chocolate-butter mixture.
10. Scale 2 pounds, 8 ounces of batter into greased, paper-lined, 9-inch cake pans.
11. Bake at 325° F until firm and dry in the center.

ICINGS

CAKES: FINISHED

CREAMS

FILLINGS

PIES

SLOW BAKING

BATTER

DOUGHS

SAUCES

PASTRY TECHNIQUES:

Chopping, Melting, Whipping, Folding

Chopping:

1. Use a sharp knife.
2. Hold the food product properly.
3. Cut with a quick downward motion.

Melting:

1. Prepare the food product to be melted.
2. Place the food product an appropriate sized pot over direct heat or over a double boiler.
3. Stir frequently or occasionally, depending on the delicacy of the product, until melted.

OR

1. Place the product on a sheet pan or in a bowl, and place in a low oven until melted.

Whipping:

1. Hold the whip at a 55-degree angle.
2. Create circles, using a circular motion.
3. The circular motion needs to be perpendicular to the bowl.

Folding:

Do steps 1, 2, and 3 in one continuous motion.
1. Run a bowl scraper under the mixture, across the bottom of the bowl.
2. Turn the bowl counterclockwise.
3. Bring the bottom mixture to the top.

HACCP:

Store at 40° F for 1 day. After 1 day, store at 0° F.

HAZARDOUS FOODS:

Egg yolks
Egg whites

Sacher Cake: Modern

YIELD:	10 pounds, 10 ounces.	31 pounds, 14½ ounces.
	5, 9-inch Cakes	15, 9-inch Cakes

INGREDIENTS:

Butter, unsalted, softened	2 pounds	6 pounds
Sugar, confectionery	12 ounces	2 pounds, 4 ounces
Chocolate, dark, semi-sweet	1 pound, 10½ ounces	5 pounds
Egg yolks	1 pound, 7½ ounces	4 pounds, 6½ ounces
Egg whites	2 pounds, 3 ounces	6 pounds, 9½ ounces
Sugar, granulated	12½ ounces	2 pounds, 5 ounces
Flour, bread	14 ounces	2 pounds, 10 ounces
Flour, cake	14 ounces	2 pounds, 10 ounces
Baking powder	½ ounce	1½ ounces

METHOD OF PREPARATION:

1. Gather the equipment and ingredients.
2. Place the butter and confectionery sugar in a bowl; whip until very light.
3. Chop the chocolate, and melt it using a double boiler.
4. Slowly add the melted chocolate to the whipped butter mixture.
5. Blend well.
6. Gradually add the egg yolks to the chocolate-butter mixture.
7. In another bowl, place the egg whites; whip to a medium stiff peak while slowly adding the granulated sugar to make a meringue.
8. Gently fold the meringue into the chocolate-butter mixture.
9. Sift the dry ingredients together.
10. Fold in the remaining sifted dry ingredients.
11. Scale 2 pounds, 2 ounces of batter into greased, parchment-lined, 9-inch cake pans.
12. Bake at 350° F, for approximately 40 minutes or until firm and dry in the center.

Spanish Vanilla Cake

PASTRY TECHNIQUES:

Whipping, Combining, Folding

Whipping:

1. Hold the whip at a 55-degree angle.
2. Create circles, using a circular motion.
3. The circular motion needs to be perpendicular to the bowl.

Combining:

Bringing together two or more components.
1. Prepare the components to be combined.
2. Add one to the other, using the appropriate mixing method (if needed).

Folding:

Do steps 1, 2, and 3 in one continuous motion.
1. Run a bowl scraper under the mixture, across the bottom of the bowl.
2. Turn the bowl counterclockwise.
3. Bring the bottom mixture to the top.

HACCP:

Store at 40° F for 1 day. After 1 day, store at 0° F.

HAZARDOUS FOODS:

Egg yolks
Egg whites

YIELD:	10 pounds, 7 ounces 5, 9-inch Cakes	20 pounds, 14 ounces 10, 9-inch Cakes

INGREDIENTS:		
Butter, unsalted	13 ounces	1 pound, 10 ounces
Almond paste	2 pounds, 10 ounces	5 pounds, 4 ounces
Egg yolks	1 pound, 8 ounces	3 pounds
Egg whites	2 pounds	4 pounds
Sugar, granulated	1 pound, 5 ounces	2 pounds, 10 ounces
Flour, cake	1 pound, 2 ounces	2 pounds, 4 ounces
Couverture, dark, semi-sweet, chopped	1 pound, 1 ounce	2 pounds, 2 ounces
Extract, vanilla	To taste	To taste
Extract, lemon	To taste	To taste
Salt	To taste	To taste

METHOD OF PREPARATION:

1. Gather the equipment and ingredients.
2. Melt the butter, and set it aside.
3. Place the almond paste and egg yolks in a bowl; whip until the color lightens.
4. Place the egg whites in another bowl, and whip to a medium peak; slowly add in the granulated sugar to make a meringue.
5. Fold the egg yolk mixture into the meringue.
6. Combine the cake flour and chopped couverture.
7. Fold into the egg mixture.
8. Fold in the melted butter and flavorings.
9. Pour the batter into greased, paper-lined, 9-inch cake pans. Each pan should hold 2 pounds, 1 ounce of batter.
10. Bake at 350° F to 360° F until firm in the center.
11. Cool.

Cakes: Bases **33**

CAKES: BASES

ICINGS

CAKES: FINISHED

CREAMS

FILLINGS

PIES

SLOW BAKING

BATTER

DOUGHS

SAUCES

Vanilla Chiffon Genoise

YIELD:	10 pounds, 6 ounces.	20 pounds, 12 ounces.
	7, 9-inch Cakes	14, 9-inch Cakes

INGREDIENTS:

Egg yolks	2 pounds	4 pounds
Sugar, granulated	3 pounds	6 pounds
Oil, vegetable	12 ounces	1 pound, 8 ounces
Egg whites	2 pounds	4 pounds
Flour, cake, sifted	2 pounds, 4 ounces	4 pounds, 8 ounces
Baking powder	1 ounce	2 ounces
Water, room temperature	5 ounces	10 ounces
Extract, vanilla	To taste	To taste

METHOD OF PREPARATION:

1. Gather the equipment and ingredients.
2. Properly grease the cake pans.
3. Place the egg yolks and half of the granulated sugar in a bowl; whip to full volume.
4. Continue mixing on medium speed, and slowly incorporate the oil.
5. In another bowl, whip the egg whites to a medium peak; slowly add the remaining granulated sugar to make a meringue.
6. Sift together the cake flour and baking powder.
7. Combine the water and vanilla extract.
8. Alternately add the flour and water mixtures into the yolk mixture by hand.
9. Fold the meringue into the batter.
10. Scale 1 pound, 8 ounces batter into a greased paper-lined 9-inch cake pan.
11. Bake at 360° F until spongy in the center.

PASTRY TECHNIQUES:
Whipping, Combining

Whipping:
1. Hold the whip at a 55-degree angle.
2. Create circles, using a circular motion.
3. The circular motion needs to be perpendicular to the bowl.

Combining:
Bringing together two or more components.
1. Prepare the components to be combined.
2. Add one to the other, using the appropriate mixing method (if needed).

HACCP:
Store at 40° F for 1 day. After 1 day, store at 0° F.

HAZARDOUS FOODS:
Egg yolks
Egg whites

Vanilla Genoise

PASTRY TECHNIQUES:
Whipping, Melting, Folding

Whipping:
1. Hold the whip at a 55-degree angle.
2. Create circles, using a circular motion.
3. The circular motion needs to be perpendicular to the bowl.

Melting:
1. Prepare the food product to be melted.
2. Place the food product an appropriate sized pot over direct heat or over a double boiler.
3. Stir frequently or occasionally, depending on the delicacy of the product, until melted.

OR
1. Place the product on a sheet pan or in a bowl, and place in a low-temperature oven until melted.

Folding:
Do steps 1, 2, and 3 in one continuous motion.
1. Run a bowl scraper under the mixture, across the bottom of the bowl.
2. Turn the bowl counterclockwise.
3. Bring the bottom mixture to the top.

HACCP:
Store at 40° F for 1 day. After 1 day, store at 0° F.

HAZARDOUS FOOD:
Eggs

YIELD:	3 pounds, 10½ ounces.	7 pounds, 5 ounces.
	22, 9-inch by 3-inch Pans	4, 9-inch by 3-inch Pans

INGREDIENTS:

Flour, cake	8 ounces	1 pound
Cornstarch	6 ounces	12 ounces
Butter, unsalted	6 ounces	12 ounces
Eggs, whole	1 pound, 8 ounces	3 pounds
Salt	⅛ ounce	¼ ounce
Extract, vanilla	¼ ounce	½ ounce
Extract, lemon	⅛ ounce	¼ ounce
Sugar, granulated	14 ounces	1 pound, 12 ounces

METHOD OF PREPARATION:

1. Gather the equipment and ingredients.
2. Properly grease the cake pans.
3. Sift the cake flour and cornstarch together; set aside.
4. Melt the butter, and set aside. (Butter should be only lukewarm.)
5. Place the whole eggs, salt, vanilla extract, lemon extract, and granulated sugar in a bowl; immediately whisk over a warm water bath. (Never scale the ingredients together in advance, or lumping will occur when the dry sugar comes into contact with the eggs.)
6. Heat the mixture to 110° F constantly mixing at all times. *Do not cook* the mixture.
7. Remove the bowl from the warm bath, and place on a mixer; whip on high speed to full volume. (Full volume can be determined by the "5 second track method." See chef note 3.)
8. When full volume is reached, remove the bowl from the mixer, and immediately fold the dry ingredients into the whipped egg mixture. Use your hand along with a plastic scraper to distribute the sifted dry ingredients evenly. This is a combination of the folding technique (turning the bowl counterclockwise with the left hand and scraping up from the bottom with the right hand in a clockwise rotation; finish out on top of the batter with your right hand and scraper palm up and shaking vigorously to distribute the flour and starch). Work quickly. Continue mixing until all of the ingredients are completely incorporated. (The longer it takes to combine ingredients, the greater the chance that lumps will be trapped in the batter.)
9. Place a small amount of batter in another small bowl.
10. Using your fingers, quickly whisk the melted butter into this batter until completely incorporated.

ICINGS

CAKES: FINISHED

CREAMS

FILLINGS

PIES

SLOW BAKING

BATTER

DOUGHS

SAUCES

CHEF NOTES:
1. The following methods test for doneness:
   (a) Check for color; a golden brown is good.
   (b) Check to see if the cake is pulling away from the sides of the pan.
   (c) Touch the center of the cake; it should spring back.
2. Sponge cake is a very delicate cake; do not slam the door or knock the pans together.
3. The following is the "5-second track method":
   Put ½ inch of your fingertip through the batter. If it holds a track for 5 seconds before closing, it is done. If it fails to hold a track, whip more. Check several times during mixing. Stay with the machine to monitor its progress. Keep track of mixing times and speeds. As the batter thickens, reduce the speed to medium, and check more frequently. *Do not overmix;* this will result in loss of volume or total collapse. Eggs should be cool at the end of this process.

11. Fold this butter mixture, gently, back into the remaining batter.
12. Scale the batter at 1 pound, 11 ounces per 9-inch by 3-inch pan, approximately two-thirds full.
13. Bake at 350° F for approximately 35 to 40 minutes. Test for doneness. (See chef note 1.)
14. When done, remove from the oven, and place on a cooling rack.

Walnut Chiffon Genoise

PASTRY TECHNIQUES:
Whipping, Combining

Whipping:
1. Hold the whip at a 55-degree angle.
2. Create circles, using a circular motion.
3. The circular motion needs to be perpendicular to the bowl.

Combining:
Bringing together two or more components.
1. Prepare the components to be combined.
2. Add one to the other, using the appropriate mixing method (if needed).

HACCP:
Store at 40° F for 1 day. After 1 day, store at 0° F.

HAZARDOUS FOODS:
Egg yolks
Egg whites

YIELD:	5 pounds, 10 ounces.	11 pounds, 4 ounces.
	4, 9-inch Cakes.	8, 9-inch Cakes.

INGREDIENTS:

Egg yolks	1 pound	2 pounds
Sugar, granulated	1 pound, 8 ounces	3 pounds
Oil, vegetable	6 ounces	12 ounces
Egg whites	1 pound	2 pounds
Walnuts or hazelnuts, finely chopped	7 ounces	14 ounces
Flour, cake, sifted	1 pound, 2 ounces	2 pounds, 4 ounces
Baking powder	½ ounce	1 ounce
Water, room temperature	2½ ounces	5 ounces
Extract, vanilla	To taste	To taste

METHOD OF PREPARATION:

1. Gather the equipment and ingredients.
2. Properly grease the cake pans.
3. Place the egg yolks and half of the granulated sugar in a bowl; whip to full volume.
4. Continue mixing on medium speed, and slowly incorporate the oil.
5. In another bowl, whip the egg whites to a medium peak; slowly add the remaining granulated sugar to make a meringue.
6. Combine the nuts, sifted cake flour, and baking powder.
7. Combine the water and vanilla extract.
8. Alternately add the flour and water mixtures into the yolk mixture by hand.
9. Fold the meringue into the batter.
10. Fill each 9-inch greased cake pan with 1 pound, 6 ounces of batter.
11. Bake at 360° F until spongy in the center.

CHEF NOTE:
If hazelnut is used, the product will be *Hazelnut Chiffon Genoise.*

CAKES: BASES

ICINGS

CAKES: FINISHED

CREAMS

FILLINGS

PIES

SLOW BAKING

BATTER

DOUGHS

SAUCES

PASTRY TECHNIQUE:
Blending

Blending:
1. Combine the dry ingredients on low speed.
2. Add the softened fat(s) and liquid(s).
3. Mix the ingredients on low speed.
4. Increase the speed gradually.

HACCP:
Store at 40° F for 1 day. After 1 day, store at 0° F.

HAZARDOUS FOOD:
Eggs

Yellow Layer Cake
(High-Ratio)

YIELD:	5 pounds, 2½ ounces.	10 pounds, 5 ounces.
	2½, 9-inch Cakes.	5, 9-inch Cakes.
	1 Full Sheet Pan.	2 Full Sheet Pans.

INGREDIENTS:

Eggs, whole	1 pound	2 pounds
Water, cold	12 ounces	1 pound, 8 ounces
Flour, cake	1 pound, 5 ounces	2 pounds, 10 ounces
Salt	½ ounce	1 ounce
Dry milk solids (DMS)	2 ounces	4 ounces
Baking powder	1 ounce	2 ounces
Shortening, high-ratio	9 ounces	1 pound, 2 ounces
Sugar, granulated	1 pound, 5 ounces	2 pounds, 10 ounces

METHOD OF PREPARATION:

1. Gather the equipment and ingredients.
2. Combine together the whole eggs and two thirds of the water; whisk together, and set aside.
3. Sift together the cake flour, salt, DMS, and baking powder.
4. Place the sifted ingredients, shortening, sugar, and one third of the egg-water mixture into a mixing bowl.
5. Blend on low speed, with a paddle, for 4 minutes; scrape the bowl well.
6. Add one third more of the egg-water mixture, and mix for 4 minutes; scrape the bowl well.
7. Add the remaining third of the egg-water mixture, and mix for 4 minutes; scrape the bowl well.
8. Add the remaining one third of water, and mix until smooth.
9. Bake at 375° F for 30 to 40 minutes, or until golden brown.

Scale:

1. 2 pounds, 1 ounce for 9-inch by 3-inch cake pans.
2. 5 pounds, 2½ ounces for full sheet pan.

2

Buttercreams and Icings

Buttercreams and Icings

Basic Buttercream

PASTRY TECHNIQUES:
Creaming, Whipping

Creaming:
1. Soften the fats on low speed.
2. Add the sugar(s) and cream; increase the speed slowly.
3. Add the eggs one at a time; scrape the bowl frequently.
4. Add the dry ingredients in stages.

Whipping:
1. Hold the whip at a 55-degree angle.
2. Create circles, using a circular motion.
3. The circular motion needs to be perpendicular to the bowl.

HACCP:
Store at 40° F.

HAZARDOUS FOOD:
Egg whites

YIELD:		4 pounds, 8 ounces.	18 pounds.

INGREDIENTS:			
Butter, unsalted		12 ounces	3 pounds
Sugar, confectionery		2 pounds, 8 ounces	10 pounds
Shortening, high-ratio		12 ounces	3 pounds
Egg whites (pasteurized)		8 ounces	2 pounds
Extract, vanilla		To taste	To taste
Lemon juice		To taste	To taste

METHOD OF PREPARATION:
1. Gather the equipment and ingredients.
2. Place the butter in a bowl with half of the confectionery sugar; cream using a paddle to the consistency of the shortening.
3. Scrape bowl well.
4. Add the shortening and remaining confectionery sugar; cream using a paddle until light and airy.
5. Remove the paddle attachment, and replace with the whip attachment.
6. While whipping, slowly add the egg whites and flavorings in stages; scrape the bowl between additions.
7. Combine ingredients well.
8. Continue whipping until light and airy.

CAKES: BASES

ICINGS

CAKES: FINISHED

CREAMS

FILLINGS

PIES

SLOW BAKING

BATTER

DOUGHS

SAUCES

Buttercream with Fondant

PASTRY TECHNIQUES:
Creaming, Whipping

Creaming:
1. Soften the fats on low speed.
2. Add the sugar(s) and cream; increase the speed slowly.
3. Add the eggs one at a time; scrape the bowl frequently.
4. Add the dry ingredients in stages.

Whipping:
1. Hold the whip at a 55-degree angle.
2. Create circles, using a circular motion.
3. The circular motion needs to be perpendicular to the bowl.

HACCP:
Store at 40° F.

YIELD:	5 pounds.	10 pounds.
INGREDIENTS:		
Butter, unsalted, room temperature	1 pound	2 pounds
Shortening, high-ratio	1 pound	2 pounds
Fondant, prepared	3 pounds	6 pounds

METHOD OF PREPARATION:

1. Gather the equipment and ingredients.
2. Scale all of the ingredients.
3. Place the firmest ingredient in the bowl; paddle to the consistency of the next ingredient's consistency.
4. Scrape the bowl well.
5. Add the next ingredient, and paddle to the consistency of the last ingredient.
6. Scrape the bowl well.
7. Add the last ingredient; paddle until light and fluffy.
8. Remove the paddle attachment, and replace with the whip attachment.
9. Whip until light in consistency.

CHEF NOTE:
Dry fondant can be substituted for prepared fondant by combining 2 pounds, 11 ounces of dry fondant with 5 ounces of warm water until it has a smooth consistency.

CAKES: BASES

ICINGS

CAKES: FINISHED

CREAMS

FILLINGS

PIES

SLOW BAKING

BATTER

DOUGHS

SAUCES

PASTRY TECHNIQUES:

Cooking, Creaming, Whipping, Combining

Cooking:

Preparing food through the use of various sources of heating.
1. Choose the appropriate heat application: baking, boiling, simmering, etc.
2. Prepare the formula according to instructions.
3. Cook according to instructions.

Creaming:

1. Soften the fats on low speed.
2. Add the sugar(s) and cream; increase the speed slowly.
3. Add the eggs one at a time; scrape the bowl frequently.
4. Add the dry ingredients in stages.

Whipping:

1. Hold the whip at a 55-degree angle.
2. Create circles, using a circular motion.
3. The circular motion needs to be perpendicular to the bowl.

Combining:

Bringing together two or more components.
1. Prepare the components to be combined.
2. Add one to the other, using the appropriate mixing method (if needed).

HACCP:

Store at 40° F.

HAZARDOUS FOOD:

Egg whites

CHEF NOTE:

To rewhip cold buttercream: Melt one third of the amount. Place the remaining cold buttercream in a bowl. Add the melted buttercream, and, using a whip, combine at low speed. Whip at high speed until the cream becomes smooth again. If it is still lumpy, melt more buttercream, and add it to the bowl. Continue whipping the mixture.

Buttercream with Meringue

YIELD: 17 pounds, 8½ ounces. 26 pounds, 4¾ ounces.

INGREDIENTS:

Water, hot	1 pound, 8 ounces	2 pounds, 4 ounces
Sugar, granulated	6 pounds	9 pounds
Egg whites (70° F)	3 pounds	4 pounds, 8 ounces
Butter, unsalted, room temperature	7 pounds	10 pounds, 8 ounces
Salt	½ ounce	¾ ounce
Extract, vanilla	To taste	To taste

METHOD OF PREPARATION:

1. Gather the equipment and ingredients.
2. Place the water and two thirds of the granulated sugar in a pot, and bring to a boil. As it begins to boil, skim the scum (impurities in foam on surface) with a ladle. Boil; do not stir. Wash down the sides of pot with a brush dipped in water to prevent crystals from forming.
3. Heat to 250° F.
4. Place the egg whites in a bowl, and whip to a stiff consistency; slowly add the remaining granulated sugar to form a meringue.
5. When the sugar syrup reaches 250° F, pour slowly into the meringue at medium speed.
6. Whip until cool.
7. In another bowl, cream the butter, salt, and vanilla extract until light and fluffy.
8. Add the creamed butter to the cooled meringue; whip on medium-to-high speed until all of the ingredients are well combined and the mixture is creamy.

Pastry Techniques:

Pastry Techniques:
Whipping, Combining

Whipping:
1. Hold the whip at a 55-degree angle.
2. Create circles, using a circular motion.
3. The circular motion needs to be perpendicular to the bowl.

Combining:
Bringing together two or more components.
1. Prepare the components to be combined.
2. Add one to the other, using the appropriate mixing method (if needed).

HACCP:
Store at 40° F.

Buttercream with Pâté à Bombe

YIELD:	4 pounds, 2½ ounces	8 pounds, 5 ounces

INGREDIENTS:		
Pâté à bombe (see page 98)	2 pounds, 2½ ounces	4 pounds, 5 ounces
Butter, unsalted	2 pounds	4 pounds

METHOD OF PREPARATION:

1. Gather the equipment and ingredients.
2. Prepare the pâté à bombe.
3. Place the butter in a bowl, and paddle until light.
4. Add the pâté à bombe to the whipped butter.
5. Combine well.

CAKES: BASES
ICINGS
CAKES: FINISHED
CREAMS
FILLINGS
PIES
SLOW BAKING
BATTER
DOUGHS
SAUCES

PASTRY TECHNIQUES:

Chopping, Melting, Whipping

Chopping:

1. Use a sharp knife.
2. Hold the food product properly.
3. Cut with a quick downward motion.

Melting:

1. Prepare the food product to be melted.
2. Place the food product in an appropriate-sized pot over direct heat or over a double boiler.
3. Stir frequently or occasionally, depending on the delicacy of the product, until melted.

OR

1. Place the product on a sheet pan or in a bowl, and place in a low-temperature oven until melted.

Whipping:

1. Hold the whip at a 55-degree angle.
2. Create circles, using a circular motion.
3. The circular motion needs to be perpendicular to the bowl.

HACCP:

Store at 40° F.

Chocolate Buttercream

YIELD:	2 pounds, 8 ounces.	5 pounds.

INGREDIENTS:

Buttercream	2 pounds	4 pounds
Chocolate, dark, semi-sweet	8 ounces	1 pound
Extract, vanilla	To taste	To taste

METHOD OF PREPARATION:

1. Gather the equipment and ingredients.
2. Prepare the buttercream according to the directions (see page 41), and leave in mixing bowl with a whip.
3. Chop and melt the dark chocolate.
4. Turn the mixer on low speed, and slowly add the chocolate in a steady stream into the buttercream without hitting the whip or the sides of the bowl.
5. Incorporate the chocolate completely.
6. Add the vanilla extract.

Variations:

1. *Fudge Base:*
   a. Soften the fudge base. (Use 30% according to the weight of the buttercream.)
   b. Add to the buttercream.
2. *Cocoa Powder:*
   a. Place the cocoa powder in a bowl. (Use according to desired taste.)
   b. Using a whisk, add either rum or brandy; add enough to create a paste.
   c. Add to the buttercream.
3. *Chocolate:*
   a. If a rich chocolate taste is desired, increase the amount of the chocolate.
   b. Follow the procedure as listed above.

Chocolate Fudge Icing

PASTRY TECHNIQUES:
Boiling, Combining

Boiling:
1. Bring the cooking liquid to a rapid boil.
2. Stir the contents.

Combining:
Bringing together two or more components.
1. Prepare the components to be combined.
2. Add one to the other, using the appropriate mixing method (if needed).

HACCP:
Store at 60° F to 65° F.

YIELD:	2 pounds, 4¼ ounces.	4 pounds, 8½ ounces.
	½ Sheet Pan.	1 Sheet Pan.

INGREDIENTS:

Ingredient		
Corn syrup	1 ounce	2 ounces
Shortening, all-purpose	¾ ounce	1½ ounces
Water	4½ ounces	9 ounces
Fudge base	8 ounces	1 pound
Sugar, confectionery, sifted	1 pound, 6 ounces	2 pounds, 12 ounces

METHOD OF PREPARATION:

1. Gather the equipment and ingredients.
2. Place the corn syrup, shortening, and water in a pot, and bring to a boil; remove from the heat.
3. Place the fudge base and confectionery sugar in a bowl; paddle until well blended.
4. Add the boiling water mixture into the fudge base in stages.
5. Combine until well blended.

CAKES: BASES

ICINGS

CAKES: FINISHED

CREAMS

FILLINGS

PIES

SLOW BAKING

BATTER

DOUGHS

SAUCES

PASTRY TECHNIQUES:
Chopping, Melting, Combining

Chopping:
1. Use a sharp knife.
2. Hold the food product properly.
3. Cut with a quick downward motion.

Melting:
1. Prepare the food product to be melted.
2. Place the food product in an appropriate-sized pot over direct heat or over a double boiler.
3. Stir frequently or occasionally, depending on the delicacy of the product, until melted.

OR

1. Place the product on a sheet pan or in a bowl, and place in a low-temperature oven until melted.

Combining:
Bringing together two or more components.
1. Prepare the components to be combined.
2. Add one to the other, using the appropriate mixing method (if needed).

HACCP:
Store at 60° F to 65° F.

Chocolate Glaze/ Coating

YIELD:	1 pound, 14 ounces.	3 pounds, 12 ounces.

INGREDIENTS:

Ingredient		
Chocolate, dark, semi-sweet, finely chopped	1 pound, 4 ounces	2 pounds, 8 ounces
Shortening, all-purpose	10 ounces	1 pound, 4 ounces

METHOD OF PREPARATION:

1. Gather the equipment and ingredients.
2. Melt the chopped chocolate over a double boiler.
3. Melt the shortening in a pot.
4. Combine the chocolate and shortening; mix well.
5. If necessary, strain through a chinois mousseline or cheesecloth.
6. Store covered in a dry storage area.
7. To use, heat over a double boiler.

CHEF NOTE:
Do not, under any circumstances, *heat* the chocolate or chocolate coating above 122° F.

Cream Cheese Icing

PASTRY TECHNIQUE:
Creaming

Creaming:
1. Soften the fats on low speed.
2. Add the sugar(s) and cream; increase the speed slowly.
3. Add the eggs one at a time; scrape the bowl frequently.
4. Add the dry ingredients in stages.

HACCP:
Store at 40° F.

HAZARDOUS FOOD:
Cream cheese

YIELD:	1 pound, 11 ounces.	3 pounds, 6 ounces.
INGREDIENTS:		
Butter, unsalted, room temperature	4 ounces	8 ounces
Cream cheese	8 ounces	1 pound
Shortening, high-ratio	1¾ ounces	3½ ounces
Sugar, confectionery, sifted	13 ounces	1 pound, 10 ounces
Lemon juice	¼ ounce	½ ounce

METHOD OF PREPARATION:

1. Gather the equipment and ingredients.
2. Place the butter in a bowl, and soften; remove.
3. Place the cream cheese in a bowl, and soften.
4. Add the shortening in stages to the softened cream cheese, and scrape the bowl well.
5. Add the softened butter in stages to the cream cheese and shortening mixture, and scrape the bowl well.
6. Add the sifted confectionery sugar and lemon juice; mix only until incorporated.

CHEF NOTE:
Excessive mixing will soften the mixture greatly.

CAKES: BASES
ICINGS
CAKES: FINISHED
CREAMS
FILLINGS
PIES
SLOW BAKING
BATTER
DOUGHS
SAUCES

French Cream Icing

PASTRY TECHNIQUES:
Creaming, Whipping

Creaming:
1. Soften the fats on low speed.
2. Add the sugar(s) and cream; increase the speed slowly.
3. Add the eggs one at a time; scrape the bowl frequently.
4. Add the dry ingredients in stages.

Whipping:
1. Hold the whip at a 55-degree angle.
2. Create circles, using a circular motion.
3. The circular motion needs to be perpendicular to the bowl.

HACCP:
Store at 40° F.

YIELD:	7 pounds, 9¼ ounces.	15 pounds, 2½ ounces.
INGREDIENTS:		
Sugar, confectionery	3 pounds, 12 ounces	7 pounds, 8 ounces
Dry milk solids (DMS)	4½ ounces	9 ounces
Shortening, high-ratio	2 pounds, 8 ounces	5 pounds
Emulsion, lemon	To taste	To taste
Extract, vanilla	To taste	To taste
Water	1 pound	2 pounds
Color, egg shade (optional)	As needed	As needed

METHOD OF PREPARATION:
1. Gather the equipment and ingredients.
2. Sift together the confectionery sugar and DMS.
3. Place the sifted ingredients in a bowl, and add the shortening; using a paddle, combine well.
4. Cream the mixture until light.
5. Combine the lemon emulsion, vanilla extract, water, and egg color (optional) into one container.
6. Slowly add the liquids in stages to the creamed sugar mixture.
7. Incorporate well.
8. Allow to whip until light and fluffy.

Pastry Technique:
Blooming

Blooming:
Gelatin sheets or leaves:
1. Fan the sheets out.
2. Cover the sheets in liquid.
3. Sheets are bloomed when softened.
Granular gelatin:
1. Sprinkle the gelatin.
2. Gelatin is ready when it is cream of wheat consistency.

HACCP:
Store at 60° F to 65° F.

Honey Glaze for Doughnuts

YIELD: 6 pounds, 9¼ ounces.   13 pounds, 2½ ounces.

INGREDIENTS:

Gelatin	½ ounce	1 ounce
Water	1 pound, 4 ounces	2 pounds, 8 ounces
Honey	4 ounces	8 ounces
Sugar, confectionery	5 pounds	10 pounds
Salt	¼ ounce	½ ounce
Extract, vanilla	½ ounce	1 ounce

METHOD OF PREPARATION:

1. Gather the equipment and ingredients.
2. Bloom the gelatin in a dry bowl with a small amount of water; set aside.
3. Heat the remaining water to 140° F.
4. Add the honey to the hot water, and stir.
5. Add the bloomed gelatin, and stir.
6. Place the confectionery sugar, salt, and vanilla extract in a bowl.
7. Slowly pour the hot water mixture into the sugar mixture; whisk constantly until well combined and sugar is melted.
8. Ready for icing.

Royal Icing

CAKES: BASES

ICINGS

CAKES: FINISHED

CREAMS

FILLINGS

PIES

SLOW BAKING

BATTER

DOUGHS

SAUCES

PASTRY TECHNIQUE:
Mixing

Mixing:
1. Follow the proper mixing procedure: creaming, blending, whipping, or combination.

HACCP:
Store at 40° F.

HAZARDOUS FOOD:
Egg whites

YIELD: 4 pounds, 12¼ ounces. 9 pounds, 8½ ounces.

INGREDIENTS:

Egg whites, room temperature	12 ounces	1 pound, 8 ounces
Sugar, confectionery	4 pounds	8 pounds
Cream of tartar	¼ ounce	½ ounce

METHOD OF PREPARATION:

1. Gather the equipment and ingredients.
2. Place the egg whites in a mixing bowl.
3. Sift all of the dry ingredients together twice or more until very fine.
4. Add half of the dry ingredients into the egg whites, and mix at low speed; use a paddle until well incorporated.
5. Add the remaining dry ingredients, and continue to mix on low speed; scrape the bowl often.
6. Mix for an additional 5 to 7 minutes on medium speed, or to a desired consistency.
7. Royal icing is ready for use, but if stored, it should be wrapped airtight and be refrigerated.

3

Cakes and Tortes: Finished

3

Cakes and Tortes: Finished

Baumkuchen Yogurt Cream Torte

YIELD: 2, 9-inch Tortes.

INGREDIENTS:

Baumkuchen sheets (see page 5)	As needed
Preserves, apricot	As needed
Oranges, mandarin, segments	As needed
Chocolate chiffon genoise (see page 11)	2, 9-inch layers, ⅛-inch thick
Vanilla chiffon genoise (see page 33)	2, 9-inch layers, ⅛-inch thick
Apricot, coating	As needed
Chantilly cream (see page 94)	As needed
Chocolate, dark, semi-sweet, stencils	16 each

Filling:

Gelatin	½ ounce
Water	8 ounces
Cream, heavy	1 pound
Egg yolks	4 ounces
Sugar, granulated	4 ounces
Yogurt, plain	1 pound
Compound, orange	To taste

METHOD OF PREPARATION:

Gather the equipment and ingredients.

Preparation of Filling:

1. Bloom the gelatin in water, and set aside.
2. Whip the heavy cream to a soft peak, and set aside.
3. Heat the egg yolks and sugar in a bowl over a double boiler to 140° F while stirring.
4. Add the egg mixture into the yogurt, and combine well.
5. Add the compound, and combine well.

Sidebar

PASTRY TECHNIQUES:
Blooming, Whipping, Tempering, Folding, Filling

Blooming:
Gelatin sheets or leaves:
1. Fan the sheets out.
2. Cover the sheets in liquid.
3. Sheets are bloomed when softened.
Granular gelatin:
1. Sprinkle the gelatin.
2. Gelatin is ready when it is cream of wheat consistency.

Whipping:
1. Hold the whip at a 55-degree angle.
2. Create circles, using a circular motion.
3. The circular motion needs to be perpendicular to the bowl.

Tempering:
1. Whisk the eggs vigorously while ladling hot liquid.

Folding:
Do steps 1, 2, and 3 in one continuous motion.
1. Run a bowl scraper under the mixture, across the bottom of the bowl.
2. Turn the bowl counterclockwise.
3. Bring the bottom mixture to the top.

Filling:
1. Cut open the food product.
2. Carefully spread the filling using an icing spatula.
3. Carefully pipe the filling using a pastry bag.

HACCP:
Store at 40° F.

HAZARDOUS FOODS:
Heavy cream
Egg yolks
Yogurt

Tab

CAKES: BASES

ICINGS

CAKES: FINISHED

CREAMS

FILLINGS

PIES

SLOW BAKING

BATTER

DOUGHS

SAUCES

6. Heat the gelatin, and temper into the yogurt mixture.

7. Fold the whipped cream into the yogurt mixture.

To Assemble (1, 9-inch torte):

1. Cut the baumkuchen sheets into thin slices, as instructed.

2. Brush the sides of the cake ring with apricot preserves.

3. Lay the slices of baumkuchen on the bottom and sides of the cake ring.

4. Fill the prepared yogurt cream into the ring one third of the way up.

5. Place the mandarin oranges in two circles in the cream.

6. Place a thin, trimmed, chocolate chiffon genoise layer on top.

7. Add more yogurt cream.

8. Place two circles of mandarin orange segments on top of the cream.

9. Place a thin, vanilla chiffon genoise layer on top.

10. Chill for at least 4 hours.

11. Turn upside down on a cake circle.

12. Remove the cake ring.

13. Brush with apricot coating over the top and sides of the cake.

14. Mark into 16 portions.

15. Decorate each portion with a rosette of chantilly cream.

16. Place a small chocolate stencil against each rosette.

Birthday Torte

YIELD: 1, 9-inch Torte.

CAKES: BASES

ICINGS

CAKES: FINISHED

CREAMS

FILLINGS

PIES

SLOW BAKING

BATTER

DOUGHS

SAUCES

PASTRY TECHNIQUES:

Filling, Icing, Piping

Filling:

1. Cut open the food product.
2. Carefully spread the filling using an icing spatula.
3. Carefully pipe the filling using a pastry bag.

Icing:

1. Use a clean icing spatula.
2. Work quickly and neatly.

Piping:

With bag:
1. Use a bag with a disposable tip; cut the bag at 45-degree angle.
2. Fill to no more than half full.
3. Burp the bag.
With cone:
1. Cut and fold the piping cone to the appropriate size.
2. Fill the cone with a small amount.
3. Fold the ends to form a triangle.
4. Pipe the desired designs.

HACCP:

Store at 40° F.

Top view

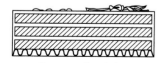

Cross-sectional view

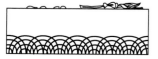

Side view

INGREDIENTS:

Cake layers, vanilla or chocolate	3, 9-inch layers, ⅜-inch thick
Simple syrup, flavored (see page 415)	3 ounces
Buttercream, vanilla	1 pound, 8 ounces
Buttercream, colored pink	6 ounces
Buttercream, colored green	2 ounces
Piping gel, chocolate-flavored	½ ounce

METHOD OF PREPARATION:

1. Gather the equipment and ingredients.
2. Moisten each cake layer with syrup during assembly.
3. Spread vanilla buttercream evenly over the bottom sponge layer.
4. Place the second layer on top; center and level.
5. Spread vanilla buttercream evenly over the second layer.
6. Place the last layer on top; center and level.
7. Cover the entire torte with vanilla buttercream; ice straight and level, leaving no more than one eighth of an inch of buttercream on top.
8. Pipe roses on nails with pink buttercream, as directed, and freeze.
9. Pipe flower stems, with green buttercream, on top of the cake.
10. Pipe half roses and buds on several stems.
11. Remove firm roses from the freezer; place on any open stems.
12. Pipe "Happy Birthday" on top of the cake.

PASTRY TECHNIQUES:
Filling, Icing, Piping

Filling:
1. Cut open the food product.
2. Carefully spread the filling using an icing spatula, or
3. Carefully pipe the filling using a pastry bag.

Icing:
1. Use a clean icing spatula.
2. Work quickly and neatly.

Piping:
With bag:
1. Use a bag with a disposable tip; cut the bag at 45-degree angle.
2. Fill to no more than half full.
3. Burp the bag.
With cone:
1. Cut and fold the piping cone to the appropriate size.
2. Fill the cone with a small amount.
3. Fold the ends to form a triangle.
4. Pipe the desired designs.

HACCP:
Store at 40° F.

HAZARDOUS FOOD:
Heavy cream

Black Forest Torte

YIELD: 1, 9-inch Torte.

INGREDIENTS:

Cake layers, chocolate	3, 9-inch layers, ⅜-inch thick
Simple syrup, Kirschwasser (see page 415)	3 ounces
Cream, heavy, whipped	1 pound
Black forest cherry filling (see page 199)	4 ounces
Chocolate, dark, semi-sweet, shaved	1 ounce
Glazé red cherries	As needed

METHOD OF PREPARATION:

1. Gather the equipment and ingredients.
2. Moisten each cake layer with syrup during assembly.
3. Ice inside of the ring with whipped cream, about ¼-inch thick.
4. Place the ring over the cardboard circle (cut to fit the ring).
5. Cut the cake layers in half.
6. Using the seam of the ring as a guide, grasp half of the cake layer along the cut side, and place it into the ring. The cut should line up with the seam, and the outside edge should be up against the whipped cream.
7. Turn the ring 180 degrees, and repeat with the second half of the cake layer.
8. Pipe a target pattern of whipped cream on the cake layer. Pipe a dot in the center, a ¼-inch bead around the outside edge, and finally a ¼-inch circle between the dot and the perimeter.
9. In between these lines of whipped cream, spoon in the filling; place the halved cherries next to each other to completely fill in all of the space. You should now have alternating circles of whipped cream and cherries.
10. Give the ring a third turn, and place the second cake layer in it. Press to level.
11. Pipe a ¼-inch layer of whipped cream on top of the cake, in a spiral pattern, from the center to the outside.
12. Give the ring a third turn, and repeat the process with the final layer. Be sure to level the cake layer as you build.
13. There should be about an ⅛ inch of space left between the top of the cake and the top edge of the ring. Fill it with whipped cream, and level.
14. Refrigerate the torte for about 5 minutes, or until firm.
15. Unmold by setting the torte on a platform of smaller diameter. Heat the outside of the ring carefully with a torch or hot towel. Carefully slide the ring down.
16. Repair any defects.
17. Divide and mark 16 portions evenly.

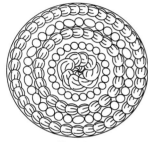

Top view

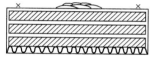

Cross-sectional view

Side view

18. Using whipped cream, pipe rosettes with a no. 3 star tube, ¼ inch from the edge of the torte, in the center of each portion.

19. Garnish the center of the torte and the outside bottom edge with shaved chocolate; reserve the largest pieces for the top and the crushed pieces for the bottom edge.

20. Garnish the top of the torte with glazé and cherries.

CAKES: BASES

ICINGS

CAKES: FINISHED

CREAMS

FILLINGS

PIES

SLOW BAKING

BATTER

DOUGHS

SAUCES

PASTRY TECHNIQUES:
Whipping, Folding, Filling, Icing

Whipping:
1. Hold the whip at a 55-degree angle.
2. Create circles, using a circular motion.
3. The circular motion needs to be perpendicular to the bowl.

Folding:
Do steps 1, 2, and 3 in one continuous motion.
1. Run a bowl scraper under the mixture, across the bottom of the bowl.
2. Turn the bowl counterclockwise.
3. Bring the bottom mixture to the top.

Filling:
1. Cut open the food product.
2. Carefully spread the filling using an icing spatula.
3. Carefully pipe the filling using a pastry bag.

Icing:
1. Use a clean icing spatula.
2. Work quickly and neatly.

HACCP:
Store at 40° F.

HAZARDOUS FOODS:
Egg yolks
Egg whites

Budapester Torte

YIELD: 5 pounds, 3½ ounces. 16 Layers/4 Tortes.

INGREDIENTS:

Layers:

Egg yolks	1 pound, 14 ounces
Sugar, granulated	22 ounces
Egg whites	1 pound, 4 ounces
Flour, cake, sifted	6 ounces
Cocoa powder, sifted	5½ ounces

For One Torte:

Simple syrup, rum or brandy-flavored (see page 415)	3 ounces
Preserves, raspberry	8 ounces
Buttercream, chocolate	2 pounds
Chocolate, dark, semi-sweet, shaved	As needed
Buttercream, vanilla	3 ounces

METHOD OF PREPARATION:

Gather the equipment and ingredients.

Preparation of Layers:
1. Place the egg yolks and 10 ounces of the granulated sugar in a bowl; whip to full volume.
2. Place the egg whites in another bowl; whip to a medium-stiff peak; slowly add 12 more ounces of the granulated sugar to make a meringue.
3. Sift together the cake flour and cocoa powder.
4. Fold together the whipped egg yolk mixture and the meringue.
5. Add the sifted dry ingredients into the egg mixture.
6. Divide into 16 portions; spread each portion to fill 9-inch circles on lightly greased parchment paper.
7. Bake at 380° F until firm in the center.
8. Cool.

To assemble (1, 9-inch torte):
1. Moisten four cake layers with simple syrup, as needed, during assembly of the torte.
2. Sandwich the cake layers together with a thin layer of raspberry preserves topped by a thin layer of chocolate buttercream.
3. Cover the torte with chocolate buttercream.
4. Decorate the sides and top with chocolate shavings.
5. Mark the top in 16 equal portions.
6. Decorate each portion with a vanilla buttercream dot, covered with chocolate shavings.

Carrot Torte

YIELD: 1, 9-inch Torte.

PASTRY TECHNIQUES:
Filling, Icing, Piping

Filling:
1. Cut open the food product.
2. Carefully spread the filling using an icing spatula.
3. Carefully pipe the filling using a pastry bag.

Icing:
1. Use a clean icing spatula.
2. Work quickly and neatly.

Piping:
With bag:
1. Use a bag with a disposable tip; cut the bag at 45-degree angle.
2. Fill to no more than half full.
3. Burp the bag.
With cone:
1. Cut and fold the piping cone to the appropriate size.
2. Fill the cone with a small amount.
3. Fold the ends to form a triangle.
4. Pipe the desired designs.

HACCP:
Store at 40° F.

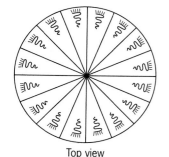
Top view

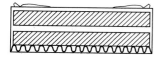
Cross-sectional view

Side view

INGREDIENTS:

Ingredient	Amount
Buttercream, vanilla	1 pound, 4 ounces
Cream cheese icing (see page 48)	5 ounces
Carrot cake (see page 9)	2, 9-inch layers
Buttercream, orange or colored orange	2¼ ounces
Buttercream, pistachio or colored green	1¼ ounces
Walnuts, chopped, ⅛-inch pieces	1½ ounces

METHOD OF PREPARATION:

1. Gather the equipment and ingredients.
2. Ice the inside of the ring with vanilla buttercream about ¼-inch thick.
3. Place the ring over the cardboard circle (cut to fit the ring.)
4. Spread cream cheese icing evenly over the bottom layer of the carrot cake. Cut in half.
5. Using the seam of the ring as a guide, lift half of the cake from the cut edge, and place into the ring. The cut should line up with the seam, and the outside edge should be up against the buttercream.
6. Turn the ring 180 degrees and in the same way; lift and place the second half of cake into its place, making a smooth center seam.
7. Turn the ring 180 degrees so the seam of cake is now running horizontally in front of you.
8. Cut the second layer of carrot cake in half.
9. Place each half on top of the first, as with the first layer. Be sure the seam is smooth and cake is level in the ring.
10. If there is more than one eighth of an inch of space between the top of the cake and the top edge of the ring, add spacers to bring it up into position.
11. Cover the top with vanilla buttercream, and level, using the ring as a guide and a long, straight edge.
12. Refrigerate the torte in the ring for about 5 minutes, or until the buttercream is firm.
13. Unmold by setting the torte on a platform of smaller diameter. Using a hand-held torch or a hot towel, heat the outside of the ring slightly; carefully slide the ring down.
14. Repair any defects.
15. Divide and mark 16 even portions.
16. Use orange buttercream to pipe carrots in the center of each portion, about ½ inch from the edge of the torte, using a no. 1 plain tube.
17. Using a leaf cut bag and green buttercream, pipe greens at the top of the carrot, leaving ¼-inch space from the edge of the torte.
18. Garnish the bottom outside edge with walnuts about evenly, ½ inch up the side of the torte.

PASTRY TECHNIQUES:
Whipping, Filling, Icing, Piping

Whipping:
1. Hold the whip at a 55-degree angle.
2. Create circles, using a circular motion.
3. The circular motion needs to be perpendicular to the bowl.

Filling:
1. Cut open the food product.
2. Carefully spread the filling using an icing spatula.
3. Carefully pipe the filling using a pastry bag.

Icing:
1. Use a clean icing spatula.
2. Work quickly and neatly.

Piping:
With bag:
1. Use a bag with a disposable tip; cut the bag at 45-degree angle.
2. Fill to no more than half full.
3. Burp the bag.
With cone:
1. Cut and fold the piping cone to the appropriate size.
2. Fill the cone with a small amount.
3. Fold the ends to form a triangle.
4. Pipe the desired designs.

HACCP:
Store at 40° F.

HAZARDOUS FOOD:
Heavy cream

Crispy Coffee Cream Torte

YIELD: 1, 9-inch Torte.

INGREDIENTS:

Vanilla chiffon genoise (see page 33)	2, 9-inch layers, ⅓-inch thick
Simple syrup, brandy-flavored (see page 415)	2 ounces
Japonaise (see page 170)	1, 9-inch layer
Marzipan (see page 422)	1, 9-inch disk
Almonds, blanched, toasted, and sliced	As needed
Chocolate, dark, semi-sweet, piping	As needed
Marzipan, pink flower	1 each
Marzipan, green leaves	3 each

Flavored Chantilly Cream:

Cream, heavy	1 pound, 4 ounces
Sugar, confectionery	1¼ ounces
Compound, coffee-flavored	To taste

METHOD OF PREPARATION:

1. Gather the equipment and ingredients.
2. Moisten each layer of genoise with flavored simple syrup, as needed, during assembly.

Preparation of Flavored Chantilly Cream:

1. Whip the heavy cream.
2. Add the confectionery sugar and coffee compound.

To Assemble (1, 9-inch torte):

1. Moisten a layer of genoise with the syrup.
2. Spread the flavored chantilly cream on a layer of genoise.
3. Top with a layer of japonaise.
4. Spread the flavored chantilly cream on top of the japonaise.
5. Top with the remaining layer of genoise.
6. Cover the entire torte with the remaining flavored chantilly cream.
7. Place a marzipan disk on top of the torte.
8. Press almonds on the side.
9. Pipe a border along the edge of the marzipan; use dark piping chocolate.
10. Place a marzipan flower and leaves in the center of the torte.

PASTRY TECHNIQUES:

Filling, Icing

Filling:

1. Cut open the food product.
2. Carefully spread the filling using an icing spatula.
3. Carefully pipe the filling using a pastry bag.

Icing:

1. Use a clean icing spatula.
2. Work quickly and neatly.

HACCP:

Store at 40° F.

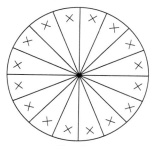

Top view

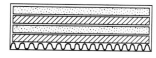
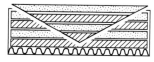
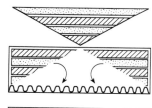
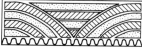

Cross-sectional views

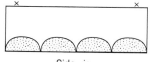

Side view

Crush Torte

YIELD: 1, 9-inch Torte.

INGREDIENTS:

Cake layers, chocolate and vanilla	2 each, 9-inch layers, ¼-inch thick
Buttercream, coconut	1 pound, 6 ounces
Buttercream, chocolate	2 ounces
Simple syrup, coconut (see page 415)	3 ounces
Macaroon coconut	2 ounces

METHOD OF PREPARATION:

1. Gather the equipment and ingredients.
2. Moisten each layer of sponge cake with syrup during assembly.
3. Spread coconut buttercream evenly on the first *chocolate* layer.
4. Place a *vanilla* layer on top; center and level.
5. Spread coconut buttercream evenly on the second layer.
6. Place a *chocolate* layer on top; center and level.
7. Spread coconut buttercream evenly on the third layer.
8. Place a *vanilla* layer on top; center and level.
9. Refrigerate the torte for about 5 minutes, or until firm.
10. Make a cut, starting from the top outside edge, through the torte, to a point in the bottom center. Turn the torte as you cut 365 degrees. Lift out the center "core"; reserve.
11. Place a cardboard on the top of the remaining torte, and flip the torte over completely.
12. Press down, with your hands, to force the center of the torte inward and down against the cardboard.
13. Spread the surface with a thin coating of coconut buttercream.
14. Place the "core" back inside, and press to ensure a good seal and a flat surface.
15. Straighten the sides and top, as necessary.
16. Cover the entire torte with coconut buttercream; ice straight and level, leaving no more than one eighth of an inch of buttercream on top.
17. Divide and mark 16 portions evenly.
18. Prepare a piping bag with a no. 3 star tube; stripe the bag with chocolate buttercream from the tip, running up one side. Fill the bag with coconut buttercream.
19. Pipe 16 stripped rosettes, one fourth inch from the edge of the torte, in the center of each portion.
20. Using your hand, decorate the sides with half circles of coconut. The divisions on top will serve as a guide to spacing eight uniform halves.

CAKES: BASES
ICINGS
CAKES: FINISHED
CREAMS
FILLINGS
PIES
SLOW BAKING
BATTER
DOUGHS
SAUCES

Dobos Torte

PASTRY TECHNIQUES:

Filling, Icing, Melting, Pouring, Cutting

Filling:

1. Cut open the food product.
2. Carefully spread the filling using an icing spatula.
3. Carefully pipe the filling using a pastry bag.

Icing:

1. Use a clean icing spatula.
2. Work quickly and neatly.

Melting:

1. Prepare the food product to be melted.
2. Place the food product in an appropriately sized pot over direct heat or over a double boiler.
3. Stir frequently or occasionally, depending on the delicacy of the product, until melted.

OR

1. Place the product on a sheet pan or in a bowl, and place in a low-temperature oven until melted.

Pouring:

1. Place the product in an appropriate container for pouring: a pitcher or large ladle.
2. Pour the product into desired containers or over another product.

Cutting:

Using a sharp knife to cut to the directed size.

HACCP:

Store at 40° F.

YIELD: 1, 9-inch Torte.

INGREDIENTS:

Dobos layers (see page 18)	6, 9-inch layers, ⅛-inch thick
Buttercream, chocolate	2 pounds, 2 ounces
Sugar, granulated	5 ounces
Lemon juice	3 drops
Dobos layer, additional	1, 7-inch layer, ⅛-inch thick
Almonds, lightly toasted and sliced	As needed

METHOD OF PREPARATION:

1. Gather the equipment and ingredients.
2. Trim all 9-inch dobos layers so that they are equal in size.
3. Place the 6, 9-inch trimmed dobos layers together with chocolate buttercream between each layer.
4. Cover the top and sides with chocolate buttercream.
5. Set aside.
6. Place the granulated sugar and lemon juice in a pot, over medium heat; stir constantly until the sugar becomes a golden carmel color.
7. Pour the caramel evenly on top of 1, 7-inch dobos layer.
8. With a greased knife, cut the 7-inch disk into 16 wedges while the caramel is still hot.
9. Cool the wedges.
10. Mark the 9-inch torte into 16 sections.
11. Pipe a spiral decoration on each section; use the chocolate buttercream.
12. Arrange the caramel wedges, slightly tilted, on top of the 9-inch torte.
13. Ice the sides of the torte with chocolate buttercream.
14. Place sliced almonds around bottom edge and center of the torte.

CHEF NOTE:

The finished dobos torte is only 2 inches high.

Fresh Fruit Torte

Frasier

YIELD: 1, 9-inch Torte.

INGREDIENTS:

Cake layers, vanilla	2, 9-inch layers, ½-inch thick
Simple syrup, Kirschwasser (see page 415)	3 ounces
Strawberries, fresh, clean, trimmed	1½ pints, each 1-inch high
Buttercream, vanilla	10 ounces
Pastry cream (see page 97)	5 ounces
Cream, heavy, whipped, sweetened	4 ounces
Piping gel, chocolate-flavored	½ ounce

METHOD OF PREPARATION:

1. Gather the equipment and ingredients.
2. During assembly, moisten each cake layer with syrup.
3. Cut the strawberries using a ring so they will have the same curve. Cut enough to fit, side by side, around the inside edge of the ring. (Cut two pieces from each berry, no more than 1-inch high.)
4. Place the bottom cake layer into the ring.
5. Place the curved strawberries on the edge of the cake layer, touching the ring. They should sit flat and tightly together.
6. Combine the softened buttercream and pastry cream quickly with a whisk to make a filling.
7. Pipe or spread this filling in and around all of the berries, filling in any spaces, and press against the ring to close any gaps.
8. Spread a little filling in the center of the cake; fill the entire center with the 1-inch cut, whole strawberries and any other pieces from trimming.
9. Cover the berries with the filling, taking up all of the space in and around them. Level the surface.
10. Place the second cake layer on top.
11. Use spacers to adjust the level of the torte, leaving ⅛-inch space between the top of the cake and the top edge of the ring.
12. Level with whipped cream. Refrigerate for 5 minutes, or until firm.

PASTRY TECHNIQUES:
Filling, Covering

Filling:
1. Cut open the food product.
2. Carefully spread the filling using an icing spatula.
3. Carefully pipe the filling using a pastry bag.

Covering:
Sealing a product with a layering of another product such as marzipan or rolled fondant.
1. Prepare the product to be covered with a sticky layer of buttercream, food gel, or other medium that is called for in the formula.
2. Roll out the covering material.
3. Cover the product with the covering material.
4. Smooth the covered product with a bowl scraper to remove wrinkles and air bubbles.

HACCP:
Store at 40° F.

HAZARDOUS FOOD:
Heavy cream

Top view

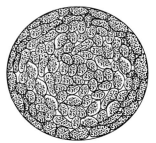

Middle layer, top view

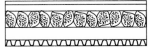

Cross-sectional views

Side view

13. Unmold by setting the torte on a platform of smaller diameter. Heat the outside of the ring carefully with a torch or hot towel; carefully slide the ring down.

14. Repair any defects.

15. Using a small, narrow piping bag, pipe the decoration about ¼ inch from the edge of the torte, completely around to a seamless finish.

Ganache Torte

CAKES: BASES

ICINGS

CAKES: FINISHED

CREAMS

FILLINGS

PIES

SLOW BAKING

BATTER

DOUGHS

SAUCES

PASTRY TECHNIQUES:
Filling, Icing, Rolling

Filling:
1. Cut open the food product.
2. Carefully spread the filling using an icing spatula, or
3. Carefully pipe the filling using a pastry bag.

Icing:
1. Use a clean icing spatula.
2. Work quickly and neatly.

Rolling:
1. Prepare the rolling surface by dusting with the appropriate medium (flour, cornstarch, etc.).
2. Use the appropriate style pin (stick pin or ball bearing pin) to roll the dough to desired thickness; rotate the dough during rolling to prevent sticking.

HACCP:
Store at 40° F.

YIELD: 1, 9-inch Torte.

INGREDIENTS:

Vanilla chiffon genoise (see page 33)	3, 9-inch layers, ⅓-inch thick
Simple syrup, rum-flavored (see page 415)	3 ounces
Ganache, dark (see pages 362, 363)	1 pound, 15 ounces
White chocolate, shaved	As needed
Marzipan (see page 422)	As needed
White chocolate, coating	As needed
Chocolate, dark, semi-sweet, piping	As needed

METHOD OF PREPARATION:

1. Gather the equipment and ingredients.
2. Moisten three vanilla chiffon genoise layers with flavored simple syrup, as needed, during assembly.
3. Fill each chiffon genoise layer with ganache; stack the layers.
4. Cover the cake with ganache.
5. Place the white chocolate shavings around the bottom edge of the torte.
6. Mark the cake into 16 portions.
7. Using a small, round tip, pipe a spiral of ganache. Start the spiral about 1½ inches away from the center until the outer edge is reached.
8. Set the torte aside.
9. Roll out the marzipan ¹⁄₁₂-inch thick.
10. Cut an 8⁷⁄₁₆-inch disk out of the marzipan.
11. Let the marzipan disk dry for 10 minutes before using.
12. Coat the marzipan disk with white chocolate.
13. Let it set, and then cut into 16 equal wedges.
14. Decorate each wedge of marzipan with dark piping chocolate, as instructed.
15. Place a marzipan wedge on top of each slice, slightly angled.

PASTRY TECHNIQUES:

Whipping, Folding, Piping, Coating, Icing

Folding:

Do steps 1, 2, and 3 in one continuous motion.
1. Run a bowl scraper under the mixture, across the bottom of the bowl.
2. Turn the bowl counterclockwise.
3. Bring the bottom mixture to the top.

Piping:

With bag:
1. Use a bag with a disposable tip; cut the bag at 45-degree angle.
2. Fill to no more than half full.
3. Burp the bag.
With cone:
1. Cut and fold the piping cone to the appropriate size.
2. Fill the cone with a small amount.
3. Fold the ends to form a triangle.
4. Pipe the desired designs.

Coating:

1. Use a coating screen, with a sheet pan underneath.
2. Ensure that the product is the correct temperature.
3. Coat the product; use an appropriately-sized utensil.

Icing:

1. Use a clean icing spatula.
2. Work quickly and neatly.

HACCP:

Store at 40° F.

HAZARDOUS FOODS:

Eggs
Egg whites

Havana Torte

YIELD: 10 pounds, 10 ounces.   4, 9-inch Tortes.

INGREDIENTS:

Mixture One:

Butter, room temperature	15 ounces
Sugar, granulated	15 ounces
Almond paste	13 ounces
Salt	Pinch
Lemon juice	1 ounce
Eggs, whole	1 pound, 3 ounces
Almonds, toasted, finely ground	1 pound, 1 ounce
Flour, bread, sifted	9 ounces

Mixture Two:

Egg whites	1 pound, 12 ounces
Sugar, granulated	1 pound, 8 ounces
Hazelnuts, toasted, finely ground	1 pound, 7 ounces
Cocoa powder, sifted	5½ ounces
Cinnamon, ground	½ ounce

For 1 Torte:

Simple syrup, brandy-flavored (see page 415)	As needed
Buttercream, vanilla	14 ounces
Dark chocolate, coating	As needed
Marzipan, yellow (see page 422)	As needed
Chocolate, dark, semi-sweet, piping	As needed

METHOD OF PREPARATION:

Gather the equipment and ingredients.

Preparation of Mixture One:

1. Place the butter, granulated sugar, almond paste, salt, and lemon juice in a bowl with a paddle.
2. Paddle until smooth.
3. Change the paddle to a whip.
4. Slowly add the eggs; whip to a medium-stiff peak.
5. Combine the almonds and flour; fold into the egg mixture by hand.

Preparation of Mixture Two:

1. Place the egg whites in a bowl; whip to a medium-stiff peak; slowly add the granulated sugar to make a meringue.
2. Combine the hazelnuts, cocoa powder, and cinnamon; fold into the meringue by hand.
3. Lightly grease the 9-inch cake pans, and place parchment paper on the bottoms.
4. Take half of mixture 2, and divide equally into four 9-inch cake pans.
5. Divide mixture 1 equally among four 9-inch cake pans; pipe on mixture 2 in each of the 9-inch cake pans with the use of a pastry bag.
6. Top with the other half of mixture 2; divide equally among the four 9-inch cake pans.
7. Bake at 360° F to 375° F until firm in the center.
8. Cool

To Assemble (1, 9-inch torte):

1. Moisten the cake with flavored simple syrup, if desired.
2. Cover the cake with a thin layer of plain buttercream.
3. Chill for about 20 minutes.
4. Coat the top and sides with dark chocolate coating.
5. Mark the top into 16 equal portions.
6. Roll out the yellow marzipan to a $\frac{1}{12}$-inch thickness.
7. Cut out round circles, 1-inch in diameter, 16 per cake, from the marzipan.
8. Place one marzipan circle on each slice.
9. Pipe the capital letter "H" on each marzipan circle; use dark piping chocolate.

CAKES: BASES

ICINGS

CAKES: FINISHED

CREAMS

FILLINGS

PIES

SLOW BAKING

BATTER

DOUGHS

SAUCES

PASTRY TECHNIQUES:

Whipping, Folding, Filling, Icing, Coating

Whipping:

1. Hold the whip at a 55-degree angle.
2. Create circles, using a circular motion.
3. The circular motion needs to be perpendicular to the bowl.

Folding:

Do steps 1, 2, and 3 in one continuous motion.
1. Run a bowl scraper under the mixture, across the bottom of the bowl.
2. Turn the bowl counterclockwise.
3. Bring the bottom mixture to the top.

Filling:

1. Cut open the food product.
2. Carefully spread the filling using an icing spatula.
3. Carefully pipe the filling using a pastry bag.

Icing:

1. Use a clean icing spatula.
2. Work quickly and neatly.

Coating:

1. Use a coating screen, with a sheet pan underneath.
2. Ensure that the product is the correct temperature.
3. Coat the product; use an appropriately-sized utensil.

HACCP:

Store at 40° F.

Hazelnut Special Torte

YIELD: 1, 9-inch Torte.

INGREDIENTS:

Hazelnut cake (see page 22)	1, 9-inch cake
Simple syrup, brandy-flavored (see page 415)	As needed
Buttercream, hazelnut	5 ounces
Buttercream, vanilla	1 pound, 1 ounce
Praline, coating	As needed
Hazelnuts, whole, blanched, toasted	As needed

METHOD OF PREPARATION:

1. Gather the equipment and ingredients.
2. Slice the cake into two equal layers.
3. Moisten each layer with brandy-flavored simple syrup, if desired.
4. Fill with hazelnut-flavored buttercream.
5. Cover the torte thinly with plain buttercream.
6. Chill for about 20 minutes.
7. Coat the torte with the praline coating.
8. Mark the top of the torte into 16 equal portions.
9. Using a medium-star tip, pipe a small rosette of plain buttercream on each slice.
10. Decorate each rosette with a lightly toasted, blanched hazelnut.

Jelly Roll Torte

YIELD: 3, 8-inch Rolls.

PASTRY TECHNIQUES:

Filling, Icing, Piping

Filling:

1. Cut open the food product.
2. Carefully spread the filling using an icing spatula.
3. Carefully pipe the filling using a pastry bag.

Icing:

1. Use a clean icing spatula.
2. Work quickly and neatly.

Piping:

With bag:
1. Use a bag with a disposable tip; cut the bag at 45-degree angle.
2. Fill to no more than half full.
3. Burp the bag.
With cone:
1. Cut and fold the piping cone to the appropriate size.
2. Fill the cone with a small amount.
3. Fold the ends to form a triangle.
4. Pipe the desired designs.

HACCP:

Store at 40° F.

INGREDIENTS:

Jelly roll spongecake (see page 23)	1, 18-inch by 24-inch sponge
Simple syrup, flavored (see page 415)	3½ ounces
Preserves, raspberry, seeded	6 ounces
Buttercream, flavored (as desired)	3 pounds

METHOD OF PREPARATION:

1. Gather the equipment and ingredients.
2. Moisten the jelly roll sponge with syrup.
3. Spread the raspberry preserves thinly over the jelly roll sponge.
4. Spread buttercream thinly over the top of the preserves.
5. Begin rolling at the top of the sheet, evenly across; then roll down, gradually tightening the roll as you go.
6. Wrap the roll in sheetpaper, and place it seam-side down on a sheet pan. Refrigerate until firm.
7. Remove the roll, and place it on a 2-inch cardboard strip.
8. Ice with buttercream, and smooth with thin paper strip, as directed.
9. Pipe a shell border down the top, center of the roll using a no. 3 star tube.
10. Divide the roll into three equal lengths, approximately 8 inches.
11. Cut the roll; then cut the cardboard.
12. Box two rolls per 9-inch by 9-inch by 5-inch cake box.

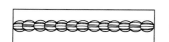

Top view

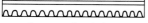

Cross-sectional view, before rolling

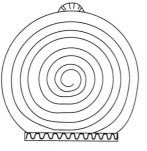

Cross-sectional view, after rolling

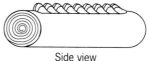

Side view

CAKES: BASES

ICINGS

CAKES: FINISHED

CREAMS

FILLINGS

PIES

SLOW BAKING

BATTER

DOUGHS

SAUCES

Linzer Torte

PASTRY TECHNIQUES:

Rolling, Spreading

Rolling:

1. Prepare the rolling surface by dusting with the appropriate medium (flour, cornstarch, etc.).
2. Use the appropriate style pin (stick pin or ball bearing pin) to roll the dough to desired thickness; rotate the dough during rolling to prevent sticking.

Spreading:

1. Using an icing spatula or off-set spatula, smooth the icing or other spreading medium over the surface area.

HACCP:

Store at 40° F.

YIELD: 1, 8½-inch Torte.

INGREDIENTS:

Linzer dough, bottom shell (see page 181)	1 pound, ½ ounce
Preserves, raspberry	3 ounces
Linzer dough, lattice top	1 pound, ¼ ounce
Egg wash (see page 411)	As needed

METHOD OF PREPARATION:

1. Gather the equipment and ingredients.
2. Roll out the dough for the bottom shell to ¼-inch thick.
3. Cut the dough to the shape of the pan, and place in the pan.
4. Spread 3 ounces of raspberry preserves on the dough.
5. Roll out the dough for the crust to ¼-inch thick; make a diamond-lattice top crust. Use the egg wash to glue the lattice top together.
6. Bake at 350° F until golden brown.
7. Cool in the pans.

Lutetia Torte

YIELD: 1, 9-inch Torte.

PASTRY TECHNIQUES:
Filling, Icing, Coating

Filling:
1. Cut open the food product.
2. Carefully spread the filling using an icing spatula, or
3. Carefully pipe the filling using a pastry bag.

Icing:
1. Use a clean icing spatula.
2. Work quickly and neatly.

Coating:
1. Use a coating screen, with a sheet pan underneath.
2. Ensure that the product is the correct temperature.
3. Coat the product; use an appropriately-sized utensil.

HACCP:
Store at 40° F.

INGREDIENTS:

Walnut chiffon genoise (see page 36)	3, 9-inch layers, ⅓-inch thick
Simple syrup, rum-flavored (see page 415)	2½ ounces
Preserves, raspberry	2½ ounces
Ganache (see pages 362, 363)	1 pound, 9 ounces
Chantilly cream (see page 94)	4 ounces
Dark chocolate, coating	As needed
Walnuts, halves	16 each
Royal icing (see page 51)	As needed
Marzipan, yellow carnation (see page 423)	1 each
Marzipan, green leaves	3 each

METHOD OF PREPARATION:

1. Gather the equipment and ingredients.
2. Moisten three layers of walnut chiffon genoise cakes with flavored simple syrup during assembly.
3. Spread the raspberry preserves on the first layer of genoise.
4. Spread ganache on top of the raspberry preserves.
5. Place a second layer of genoise on top of the ganache.
6. Spread a layer of chantilly cream on top.
7. Top with a third layer of genoise.
8. Cover the cake with ganache.
9. Chill for about 20 minutes.
10. Coat the cake with a dark chocolate coating.
11. Mark into 16 portions.
12. Decorate with walnut halves and royal icing.
13. Place a marzipan carnation with leaves in the center.

CAKES: BASES

ICINGS

CAKES: FINISHED

CREAMS

FILLINGS

PIES

SLOW BAKING

BATTER

DOUGHS

SAUCES

PASTRY TECHNIQUES:
Filling, Icing, Piping

Filling:
1. Cut open the food product.
2. Carefully spread the filling using an icing spatula.
3. Carefully pipe the filling using a pastry bag.

Icing:
1. Use a clean icing spatula.
2. Work quickly and neatly.

Piping:
With bag:
1. Use a bag with a disposable tip; cut the bag at 45-degree angle.
2. Fill to no more than half full.
3. Burp the bag.
With cone:
1. Cut and fold the piping cone to the appropriate size.
2. Fill the cone with a small amount.
3. Fold the ends to form a triangle.
4. Pipe the desired designs.

HACCP:
Store at 40° F.

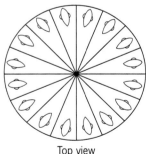

Top view

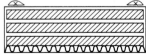

Cross-sectional view

Side view

Mandarin Orange Torte

YIELD: 1, 9-inch Torte.

INGREDIENTS:

Cake layers, vanilla	3, 9-inch layers, ⅜-inch thick
Simple syrup, mandarin orange flavored	3 ounces
Buttercream, orange	1 pound, 12 ounces
Orange, mandarin, segments, drained, dry	16 each
Macaroon coconut	½ ounce

METHOD OF PREPARATION:

1. Gather the equipment and ingredients.
2. Moisten each cake layer with simple syrup.
3. Spread orange buttercream evenly on top.
4. Place a second layer of cake on top; center and level.
5. Spread orange buttercream evenly on top.
6. Place the third layer of cake on top; center and level.
7. Cover the entire torte with orange buttercream; ice straight and level, leaving no more than one eighth of an inch of buttercream on top.
8. Divide and mark 16 portions evenly.
9. Using orange buttercream, pipe 16 rosettes with a no. 3 star tube, ¼ inch from the edge of the torte, in the center of each portion.
10. Stand each orange segment, narrow end down, wide end up, pointing toward the center of the torte in each rosette.
11. Garnish the bottom half with macaroon coconut.

CAKES: BASES
ICINGS
CAKES: FINISHED
CREAMS
FILLINGS
PIES
SLOW BAKING
BATTER
DOUGHS
SAUCES

Marzipan Dome Torte

PASTRY TECHNIQUES:
Filling, Icing, Rolling

Filling:
1. Cut open the food product.
2. Carefully spread the filling using an icing spatula.
3. Carefully pipe the filling using a pastry bag.

Icing:
1. Use a clean icing spatula.
2. Work quickly and neatly.

Rolling:
1. Prepare the rolling surface by dusting with the appropriate medium (flour, cornstarch, etc.).
2. Use the appropriate style pin (stick pin or ball bearing pin) to roll the dough to desired thickness; rotate the dough during rolling to prevent sticking.

HACCP:
Store at 40° F.

YIELD: 1, 9-inch Torte.

INGREDIENTS:

Walnut chiffon genoise (see page 36)	2, 9-inch layers, ⅓-inch thick
Walnut chiffon genoise	2, 7-inch layers, ⅓-inch thick
Simple syrup, brandy-flavored (see page 415)	3 ounces
Preserves, raspberry	4 ounces
Marzipan (see page 422)	1, 9-inch disk, ¹⁄₁₂-inch thick
Buttercream, praline-flavored	1 pound
Marzipan, additional, colored	As needed
Marzipan, yellow rose	1 each
Marzipan, green leaves	3 each
Chocolate, dark, semi-sweet, piping	As needed

METHOD OF PREPARATION:

1. Gather the equipment and ingredients.
2. Moisten each layer of walnut chiffon genoise with flavored simple syrup during assembly.
3. Spread a thin layer of raspberry preserves on the first 9-inch layer.
4. Place a 9-inch round disk of thin marzipan over the preserves.
5. Place the second 9-inch layer of walnut chiffon genoise on top of the marzipan disk.
6. Spread praline-flavored buttercream on top.
7. Place a 7-inch walnut chiffon genoise on top.
8. Spread raspberry preserves on top of this layer.
9. Spread praline-flavored buttercream on top.
10. Place the final 7-inch layer on top.
11. Trim the torte to create a dome effect.
12. After it is trimmed, coat the entire torte with praline buttercream.
13. Roll out the colored marzipan until it is large enough to cover the entire torte.
14. Trim the excess marzipan around the bottom.
15. Mark the torte into 16 portions.
16. Decorate with a yellow marzipan rose and green marzipan leaves.
17. Decorate with dark piping chocolate.

PASTRY TECHNIQUES:

Filling, Icing

Filling:

1. Cut open the food product.
2. Carefully spread the filling using an icing spatula.
3. Carefully pipe the filling using a pastry bag.

Icing:

1. Use a clean icing spatula.
2. Work quickly and neatly.

HACCP:

Store at 40° F.

HAZARDOUS FOOD:

Egg whites

CHEF NOTE:

In cheese filling (see recipe, page 110), substitute bakers' cheese for Mascarpone.

Top view

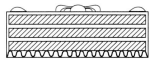

Cross-sectional view

Side view

Meringue Torte

YIELD: 1, 9-inch Torte.

INGREDIENTS:

Cake layers, vanilla	3, 9-inch layers, ⅜-inch thick
Simple syrup, flavored (see page 415)	2½ ounces
Chesse filling (see page 110)	10 ounces
Amaretto, gel	To taste
Egg whites	6 ounces
Sugar, granulated	6 ounces
Cream of tartar	Pinch

METHOD OF PREPARATION:

1. Gather the equipment and ingredients.
2. Moisten each layer of vanilla cake with flavored simple syrup during assembly.
3. Spread half of the cheese filling on the first layer.
4. Place a second layer of cake on top; center and level.
5. Spread the remaining cheese filling on the second layer; center and level.
6. Place the final layer of cake on top; center and level.
7. Trim the edges, if necessary.
8. Whip the egg whites, sugar, and cream of tartar to a stiff peak to make a meringue.
9. Ice the torte, top and sides, with meringue; decorate using a no. 3 star tube.
10. Brown using the hand torch.

PASTRY TECHNIQUES:

Filling, Icing

Filling:

1. Cut open the food product.
2. Carefully spread the filling using an icing spatula, or
3. Carefully pipe the filling using a pastry bag.

Icing:

1. Use a clean icing spatula.
2. Work quickly and neatly.

HACCP:

Store at 40° F.

Mocha Buttercream Torte No. 1

YIELD: 1, 9-inch Torte.

INGREDIENTS:

Cake layers, vanilla	3, 9-inch layers, ⅜-inch thick
Simple syrup, kahlua (see page 415)	3 ounces
Preserves, apricot	2½ ounces
Buttercream, mocha	1 pound, 8 ounces
Buttercream, vanilla	4 ounces
Mocha beans	16 each
Chocolate, decorettes	As needed

METHOD OF PREPARATION:

1. Gather the equipment and ingredients.
2. Moisten each layer of cake with syrup during assembly.
3. Spread the preserves evenly on the first layer of cake.
4. Spread mocha buttercream evenly on top.
5. Place a second layer of cake on top; center and level.
6. Spread mocha buttercream evenly on the second layer.
7. Place a third layer of cake on top; center and level.
8. Cover the entire torte with mocha buttercream; ice straight and level; leave no more than ⅛ inch of buttercream on top.
9. Divide and mark 16 portions evenly.
10. Using vanilla buttercream, pipe 16 rosettes with a no. 3 star tube, ¼ inch from the edge of the torte, in the center of each portion.
11. Place the mocha beans on the rosettes, with the dimple on the bean pointed toward the center of the torte.
12. Garnish the bottom outside edge with chocolate decorettes about ½ inch up the side of the torte.

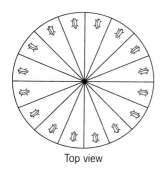

Top view

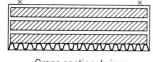

Cross-sectional view

Side view

CAKES: BASES

ICINGS

CAKES: FINISHED

CREAMS

FILLINGS

PIES

SLOW BAKING

BATTER

DOUGHS

SAUCES

PASTRY TECHNIQUES:
Filling, Icing

Filling:
1. Cut open the food product.
2. Carefully spread the filling using an icing spatula, or
3. Carefully pipe the filling using a pastry bag.

Icing:
1. Use a clean icing spatula.
2. Work quickly and neatly.

HACCP:
Store at 40° F.

Mocha Buttercream Torte No. 2

YIELD: 1, 9-inch Torte.

INGREDIENTS:

Vanilla chiffon genoise (see page 33)	3, 9-inch layers, ⅓-inch thick
Simple syrup, brandy-flavored (see page 415)	3 ounces
Preserves, apricot	2½ ounces
Buttercream, mocha	2 pounds
Mocha beans	16 each
Chocolate, dark, semi-sweet, piping	As needed
Almonds, light, blanched, sliced, and toasted	As needed

METHOD OF PREPARATION:

1. Gather the equipment and ingredients.
2. Moisten each layer of vanilla chiffon genoise with flavored simple syrup during assembly.
3. Spread the apricot preserves on the first layer of genoise, and top with mocha buttercream.
4. Top with the second layer of genoise.
5. Spread mocha buttercream on top.
6. Place the third layer of genoise.
7. Cover the torte with mocha buttercream; ice straight and level; leave no more than ⅛ inch of buttercream on top.
8. Mark into 16 portions.
9. Decorate with mocha buttercream lines and mocha beans.
10. Finish with piping chocolate over buttercream lines.
11. Place sliced almonds around the bottom edge and in the center of the torte.

CAKES: BASES

ICINGS

CAKES: FINISHED

CREAMS

FILLINGS

PIES

SLOW BAKING

BATTER

DOUGHS

SAUCES

PASTRY TECHNIQUES:
Filling, Icing

Filling:
1. Cut open the food product.
2. Carefully spread the filling using an icing spatula.
3. Carefully pipe the filling using a pastry bag.

Icing:
1. Use a clean icing spatula.
2. Work quickly and neatly.

HACCP:
Store at 40° F.

Pistachio Torte No. 1

YIELD: 1, 9-inch Torte.

INGREDIENTS:

Cake layers, vanilla	3, 9-inch layers, ⅜-inch thick
Simple syrup, pistachio (see page 415)	3 ounces
Buttercream, pistachio	1 pound, 8 ounces
Buttercream, vanilla	4 ounces
Pistachios, ground, sieved	1½ ounces

METHOD OF PREPARATION:

1. Gather the equipment and ingredients.
2. Moisten each layer of cake with simple syrup during assembly.
3. Spread pistachio buttercream evenly on the first layer of cake.
4. Place a second layer of cake on top; center and level.
5. Spread pistachio buttercream evenly on the second layer.
6. Place the third layer of cake on top; center and level. Trim, as needed.
7. Cover the entire torte with pistachio buttercream; ice straight and level, leaving no more than ⅛ inch of buttercream on top.
8. Mark the top of the cake in the center with a 5-inch circle.
9. Completely cover the sides and top, with the exception of the 5-inch circle, with ground, sieved pistachios to hide all of the buttercream; remove all excess with a clean brush.
10. Using vanilla buttercream, pipe a reverse scroll along the marked center to make a complete circle.
11. Sprinkle a pinch of ground pistachios into the center of the torte.

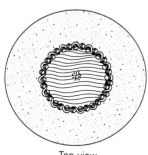

Top view

Cross-sectional view

Side view

Pistachio Torte No. 2

YIELD: 1, 9-inch Torte.

PASTRY TECHNIQUES:
Filling, Icing

Filling:
1. Cut open the food product.
2. Carefully spread the filling using an icing spatula.
3. Carefully pipe the filling using a pastry bag.

Icing:
1. Use a clean icing spatula.
2. Work quickly and neatly.

HACCP:
Store at 40° F.

INGREDIENTS:

Vanilla chiffon genoise (see page 33)	2, 9-inch layers, ⅓-inch thick
Simple syrup, brandy-flavored (see page 415)	2 ounces
Preserves, apricot	2½ ounces
Buttercream, pistachio	1 pound, 12 ounces
Japonaise (see page 170)	1, 9-inch layer, ½-inch thick
Marzipan, green (see page 422)	1, 9-inch disk
Pistachios, chopped	As needed
Chocolate, dark, semi-sweet, piping	As needed
Pistachios, whole, blanced	16 each
Marzipan, pink rose	1 each
Marzipan, green leaves	3 each

METHOD OF PREPARATION:

1. Gather the equipment and ingredients.
2. Moisten each layer of vanilla chiffon genoise with flavored simple syrup during assembly.
3. Spread the apricot preserves on the first layer of vanilla chiffon genoise.
4. Top with pistachio-flavored buttercream.
5. Place the japonaise layer on top.
6. Spread pistachio-flavored buttercream on top.
7. Place the second layer of vanilla chiffon genoise on top.
8. Cover the entire torte with pistachio-flavored buttercream.
9. Place a prepared marzipan disk on top of the torte.
10. Decorate the bottom edge of the torte with chopped pistachio nuts.
11. Place lines of dark piping chocolate on the marzipan as decoration.
12. Place whole pistachios on the torte, as instructed.
13. Place a pink marzipan rose with green marzipan leaves in the center of the torte.

Praline Torte

CAKES: BASES

ICINGS

CAKES: FINISHED

CREAMS

FILLINGS

PIES

SLOW BAKING

BATTER

DOUGHS

SAUCES

PASTRY TECHNIQUES:
Filling, Icing

Filling:
1. Cut open the food product.
2. Carefully spread the filling using an icing spatula.
3. Carefully pipe the filling using a pastry bag.

Icing:
1. Use a clean icing spatula.
2. Work quickly and neatly.

HACCP:
Store at 40° F.

YIELD: 1, 9-inch Torte.

INGREDIENTS:

Preserves, apricot	2½ ounces
Short dough (see page 183)	1, 9-inch disk, ⅛-inch thick, baked
Ganache, dark (see pages 362, 363)	5 ounces
Japonaise (see page 170)	1, 9-inch disk, ⅓-inch thick
Buttercream, praline-flavored	2 pounds
Vanilla chiffon genoise (see page 33)	1, 9-inch layer, 1-inch thick
Simple syrup, brandy-flavored (see page 415)	2 ounces
Hazelnuts, ground, blanched and toasted	As needed
Hazelnuts, whole, blanched and toasted	As needed

METHOD OF PREPARATION:

1. Gather the equipment and ingredients.
2. Spread the apricot preserves on the baked short dough disk.
3. Spread the ganache over the apricot preserves.
4. Place a japonaise layer on top.
5. Spread a layer of praline-flavored buttercream on top.
6. Place a vanilla chiffon genoise layer on top.
7. Moisten with flavored simple syrup.
8. Cover the entire torte with praline-flavored buttercream.
9. Place ground hazelnuts around the bottom edge of the torte.
10. Decorate by piping praline buttercream in a lattice pattern on top of the torte.
11. Place whole toasted hazelnuts in the open areas of lattice work.
12. Pipe a shell border with a small star tip around the outside top edge, using praline buttercream.

PASTRY TECHNIQUES:
Filling, Icing, Combing, Piping

Filling:
1. Cut open the food product.
2. Carefully spread the filling using an icing spatula.
3. Carefully pipe the filling using a pastry bag.

Icing:
1. Use a clean icing spatula.
2. Work quickly and neatly.

Combing:
1. Prepare the item with the appropriate amount of icing.
2. Drag a clean comb across the surface.

Piping:
With bag:
1. Use a bag with a disposable tip; cut the bag at 45-degree angle.
2. Fill to no more than half full.
3. Burp the bag.
With cone:
1. Cut and fold the piping cone to the appropriate size.
2. Fill the cone with a small amount.
3. Fold the ends to form a triangle.
4. Pipe the desired designs.

HACCP:
Store at 40° F.

Raspberry Chocolate Torte

YIELD: 1, 9-inch Torte.

INGREDIENTS:

Cake layers, chocolate	3, 9-inch layers, ⅜-inch thick
Simple syrup, raspberry, (see page 415)	3½ ounces
Preserves, raspberry, seeded	2½ ounces
Buttercream, chocolate	1 pound, 8 ounces
Buttercream, vanilla	4 ounces
Almonds, blanched, sliced, and toasted	½ ounce

METHOD OF PREPARATION:

1. Gather the equipment and ingredients.
2. Moisten each layer of sponge cake with simple syrup during assembly.
3. Spread 3 ounces of the raspberry preserves on the first layer of sponge cake.
4. Spread chocolate buttercream evenly on top of the preserves.
5. Place a second layer of sponge cake on top; center and level.
6. Spread chocolate buttercream evenly on the second layer.
7. Place a third layer of sponge cake on top; center and level.
8. Cover the entire torte with chocolate buttercream; ice straight and level, leaving no more than one eighth of an inch of buttercream on top.
9. Divide and mark 16 portions evenly.
10. Using the vanilla buttercream, pipe 16 rosettes with a no. 3 star tube, ¼ inch from the edge of the torte, in the center of each portion.
11. Pipe a small dot of the remaining raspberry preserves in the center of each rosette.
12. Comb the sides of the torte horizontally using the medium tooth edge.
13. Garnish the bottom half of the torte with the toasted almond slices.

Top view

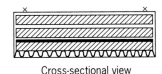

Cross-sectional view

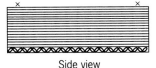

Side view

Raspberry Windmill Torte

YIELD: 1, 9-inch Torte.

INGREDIENTS:

Vanilla chiffon genoise (see page 33)	2, 9-inch layers, ⅓-inch thick
Chocolate chiffon genoise (see page 11)	2, 9-inch layers, ⅓-inch thick
Simple syrup, brandy-flavored (see page 415)	3 ounces
Buttercream, raspberry	2 pounds
Almonds, blanched, sliced, and toasted	As needed
Marzipan, tinted pink (see page 422)	As needed
Dark chocolate, coating	As needed
White chocolate, coating	As needed

METHOD OF PREPARATION:

1. Gather the equipment and ingredients.
2. Cut each one of the four genoise layers into one 9-inch ring, one 6-inch ring, and one 3-inch circle per layer.
3. Replace the 6-inch ring on each layer with the opposite-colored, 6-inch ring.
4. Take a layer with a vanilla genoise outer ring, moisten with flavored simple syrup, and spread with raspberry buttercream.
5. For the second layer, use a layer with a chocolate chiffon genoise outer ring; moisten with flavored simple syrup, and spread with raspberry buttercream.
6. Repeat step 4.
7. Repeat step 5.
8. Cover the entire torte with raspberry buttercream.
9. Mark the cake into 16 portions.
10. Use a small, round tip to pipe a spiral of buttercream, beginning approximately 1½ inches from the center and ending at the outer edge of the torte.
11. Place sliced almonds around the bottom edge of the torte.
12. Roll out pink marzipan to a ½-inch thickness, and cut a disk 8⁷⁄₁₆-inches wide.
13. Allow to dry for about 10 minutes.
14. Cut the marzipan disk in half.

Filling, Icing, Combing

Filling:
1. Cut open the food product.
2. Carefully spread the filling using an icing spatula.
3. Carefully pipe the filling using a pastry bag.

Icing:
1. Use a clean icing spatula.
2. Work quickly and neatly.

Combining:
Bringing together two or more components.
1. Prepare the components to be combined.
2. Add one to the other, using the appropriate mixing method (if needed).

HACCP:
Store at 40° F.

15. Coat half of the disk with dark chocolate and the other half with white chocolate.
16. Use a decorating comb on both halves to create a wave design before the chocolate sets.
17. When the chocolate sets, cut each half into eight equal wedges.
18. Place the wedges on top of the torte, alternating colors.
19. Place the wedges on marked lines, aligned with the outer edges, leaning against a piped spiral. *Do not overlap* the tips of the wedges at the center.

Roulade Torte

YIELD: 1, 9-inch Torte.

CAKES: BASES
ICINGS
CAKES: FINISHED
CREAMS
FILLINGS
PIES
SLOW BAKING
BATTER
DOUGHS
SAUCES

PASTRY TECHNIQUES:
Cutting, Filling, Rolling, Icing, Piping

Cutting:
Using a sharp knife to cut to the directed size.

Filling:
1. Cut open the food product.
2. Carefully spread the filling using an icing spatula.
3. Carefully pipe the filling using a pastry bag.

Rolling:
1. Prepare the rolling surface by dusting with the appropriate medium (flour, cornstarch, etc.).
2. Use the appropriate style pin (stick pin or ball-bearing pin) to roll the dough to desired thickness; rotate the dough during rolling to prevent sticking.

Icing:
1. Use a clean icing spatula.
2. Work quickly and neatly.

Piping:
With bag:
1. Use a bag with a disposable tip; cut the bag at 45-degree angle.
2. Fill to no more than half full.
3. Burp the bag.
With cone:
1. Cut and fold the piping cone to the appropriate size.
2. Fill the cone with a small amount.
3. Fold the ends to form a triangle.
4. Pipe the desired designs.

HACCP:
Store at 40° F.

INGREDIENTS:

Luisenroulade (see page 27)	¾ sheet pan
Buttercream, chocolate	2 pounds, 10 ounces
Vanilla chiffon genoise (see page 33)	2, 9-inch layers, ⅛-inch thick
Fondant, heated	As needed
Cherries, candied, red	8 each
Almonds, blanched, sliced, toasted	As needed

METHOD OF PREPARATION:

1. Gather the equipment and ingredients.
2. Cut the luisenroulade into 1½-inch strips.
3. Spread chocolate buttercream on each strip the same thickness as the roulade.
4. Roll up the roulade strips.
5. Spread a very thin layer of chocolate buttercream on a vanilla chiffon genoise layer.
6. Place the first roll in the center of the cake, standing vertically.
7. Place the remaining rolls around the center roll until the torte is 8⁷⁄₁₆ inches in diameter.
8. Cover the top very thinly with chocolate buttercream.
9. Place the second vanilla chiffon genoise layer on top.
10. Cover the entire torte with chocolate buttercream.
11. Mark into 16 equal portions.
12. Beginning in the center, pipe a spiral about 3 inches in diameter, using chocolate buttercream and a small, round tip.
13. Pipe a buttercream-swan design on each portion; use the same tip.
14. Fill the opening of the swan decoration with prepared, heated fondant.
15. Place half of a candied cherry at the point where the lines of buttercream connect.
16. Place lightly toasted almonds around the bottom edge of the torte.

Sacher Torte

YIELD: 1, 9-inch Torte.

PASTRY TECHNIQUES:

Filling, Icing, Coating

Filling:

1. Cut open the food product.
2. Carefully spread the filling using an icing spatula, or
3. Carefully pipe the filling using a pastry bag.

Icing:

1. Use a clean icing spatula.
2. Work quickly and neatly.

Coating:

1. Use a coating screen, with a sheet pan underneath.
2. Ensure that the product is the correct temperature.
3. Coat the product; use an appropriately-sized utensil.

HACCP:

Store at 40° F.

INGREDIENTS:

Sacher cake (see pages 30 and 31)	2, 9-inch layers, 1¼-inch thick
Simple syrup, rum-flavored (see page 415)	3 ounces
Preserves, apricot	3 ounces
Chocolate, coating	As needed
Chocolate, dark, semi-sweet, piping	As needed

METHOD OF PREPARATION:

1. Gather the equipment and ingredients.
2. Moisten both cake layers with flavored simple syrup during assembly.
3. Spread the first layer with the preserves.
4. Place the second layer on top.
5. Cover the torte completely with ganache.
6. Chill for about 20 minutes.
7. Coat the torte with chocolate coating.
8. Mark the torte into 16 portions.
9. Write the word *Sacher* on each slice with dark piping chocolate.

CHEF NOTE:

Instead of using chocolate ganache to cover the torte, you could cover the cake with a thin layer of apricot glaze and then coat cake with a chocolate coating.

Spanish Vanilla Torte

YIELD: 1, 9-inch Torte.

PASTRY TECHNIQUES:

Whipping, Combining, Folding, Filling, Icing, Coating

Whipping:

1. Hold the whip at a 55-degree angle.
2. Create circles, using a circular motion.
3. The circular motion needs to be perpendicular to the bowl.

Combining:

Bringing together two or more components.
1. Prepare the components to be combined.
2. Add one to the other, using the appropriate mixing method (if needed).

Folding:

Do steps 1, 2, and 3 in one continuous motion.
1. Run a bowl scraper under the mixture, across the bottom of the bowl.
2. Turn the bowl counterclockwise.
3. Bring the bottom mixture to the top.

Filling:

1. Cut open the food product.
2. Carefully spread the filling using an icing spatula.
3. Carefully pipe the filling using a pastry bag.

Icing:

1. Use a clean icing spatula.
2. Work quickly and neatly.

Coating:

1. Use a coating screen, with a sheet pan underneath.
2. Ensure that the product is the correct temperature.
3. Coat the product; use an appropriately sized utensil.

HACCP:

Store at 40° F.

INGREDIENTS:

Spanish vanilla cake (see page 32)	1, 9-inch cake
Simple syrup, rum-flavored (see page 415)	2 ounces
Ganache, dark (see pages 362, 363)	1 pound, 13 ounces
Dark chocolate, coating	As needed
Chocolate, dark, semi-sweet, stencils	16 each
Marzipan (optional) (see page 422)	1, 5-inch disk, 1/12-inch thick

METHOD OF PREPARATION:

1. Gather the equipment and ingredients.
2. Slice the cake into two equal layers.
3. Moisten the first layer with flavored simple syrup.
4. Spread ganache on top.
5. Top with the second layer of cake.
6. Moisten with flavored simple syrup.
7. Cover the entire cake with ganache.
8. Chill for about 20 minutes.
9. Coat the top and sides with dark chocolate coating.
10. Mark the cake into 16 equal portions.
11. Decorate with a ganache rosette on each portion.
12. Prepare half moons out of dark chocolate, 16 per cake.
13. Place each moon into the rosette while the ganache is still soft. (The half moons should stand up vertically and line up with the outside edge.)
14. *Optional:* Prepare a marzipan disk decorated with writing for a special occasion, and place it in the center of the cake.

CAKES: BASES

ICINGS

CAKES: FINISHED

CREAMS

FILLINGS

PIES

SLOW BAKING

BATTER

DOUGHS

SAUCES

PASTRY TECHNIQUES:
Filling, Icing, Assembling

Filling:
1. Cut open the food product.
2. Carefully spread the filling using an icing spatula.
3. Carefully pipe the filling using a pastry bag.

Icing:
1. Use a clean icing spatula.
2. Work quickly and neatly.

Collecting and Assembling:
1. Prepare all of the ingredients to the formula.
2. Clear the area for assembly.
3. Fit the pieces together according to formula instructions or instructor's guidelines.

HACCP:
Store at 40° F.

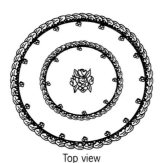

Top view

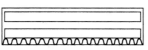

Cross-sectional view

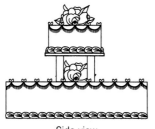

Side view

Wedding Cake
(Individual Miniature)

YIELD: 2 Tiers: 1, 9-inch Layer, 1, 6-inch Layer.

INGREDIENTS:

Pound cake (pages 28, 29)	2, 9-inch layers, 1¼-inch thick *and* 2, 5½-inch layers, 1¼-inch thick
Simple syrup, flavored (as desired) (see page 415)	8 ounces
Buttercream, Italian, vanilla	2 pounds, 8 ounces
Buttercream, Italian, pink	4 ounces
Buttercream, Italian, green	2 ounces

METHOD OF PREPARATION:

1. Gather the equipment and ingredients.
2. Moisten each layer of pound cake liberally with flavored simple syrup (top and bottom) during assembly.
3. Assemble the tortes, and cover with vanilla buttercream. Refrigerate in individual 10-inch by 10-inch by 5-inch cake boxes until firm.
4. Using a rose nail and tube, prepare 10 pink buttercream-full roses, as directed; freeze.
5. Stick two 10-inch cardboard cake circles together with gel, making sure to cross the corrugated lines in opposite directions for strength. Stick aluminum foil over the top with gel, and wrap tight. (This serves as a strong base.)
6. Stick the 9-inch torte on a covered base cardboard with gel.
7. Mark post holes in the center of the 9-inch torte with a plastic separation plate; remove. Mark 16 divisions on the 9-inch, and eight divisions on the 6-inch; leave marks only on the outside top edge.
8. Using an apple corer, cut and remove the cake core from the post sites.
9. Pipe a small mound of vanilla buttercream in the center, between the post holes, and place four roses pointing up and out between the post holes. Place a fifth rose on the top and center of the mound. Using a leaf bag and green buttercream, pipe leaves between the roses to fill the gaps.
10. Pipe the holes half full with vanilla buttercream, and insert the posts. Attach a clean plate to the posts.
11. Stick the 6-inch torte to a separator plate with gel.
12. Repeat step 9 on the 6-inch torte.
13. With the point of a piping bag, outline a shallow crescent form; start at the top edge mark, and end at the next top edge mark. It should droop about 1 inch at the lowest point. Then pipe a crescent, narrow at the ends and wide at the middle, using a no. 0 star tube in a jitter motion. Repeat until both the 9-inch and 6-inch tortes are complete.
14. At the point where the crescents end and begin, pipe a small rosette, using a no. 0 star tube, on the top of the torte.
15. At the base of each torte, pipe a shell border completely around; use the no. 0 star tube.

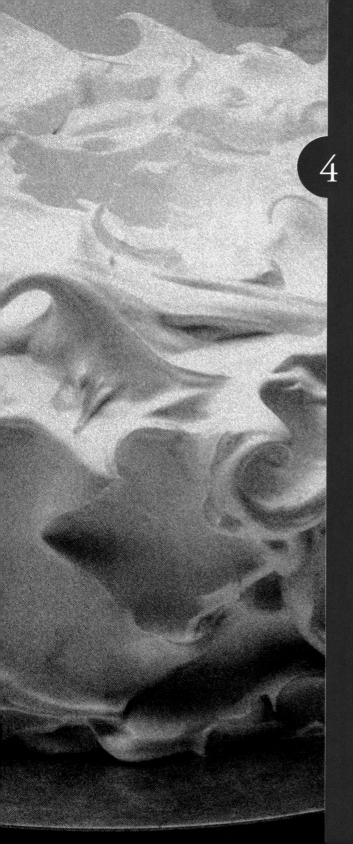

4

Creams and Mousses

4

Creams and Mousses

Almond Cream

CAKES: BASES

ICINGS

CAKES: FINISHED

CREAMS

FILLINGS

PIES

SLOW BAKING

BATTER

DOUGHS

SAUCES

PASTRY TECHNIQUES:
Combining, Piping, Combing

Combining:
Bringing together two or more components.
1. Prepare the components to be combined.
2. Add one to the other, using the appropriate mixing method (if needed).

Piping:
With bag:
1. Use a bag with a disposable tip; cut the bag at 45-degree angle.
2. Fill to no more than half full.
3. Burp the bag.
With cone:
1. Cut and fold the piping cone to the appropriate size.
2. Fill the cone with a small amount.
3. Fold the ends to form a triangle.
4. Pipe the desired designs.

Combing:
1. Prepare the item with the appropriate amount of icing.
2. Drag a clean comb across the surface.

HACCP:
Store at 40° F.

HAZARDOUS FOOD:
Eggs

YIELD:	2 pounds, 12½ ounces.	5 pounds, 9 ounces.
INGREDIENTS:		
Butter, unsalted, softened	4½ ounces	9 ounces
Sugar, powdered	5⅝ ounces	11¼ ounces
Almonds, ground, toasted	5⅝ ounces	11¼ ounces
Flour, pastry	1½ ounces	3 ounces
Eggs, whole	5 ounces	10 ounces
Liqueur (optional)	As needed	As needed
Pastry cream, softened (see page 97)	1 pound, 6¼ ounces	2 pounds, 12½ ounces

METHOD OF PREPARATION:

1. Gather the equipment and ingredients.
2. Place the butter in a bowl, and soften.
3. Sift the powdered sugar, and combine with the almonds.
4. Add the sifted sugar-almond mixture to the butter; combine.
5. Add the pastry flour, and combine.
6. Add the eggs in gradually.
7. Liqueur can be added, if desired.
8. Combine this almond mixture with approximately the same amount of softened pastry cream.
9. Fill into the unbaked pastry shells.

CHEF NOTE:
Almond cream can be used as a filling in preparing pithiviers.

PASTRY TECHNIQUES:
Blooming, Whipping, Boiling, Folding

Blooming:
Gelatin sheets or leaves:
1. Fan the sheets out.
2. Cover the sheets in liquid.
3. Sheets are bloomed when softened.
Granular gelatin:
1. Sprinkle the gelatin.
2. Gelatin is ready when it is cream of wheat consistency.

Whipping:
1. Hold the whip at a 55-degree angle.
2. Create circles, using a circular motion.
3. The circular motion needs to be perpendicular to the bowl.

Boiling:
1. Bring the cooking liquid to a rapid boil.
2. Stir the contents.

Folding:
Do steps 1, 2, and 3 in one continuous motion.
1. Run a bowl scraper under the mixture, across the bottom of the bowl.
2. Turn the bowl counterclockwise.
3. Bring the bottom mixture to the top.

HACCP:
Store at 40° F.

HAZARDOUS FOODS:
Milk
Heavy cream

CHEF NOTES:
1. Different flavorings can be added to basic bavarian cream. They can be added when folding in the pâté à bombe.
2. It is recommended to chill the molds in ice water before pouring the cream into them. They will then be easier to unmold.

Bavarian Cream No. 1

Using a Pâté à Bombe

YIELD: 2 pounds, 9 ounces. 5 pounds, 1¾ ounces.

INGREDIENTS:

Gelatin	¾ ounce	1½ ounces
Milk, whole	1 pound	2 pounds
Cream, heavy	1 pound	2 pounds
Salt	⅛ ounce	¼ ounce
Pâté à bombe (see page 98)	8 ounces	1 pound

METHOD OF PREPARATION:
1. Gather the equipment and ingredients.
2. Place the gelatin in a dry bowl, and bloom with one fourth of the milk.
3. Whip the cream to a soft-to-medium peak; set aside.
4. Place the remaining milk and salt in a pot; bring to a boil.
5. Remove from the heat, and pour over the bloomed gelatin.
6. Cool over an ice bath or in the refrigerator.
7. When it is cool, whisk in the pâté à bombe.
8. Fold in the whipped cream.
9. Pour into desired molds.
10. Refrigerate or freeze molds immediately.

CAKES: BASES
ICINGS
CAKES: FINISHED
CREAMS
FILLINGS
PIES
SLOW BAKING
BATTER
DOUGHS
SAUCES

PASTRY TECHNIQUES:
Blooming, Whipping, Boiling, Tempering, Folding

Blooming:
Gelatin sheets or leaves:
1. Fan the sheets out.
2. Cover the sheets in liquid.
3. Sheets are bloomed when softened.

Granular gelatin:
1. Sprinkle the gelatin.
2. Gelatin is ready when it is cream of wheat consistency.

Whipping:
1. Hold the whip at a 55-degree angle.
2. Create circles, using a circular motion.
3. The circular motion needs to be perpendicular to the bowl.

Boiling:
1. Bring the cooking liquid to a rapid boil.
2. Stir the contents.

Tempering:
1. Whisk the eggs vigorously while ladling hot liquid.

Folding:
Do steps 1, 2, and 3 in one continuous motion.
1. Run a bowl scraper under the mixture, across the bottom of the bowl.
2. Turn the bowl counterclockwise.
3. Bring the bottom mixture to the top.

HACCP:
Store at 40° F.

HAZARDOUS FOODS:
Milk
Egg yolks
Heavy cream

Bavarian Cream No. 2

Using English Sauce

YIELD: 2 pounds, 9 ounces. 5 pounds, 3 ounces.

INGREDIENTS:

Gelatin	½ ounce	1 ounce
Milk, whole	1 pound	2 pounds
Cream, heavy	1 pound	2 pounds
Sugar, granulated	4 ounces	8 ounces
Egg yolks	5 ounces	10 ounces
Extract, vanilla	To taste	To taste
Flavorings, as desired	To taste	To taste

METHOD OF PREPARATION:

1. Gather the equipment and ingredients.
2. Place the gelatin in a dry bowl, and bloom with one fourth of the milk.
3. Whip the cream to a soft-to-medium peak. Set aside.
4. Place the remaining milk and sugar in a pot; bring to a boil.
5. Temper the egg yolks, and add to the boiling milk. Heat, stirring constantly, until the liquid coats the back of a spoon; do not boil.
6. Remove from the heat, and strain.
7. Melt the bloomed gelatin over a double boiler.
8. Add the melted gelatin to the egg yolk mixture.
9. To quickly stop the cooking process, cool in an ice bath; stir often.
10. When cool, fold in the vanilla extract, flavorings, and whipped cream.
11. Fill the molds.
12. Refrigerate or freeze the molds immediately.

Chantilly Cream

PASTRY TECHNIQUE:

Whipping

Whipping:
1. Hold the whip at a 55-degree angle.
2. Create circles, using a circular motion.
3. The circular motion needs to be perpendicular to the bowl.

HACCP:

Store at 40° F.

HAZARDOUS FOOD:

Heavy cream

YIELD:	1 pound, 1 ounce.	2 pounds, 2 ounces.

INGREDIENTS:

Cream, heavy	1 pound	2 pounds
Sugar, granulated	1 ounce	2 ounces
Abstract, vanilla	To taste	To taste

METHOD OF PREPARATION:

1. Gather the equipment and ingredients.
2. Place all of the ingredients in a cold bowl.
3. Whip at high speed to the desired thickness and consistency.
4. Use immediately, or refrigerate until needed.

Diplomat Cream

CAKES: BASES

ICINGS

CAKES: FINISHED

CREAMS

FILLINGS

PIES

SLOW BAKING

BATTER

DOUGHS

SAUCES

PASTRY TECHNIQUES:
Blooming, Whipping

Blooming:
Gelatin sheets or leaves:
1. Fan the sheets out.
2. Cover the sheets in liquid.
3. Sheets are bloomed when softened.
Granular gelatin:
1. Sprinkle the gelatin.
2. Gelatin is ready when it is cream of wheat consistency.

Whipping:
1. Hold the whip at a 55-degree angle.
2. Create circles, using a circular motion.
3. The circular motion needs to be perpendicular to the bowl.

HACCP:
Store at 40°F.

HAZARDOUS FOODS:
Heavy cream
Pastry cream

YIELD:	1 pound.	2 pounds.

INGREDIENTS:

Gelatin	⅛ ounce	¼ ounce
Water	⅞ ounce	1¾ ounces
Pastry cream (see page 97)	8 ounces	1 pound
Cream, heavy	8 ounces	1 pound
Flavorings	As needed	As needed

METHOD OF PREPARATION:

1. Gather the equipment and ingredients.
2. Place the gelatin in a dry bowl, and bloom it with water.
3. Place the pastry cream in a bowl, and whisk until softened and creamy.
4. Whip the heavy cream until it is a soft-to-medium peak.
5. Combine the pastry cream and whipped cream.
6. Heat the bloomed gelatin over a double boiler.
7. Flavor as needed.
8. Temper the gelatin and add to the pastry cream mixture.

CHEF NOTE:
If the cream needs to be firmer, add additional gelatin.

Lemon Cream

Blooming, Whipping, Combining, Folding

Blooming:

Gelatin sheets or leaves:
1. Fan the sheets out.
2. Cover the sheets in liquid.
3. Sheets are bloomed when softened.

Granular gelatin:
1. Sprinkle the gelatin.
2. Gelatin is ready when it is cream of wheat consistency.

Whipping:

1. Hold the whip at a 55-degree angle.
2. Create circles, using a circular motion.
3. The circular motion needs to be perpendicular to the bowl.

Combining:

Bringing together two or more components.
1. Prepare the components to be combined.
2. Add one to the other, using the appropriate mixing method (if needed).

Folding:

Do steps 1, 2, and 3 in one continuous motion.
1. Run a bowl scraper under the mixture, across the bottom of the bowl.
2. Turn the bowl counterclockwise.
3. Bring the bottom mixture to the top.

HACCP:

Store at 40° F.

HAZARDOUS FOOD:

Heavy cream

YIELD:		5 pounds, 15 ounces. 3, 9-inch Tarts	11 pounds, 14 ounces. 6, 9-inch Tarts

INGREDIENTS:			
Gelatin, powdered		¾ to 1 ounce	1½ to 2 ounces
Lemon juice, fresh, strained		12 ounces	1 pound, 8 ounces
Cream, heavy		2 pounds	4 pounds
Milk, sweetened, condensed		2 pounds, 10 ounces	5 pounds, 4 ounces
Lemons, zest		1 each	2 each
Strawberries, sliced (optional)		8 ounces	1 pound

METHOD OF PREPARATION:

1. Gather the equipment and ingredients.
2. Place the gelatin in a dry bowl, and bloom it with a small amount of lemon juice.
3. Whip the cream to a soft peak, and set aside.
4. Combine the remaining lemon juice, sweetened condensed milk, and lemon zest.
5. Heat/bloom the gelatin over a double boiler.
6. Add the heated gelatin to the lemon juice mixture, and combine well.
7. Cool slightly.
8. Gently fold in the whipped cream until blended.
9. *Optional:* Fold in the sliced strawberries.
10. Pipe the cream into the desired cups or tart/tartlet shells.

CAKES: BASES

ICINGS

CAKES: FINISHED

CREAMS

FILLINGS

PIES

SLOW BAKING

BATTER

DOUGHS

SAUCES

Pastry Cream

YIELD:	3 pounds, 4½ ounces.	6 pounds, 9⅛ ounces.

INGREDIENTS:

Milk, whole	2 pounds	4 pounds
Sugar, granulated	8 ounces	1 pound
Salt	Pinch	Pinch
Cornstarch	2.5oz. 3¾ ounces	7½ ounces
Flour, cake	½ ounce	1 ounce
Egg yolks	4 ounces	8 ounces
Eggs, whole	2 ounces	4 ounces
Extract, vanilla	To taste	To taste
Butter, unsalted	2 ounces	4 ounces

METHOD OF PREPARATION:

1. Gather the equipment and ingredients.
2. Place three fourths of the milk, half of the granulated sugar, and the salt in a pot; bring to a boil.
3. Place the cornstarch and flour in a dry bowl; slowly add the remaining fourth of milk slowly to form a smooth paste.
4. Add the egg yolks and whole eggs to the cornstarch mixture. Combine well.
5. Temper the cornstarch mixture, and add to the boiling milk.
6. Bring the mixture back to a second boil, constantly stirring; cook for 3 minutes.
7. Remove from the heat; stir in the vanilla extract and butter.
8. Whisk well.
9. Cool properly, and refrigerate.

PASTRY TECHNIQUES:
Boiling, Tempering, Thickening

Boiling:
1. Bring the cooking liquid to a rapid boil.
2. Stir the contents.

Tempering:
1. Whisk the eggs vigorously while ladling hot liquid.

Thickening:
1. Mix a small amount of sugar with the starches.
2. Create a slurry.
3. Whisk vigorously until thickened and translucent.

HACCP:
Store at 40° F.

HAZARDOUS FOODS:
Milk
Egg yolks
Eggs

CHEF NOTE:
Place buttered parchment paper on top of cream to avoid forming a hard skin on top.

Pâté à Bombe

PASTRY TECHNIQUES:

Cooking, Whipping, Combining

Cooking:

Preparing food through the use of various sources of heating.
1. Choose the appropriate heat application: baking, boiling, simmering, etc.
2. Prepare the formula according to instructions.
3. Cook according to instructions.

Whipping:

1. Hold the whip at a 55-degree angle.
2. Create circles, using a circular motion.
3. The circular motion needs to be perpendicular to the bowl.

Combining:

Bringing together two or more components.
1. Prepare the components to be combined.
2. Add one to the other, using the appropriate mixing method (if needed).

HACCP:

Store at 40° F.

HAZARDOUS FOOD:

Egg yolks

YIELD:		1 pound, 1 ounce.	4 pounds, 4 ounces.
INGREDIENTS:			
Sugar, granulated		8 ounces	2 pounds
Corn syrup		2 ounces	8 ounces
Water		4 ounces	1 pound
Egg yolks		3 ounces	12 ounces
Extract, vanilla		To taste	To taste

METHOD OF PREPARATION:

1. Gather the equipment and ingredients.
2. Place the sugar, corn syrup, and water in a pot.
3. Cook to 250° F.
4. Whip the egg yolks at medium speed to full volume.
5. When the sugar has reached the correct temperature, pour it into the egg yolks; use low speed.
6. After all of the sugar has been added, continue whipping at medium speed until the mixture is cold.
7. Add the vanilla extract.
8. Store in a refrigerator.

Basic Fruit Mousse

CAKES: BASES

ICINGS

CAKES: FINISHED

CREAMS

FILLINGS

PIES

SLOW BAKING

BATTER

DOUGHS

SAUCES

PASTRY TECHNIQUES:

Blooming, Combining, Whipping, Folding

Blooming:

Gelatin sheets or leaves:
1. Fan the sheets out.
2. Cover the sheets in liquid.
3. Sheets are bloomed when softened.

Granular gelatin:
1. Sprinkle the gelatin.
2. Gelatin is ready when it is cream of wheat consistency.

Combining:

Bringing together two or more components.
1. Prepare the components to be combined.
2. Add one to the other, using the appropriate mixing method (if needed).

Whipping:

1. Hold the whip at a 55-degree angle.
2. Create circles, using a circular motion.
3. The circular motion needs to be perpendicular to the bowl.

Folding:

Do steps 1, 2, and 3 in one continuous motion.
1. Run a bowl scraper under the mixture, across the bottom of the bowl.
2. Turn the bowl counterclockwise.
3. Bring the bottom mixture to the top.

HACCP:

Store at 40° F.

HAZARDOUS FOOD:

Heavy cream

| YIELD: | 1 pound, 1¾ ounces. | 3 pounds, 10½ ounces. |

INGREDIENTS:

Gelatin	¼ ounce	½ ounce
Water	1¼ ounces	2½ ounces
Purée, fruit	9½ ounces	1 pound, 3 ounces
Cream, heavy	1 pound	2 pounds
Sugar, confectionery	2 ounces (variable)	4 ounces (variable)

METHOD OF PREPARATION:

1. Gather the equipment and ingredients.
2. Place the gelatin in a dry bowl, and bloom with water.
3. Melt the bloomed gelatin over a double boiler.
4. Add the fruit purée to the gelatin.
5. Allow the mixture to cool, but do not let it become firm.
6. Whip the cream and sugar to a medium peak.
7. Fold gently together the whipped cream and purée mixture.
8. Allow the mixture to set slightly; then pipe into a ramekin or other appropriate serving dish.

CHEF NOTES:
1. Some fruit purée, such as raspberry or strawberry, is sweeter than others and will require a reduction in the amount of sugar used.
2. Some fruits, such as pineapple and kiwi, contain acids, which interfere with the setting of the gelatin. They will require cooking to neutralize the enzymes.
3. Mousse can be made moldable by increasing the gelatin in the formula.

Chocolate Mousse No. 1

PASTRY TECHNIQUES:

Whipping, Chopping, Melting, Folding

Whipping:
1. Hold the whip at a 55-degree angle.
2. Create circles, using a circular motion.
3. The circular motion needs to be perpendicular to the bowl.

Chopping:
1. Use a sharp knife.
2. Hold the food product properly.
3. Cut with a quick downward motion.

Melting:
1. Prepare the food product to be melted.
2. Place the food product in an appropriate-sized pot over direct heat or over a double boiler.
3. Stir frequently or occasionally, depending on the delicacy of the product, until melted.

OR

1. Place the product on a sheet pan or in a bowl, and place in a low-temperature oven until melted.

Folding:

Do steps 1, 2, and 3 in one continuous motion.
1. Run a bowl scraper under the mixture, across the bottom of the bowl.
2. Turn the bowl counterclockwise.
3. Bring the bottom mixture to the top.

HACCP:

Store at 40° F.

HAZARDOUS FOODS:

Heavy cream
Egg yolks
Egg whites

YIELD:	1 pound, 8 ounces.	3 pounds.

INGREDIENTS:		
Cream, heavy	8 ounces	1 pound
Chocolate, dark, semi-sweet	6 ounces	12 ounces
Egg yolks	2 ounces	4 ounces
Sugar, granulated	4½ ounces	9 ounces
Egg whites	2½ ounces	5 ounces
Flavor, brandy or rum	1 ounce	2 ounces

METHOD OF PREPARATION:

1. Gather the equipment and ingredients.
2. Whip the heavy cream to a firm peak, and hold in a refrigerator.
3. Melt the chocolate over a water bath, and hold at 98° F.
4. Heat the egg yolks with half of the sugar over a double boiler; whip constantly to prevent overheating. The egg yolks must reach 145° F.
5. In another bowl, whip the egg whites, and gradually add the remaining granulated sugar to make a meringue. Whip to a wet, medium peak.
6. Fold the chocolate into the whipped yolk mixture.
7. Add either the brandy or rum flavoring.
8. Fold the whipped cream into the chocolate mixture.
9. Add the whipped meringue into the chocolate mixture. *Do not overfold.*
10. Let it set in a refrigerator.
11. Pipe into glasses.

CAKES: BASES
ICINGS
CAKES: FINISHED
CREAMS
FILLINGS
PIES
SLOW BAKING
BATTER
DOUGHS
SAUCES

PASTRY TECHNIQUES:

Whipping, Combining

Whipping:

1. Hold the whip at a 55-degree angle.
2. Create circles, using a circular motion.
3. The circular motion needs to be perpendicular to the bowl.

Combining:

Bringing together two or more components.
1. Prepare the components to be combined.
2. Add one to the other, using the appropriate mixing method (if needed).

HACCP:

Store at 40° F.

HAZARDOUS FOODS:

Egg yolks
Egg whites
Heavy cream

Chocolate Mousse No. 2

With Ganache, Pâté à Bombe, Italian Meringue

YIELD:	2 pounds, 14½ ounces.	5 pounds, 13 ounces.

INGREDIENTS:

Cream, heavy	1 pound, 6½ ounces	2 pounds, 13 ounces
Ganache, hard	8½ ounces	1 pound, 1 ounce
Rum	½ ounce	1 ounce
Pâté à Bombe:		
Sugar, granulated	6½ ounces	13 ounces
Water	2½ ounces	5 ounces
Egg yolks	2 ounces	4 ounces
Italian Meringue:		
Egg whites	3 ounces	6 ounces
Cream of tartar	Pinch	⅛ ounce
Sugar, granulated	1 ounce	2 ounces

METHOD OF PREPARATION:

1. Gather the equipment and ingredients.
2. Whip the cream to a soft peak.
3. Soften the ganache.
4. Add the pâté à bombe to the softened ganache.
5. Add the rum.
6. Fold in the Italian meringue.
7. Fold in the whipped cream.

Preparation of Pâté à Bombe:

1. Place the granulated sugar and water in a pot, and cook until it reaches 238° F.
2. Place the egg yolks in a bowl, and whip at high speed until light.
3. Decrease the mixer speed to medium; slowly pour 3 ounces of 238° F sugar syrup into the whipped yolks.
4. Whip until cool.

Preparation of Italian Meringue:

1. Return the remaining sugar syrup to the heat; continue to cook until a temperature of 250° F is reached.
2. Prepare a common meringue by warming the egg whites to 100° F. Whip at high speed, gradually adding the cream of tartar and granulated sugar.
3. When the sugar syrup reaches 250° F, add it to the meringue. Whip at medium speed until the meringue is cool.

PASTRY TECHNIQUES:
Blooming, Whipping, Scalding,
Melting, Folding

Blooming:
Gelatin sheets or leaves:
1. Fan the sheets out.
2. Cover the sheets in liquid.
3. Sheets are bloomed when softened.
Granular gelatin:
1. Sprinkle the gelatin.
2. Gelatin is ready when it is cream
of wheat consistency.

Whipping:
1. Hold the whip at a 55-degree
angle.
2. Create circles, using a circular
motion.
3. The circular motion needs to be
perpendicular to the bowl.

Scalding:
1. Heat the liquid on high heat.
2. Do not boil the liquid.

Melting:
1. Prepare the food product to be
melted.
2. Place the food product in an appropriate sized pot over direct
heat or over a double boiler.
3. Stir frequently or occasionally, depending on the delicacy of the
product, until melted.

OR

1. Place the product on a sheet pan
or in a bowl, and place in a low-
temperature oven until melted.

Folding:
Do steps 1, 2, and 3 in one continuous motion.
1. Run a bowl scraper under the mixture, across the bottom of the
bowl.
2. Turn the bowl counterclockwise.
3. Bring the bottom mixture to the
top.

HACCP:
Store at 40° F.

HAZARDOUS FOODS:
Egg yolks
Milk
Heavy cream

White Chocolate Mousse

YIELD:	15⅛ ounces.	1 pound, 14¼ ounces.

INGREDIENTS:

Gelatin	⅛ ounce	¼ ounce
Egg yolks	2¼ ounces	4½ ounces
Sugar, granulated	1¼ ounces	2½ ounces
Milk, whole	2½ ounces	5 ounces
Chocolate, white, chopped	2¼ ounces	4½ ounces
Cream, heavy, whipped	6¾ ounces	13½ ounces
Extract, vanilla	To taste	To taste
Triple Sec or Grand Marnier	To taste	To taste

METHOD OF PREPARATION:

1. Gather the equipment and ingredients.
2. Bloom the gelatin, and set aside.
3. Place the egg yolks and granulated sugar in a bowl over a double boiler; heat to 140° F, whipping constantly.
4. Scald the milk.
5. Place the chopped chocolate in a bowl, and pour scalded milk over it. Stir until all of the chocolate has melted.
6. Pour the hot chocolate mixture over the bloomed gelatin; stir thoroughly to dissolve the gelatin. It may be necessary to place it over a double boiler if all of the gelatin is not dissolved.
7. Fold in the flavorings.
8. Cool the chocolate mixture until it begins to thicken slightly.
9. Fold in the whipped cream.
10. Let set in refrigerator.
11. Pipe into glasses.

CAKES: BASES

ICINGS

CAKES: FINISHED

CREAMS

FILLINGS

PIES

SLOW BAKING

BATTER

DOUGHS

SAUCES

5

Fillings and Puddings

5

Fillings and Puddings

CAKES: BASES

ICINGS

CAKES: FINISHED

CREAMS

FILLINGS

PIES

SLOW BAKING

BATTER

DOUGHS

SAUCES

Almond Filling

PASTRY TECHNIQUES:
Creaming, Combining

Creaming:
1. Soften the fats on low speed.
2. Add the sugar(s) and cream; increase the speed slowly.
3. Add the eggs one at a time; scrape the bowl frequently.
4. Add the dry ingredients in stages.

Combining:
Bringing together two or more components.
1. Prepare the components to be combined.
2. Add one to the other, using the appropriate mixing method (if needed).

HACCP:
Store at 40° F.

HAZARDOUS FOOD:
Egg whites

YIELD:	2 pounds, 13 ounces.	5 pounds, 10 ounces.

INGREDIENTS:

Almond paste	2 pounds	4 pounds
Butter, unsalted	8 ounces	1 pound
Egg whites	2 ounces	4 ounces
Flour, bread	3 ounces	6 ounces

METHOD OF PREPARATION:

1. Gather the equipment and ingredients.
2. Place the almond paste and butter in a bowl with a paddle; cream together.
3. Add the egg whites slowly, and scrape well.
4. Add the bread flour, and combine well.

PASTRY TECHNIQUE:
Creaming

Creaming:
1. Soften the fats on low speed.
2. Add the sugar(s) and cream; increase the speed slowly.
3. Add the eggs one at a time; scrape the bowl frequently.

HACCP:
Store at 40° F.

HAZARDOUS FOODS:
Bakers' cheese
Eggs

Bakers' Cheese
(for Danish)

YIELD:	4 pounds, ⅝ ounce.	8 pounds, 1¼ ounces.

INGREDIENTS:

Ingredient		
Sugar, granulated	10 ounces	1 pound, 4 ounces
Cheese, bakers'	2 pounds, 8 ounces	5 pounds
Salt	⅝ ounce	1¼ ounces
Eggs, whole	8 ounces	1 pound
Butter, unsalted, soft	5 ounces	10 ounces
Flour, bread	1½ ounces	3 ounces

METHOD OF PREPARATION:

1. Gather the equipment and ingredients.
2. Cream the granulated sugar and bakers' cheese with a paddle on the first speed in a 20-quart mixer until smooth.
3. Add the eggs slowly on low speed.
4. Add the butter, salt, and flour; mix until well combined.

CAKES: BASES
ICINGS
CAKES: FINISHED
CREAMS
FILLINGS
PIES
SLOW BAKING
BATTER
DOUGHS
SAUCES

PASTRY TECHNIQUES:
Boiling, Thickening

Boiling:
1. Bring the cooking liquid to a rapid boil.
2. Stir the contents.

Thickening:
1. Mix a small amount of sugar with the starches.
2. Create a slurry.
3. Whisk vigorously until thickened and translucent.

HACCP:
Store at 40° F.

Black Forest Cherry Filling
(Dark Sweet)

YIELD:	1 pound, 8½ ounces.	3 pounds, 1 ounce.

INGREDIENTS:

Cherries, canned, dark, sweet, drained and halved	1 pound	2 pounds
Cherry syrup	8 ounces	1 pound
Cornstarch	½ ounce	1 ounce

METHOD OF PREPARATION:

1. Gather the equipment and ingredients.
2. Drain the cans of cherries, and reserve the liquid for the cherry syrup portion.
3. Place 13 ounces of syrup in a pot, and bring it to a boil.
4. Place the cornstarch in a dry bowl, and slowly add remaining syrup; whisk constantly to prevent lumps from forming.
5. Add the cornstarch mixture to the boiling syrup, and whisk constantly as it thickens. Continue to boil; whisk for 2 minutes to ensure the starch is cooked.
6. Add the halved cherries, and combine.
7. Cool.

CHEF NOTE:
If there is not enough syrup in the cherries, add water and sugar to make up the difference.

Cheese Filling

Creaming, Combining

Creaming:
1. Soften the fats on low speed.
2. Add the sugar(s) and cream; increase the speed slowly.
3. Add the eggs one at a time; scrape the bowl frequently.

Combining:
Bringing together two or more components.
1. Prepare the components to be combined.
2. Add one to the other, using the appropriate mixing method (if needed).

HACCP:
Store at 40° F.

HAZARDOUS FOODS:
Cream cheese
Bakers' cheese
Egg yolks

YIELD:	2 pounds.	6 pounds.
INGREDIENTS:		
Cream cheese, room temperature	1 pound	3 pounds
Cheese, bakers', room temperature	8 ounces	1 pound, 8 ounces
Sugar, granulated	5¼ ounces	15¾ ounces
Egg yolks	3 ounces	9 ounces
Extract, vanilla	To taste	To taste
Orange zest	To taste	To taste
Lemon zest	To taste	To taste

METHOD OF PREPARATION:

1. Gather the equipment and ingredients.
2. Place the cream cheese, bakers' cheese, and granulated sugar in a bowl with a paddle.
3. Paddle until smooth; scrape often.
4. Add the yolks and flavorings in small portions. Mix and scrape well after each addition.
5. Cover, and refrigerate until needed.

CAKES: BASES

ICINGS

CAKES: FINISHED

CREAMS

FILLINGS

PIES

SLOW BAKING

BATTER

DOUGHS

SAUCES

PASTRY TECHNIQUES:

Melting, Combining

Melting:

1. Prepare the food product to be melted.
2. Place the food product in an appropriate-sized pot over direct heat or over a double boiler.
3. Stir frequently or occasionally, depending on the delicacy of the product, until melted.

OR

1. Place the product on a sheet pan or in a bowl, and place in a low-temperature oven until melted.

Combining:

Bringing together two or more components.

1. Prepare the components to be combined.
2. Add one to the other, using the appropriate mixing method (if needed).

HACCP:

Store at 60° F to 65° F.

Chocolate Filling
(for Croissant)

YIELD:	3 pounds.	6 pounds.

INGREDIENTS:

Shortening, all-purpose	1 pound	2 pounds
Chocolate, dark, semi-sweet, chopped	2 pounds	4 pounds

METHOD OF PREPARATION:

1. Gather the equipment and ingredients.
2. Over direct heat, melt the shortening; remove from the heat.
3. Add the chopped dark chocolate to the melted shortening. Stir until dissolved; strain.
4. Store in a covered container in a dry storage area.

CHEF NOTE:

To use, heat the filling slightly to a soft, pliable paste consistency. Place the filling in the center of the croissant triangle, and roll.

PASTRY TECHNIQUES:

Combining, Boiling, Thickening

Combining:

Bringing together two or more components.
1. Prepare the components to be combined.
2. Add one to the other, using the appropriate mixing method (if needed).

Boiling:

1. Bring the cooking liquid to a rapid boil.
2. Stir the contents.

Thickening:

1. Mix a small amount of sugar with the starches.
2. Create a slurry.
3. Whisk vigorously until thickened and translucent.

HACCP:

Store at 40° F.

HAZARDOUS FOOD:

Egg yolks

German Chocolate Cake Filling

YIELD:	6 pounds, 1½ ounces.	12 pounds, 3 ounces.

INGREDIENTS:		
Milk, evaporated	1 pound, 8 ounces	3 pounds
Egg yolks, sugared	4½ ounces	9 ounces
Butter, unsalted, melted	1 pound, 8 ounces	3 pounds
Sugar, granulated	1 pound, 5 ounces	2 pounds, 10 ounces
Pecan pieces	12 ounces	1 pound, 8 ounces
Coconut flakes	12 ounces	1 pound, 8 ounces

METHOD OF PREPARATION:

1. Gather the equipment and ingredients.
2. Combine the evaporated milk and egg yolks together.
3. Melt the butter.
4. Add the granulated sugar and melted butter to the milk-yolk mixture.
5. Place in a bowl, and place over a double boiler; cook until the mixture thickens.
6. Add the pecan pieces and coconut flakes to the cooked mixture.
7. Cool.

CHEF NOTE:

Do *not* cook the filling to a caramel color; the filling should be light in color.

CAKES: BASES
ICINGS
CAKES: FINISHED
CREAMS
FILLINGS
PIES
SLOW BAKING
BATTER
DOUGHS
SAUCES

PASTRY TECHNIQUE:
Combining

Combining:
Bringing together two or more components.
1. Prepare the components to be combined.
2. Add one to the other, using the appropriate mixing method (if needed).

HACCP:
Store at 40° F.

HAZARDOUS FOOD:
Eggs

Orange Coconut Filling
(For Danish)

YIELD:	4 pounds, 12 ounces.	9 pounds, 8 ounces.

INGREDIENTS:		
Oranges, whole, seedless, washed	1 pound	2 pounds
Sugar, granulated	12 ounces	1 pound, 8 ounces
Coconut	1 pound, 8 ounces	3 pounds
Butter, unsalted, melted	6 ounces	12 ounces
Eggs, whole	6 ounces	12 ounces
Water or orange juice	6 ounces	12 ounces

METHOD OF PREPARATION:

1. Gather the equipment and ingredients.
2. In a food processor, grind the whole oranges until puréed; strain.
3. In a separate bowl, mix together the puréed oranges, granulated sugar, coconut, melted butter, eggs, and water.
4. Store covered in the refrigerator until ready to use.

Poppy Seed Filling

PASTRY TECHNIQUES:
Boiling, Reducing, Combining

Boiling:
1. Bring the cooking liquid to a rapid boil.
2. Stir the contents.

Reducing:
1. Bring the sauce to a boil; then reduce to a simmer.
2. Stir often; reduce to the desired consistency.

Combining:
Bringing together two or more components.
1. Prepare the components to be combined.
2. Add one to the other, using the appropriate mixing method (if needed).

HACCP:
Store at 40° F.

HAZARDOUS FOODS:
Milk
Heavy cream

YIELD:	1 pound, 7 ounces.	2 pounds, 14 ounces.
INGREDIENTS:		
Seeds, poppy	4 ounces	8 ounces
Sugar, granulated	2 ounces	4 ounces
Milk, whole	8 ounces	1 pound
Cream, heavy	4 ounces	8 ounces
Raisins, golden	2 ounces	4 ounces
Walnuts, chopped	2 ounces	4 ounces
Orange, peel, zest	Pinch	¼ each
Butter, unsalted	1 ounce	2 ounces
Crumbs, cake, dry	As needed	As needed

METHOD OF PREPARATION:

1. Gather the equipment and ingredients.
2. Place the poppy seeds, granulated sugar, milk, heavy cream, golden raisins, and walnuts in a pot.
3. Bring to a boil; then reduce the heat to a simmer to evaporate the liquid in the mixture.
4. Chop the orange zest in a food processor.
5. Add the chopped orange and butter to the poppy seed mixture. Stir well.
6. Add enough cake crumbs to allow the mixture to hold its shape.
7. Store refrigerated in a covered container or plastic bag.

Tiramisu Filling

YIELD:	2 pounds, 6 ounces.	4 pounds, 12 ounces.

INGREDIENTS:

Cream cheese	12 ounces	1 pound, 8 ounces
Mascarpone cheese	12 ounces	1 pound, 8 ounces
Sugar, confectionery, sifted	6 ounces	12 ounces
Cream, heavy, whipped	8 ounces	1 pound

METHOD OF PREPARATION:

1. Gather the equipment and ingredients.
2. Place the cream cheese in a bowl, and soften; scrape the bowl occasionally.
3. Add the mascarpone cheese to the cream cheese, and incorporate thoroughly.
4. Add the confectionery sugar, and combine.
5. Remove from the mixer, and fold in the whipped cream.

PASTRY TECHNIQUES:

Creaming, Combining, Whipping, Folding

Creaming:

1. Soften the fats on low speed.
2. Add the sugar(s) and cream; increase the speed slowly.
3. Add the eggs one at a time; scrape the bowl frequently.

Combining:

Bringing together two or more components.
1. Prepare the components to be combined.
2. Add one to the other, using the appropriate mixing method (if needed).

Whipping:

1. Hold the whip at a 55-degree angle.
2. Create circles, using a circular motion.
3. The circular motion needs to be perpendicular to the bowl.

Folding:

Do steps 1, 2, and 3 in one continuous motion.
1. Run a bowl scraper under the mixture, across the bottom of the bowl.
2. Turn the bowl counterclockwise.
3. Bring the bottom mixture to the top.

HACCP:

Store at 40° F.

HAZARDOUS FOODS:

Cream cheese
Mascarpone cheese
Heavy cream

CHEF NOTE:

Tiramisu is an Italian word that is translated as "pick me up." Often, the tiramisu cheese filling has espresso incorporated into the mix. Gusto Rico or espresso powder also can be used. The filling is served with espresso-soaked lady fingers.

CAKES: BASES
ICINGS
CAKES: FINISHED
CREAMS
FILLINGS
PIES
SLOW BAKING
BATTER
DOUGHS
SAUCES

Tosca Almond Mix

PASTRY TECHNIQUES:
Cooking, Combining

Cooking:
Preparing food through the use of various sources of heating.
1. Choose the appropriate heat application: baking, boiling, simmering, etc.
2. Prepare the formula according to instructions.
3. Cook according to instructions.

Combining:
Bringing together two or more components.
1. Prepare the components to be combined.
2. Add one to the other, using the appropriate mixing method (if needed).

HACCP:
Store at 40° F.

HAZARDOUS FOOD:
Half-and-half

YIELD:		2 pounds, 7 ounces.	4 pounds, 14 ounces.
INGREDIENTS:			
Butter, unsalted		8 ounces	1 pound
Sugar, granulated		8 ounces	1 pound
Corn syrup		7 ounces	14 ounces
Half-and-half		6 ounces	12 ounces
Almonds, blanched, sliced, and lightly toasted		10 ounces	1 pound, 4 ounces

METHOD OF PREPARATION:

1. Gather the equipment and ingredients.
2. Place the butter, sugar, corn syrup, and half-and-half in a pot; cook to 230° F.
3. Remove from the heat, and stir in the almonds.

CHEF NOTE:
Tosca may be used as a filling for cakes and pastries such as pinwheels, frangipane, layer cakes, tortes, and Danish.

Walnut Strudel Filling

CAKES: BASES
ICINGS
CAKES: FINISHED
CREAMS
FILLINGS
PIES
SLOW BAKING
BATTER
DOUGHS
SAUCES

PASTRY TECHNIQUE:
Boiling, Reducing, Combining

Boiling:
1. Bring the cooking liquid to a rapid boil.
2. Stir the contents.

Reducing:
1. Bring the sauce to a boil; then reduce to a simmer.
2. Stir often; reduce to the desired consistency.

Combining:
Bringing together two or more components.
1. Prepare the components to be combined.
2. Add one to the other, using the appropriate mixing method (if needed).

HACCP:
Store at 40° F.

HAZARDOUS FOOD:
Milk

YIELD:	2 pounds, 15¼ ounces.	5 pounds, 14½ ounces.
INGREDIENTS:		
Walnuts, crushed	1 pound	2 pounds
Butter, unsalted	4 ounces	8 ounces
Sugar, granulated	6 ounces	12 ounces
Raisins, golden	4 ounces	8 ounces
Lemon zest	¼ each	½ each
Milk, whole	12 ounces	1 pound, 8 ounces
Crumbs, cake, dry	4 ounces	8 ounces
Brandy	1¼ ounces	2½ ounces

METHOD OF PREPARATION:

1. Gather the equipment and ingredients.
2. Place the walnuts, butter, granulated sugar, raisins, lemon zest, and milk in a pot; bring to a boil.
3. Reduce the heat, and simmer to evaporate the liquid.
4. Remove from the heat, and add the cake crumbs and brandy; incorporate well.
5. Cool.
6. Store in a refrigerator; keep covered until used.

Bread Pudding

YIELD: 10 pounds, 1¼ ounces.

PASTRY TECHNIQUES:

Scalding, Slow Baking

Scalding:

1. Heat the liquid on high heat.
2. Do not boil the liquid.

Slow Baking:

1. Use an appropriate baking dish.
2. Use hot water in the pan.
3. Replenish the water when needed.

HACCP:

Store at 40° F.

HAZARDOUS FOODS:

Eggs
Milk
Heavy cream

INGREDIENTS:

Butter, unsalted, softened	As needed
Bread, cubed or sliced	2 pounds
Cinnamon, ground	As needed
Nutmeg, ground	As needed
Eggs, whole	2 pounds
Sugar, granulated	1 pound
Salt	¼ ounce
Extract, vanilla	1 ounce
Milk, whole	4 pounds
Cream, heavy	1 pound

METHOD OF PREPARATION:

1. Gather the equipment and ingredients.
2. Butter the hotel pan.
3. Place the cubed or sliced bread in a hotel pan.
4. Sprinkle the bread with cinnamon and nutmeg.
5. Combine and whisk together the eggs, granulated sugar, salt, and vanilla extract.
6. Scald the milk and heavy cream.
7. Temper the egg mixture with the scalded milk and heavy cream.
8. Pour the mixture over the bread.
9. Bake at 350° F in a water bath for 60 minutes, or until set.

CHEF NOTES:

1. Use two-day-old white French or Italian bread for more flavor.
2. To enrich pudding, chopped fruit and chocolate pieces can be added.

Frankfurt Pudding

CAKES: BASES

ICINGS

CAKES: FINISHED

CREAMS

FILLINGS

PIES

SLOW BAKING

BATTER

DOUGHS

SAUCES

PASTRY TECHNIQUES:

Creaming, Combining, Whipping

Creaming:
1. Soften the fats on low speed.
2. Add the sugar(s) and cream; increase the speed slowly.
3. Add the eggs one at a time; scrape the bowl frequently.
4. Add the dry ingredients in stages.

Combining:
Bringing together two or more components.
1. Prepare the components to be combined.
2. Add one to the other, using the appropriate mixing method (if needed).

Whipping:
1. Hold the whip at a 55-degree angle.
2. Create circles, using a circular motion.
3. The circular motion needs to be perpendicular to the bowl.

HAZARDOUS FOODS:
Egg yolks
Egg whites

YIELD:	12 Servings.	24 Servings.

INGREDIENTS:

	12 Servings	24 Servings
Butter, unsalted, room temperature	8 ounces	1 pound
Sugar, granulated	11 ounces	1 pound, 6 ounces
Egg yolks	9 ounces	1 pound, 2 ounces
Crumbs, vanilla cake, dried and sifted	8 ounces	1 pound
Almonds, unpeeled, finely grated	7½ ounces	15 ounces
Cinnamon, ground	Pinch	Pinch
Raisins, seedless (optional)	4½ ounces	9 ounces
Egg whites	13 ounces	1 pound, 10 ounces
Butter, unsalted, softened	As needed	As needed
Crumbs, bread, or crumbs from ladyfingers	As needed	As needed
Fruit sauce, red	As needed	As needed

METHOD OF PREPARATION:

1. Gather the equipment and ingredients.
2. Place the butter and sugar in a bowl, and paddle until fluffy; scrape the bowl often.
3. Gradually add the egg yolks, scraping the bowl down.
4. Add the sponge cake crumbs, almonds, and cinnamon; add raisins, if desired, and mix well.
5. In a separate bowl, whip the egg whites to a medium-stiff peak.
6. Carefully fold the egg whites into the butter mixture.
7. Butter a 2-inch hotel pan; pour the batter into it.
8. Sprinkle with bread crumbs or ladyfinger crumbs.
9. Place the pan in a water bath, and bake at 350° F for approximately 30 to 35 minutes.
10. Portion before inserting the pudding onto a desert plate.
11. Serve with a red fruit sauce.

Indian Pudding

PASTRY TECHNIQUES:

Scalding, Combining

Scalding:

1. Heat the liquid on high heat.
2. Do not boil the liquid.

Combining:

Bringing together two or more components.
1. Prepare the components to be combined.
2. Add one to the other, using the appropriate mixing method (if needed).

HACCP:

Store at 40° F.

HAZARDOUS FOODS:

Milk
Eggs

YIELD:

INGREDIENTS:	9 pounds, 3⅛ ounces.	18 pounds, 6¼ ounces.
Butter, unsalted	As needed	As needed
Milk, whole	6 pounds	12 pounds
Cornmeal	9½ ounces	1 pound, 3 ounces
Butter, unsalted, melted	3 ounces	6 ounces
Molasses	1 pound, 2 ounces	2 pounds, 4 ounces
Salt	¼ ounce	½ ounce
Cinnamon, ground	¼ ounce	½ ounce
Ginger, ground	⅛ ounce	¼ ounce
Eggs, whole	1 pound, 4 ounces	2 pounds, 8 ounces

METHOD OF PREPARATION:

1. Gather the equipment and ingredients.
2. Grease a hotel pan with butter.
3. Scald the milk.
4. Add the cornmeal to the milk.
5. Cook over a double boiler; stir constantly.
6. Combine the butter, molasses, salt, cinnamon, and ginger.
7. Add the eggs to the molasses mixture.
8. Combine the molasses mixture with the cornmeal mixture.
9. Pour into the greased hotel pan.
10. Bake at 350° F in a water bath for 30 to 40 minutes.

CAKES: BASES

ICINGS

CAKES: FINISHED

CREAMS

FILLINGS

PIES

SLOW BAKING

BATTER

DOUGHS

SAUCES

Rice Pudding

YIELD: 9 pounds, 12¾ ounces.

INGREDIENTS:

Butter, unsalted	As needed
Rice, medium-grain, uncooked	1 pound
Sugar, confectionery	As needed
Milk, whole	6 pounds
Extract, vanilla	½ ounce
Salt	¼ ounce
Egg yolks	12 ounces
Sugar, granulated	1 pound
Cream, heavy	1 pound
Cinnamon, ground	As needed

METHOD OF PREPARATION:

1. Gather the equipment and ingredients.
2. Butter a hotel pan.
3. Place the rice in water with a small amount of confectionery sugar.
4. Bring to a boil; blanch for 3 minutes. Drain the rice.
5. Place the blanched rice, milk, vanilla extract, and salt in a pot, and cook for approximately 30 minutes, until tender. Stir occasionally.
6. Combine the egg yolks, granulated sugar, and heavy cream.
7. Temper the egg mixture, and add to the hot milk mixture.
8. Cook for an additional 2 minutes.
9. Remove, and pour into the buttered hotel pan.
10. Sprinkle with cinnamon.
11. Place on a sheet pan, and add water (double-boiler effect).
12. Bake at 350° F for 30 to 40 minutes, or until set.

PASTRY TECHNIQUES:

Boiling, Combining, Tempering, Slow Baking

Boiling:

1. Bring the cooking liquid to a rapid boil.
2. Stir the contents.

Combining:

Bringing together two or more components.
1. Prepare the components to be combined.
2. Add one to the other, using the appropriate mixing method (if needed).

Tempering:

To equalize two extreme temperatures.
1. Whisk the eggs vigorously while ladling hot liquid.

Slow Baking:

1. Use an appropriate baking dish.
2. Use hot water in the pan.
3. Replenish the water when needed.

HAZARDOUS FOODS:

Milk
Egg yolks
Heavy cream

Rice Trauttmannsdorf

PASTRY TECHNIQUES:

Soaking, Cooking, Blooming, Folding

Soaking:

1. Place the item(s) to be soaked in a large bowl or appropriate container.
2. Pour water or other liquid over the items to be soaked.
3. Allow to sit until desired saturation or softening is achieved.

Cooking:

Preparing food through the use of various sources of heating.
1. Choose the appropriate heat application: baking, boiling, simmering, etc.
2. Prepare the formula according to instructions.
3. Cook according to instructions.

Blooming:

Gelatin sheets or leaves:
1. Fan the sheets out.
2. Cover the sheets in liquid.
3. Sheets are bloomed when softened.

Granular gelatin:
1. Sprinkle the gelatin.
2. Gelatin is ready when it is cream-of-wheat consistency.

Folding:

Do steps 1, 2, and 3 in one continuous motion.
1. Run a bowl scraper under the mixture, across the bottom of the bowl.
2. Turn the bowl counterclockwise.
3. Bring the bottom mixture to the top.

HACCP:

Store at 40° F.

HAZARDOUS FOODS:

Milk
Heavy cream

CHEF NOTE:

1. Any fruit that will not bleed may be used for rice Trauttmannsdorf.
2. Timbales must be well chilled before filling.

YIELD: 3 pounds, 10⅞ ounces. 7 pounds, 4⅞ ounces.

INGREDIENTS:

Fruit, assorted, chopped	5¼ ounces	10½ ounces
Liqueur, maraschino	¼ ounce	½ ounce
Rice, long grain, uncooked	5¼ ounces	10½ ounces
Water	1 pound, 4 ounces	2 pounds, 8 ounces
Milk, whole	1 pound, 8 ounces	3 pounds
Salt	Pinch	⅛ ounce
Extract, vanilla	To taste	To taste
Sugar, granulated	5¼ ounces	10½ ounces
Gelatin	⅝ ounce	1¼ ounces
Water, cold	2½ ounces	5 ounces
Cream, heavy, whipped to a soft peak	6 ounces	12 ounces
Melba sauce (see page 215)	As needed	As needed

METHOD OF PREPARATION:

1. Gather the equipment and ingredients.
2. Place the timbales in a freezer.
3. Soak the fruit in the maraschino liqueur.
4. Cook the rice in water until very tender. Rinse thoroughly, and drain.
5. Bring the milk, salt, and vanilla extract to a boil; add the rice, and cook until the rice is done. (Rice is done when it loses its shape under pressure.)
6. Add the sugar to the rice mixture.
7. Bloom the gelatin in cold water.
8. Add the bloomed gelatin to the hot rice mixture. Stir well to dissolve the gelatin.
9. Add the fruit to the rice mixture, and cool.
10. When cool, fold in the whipped cream.
11. Fill the timbales level; tap them lightly on a table to release air pockets, and refrigerate to set.
12. Dip the timbales two thirds in warm water for 3 seconds; unmold.
13. Place on dessert plates, and serve with melba sauce. (Keep refrigerated until service.)

CAKES: BASES

ICINGS

CAKES: FINISHED

CREAMS

FILLINGS

PIES

SLOW BAKING

BATTER

DOUGHS

SAUCES

PASTRY TECHNIQUES:
Combining, Tempering, Whipping, Folding

Combining:
Bringing together two or more components.
1. Prepare the components to be combined.
2. Add one to the other, using the appropriate mixing method (if needed).

Tempering:
1. Whisk the eggs vigorously while ladling hot liquid.

Whipping:
1. Hold the whip at a 55-degree angle.
2. Create circles, using a circular motion.
3. The circular motion needs to be perpendicular to the bowl.

Folding:
Do steps 1, 2, and 3 in one continuous motion.
1. Run a bowl scraper under the mixture, across the bottom of the bowl.
2. Turn the bowl counterclockwise.
3. Bring the bottom mixture to the top.

HACCP:
Store at 40° F.

HAZARDOUS FOODS:
Milk
Egg yolks
Heavy cream
Egg whites

Tapioca Pudding

YIELD: 8 pounds, 10¼ ounces.   17 pounds, 4¾ ounces.

INGREDIENTS:

Butter, unsalted	As needed	As needed
Tapioca	4 pounds	8 pounds
Milk, whole	3 pounds	6 pounds
Extract, vanilla	¼ ounce	½ ounce
Salt	Pinch	¼ ounce
Egg yolks	6 ounces	12 ounces
Sugar, granulated	6 ounces	12 ounces
Cream, heavy	8 ounces	1 pound
Cinnamon, ground	As needed	As needed
Egg whites	4 ounces	8 ounces
Sugar, granulated	2 ounces	4 ounces

METHOD OF PREPARATION:

1. Gather the equipment and ingredients.
2. Butter a hotel pan.
3. Place the tapioca, milk, vanilla extract, and salt in a pot; cook until tender.
4. Combine the egg yolks, granulated sugar, heavy cream, and cinnamon.
5. Temper the egg yolk mixture, and add to the milk mixture.
6. Cook for 2 to 3 minutes, stirring constantly; remove from the stove.
7. Place the egg whites in a bowl, whip to a soft peak, and slowly add the granulated sugar to make a meringue.
8. Fold the meringue into the tapioca mixture.
9. Pour into the buttered hotel pan.
10. Refrigerate until set.

Vanilla Pudding

PASTRY TECHNIQUES:
Boiling, Tempering

Boiling:
1. Bring the cooking liquid to a rapid boil.
2. Stir the contents.

Tempering:
1. Whisk the eggs vigorously while ladling hot liquid.

HACCP:
Store at 40° F.

HAZARDOUS FOODS:
Milk
Egg yolks
Eggs

YIELD:	3 pounds, 2 ounces.	6 pounds, 4 ounces.
INGREDIENTS:		
Sugar, granulated	8 ounces	1 pound
Milk, whole	2 pounds	4 pounds
Cornstarch	1½ ounces	3 ounces
Egg yolks	4 ounces	8 ounces
Eggs, whole	2 ounces	4 ounces
Butter, unsalted	2 ounces	4 ounces
Extract, vanilla	½ ounce	1 ounce

METHOD OF PREPARATION:

1. Gather the equipment and ingredients.
2. Place half of the sugar and the milk in a pot; bring to a boil.
3. Place the cornstarch and the remaining sugar in a dry bowl; slowly whisk in the egg yolks and whole eggs; combine well.
4. Temper the cornstarch mixture, and add to the boiling milk.
5. Bring the mixture back to a second boil, stirring constantly.
6. Remove from the heat, and stir in the butter and vanilla extract.
7. Cover, and refrigerate.

6

Pies

6

Pies

Basic Pie Dough No. 1

CAKES: BASES

ICINGS

CAKES: FINISHED

CREAMS

FILLINGS

PIES

SLOW BAKING

BATTER

DOUGHS

SAUCES

PASTRY TECHNIQUES:
Combining

Combining:
Bringing together two or more components.
1. Prepare the components to be combined.
2. Add one to the other, using the appropriate mixing method (if needed).

HACCP:
Store at 40° F.

YIELD:	1 pound, 8¼ ounces.	3 pounds, ½ ounce.
	3, 8-ounce Crusts.	6, 8-ounce Crusts.

INGREDIENTS:

Flour, pastry	12 ounces	1 pound, 8 ounces
Shortening, all-purpose	8 ounces	1 pound
Salt	¼ ounce	½ ounce
Water, ice-cold	4 ounces	8 ounces
Dried milk solids (DMS) (optional)	0 to 1 ounce	0 to 2 ounces
Sugar, granulated (optional)	0 to 1 ounce	0 to 2 ounces

METHOD OF PREPARATION:

1. Gather the equipment and ingredients.
2. Sift the flour to aerate it; remove lumps and impurities.
3. Break the shortening, by hand, into the flour.
4. Dissolve the salt in the cold water.
5. Incorporate the water into the flour until it is sticky. *Do not overwork* the dough.
6. Allow the dough to rest, and chill properly, preferably overnight.

CHEF NOTE:
The DMS and the sugar can be sifted at the beginning with the pastry flour. The process would be continued in the same manner.

127

Basic Pie Dough No. 2

PASTRY TECHNIQUE:
Blending

Blending:
1. Combine the dry ingredients on low speed.
2. Add the softened fat(s) and liquid(s).
3. Mix the ingredients on low speed.
4. Increase the speed gradually.

HACCP:
Store at 40° F.

| YIELD: | 2 pounds, 8 ounces. |
| | 5, 8-ounce Crusts. |

INGREDIENTS:

Flour, pastry	1 pound, 4 ounces
Salt	⅜ ounce
Dry milk solids (DMS)	¾ ounce
Fat (shortening, unsalted butter, or margarine)	14 ounces
Water, ice cold	6 ounces

METHOD OF PREPARATION:

1. Gather the equipment and ingredients.
2. Sift the pastry flour, salt, and DMS together.
3. Place all of the dry ingredients into a mixing bowl with a paddle.
4. Place the fat in the bowl; mix slowly to crumble the fat into large pieces.
5. Add the water slowly, to incorporate all ingredients together.
6. Blend together, but *do not overmix*.
7. Remove the dough from the mixer.
8. Allow the dough to rest and chill properly (preferably overnight).

CHEF NOTES:
1. For a 9-inch pie, scale two (8-ounce) pieces of dough for the bottom and top crusts.
2. The fat can be a mixture of all shortenings indicated or a choice of one listed.
3. Scraps can be reworked into the next dough or roll.

CAKES: BASES

ICINGS

CAKES: FINISHED

CREAMS

FILLINGS

PIES

SLOW BAKING

BATTER

DOUGHS

SAUCES

PASTRY TECHNIQUE:
Combining

Combining:
Bringing together two or more components.
1. Prepare the components to be combined.
2. Add one to the other, using the appropriate mixing method (if needed).

Graham Cracker Crust No. 1

YIELD:	15¾ ounces.	1 pound, 15½ ounces.
	2, 9-inch Pans.	4, 9-inch Pans.

INGREDIENTS:

Butter (unsalted) or margarine	5 ounces	10 ounces
Flour, cake	1 ounce	2 ounces
Crumbs, graham cracker	8 ounces	1 pound
Sugar, confectionery	1¾ ounces	3½ ounces

METHOD OF PREPARATION:

1. Gather the equipment and ingredients.
2. Melt the butter.
3. Combine the cake flour, graham cracker crumbs, and sugar in a bowl.
4. Add the melted butter into the dry ingredients.
5. Combine well.
6. Press into 9-inch pans.
7. Bake at 350° F for 8 to 10 minutes, until firm.
8. Remove from the oven, and cool.

Graham Cracker Crust No. 2

PASTRY TECHNIQUE:
Combining

Combining:
Bringing together two or more components.
1. Prepare the components to be combined.
2. Add one to the other, using the appropriate mixing method (if needed).

YIELD: 1 pound, 11¼ ounces.
                          3, 9-inch Pans.

INGREDIENTS:

Butter (unsalted) or margarine	5 ounces
Sugar, confectionery or granulated	6 ounces
Crumbs, graham cracker	1 pound
Cinnamon, ground (optional)	¼ ounce

METHOD OF PREPARATION:

1. Gather the equipment and ingredients.
2. Melt the butter.
3. Combine the sugar, graham cracker crumbs, and cinnamon.
4. Add the melted butter to the dry ingredients.
5. Combine well.
6. Press into 9-inch pans.

CAKES: BASES
ICINGS
CAKES: FINISHED
CREAMS
FILLINGS
PIES
SLOW BAKING
BATTER
DOUGHS
SAUCES

PASTRY TECHNIQUES:
Rolling, Baking

Rolling:
1. Prepare the rolling surface by dusting with the appropriate medium (flour, cornstarch, etc.).
2. Use the appropriate style pin (stick pin or ball bearing pin) to roll the dough to desired thickness; rotate the dough during rolling to prevent sticking.

Baking:
1. Preheat the oven.
2. Position the item appropriately in the oven.
3. Check for appropriate firmness and/or color.

Prebaked Pie Shells

YIELD: 1, 9-inch Shell.

INGREDIENTS:

Pie dough (see pages 127, 128)   8 ounces

METHOD OF PREPARATION:

1. Gather the equipment and ingredients.
2. Weigh out the dough into 8-ounce portions.
3. Using a rolling pin, roll out 8 ounces of pie dough, slightly larger around than a 9-inch pie pan.
4. Using a dough docker, dock the entire surface of the dough.
5. Fold the dough in half, and lift up; place over a pie pan.
6. Unfold the dough to fit the pan.
7. Remove the air between the dough and the pan by shaking slightly.
8. Trim the edges.
9. Place another pie pan on top of the dough; turn upside down.
10. Place four pie pans on a sheet pan.
11. Place the sheet pan in the oven; place a second sheet pan, upside down, on top of the pie pans to keep the pie bottoms flat.
12. Bake at 400° F for 10 minutes, or until the edges begin to brown.
13. Remove the top sheet pan, and continue baking until the dough is golden brown.
14. Remove from the oven.
15. Cool.
16. Turn over onto a single pie pan.

PASTRY TECHNIQUES:
Creaming, Combining

Creaming:
1. Soften the fats on low speed.
2. Add the sugar(s) and cream; increase the speed slowly.
3. Add the eggs one at a time; scrape the bowl frequently.
4. Add the dry ingredients in stages.

Combining:
Bringing together two or more components.
1. Prepare the components to be combined.
2. Add one to the other, using the appropriate mixing method (if needed).

Streusel Topping No. 1

YIELD:	1 pound, 8 ounces.	3 pounds.

INGREDIENTS:

Butter (unsalted) or margarine	6 ounces	12 ounces
Sugar, brown	6 ounces	12 ounces
Cinnamon, ground	To taste	To taste
Salt	To taste	To taste
Flour, bread	12 ounces	1 pound, 8 ounces

METHOD OF PREPARATION:

1. Gather the equipment and ingredients.
2. Place the butter and brown sugar in a bowl; cream together with a paddle until light and well blended.
3. Add the cinnamon and salt; combine well.
4. Add the bread flour, and mix until the mixture becomes crumbly.

CHEF NOTE:
Streusel may be used on a variety of pies, bread pudding, or cobblers. Nuts may be added for extra flavor and texture.

PASTRY TECHNIQUE:
Combining

Combining:
Bringing together two or more components.
1. Prepare the components to be combined.
2. Add one to the other, using the appropriate mixing method (if needed).

Streusel Topping No. 2

YIELD:	4 pounds, 11 ounces.	9 pounds, 6 ounces.
INGREDIENTS:		
Sugar, granulated	10 ounces	1 pound, 4 ounces
Sugar, brown	8 ounces	1 pound
Shortening, all-purpose	1 pound	2 pounds
Flour, cake	2 pound, 8 ounces	5 pounds
Extract, vanilla	1 ounce	2 ounces

METHOD OF PREPARATION:

1. Gather the equipment and ingredients.
2. In a large bowl, combine all of the ingredients by hand.

Apple Pie Filling
Canned Apples

PASTRY TECHNIQUES:
Boiling, Thickening

Boiling:
1. Bring the cooking liquid to a rapid boil.
2. Stir the contents.

Thickening:
1. Mix a small amount of sugar with the starches.
2. Create a slurry.
3. Whisk vigorously until thickened and translucent.

HACCP:
Store at 40° F.

YIELD:	2 pounds, 14 ounces.	5 pounds, 12 ounces.
	2, 9-inch Pies.	4, 9-inch Pies.

INGREDIENTS:

Ingredient		
Apples, canned, sliced	1 pound, 10 ounces	3 pounds, 4 ounces
Water, cold	12 ounces	1 pound, 8 ounces
Sugar, granulated	6 ounces	12 ounces
Salt	Pinch	Pinch
Cinnamon, ground	Pinch	Pinch
Nutmeg, ground	Pinch	Pinch
Cornstarch	1½ ounces	3 ounces

METHOD OF PREPARATION:

1. Gather the equipment and ingredients.
2. Place the sliced apples, half of the amount of water, half of the amount of sugar, the salt, cinnamon, and nutmeg in a pot.
3. Bring to a boil.
4. In a dry bowl, place the cornstarch and the remaining amount of sugar; combine.
5. Add the remaining water to the cornstarch mixture slowly to prevent lumps from occurring.
6. When the apple mixture has boiled, stir in the starch mixture slowly to thicken.
7. Continue to cook and stir for 1 minute.
8. Remove from the heat.
9. Pour onto clean sheet pans, and cool.
10. Cover. Store for later use.

CHEF NOTE:
Place the filling in an unbaked pie shell; bake until the crust is golden brown.

CAKES: BASES

ICINGS

CAKES: FINISHED

CREAMS

FILLINGS

PIES

SLOW BAKING

BATTER

DOUGHS

SAUCES

PASTRY TECHNIQUES:
Boiling, Thickening

Boiling:
1. Bring the cooking liquid to a rapid boil.
2. Stir the contents.

Thickening:
1. Mix a small amount of sugar with the starches.
2. Create a slurry.
3. Whisk vigorously until thickened and translucent.

HACCP:
Store at 40° F.

Apple Pie Filling
Fresh Apples

YIELD:	4 pounds, 4 ounces.	8 pounds, 8 ounces.
	2, 9-inch Pies.	4, 9-inch Pies.

INGREDIENTS:

Apples, fresh, peeled and sliced	2 pounds, 8 ounces	5 pounds
Water	1 pound, 4 ounces	2 pounds, 8 ounces
Sugar, granulated	6 ounces	12 ounces
Salt	Pinch	Pinch
Cinnamon, ground	To taste	To taste
Cornstarch	2 ounces	4 ounces

METHOD OF PREPARATION:

1. Gather the equipment and ingredients.
2. Combine the apples with two thirds of the water, all of the sugar, salt, and cinnamon; place in a pot.
3. Bring to a boil.
4. Place the cornstarch in a dry bowl; slowly add the other third of water; whisk constantly to prevent lumps from occurring.
5. Once the apple mixture boils, slowly add the cornstarch mixture, and stir constantly.
6. Bring the mixture back to a boil; boil for approximately 1 minute.
7. Remove from the heat.
8. Cool the filling; store for later use.

CHEF NOTE:
Place the filling in an unbaked pie shell; bake until the crust is golden brown.

PASTRY TECHNIQUES:
Boiling, Thickening

Boiling:
1. Bring the cooking liquid to a rapid boil.
2. Stir the contents.

Thickening:
1. Mix a small amount of sugar with the starches.
2. Create a slurry.
3. Whisk vigorously until thickened and translucent.

HACCP:
Store at 40° F.

Blueberry Pie Filling
Frozen/Canned

YIELD:	1 pound, 12½ ounces.	3 pounds, 9 ounces.
	1, 9-inch Pie.	2, 9-inch Pies.

INGREDIENTS:

Ingredient		
Blueberries, canned or frozen	1 pound	2 pounds
Water or juice from blueberries	7 ounces	14 ounces
Sugar, granulated	4½ ounces	9 ounces
Cornstarch	1⅛ ounces	2¼ ounces
Nutmeg	To taste	To taste
Lemon juice	To taste	To taste

METHOD OF PREPARATION:

1. Gather the equipment and ingredients.
2. If the blueberries are packed in water, drain completely; reserve the water. If the blueberries are frozen, defrost them, and drain well.
3. Place three fourths of the water or juice in a pot; add the granulated sugar.
4. Bring the mixture to a boil.
5. Place the cornstarch in a dry bowl; slowly add the remaining water to prevent lumps from forming. Make sure there are no lumps.
6. Add the nutmeg and lemon juice to the cornstarch mixture.
7. When the sugar-water mixture begins to boil, slowly add the cornstarch mixture; whisk constantly, and return to a second boil.
8. Cook until thickened properly, approximately 1 minute. The mixture will turn translucent.
9. Remove from the heat.
10. Fold in the blueberries gently so they do not become crushed.
11. Cool the filling; store for later use.

CHEF NOTE:
Place the filling in an unbaked pie shell; bake until the crust is golden brown.

PASTRY TECHNIQUES:
Boiling, Thickening

Boiling:
1. Bring the cooking liquid to a rapid boil.
2. Stir the contents.

Thickening:
1. Mix a small amount of sugar with the starches.
2. Create a slurry.
3. Whisk vigorously until thickened and translucent.

HACCP:
Store at 40° F.

Cherry Pie Filling
Canned/Frozen/Fresh

YIELD:	1 pound, 13 ounces.	3 pounds, 10 ounces.
	1, 9-inch Pie.	2, 9-inch Pies.

INGREDIENTS:

Cherries, dark, canned, frozen or fresh	1 pound	2 pounds
Water or cherry juice	7½ ounces	15 ounces
Sugar, granulated	4½ ounces	9 ounces
Cornstarch	1 ounce	2 ounces
Lemon juice	To taste	To taste
Salt	To taste	To taste

METHOD OF PREPARATION:

1. Gather the equipment and ingredients.
2. If the cherries are packed in water, drain completely; reserve the water. If the cherries are frozen, keep them frozen.
3. Place three fourths of the water or juice and the granulated sugar in a pot.
4. Bring this mixture to a boil.
5. Place the cornstarch in a dry bowl, and slowly add the remaining juice or water; whisk to prevent lumps from forming.
6. Add the lemon juice and salt to the cornstarch mixture.
7. When the sugar-water mixture begins to boil, slowly add the cornstarch mixture; stir constantly, and return to a second boil.
8. Cook until thickened properly and the mixture is translucent, approximately 1 minute.
9. Remove from the heat.
10. Gently fold in the cherries.
11. Cool the filling; store for later use.

CHEF NOTE:
Place the filling in an unbaked pie shell; bake until the crust is golden brown.

CAKES: BASES
ICINGS
CAKES: FINISHED
CREAMS
FILLINGS
PIES
SLOW BAKING
BATTER
DOUGHS
SAUCES

Banana Cream Pie

PASTRY TECHNIQUES:

PASTRY TECHNIQUES:
Boiling, Tempering, Thickening

Boiling:
1. Bring the cooking liquid to a rapid boil.
2. Stir the contents.

Tempering:
1. Whisk the eggs vigorously while ladling hot liquid.

Thickening:
1. Mix a small amount of sugar with the starches.
2. Create a slurry.
3. Whisk vigorously until thickened and translucent.

HACCP:
Store at 40° F.

HAZARDOUS FOODS:
Eggs
Heavy cream

YIELD:	1, 9-inch Pie.	2, 9-inch Pies.

INGREDIENTS:

Pie shell, prebaked (see page 131)	1, 9-inch shell	2, 9-inch shells
Bananas	3 each	6 each

Filling:

Cornstarch	1½ ounces	3 ounces
Water	1 pound	2 pounds
Eggs, whole	4 ounces	8 ounces
Dried milk solids (DMS)	2 ounces	4 ounces
Sugar, granulated	4 ounces	8 ounces
Salt	⅛ ounce	¼ ounce
Butter, unsalted	1½ ounces	3 ounces
Extract, vanilla	To taste	To taste

Garnish:

Cream, heavy, whipped	As needed	As needed

METHOD OF PREPARATION:

1. Gather the equipment and ingredients.
2. Prepare the pie shells, as needed.
3. Slice the bananas, and place evenly in the bottom of a pie shell.
4. Place the cornstarch in a dry bowl, and add a small amount of the water to dissolve it. Make sure there are no lumps.
5. Whisk the eggs with the cornstarch mixture; set aside.
6. Place the DMS in a pot; slowly add the remaining water to prevent the mixture from forming lumps.
7. Add the sugar and salt to the pot.
8. Bring this to a boil.
9. Temper the cornstarch mixture, and add to the boiling milk.
10. Bring the mixture to a second boil, and allow it to thicken; whisk constantly.
11. Remove from the heat.
12. Add the butter and vanilla extract.
13. Pour immediately on top of the sliced bananas in a prebaked pie shell.
14. Let the pie cool completely.
15. Garnish with whipped cream, as desired.

PASTRY TECHNIQUES:
Filling, Covering, Baking

Filling:
1. Cut open the food product.
2. Carefully spread the filling using an icing spatula, or
3. Carefully pipe the filling using a pastry bag.

Covering:
Sealing a product with a layering of another product such as marzipan or rolled fondant.
1. Prepare the product to be covered with a sticky layer of buttercream, food gel, or other medium that is called for in the formula.
2. Roll out the covering material.
3. Cover the product with the covering material.
4. Smooth the covered product with a bowl scraper to remove wrinkles and air bubbles.

Baking:
1. Preheat the oven.
2. Position the item appropriately in the oven.
3. Check for appropriate firmness and/or color.

HACCP:
Store at 40° F.

Boston Cream Pie

YIELD:	1, 9-inch Pie.	2, 9-inch Pies.

INGREDIENTS:

Liquid-shortening sponge cake mix, vanilla (see page 26)	10 ounces	1 pound, 4 ounces
Pastry cream, vanilla (see page 97)	8 ounces	1 pound
Chocolate fudge icing (see page 46)	8 ounces	1 pound
Fondant, warmed	As needed	As needed

METHOD OF PREPARATION:

1. Gather the equipment and ingredients.
2. Scale 10 ounces of vanilla sponge cake batter into a greased pie pan.
3. Bake the batter at 350° F, until golden brown, approximately 25 minutes.
4. Let it cool in the pan; remove completely.
5. After the cake is removed from the pan, turn the cake upside down, and cut in half. (The bottom of the cake becomes the top of the cake.)
6. Place the cake on a circle.
7. Fill the center of the cake with the 8 ounces of pastry cream.
8. Spread the 8 ounces of chocolate fudge icing on top of the cake; make it nice and smooth.
9. Use the warm fondant to garnish the top of the cake.

PASTRY TECHNIQUES:
Melting, Boiling, Tempering, Thickening

Melting:
1. Prepare the food product to be melted.
2. Place the food product in an appropriate-sized pot over direct heat or over a double boiler.
3. Stir frequently or occasionally, depending on the delicacy of the product, until melted.

OR

1. Place the product on a sheet pan or in a bowl, and place in a low-temperature oven until melted.

Boiling:
1. Bring the cooking liquid to a rapid boil.
2. Stir the contents.

Tempering:
1. Whisk the eggs vigorously while ladling hot liquid.

Thickening:
1. Mix a small amount of sugar with the starches.
2. Create a slurry.
3. Whisk vigorously until thickened and translucent.

HACCP:
Store at 40° F.

HAZARDOUS FOOD:
Egg yolks
Eggs
Milk

Butterscotch Cream Pie

YIELD:	1, 9-inch Pie.	2, 9-inch Pies.

INGREDIENTS:

	1, 9-inch shell	2, 9-inch shells
Pie shell, prebaked (see page 131)	1, 9-inch shell	2, 9-inch shells

Filling:

Butter, unsalted	3½ ounces	7 ounces
Sugar, brown	4 ounces	8 ounces
Cornstarch	1½ ounces	3 ounces
Milk, whole	1 pound	2 pounds
Eggs, whole	1¾ ounces	3½ ounces
Egg yolks	1¼ ounces	2½ ounces
Sugar, granulated	4 ounces	8 ounces
Extract, vanilla	To taste	To taste

METHOD OF PREPARATION:

1. Gather the equipment and ingredients.
2. Prepare the pie shells, as needed.
3. Melt the butter in a pot.
4. Add the brown sugar to the melted butter; cook until the color is slightly browner; set aside.
5. Place the cornstarch in a dry bowl, and slowly add some milk to dissolve it. Whisk to make sure there are no lumps.
6. Whisk the eggs and egg yolks together; add to the cornstarch mixture.
7. Place the remaining milk and granulated sugar in a pot; bring to a boil.
8. Temper the dissolved cornstarch mixture and pour into the boiling milk; reduce the heat.
9. Bring the milk mixture back to a second boil; whisk constantly.
10. Remove from the heat.
11. Add the vanilla extract.
12. Fold in the brown sugar mixture.
13. Pour immediately into the prebaked pie shell.
14. Let cool.
15. Garnish, as desired.

CAKES: BASES

ICINGS

CAKES: FINISHED

CREAMS

FILLINGS

PIES

SLOW BAKING

BATTER

DOUGHS

SAUCES

Chocolate Cream Pie

PASTRY TECHNIQUES:

Chopping, Boiling, Tempering, Thickening

Chopping:

1. Use a sharp knife.
2. Hold the food product properly.
3. Cut with a quick downward motion.

Boiling:

1. Bring the cooking liquid to a rapid boil.
2. Stir the contents.

Tempering:

1. Whisk the eggs vigorously while ladling hot liquid.

Thickening:

1. Mix a small amount of sugar with the starches.
2. Create a slurry.
3. Whisk vigorously until thickened and translucent.

HACCP:

Store at 40° F.

HAZARDOUS FOOD:

Egg yolks
Eggs
Milk

YIELD:	1, 9-inch Pie.	2, 9-inch Pies.

INGREDIENTS:		
Pie shell, prebaked (see page 131)	1, 9-inch shell	2, 9-inch shells
Filling:		
Chocolate, dark, semi-sweet	4 ounces	8 ounces
Cornstarch	1½ ounces	3 ounces
Milk, whole	1 pound, 2 ounces	2 pounds, 4 ounces
Egg yolks	2 ounces	4 ounces
Eggs, whole	2 ounces	4 ounces
Sugar, granulated	4 ounces	8 ounces
Butter, unsalted, chopped	1 ounce	2 ounces
Extract, vanilla	To taste	To taste

METHOD OF PREPARATION:

1. Gather the equipment and ingredients.
2. Prepare the pie shells, as needed.
3. Chop the chocolate very fine; set aside.
4. Place the cornstarch in a dry bowl, and add a small amount of the milk to dissolve it; make sure there are no lumps.
5. Add the egg yolks and whole eggs to the cornstarch mixture.
6. Place the remaining milk and granulated sugar in a pot; bring to a boil.
7. Temper the cornstarch mixture, and add to the boiling milk.
8. Bring the liquid back to a second boil, and allow it to thicken; whisk constantly.
9. Remove from the heat.
10. Add the butter and vanilla extract.
11. Add the chopped chocolate.
12. Stir well to melt the chocolate completely.
13. Pour immediately into a pie shell.
14. Let the pie cool completely.
15. Garnish, as desired.

Coconut Cream Pie

YIELD:	1, 9-inch Pie.	2, 9-inch Pies.

INGREDIENTS:

Pie shell, prebaked (see page 131)	1, 9-inch shell	2, 9-inch shells

Filling:

Dry milk solids (DMS)	2 ounces	4 ounces
Water, cool	1 pound	2 pounds
Cornstarch	1½ ounces	3 ounces
Eggs, whole	4 ounces	8 ounces
Salt	Pinch	Pinch
Sugar, granulated	4 ounces	8 ounces
Butter (unsalted) or shortening, chopped into small pieces	1½ ounces	3 ounces
Extract, vanilla	To taste	To taste
Coconut, plain	2½ ounces	5 ounces

Garnish:

Coconut, toasted	2½ ounces	5 ounces
Cream, heavy, whipped	As needed	As needed

METHOD OF PREPARATION:

1. Gather the equipment and ingredients.
2. Prepare the pie shells, as needed.
3. Place the DMS in a dry bowl; slowly add water to dissolve them; whisk to make sure there are no lumps; add the rest of the water, and whisk.
4. Place the cornstarch in a dry bowl, and add a small amount of milk to dissolve it; make sure there are no lumps.
5. Add the eggs and salt to the cornstarch mixture; whisk completely.
6. Place the rest of the milk and all of the sugar in a pot, and bring to a boil.
7. Once the milk boils, temper the cornstarch mixture, and add it to the boiling milk.
8. Bring to a second boil; allow to boil for 2 minutes; whisk constantly.
9. Remove from the stove, and whisk in the butter and vanilla extract.
10. Add the plain coconut and stir well.
11. Immediately pour the filling into the prebaked pie shell; cool.
12. Garnish with toasted coconut and whipped heavy cream.

PASTRY TECHNIQUES:
Boiling, Tempering, Thickening

Boiling:
1. Bring the cooking liquid to a rapid boil.
2. Stir the contents.

Tempering:
1. Whisk the eggs vigorously while ladling hot liquid.

Thickening:
1. Mix a small amount of sugar with the starches.
2. Create a slurry.
3. Whisk vigorously until thickened and translucent.

HACCP:
Store at 40° F.

HAZARDOUS FOOD:
Eggs
Heavy cream

Dutch Apple Pie

CAKES: BASES
ICINGS
CAKES: FINISHED
CREAMS
FILLINGS
PIES
SLOW BAKING
BATTER
DOUGHS
SAUCES

PASTRY TECHNIQUES:
Dredging, Filling

Dredging:
1. Coat the food product.
2. Sprinkle or toss the product in an appropriate dredging application.

Filling:
1. Cut open the food product.
2. Carefully spread the filling using an icing spatula, or
3. Carefully pipe the filling using a pastry bag.

YIELD:	1, 9-inch Pie.	2, 9-inch Pies.

INGREDIENTS:

	1, 9-inch Pie.	2, 9-inch Pies.
Pie shell, unbaked (see pages 127, 128)	1, 9-inch shell	2, 9-inch shells

Filling:

Apples	8 to 9 each	16 to 18 each
Sugar, granulated	As needed	As needed
Cinnamon, ground	As needed	As needed
Flour, cake	As needed	As needed
Raisins	4 ounces	8 ounces

Streusel Topping:

Butter, unsalted	8 ounces	1 pound
Sugar, granulated	5 ounces	10 ounces
Sugar, brown	4 ounces	8 ounces
Salt	Pinch	Pinch
Cinnamon, ground	To taste	To taste
Flour, pastry	15 ounces	1 pound, 14 ounces

METHOD OF PREPARATION:

1. Gather the equipment and ingredients.
2. Prepare an unbaked pie shell.
3. Peel and core the apples.
4. Cut the apples into medium-size slices.
5. Combine the sugar and cinnamon.
6. Dredge the apples in the cinnamon and sugar mixture.
7. Dredge the apples in the flour.
8. Place the apples and raisins in the unbaked pie shell.
9. Sprinkle the topping over the apples.
10. Bake at 400° F to 425° F for 45 minutes, or until done.

Preparation of Topping:

1. Cream together the butter, sugars, salt, and cinnamon.
2. Add the flour.

PASTRY TECHNIQUE:
Combining

Combining:
Bringing together two or more components.
1. Prepare the components to be combined.
2. Add one to the other, using the appropriate mixing method (if needed).

HACCP:
Store at 40° F.

HAZARDOUS FOODS:
Milk
Eggs

Fruit Cobbler with Topping

YIELD:		3 pounds, 5½ ounces.	6 pounds, 11 ounces.
INGREDIENTS:			
Milk, whole		12 ounces	1 pound, 8 ounces
Extract, vanilla		1 ounce	2 ounces
Eggs, whole		8 ounces	1 pound
Sugar, granulated		1 pound	2 pounds
Flour, bread		1 pound	2 pounds
Baking powder		¼ ounce	½ ounce
Cinnamon, ground		¼ ounce	½ ounce
Short dough (see page 183)		As needed	As needed
Fruit filling, as desired		As needed	As needed

METHOD OF PREPARATION:

1. Gather the equipment and ingredients.
2. Roll out the short dough crust, and place in a well-greased pan.
3. Place the fruit filling on the top of the short crust.
4. Sprinkle with topping.
5. Bake at 350° F for approximately 35 minutes.

Preparation of Cobbler Topping:

1. Place the milk, vanilla extract, eggs, and granulated sugar in a bowl with a paddle.
2. Combine well.
3. Sift together the bread flour, baking powder, and cinnamon.
4. Add the dry ingredients in the sugar mixture.
5. Combine well. *Do not overmix.*

Fruit Pie

PASTRY TECHNIQUES:
Rolling, Filling

Rolling:
1. Prepare the rolling surface by dusting with the appropriate medium (flour, cornstarch, etc.).
2. Use the appropriate style pin (stick pin or ball bearing pin) to roll the dough to desired thickness; rotate the dough during rolling to prevent sticking.

Filling:
1. Cut open the food product.
2. Carefully spread the filling using an icing spatula, or
3. Carefully pipe the filling using a pastry bag.

YIELD:	1, 9-inch Pie.	2, 9-inch Pies.
INGREDIENTS:		
Pie dough (see pages 127, 128)	1 pound	2 pounds
Pie filling	1 pound, 12 ounces	3 pounds, 8 ounces
Egg wash (see page 44)	As needed	As needed

METHOD OF PREPARATION:

1. Gather the equipment and ingredients.
2. Divide the dough into two (8-ounce) portions.
3. Roll out one (8-ounce) portion, and place it in a pie pan; be sure that all of the air between the pan and the dough is released.
4. Trim the edges. (Do not dock.)
5. Fill the shell with pie filling.
6. Wet the edges of the pie with egg wash; use a pastry brush.
7. Roll out the remaining 8-ounce portion of pie dough, and place it over the top of the pie; seal the bottom and top layers of dough completely.
8. Trim the edges.
9. Using a pastry brush, brush the top of the pie completely with the egg wash. Do not brush too heavily. (Granulated sugar may be sprinkled on top, if desired.)
10. Cut a hole in the center of the top.
11. Bake the pie at 400° F 45 minutes, or until the crust is golden brown and the filling is bubbling.
12. Cool the pie before serving.

Variations:

1. Cherry Pie Filling
   a. Canned
   b. Frozen
   c. Fresh
2. Blueberry Pie Filling
   a. Canned
   b. Frozen
3. Apple Pie Filling
   a. Canned
   b. Fresh

CHEF NOTE:
Before removing pie from oven, make sure that the shell is baked. Top color is not an indication of doneness.

CAKES: BASES

ICINGS

CAKES: FINISHED

CREAMS

FILLINGS

PIES

SLOW BAKING

BATTER

DOUGHS

SAUCES

PASTRY TECHNIQUES:
Filling, Rolling

Filling:
1. Cut open the food product.
2. Carefully spread the filling using an icing spatula.
3. Carefully pipe the filling using a pastry bag.

Rolling:
1. Prepare the rolling surface by dusting with the appropriate medium (flour, cornstarch, etc.).
2. Use the appropriate style pin (stick pin or ball bearing pin) to roll the dough to desired thickness; rotate the dough during rolling to prevent sticking.

Homestyle Apple Pie

Fresh Apples

YIELD:		1, 9-inch Pie.	2, 1-inch Pies.

INGREDIENTS:

Pie shell, unbaked		1, 9-inch shell	2, 9-inch shells
Pie dough, top crust		8 ounces	16 ounces

Filling:

Apples, fresh		6 to 8 each	12 to 16 each
Sugar, granulated		To taste	To taste
Cinnamon, ground		To taste	To taste
Flour, cake		As needed	As needed
Butter, unsalted, chopped		2 to 3 ounces	4 to 6 ounces

METHOD OF PREPARATION:

1. Gather the equipment and ingredients.
2. Prepare an unbaked pie shell, and roll out the top crust; use 8 ounces of pie dough.
3. Peel and core the apples.
4. Cut the apples into medium-size slices.
5. Combine the sugar and cinnamon.
6. Dredge the apples in the cinnamon and sugar mixture.
7. Dredge the apples in the flour.
8. Place the apples in the unbaked pie shell.
9. Place the pieces of butter on top of the apples.
10. Add a top crust over the apples.
11. Trim and flute the edges of the pie shell.
12. Make steam holes on the top crust.
13. Bake at 400° F to 425° F for 45 minutes, or until done.

CHEF NOTE:
Any readily available apple may be used for this recipe. Adjust the amount of sugar according to the sweetness or tartness of the apple.

CAKES: BASES
ICINGS
CAKES: FINISHED
CREAMS
FILLINGS
PIES
SLOW BAKING
BATTER
DOUGHS
SAUCES

PASTRY TECHNIQUES:

Blooming, Whipping, Melting, Combining

Blooming:

Gelatin sheets or leaves:
1. Fan the sheets out.
2. Cover the sheets in liquid.
3. Sheets are bloomed when softened.

Granular gelatin:
1. Sprinkle the gelatin.
2. Gelatin is ready when it is cream of wheat consistency.

Whipping:

1. Hold the whip at a 55-degree angle.
2. Create circles, using a circular motion.
3. The circular motion needs to be perpendicular to the bowl.

Melting:

1. Prepare the food product to be melted.
2. Place the food product in an appropriately-sized pot over direct heat or over a double boiler.
3. Stir frequently or occasionally, depending on the delicacy of the product, until melted.

OR
1. Place the product on a sheet pan or in a bowl, and place in a low-temperature oven until melted.

Combining:

Bringing together two or more components.
1. Prepare the components to be combined.
2. Add one to the other, using the appropriate mixing method (if needed).

HACCP:

Store at 40° F.

HAZARDOUS FOOD:

Eggs
Heavy cream

Kahlua White Russian Pie

YIELD:	1, 9-inch Pie.	2, 9-inch Pies.

INGREDIENTS:

	1, 9-inch Pie.	2, 9-inch Pies.
Graham cracker crust (see pages 129, 130)	1, 9-inch crust	2, 9-inch crusts
Filling:		
Gelatin, powdered	¼ ounce	½ ounce
Water, cold	2 ounces	4 ounces
Eggs, whole	3 each	6 each
Cream, heavy	4 ounces	8 ounces
Sugar, granulated	3½ ounces	7 ounces
Kahlua	1½ ounces	3 ounces
Vodka	1 ounce	2 ounces
Extract, vanilla	To taste	To taste
Garnish:		
Chocolate, curls	As needed	As needed
Cream, heavy	As needed	As needed

METHOD OF PREPARATION:

1. Gather the equipment and ingredients.
2. Prepare a 9-inch pie pan with a graham cracker crust.
3. Place the gelatin in a dry bowl; bloom with cold water.
4. Separate the eggs.
5. Whip the heavy cream to a soft-peak consistency.
6. Take half of the amount of sugar and all of the yolks, and place over a double boiler; whisk continuously over medium heat until the yolks reach full volume. They should be pale in color and create a ribbon effect when dropped from the whisk.
7. Melt the bloomed gelatin.
8. Once the gelatin is melted, add to the egg yolk mixture; set aside to cool. As it cools, it will become thicker.
9. Once the yolk mixture has thickened, slightly whip the egg whites. Slowly add the other half of the sugar to the whites; whip to full volume. (It peaks when firm.)
10. Fold together the yolk mixture and the soft peaked whipped cream; use a whip.
11. Fold the egg whites gently into the cream-yolk mixture.
12. Add the flavorings: Kahlua, vodka, and vanilla extract.
13. Pour into the crust.
14. Chill.
15. Garnish with chocolate curls and whipped heavy cream, if desired.

Lemon Chiffon Pie

YIELD:	1, 9-inch Pie.	2, 9-inch Pies.

INGREDIENTS:

Pie shell, prebaked (see page 131)	1, 9-inch shell	2, 9-inch shells
Filling:		
Water	7 ounces	14 ounces
Lemon juice, fresh	2½ ounces	5 ounces
Sugar, granulated	2 ounces	4 ounces
Salt	Pinch	Pinch
Lemon, rind	¼ lemon	½ lemon
Cornstarch	1 ounce	2 ounces
Water (used for the cornstarch)	1 ounce	2 ounces
Egg yolks	1 ounce	2 ounces
Butter, unsalted	¼ ounce	½ ounce
Chiffon:		
Egg whites	2½ ounces	5 ounces
Sugar, granulated	1½ ounces	3 ounces

METHOD OF PREPARATION:

1. Gather the equipment and ingredients.
2. Prepare the prebaked pie shells, as needed.
3. Place the water, lemon juice, sugar, salt, and lemon rind in a pot; bring to a boil.
4. Place the cornstarch in a dry bowl, and use the water indicated for the cornstarch; slowly add it into the cornstarch, a little at a time, and whisk until all of the cornstarch is dissolved. Make sure there are no lumps.
5. Add the egg yolks to the cornstarch mixture.
6. Once the juice mixture comes to a boil, temper the egg-cornstarch mixture, and add to the boiling liquid.
7. Bring the liquid back to a boil, and cook for 2 minutes; whisk constantly.
8. Remove from the heat, and add in the butter.
9. Whisk until all of the butter is melted.
10. Whip up the egg whites with the amount of sugar indicated for the chiffon.
11. Once the egg whites have reached a stiff peak, take them off the mixer, and fold into the lemon filling with a spatula (while the lemon mixture is still hot).
12. Pour this mixture into the prebaked pie shell.
13. Smooth slightly, and let cool.
14. Garnish, as desired.

PASTRY TECHNIQUES:
Boiling, Tempering, Thickening, Whipping, Folding

Boiling:
1. Bring the cooking liquid to a rapid boil.
2. Stir the contents.

Tempering:
1. Whisk the eggs vigorously while ladling hot liquid.

Thickening:
1. Mix a small amount of sugar with the starches.
2. Create a slurry.
3. Whisk vigorously until thickened and translucent.

Whipping:
1. Hold the whip at a 55-degree angle.
2. Create circles, using a circular motion.
3. The circular motion needs to be perpendicular to the bowl.

Folding:
Do steps 1, 2, and 3 in one continuous motion.
1. Run a bowl scraper under the mixture, across the bottom of the bowl.
2. Turn the bowl counterclockwise.
3. Bring the bottom mixture to the top.

HACCP:
Store at 40° F.

HAZARDOUS FOOD:
Egg yolks
Egg whites

CAKES: BASES

ICINGS

CAKES: FINISHED

CREAMS

FILLINGS

PIES

SLOW BAKING

BATTER

DOUGHS

SAUCES

PASTRY TECHNIQUES:

Baking, Boiling, Tempering, Thickening, Whipping

Baking:

1. Preheat the oven.
2. Position the item appropriately in the oven.
3. Check for appropriate firmness and/or color.

Boiling:

1. Bring the cooking liquid to a rapid boil.
2. Stir the contents.

Tempering:

1. Whisk the eggs vigorously while ladling hot liquid.

Thickening:

1. Mix a small amount of sugar with the starches.
2. Create a slurry.
3. Whisk vigorously until thickened and translucent.

Whipping:

1. Hold the whip at a 55-degree angle.
2. Create circles, using a circular motion.
3. The circular motion needs to be perpendicular to the bowl.

HACCP:

Store at 40° F.

HAZARDOUS FOODS:

Eggs
Egg whites

Lemon Meringue Pie

YIELD:	1, 9-inch Pie.	2, 9-inch Pies.

INGREDIENTS:

Pie shell, prebaked (see page 131)	1, 9-inch shell	2, 9-inch shells

Filling:

Cornstarch	1¾ ounces	3½ ounces
Water	1 pound	2 pounds
Eggs, whole	4 ounces	8 ounces
Sugar, granulated	6 ounces	12 ounces
Salt	To taste	To taste
Lemon rind	1½ lemons	3 lemons
Lemon juice, fresh	2½ lemons	5 lemons
Butter, unsalted	1 ounce	2 ounces

Meringue:

Egg whites	2½ ounces	5 ounces
Sugar, granulated	3 ounces	6 ounces

METHOD OF PREPARATION:

1. Gather the equipment and ingredients.
2. Prepare the prebaked pie shells, as needed.
3. Place the cornstarch in a dry bowl; slowly add some water into the cornstarch, a little at a time, and whisk until all is dissolved. Make sure no lumps are present.
4. Add the eggs to the cornstarch mixture.
5. Combine the remaining water, sugar, salt, and lemon rind into a pot, and bring to a boil.
6. When boiling, temper the cornstarch mixture; add to the hot mixture.
7. Bring back to a second boil; allow the mixture to thicken.
8. Remove from the heat.
9. Add the lemon juice and butter.
10. Pour the filling into a prebaked pie shell.
11. Allow to cool.
12. Place the egg whites in a bowl, whip, and slowly add the granulated sugar; whip to a soft peak.
13. Garnish the top of the pie with meringue.
14. Bake the pie until the meringue turns brown, or use a propane torch to brown the meringue.

Pecan Pie

PASTRY TECHNIQUE:
Combining

Combining:
Bringing together two or more components.
1. Prepare the components to be combined.
2. Add one to the other, using the appropriate mixing method (if needed).

HACCP:
Store at 40° F.

HAZARDOUS FOOD:
Eggs

YIELD:	1, 9-inch Pie.	2, 9-inch Pies.

INGREDIENTS:

	1, 9-inch Pie.	2, 9-inch Pies.
Pie shell, unbaked (see pages 127, 128)	1, 9-inch shell	2, 9-inch shells

Filling:

Eggs, whole	6 ounces	12 ounces
Butter, unsalted	2 ounces	4 ounces
Corn syrup, light	12 ounces	1 pound, 8 ounces
Sugar, granulated	3½ ounces	7 ounces
Bourbon	To taste	To taste
Extract, vanilla	To taste	To taste
Pecan, pieces	5½ ounces	11 ounces

METHOD OF PREPARATION:

1. Gather the equipment and ingredients.
2. Prepare the pie shells, as needed.
3. Place the eggs in bowl, and slightly beat.
4. Melt the butter.
5. Add the melted butter, corn syrup, sugar, bourbon, and vanilla extract into the eggs; mix well using a whisk.
6. Place the pecans into an unbaked pie shell.
7. Pour the liquid mixture on top of the pecans.
8. Bake at 425° F for 15 minutes; reduce the oven temperature to 350° F. Bake for an additional 20 to 30 minutes, or until set but still slightly loose in the center.

Pineapple Chiffon Pie

PASTRY TECHNIQUES:

Boiling, Thickening, Whipping, Filling

Boiling:

1. Bring the cooking liquid to a rapid boil.
2. Stir the contents.

Thickening:

1. Mix a small amount of sugar with the starches.
2. Create a slurry.
3. Whisk vigorously until thickened and translucent.

Whipping:

1. Hold the whip at a 55-degree angle.
2. Create circles, using a circular motion.
3. The circular motion needs to be perpendicular to the bowl.

Filling:

1. Cut open the food product.
2. Carefully spread the filling using an icing spatula.
3. Carefully pipe the filling using a pastry bag.

HACCP:

Store at 40° F.

HAZARDOUS FOOD:

Egg whites

YIELD:	1, 9-inch Pie.	2, 9-inch Pies.

INGREDIENTS:

Pie shell, prebaked (see page 131)	1, 9-inch shell	2, 9-inch shells

Filling:

Cornstarch	1¼ ounces	2½ ounces
Water	3 ounces	6 ounces
Pineapple, crushed	8 ounces	1 pound
Sugar, granulated	4 ounces	8 ounces
Water	8 ounces	1 pound
Salt	⅛ ounce	¼ ounce
Gelatin	1/16 ounce	⅛ ounce
Coloring, yellow (optional)	½ drop	1 drop

Chiffon:

Egg whites	3 ounces	6 ounces
Sugar, granulated	3 ounces	6 ounces

METHOD OF PREPARATION:

1. Gather the equipment and ingredients.
2. Place the cornstarch in a dry bowl, and add a small amount of water to dissolve it.
3. Place the crushed pineapple, sugar, water, salt, gelatin, and coloring in a pot, and bring to a boil.
4. Add the cornstarch to the boiling mixture.
5. Bring it to a second boil, and allow to thicken; whisk constantly.
6. Remove from the heat.
7. Allow to cool.
8. Place the egg whites in a bowl, and whip to full volume; slowly add the sugar.
9. Fold egg whites into cooked pineapple mixture.
10. Pour the filling into the prebaked pie shell.
11. Allow to cool.
12. Garnish, as desired.

CAKES: BASES

ICINGS

CAKES: FINISHED

CREAMS

FILLINGS

PIES

SLOW BAKING

BATTER

DOUGHS

SAUCES

Pumpkin Pie

PASTRY TECHNIQUES:
Combining, Filling

Combining:

Bringing together two or more components.
1. Prepare the components to be combined.
2. Add one to the other, using the appropriate mixing method (if needed).

Filling:

1. Cut open the food product.
2. Carefully spread the filling using an icing spatula, or
3. Carefully pipe the filling using a pastry bag.

HACCP:
Store at 40° F.

HAZARDOUS FOOD:
Eggs

YIELD:	1, 9-inch Pie.	2, 9-inch Pies.

INGREDIENTS:

Pie shell, unbaked (see pages 127, 128)	1, 9-inch shell	2, 9-inch shells

Filling:

Milk, evaporated	8 ounces	1 pound
Sugar, brown, packed	5 ounces	10 ounces
Corn syrup	2 ounces	4 ounces
Eggs, whole	2 each	4 each
Pumpkin pie filling, solid pack	12 ounces	1 pound, 8 ounces
Salt	To taste	To taste
Extract, vanilla	To taste	To taste
Cinnamon, ground	To taste	To taste
Cloves, ground	To taste	To taste
Mace, ground	To taste	To taste
Ginger, ground	To taste	To taste
Nutmeg, ground	To taste	To taste
Allspice, ground	To taste	To taste

METHOD OF PREPARATION:

1. Gather the equipment and ingredients.
2. Prepare a 9-inch unbaked pie shell.
3. Combine the evaporated milk, sugar, corn syrup, and eggs.
4. Add the pumpkin pie filling.
5. Combine.
6. Add the flavorings: salt, vanilla extract, cinnamon, clove, mace, ginger, nutmeg, and allspice.
7. Place in an unbaked pie shell.
8. Bake at 350° F or bake at 425° F until the crust begins to brown; reduce the heat to 350° F, until slightly firm, approximately 40 minutes.

CAKES: BASES
ICINGS
CAKES: FINISHED
CREAMS
FILLINGS
PIES
SLOW BAKING
BATTER
DOUGHS
SAUCES

PASTRY TECHNIQUES:
Mixing, Filling

Mixing:
1. Follow the proper mixing procedure: creaming, blending, whipping, or combination.

Filling:
1. Cut open the food product.
2. Carefully spread the filling using an icing spatula, or
3. Carefully pipe the filling using a pastry bag.

HACCP:
Store at 40° F.

HAZARDOUS FOODS:
Sour cream
Eggs

Sour Cream Apple Pie

YIELD:	1, 9-inch Pie.	2, 9-inch Pies.

INGREDIENTS:

Pie shell, unbaked (see pages 127, 128)	1, 9-inch shell	2, 9-inch shells

Walnut Streusel:

Sugar, granulated	1 ounce	2 ounces
Cinnamon, ground	To taste	To taste
Salt	Pinch	Pinch
Butter, unsalted	1½ ounces	3 ounces
Sugar, brown	1 ounce	2 ounces
Flour, bread	1½ ounces	3 ounces
Walnuts, chopped or pieces	1½ ounces	3 ounces

Filling:

Apples, Granny Smith	1 pound, 8 ounces	3 pounds
Sour cream	5½ ounces	11 ounces
Sugar, granulated	2¾ ounces	5½ ounces
Flour, bread	¾ ounce	1½ ounces
Eggs, whole	1 ounce	2 ounces
Extract, vanilla	To taste	To taste
Salt	Pinch	Pinch

METHOD OF PREPARATION:

1. Gather the equipment and ingredients.
2. Prepare an unbaked pie shell with fluted edges.

Preparation of Walnut Streusel:

1. Place the granulated sugar, cinnamon, salt, butter, and brown sugar in bowl.
2. Combine well.
3. Add the bread flour and walnuts.
4. Combine well, and set aside.

Preparation of Filling:

1. Peel and core the apples.
2. Slice the apples into ⅛-inch-thick slices.
3. Combine the sour cream, granulated sugar, bread flour, eggs, vanilla extract, and salt.
4. Combine the apples with the sour cream mixture.

Baking Instructions:

1. Place the apple mixture into an unbaked 9-inch pie shell.
2. Bake at 450° F for 10 minutes.
3. Reduce the oven temperature to 375° F, and continue to bake until the apples are cooked. (The apples will be done when soft to the touch with a fork.)
4. Remove the pie from the oven when it is done.
5. Cover the pie with the streusel topping. (Do not cover the edges.)
6. Return the pie to the oven, and bake at 375° F for an additional 10 minutes.

Strawberry Chiffon Pie

PASTRY TECHNIQUES:

Boiling, Thickening, Blooming,
Folding, Whipping

Boiling:
1. Bring the cooking liquid to a rapid
boil.
2. Stir the contents.

Thickening:
1. Mix a small amount of sugar with
the starches.
2. Create a slurry.
3. Whisk vigorously until thickened
and translucent.

Blooming:
Gelatin sheets or leaves:
1. Fan the sheets out.
2. Cover the sheets in liquid.
3. Sheets are bloomed when softened.
Granular gelatin:
1. Sprinkle the gelatin.
2. Gelatin is ready when it is cream
of wheat consistency.

Folding:
Do steps 1, 2, and 3 in one continuous motion.
1. Run a bowl scraper under the mixture, across the bottom of the
bowl.
2. Turn the bowl counterclockwise.
3. Bring the bottom mixture to the
top.

Whipping:
1. Hold the whip at a 55-degree
angle.
2. Create circles, using a circular
motion.
3. The circular motion needs to be
perpendicular to the bowl.

HACCP:
Store at 40° F.

HAZARDOUS FOOD:
Egg whites

YIELD:	1, 9-inch Pie.	2, 9-inch Pies.

INGREDIENTS:

Pie shell, prebaked (see page 131)	1, 9-inch shell	2, 9-inch shells

Filling:

Strawberries, frozen and drained *or*	10½ ounces	1 pound, 5 ounces
fresh, halved	8 ounces	1 pound
Sugar, granulated	2½ ounces	5 ounces
Salt	Pinch	Pinch
Cornstarch	⅛ ounce	¼ ounce
Water	½ ounce	1 ounce
Gelatin	⅛ ounce	¼ ounce
Water	¾ ounce	1½ ounces
Lemon juice	⅛ ounce	¼ ounce

Chiffon:

Egg whites	2½ ounces	5 ounces
Sugar, granulated	2 ounces	4 ounces

METHOD OF PREPARATION:

1. Gather the equipment and ingredients.
2. Prepare a prebaked pie shell, and cool properly.

Filling:

1. Place two thirds of the strawberries, the granulated sugar, and the salt in a pot; bring to a boil.
2. In a dry bowl, place the cornstarch, and slowly add a small amount of water to dissolve it; set aside.
3. In another dry bowl, place the gelatin, and bloom with water; set aside.
4. When the strawberry mixture comes to a boil, vigorously whisk the corn-starch mixture into the boiling strawberries.
5. Bring to a second boil, and let thicken.

CAKES: BASES

ICINGS

CAKES: FINISHED

CREAMS

FILLINGS

PIES

SLOW BAKING

BATTER

DOUGHS

SAUCES

6. Remove from the heat.
7. Add the lemon juice.
8. Add the bloomed gelatin to the strawberry mixture; combine well.
9. Cool slightly.
10. Fold in the remaining strawberries.
11. Set aside until cool but not cold.

Chiffon:

1. Place the egg whites in a bowl, and whip to full volume; slowly add the granulated sugar to the egg whites.
2. Fold the meringue into the strawberry filling.
3. Place in a prebaked pie shell.
4. Chill well prior to serving.

Sweet Potato Pie

CAKES: BASES
ICINGS
CAKES: FINISHED
CREAMS
FILLINGS
PIES
SLOW BAKING
BATTER
DOUGHS
SAUCES

PASTRY TECHNIQUE:
Combining

Combining:
Bringing together two or more components.
1. Prepare the components to be combined.
2. Add one to the other, using the appropriate mixing method (if needed).

HACCP:
Store at 40° F.

HAZARDOUS FOOD:
Eggs
Half-and-half
Heavy cream

YIELD:	1, 9-inch Pie.	2, 9-inch Pies.

INGREDIENTS:

Pie shell, unbaked (see pages 127, 128)	1, 9-inch shell	2, 9-inch shells

Filling:

Eggs, whole	2½ ounces	5 ounces
Sugar, granulated	3 ounces	6 ounces
Molasses	½ ounce	1 ounce
Half-and-half	6 ounces	12 ounces
Cream, heavy	2½ ounces	5 ounces
Flour, pastry	½ ounce	1 ounce
Cinnamon, ground	To taste	To taste
Ginger, ground	To taste	To taste
Sweet potatoes, cooked and mashed	1 pound, 5¼ ounces	2 pounds, 10½ ounces

METHOD OF PREPARATION:

1. Gather the equipment and ingredients.
2. Combine the eggs and granulated sugar.
3. Add the molasses, half-and-half, and heavy cream to the egg mixture.
4. Add the flour, cinnamon, and ginger into the egg mixture.
5. Add the sweet potatoes to the mixture; blend well in a mixer or blender.
6. Pour the filling into the unbaked pie shell; leave a little space at the top of the shell.
7. Bake at 350° F for 40 minutes, or until set in the center.

Turtle Pie

PASTRY TECHNIQUES:

Melting, Whipping, Folding

Melting:

1. Prepare the food product to be melted.
2. Place the food product in an appropriately-sized pot over direct heat or over a double boiler.
3. Stir frequently or occasionally, depending on the delicacy of the product, until melted.

OR

1. Place the product on a sheet pan or in a bowl, and place in a low-temperature oven until melted.

Whipping:

1. Hold the whip at a 55-degree angle.
2. Create circles, using a circular motion.
3. The circular motion needs to be perpendicular to the bowl.

Folding:

Do steps 1, 2, and 3 in one continuous motion.

1. Run a bowl scraper under the mixture, across the bottom of the bowl.
2. Turn the bowl counterclockwise.
3. Bring the bottom mixture to the top.

HACCP:

Store at 40° F.

HAZARDOUS FOOD:

Heavy cream
Egg yolks
Egg whites

YIELD:	1, 9-inch Pie.	2, 1-inch Pies.

INGREDIENTS:

Pie shell, prebaked (see page 131)	1, 9-inch shell	2, 9-inch shells

Filling:

Butter, unsalted	2½ ounces	5 ounces
Sugar, granulated	7¾ ounces	15½ ounces
Cream, heavy	11 ounces	1 pound, 6 ounces
Hazelnuts, toasted	4 ounces	8 ounces
Chocolate	8 ounces	1 pound
Egg yolks	1½ ounces	3 ounces
Egg whites	3 ounces	6 ounces

Garnish:

Cream, heavy, whipped	As needed	As needed

METHOD OF PREPARATION:

1. Gather the equipment and ingredients.
2. In a pan, place two thirds of the butter, and melt it.
3. Add 7 ounces of granulated sugar to the butter, and cook; stir constantly until the sugar dissolves and the mixture becomes golden brown.
4. Remove the sugar from the heat; add 3 ounces of heavy cream to the cooked sugar.
5. Add the hazelnuts to this mixture, and stir slightly.
6. Pour this mixture into a prebaked pie shell.
7. Let it cool and set.
8. Chop the chocolate fine.
9. Melt the chocolate over a double boiler.
10. Heat the egg yolks over a double boiler to 140° F and cool.
11. Place the remaining butter and cooled egg yolks into a bowl; whip until light.
12. Place the egg whites in a bowl, and whip to full volume; slowly add the remaining granulated sugar.
13. Whip the heavy cream to a medium peak.
14. Temper the heavy cream; add to the chocolate.
15. Add the yolk and butter mixture to the cream mixture.
16. Fold the egg whites into the cream mixture.
17. Spread the mixture over the soft caramel.
18. Chill to set.
19. Decorate with whipped cream.

CAKES: BASES
ICINGS
CAKES: FINISHED
CREAMS
FILLINGS
PIES
SLOW BAKING
BATTER
DOUGHS
SAUCES

Vanilla Cream Pie

PASTRY TECHNIQUES:
Boiling, Tempering, Thickening, Combining

Boiling:
1. Bring the cooking liquid to a rapid boil.
2. Stir the contents.

Tempering:
1. Whisk the eggs vigorously while ladling hot liquid.

Thickening:
1. Mix a small amount of sugar with the starches.
2. Create a slurry.
3. Whisk vigorously until thickened and translucent.

Combining:
Bringing together two or more components.
1. Prepare the components to be combined.
2. Add one to the other, using the appropriate mixing method (if needed).

HACCP:
Store at 40° F.

HAZARDOUS FOOD:
Milk
Egg yolks
Eggs

YIELD:	1, 9-inch Pie.	2, 9-inch Pies.

INGREDIENTS:

	1, 9-inch shell	2, 9-inch shells
Pie shell, prebaked (see page 131)	1, 9-inch shell	2, 9-inch shells

Filling:

Cornstarch	1½ ounces	3 ounces
Milk, whole	1 pound, 2 ounces	2 pounds, 4 ounces
Eggs, whole	2 ounces	4 ounces
Egg yolks	2 ounces	4 ounces
Sugar, granulated	4 ounces	8 ounces
Butter, unsalted	1 ounce	2 ounces
Extract, vanilla	To taste	To taste

METHOD OF PREPARATION:

1. Gather the equipment and ingredients.
2. Place the cornstarch in a dry bowl; slowly add a small amount of milk to dissolve it.
3. Whisk the eggs and egg yolks; add to the cornstarch mixture.
4. Place the remaining milk and granulated sugar in a pot; bring to a boil.
5. Temper the dissolved cornstarch mixture and add into the boiling milk; reduce the heat.
6. Bring the milk mixture back to a second boil, and cook the mixture until it thickens.
7. Remove from the heat.
8. Add the butter and vanilla extract to the mixture.
9. Pour the filling into a prebaked pie shell.
10. Chill to set.
11. Garnish, as desired.

7

Slow Baking

7

Slow Baking

Basic Custard

CAKES: BASES

ICINGS

CAKES: FINISHED

CREAMS

FILLINGS

PIES

SLOW BAKING

BATTER

DOUGHS

SAUCES

PASTRY TECHNIQUES:
Combining, Slow Baking

Combining:
Bringing together two or more components.
1. Prepare the components to be combined.
2. Add one to the other, using the appropriate mixing method (if needed).

Slow Baking:
1. Use an appropriate baking dish.
2. Use hot water in the pan.
3. Replenish the water when needed.

HACCP:
Store at 40° F.

HAZARDOUS FOODS:
Eggs
Milk

YIELD:

	1 pound, 6½ ounces.	2 pounds, 13 ounces.
INGREDIENTS:		
Eggs, whole	6 ounces	12 ounces
Sugar, granulated	3¼ ounces	6½ ounces
Milk, whole	13 ounces	1 pound, 10 ounces
Extract, vanilla	¼ ounce	½ ounce

METHOD OF PREPARATION:

1. Gather the equipment and ingredients.
2. Combine all of the ingredients, and strain through a chinois.
3. Pour the custard mixture into custard cups.
4. Place the cups in hotel pans containing hot water.
5. Bake at 325° F, until firm.
6. Cool thoroughly.

Variations:

1. Crème Caramel
2. Crème Brûlée
3. Bread Pudding

CHEF NOTE:
Do not overbake. Overbaking creates steam in the mixture which will cause air bubbles in the custard.

Cheesecake, French Style

PASTRY TECHNIQUES:
Creaming, Combining, Whipping,
    Slow Baking

Creaming:
1. Soften the fats on low speed.
2. Add the sugar(s) and cream; increase the speed slowly.
3. Add the eggs one at a time; scrape the bowl frequently.
4. Add the dry ingredients in stages.

Combining:
Bringing together two or more components.
1. Prepare the components to be combined.
2. Add one to the other, using the appropriate mixing method (if needed).

Whipping:
1. Hold the whip at a 55-degree angle.
2. Create circles, using a circular motion.
3. The circular motion needs to be perpendicular to the bowl.

Slow Baking:
1. Use an appropriate baking dish.
2. Use hot water in the pan.
3. Replenish the water when needed.

HACCP:
Store at 40° F.

HAZARDOUS FOODS:
Cream cheese
Egg yolks
Eggs
Heavy cream
Egg whites

CHEF NOTE:
French-style cheesecake can be baked without lining the pans with vanilla layer cake or by lining the pans with cake crumbs.

YIELD:	2 pounds, 2 ounces. 1, 9-inch Cake	4 pounds, 4 ounces. 2, 9-inch Cakes

INGREDIENTS:		
Cream cheese, room temperature	1 pound	2 pounds
Sugar, granulated	5 ounces	10 ounces
Butter, unsalted, softened	2½ ounces	5 ounces
Flour, bread	1¼ ounces	2½ ounces
Salt	Pinch	Pinch
Extract, vanilla	To taste	To taste
Lemon juice	To taste	To taste
Extract, lemon (optional)	To taste	To taste
Egg yolks	1⅛ ounces	2¼ ounces
Eggs, whole	1⅜ ounces	2¾ ounces
Cream, heavy	6 ounces	12 ounces
Egg whites	1⅜ ounces	2¾ ounces
Butter, additional, unsalted	As needed	As needed
Cake layers, vanilla	1, 9-inch layer, ¼-inch thick	2, 9-inch layers, ¼-inch thick

METHOD OF PREPARATION:

1. Gather the equipment and ingredients.
2. Place the cream cheese, half the amount of granulated sugar, butter, flour, salt, vanilla extract, lemon juice, and lemon extract in a bowl with a paddle.
3. Paddle until smooth; scrape the bowl often.
4. Add the egg yolks and whole eggs; combine, and scrape well.
5. Add the heavy cream; combine, and scrape well.
6. In a separate bowl, whip the egg whites to a medium peak; slowly add the remaining amount of granulated sugar.
7. Add a small amount of the cheese mixture to the egg white mixture.
8. Gently fold the remaining cheese and egg mixtures together.
9. Prepare the 9-inch cake pans by greasing them with butter and lining the bottoms with a vanilla cake layer.

10. Fill the prepared pans with 2 pounds, 2 ounces of filling.
11. Place the pan in a water bath.
12. Bake at 325° F for 45 minutes, or until firm.
13. Allow to cool properly and refrigerate overnight.

CAKES: BASES

ICINGS

CAKES: FINISHED

CREAMS

FILLINGS

PIES

SLOW BAKING

BATTER

DOUGHS

SAUCES

Crème Brûlée

PASTRY TECHNIQUES:
Combining, Slow Baking

Combining:
Bringing together two or more components.
1. Prepare the components to be combined.
2. Add one to the other, using the appropriate mixing method (if needed).

Slow Baking:
1. Use an appropriate baking dish.
2. Use hot water in the pan.
3. Replenish the water when needed.

HACCP:
Store at 40° F.

HAZARDOUS FOODS:
Egg yolks
Heavy cream

YIELD:	2 pounds, 9 ounces.	5 pounds, 2 ounces.

INGREDIENTS:

Egg yolks	6 ounces	12 ounces
Sugar, granulated	3 ounces	6 ounces
Extract, vanilla	To taste	To taste
Cream, heavy	2 pounds	4 pounds
Sugar, additional, granulated	As needed	As needed

METHOD OF PREPARATION:

1. Gather the equipment and ingredients.
2. Whisk the egg yolks and sugar together.
3. Add the vanilla extract.
4. Add the heavy cream.
5. Strain the mixture; remove any foam on top.
6. Fill the custard molds.
7. Place the molds in a hot-water bath.
8. Bake at 325° F, until firm.
9. Chill.
10. When the custard is chilled thoroughly, sprinkle some granulated sugar on top of it, and caramelize.

CHEF NOTE:
Other flavorings may be added to the mixture, such as praline paste.

Deli Cheesecake

(New York Style)

CAKES: BASES
ICINGS
CAKES: FINISHED
CREAMS
FILLINGS
PIES
SLOW BAKING
BATTER
DOUGHS
SAUCES

PASTRY TECHNIQUES:
Creaming, Slow Baking

Creaming:
1. Soften the fats on low speed.
2. Add the sugar(s) and cream; increase the speed slowly.
3. Add the eggs one at a time; scrape the bowl frequently.
4. Add the dry ingredients in stages.

Slow Baking:
1. Use an appropriate baking dish.
2. Use hot water in the pan.
3. Replenish the water when needed.

HACCP:
Store at 40° F.

HAZARDOUS FOODS:
Cream cheese
Heavy cream
Eggs
Sour cream
Half-and-half

YIELD:	2 pounds, 15 ounces.	5 pounds, 14 ounces.
	1, 9-inch Cake	2, 9-inch Cakes

INGREDIENTS:

Crust:

Graham cracker crust (see pages 129, 130)	As needed	As needed

Filling:

Cream cheese, room temperature	1 pound, 8 ounces	3 pounds
Lemon rind, grated	2 each	4 each
Sugar, granulated	8 ounces	1 pound
Cream, heavy	4 ounces	8 ounces
Eggs, whole	8 ounces	1 pound
Sour cream	1 ounce	2 ounces
Half-and-half	2 ounces	4 ounces
Extract, vanilla	To taste	To taste

METHOD OF PREPARATION:

1. Gather the equipment and ingredients.
2. Prepare the cake pan with the graham cracker crust.
3. Place the cream cheese in a bowl with the lemon rind.
4. Paddle until smooth.
5. Add the sugar, and paddle until smooth; scrape often.
6. Add the heavy cream gradually; scrape often.
7. Add the eggs in small amounts, incorporating well after each addition.
8. Scrape well.
9. Add the sour cream, half-and-half, and vanilla extract; scrape well; combine.
10. Pour 2 pounds, 15 ounces of mixture into a prepared cake pan.
11. Place in a water bath.
12. Bake at 375° F for approximately 1½ hours, or until the center is firm.
13. Remove, and cool.

PASTRY TECHNIQUE:

Whipping

Whipping:

1. Hold the whip at a 55-degree angle.
2. Create circles, using a circular motion.
3. The circular motion needs to be perpendicular to the bowl.

HAZARDOUS FOOD:

Egg whites

Common Meringue

YIELD:	1 pound, 8 ounces.	3 pounds.

INGREDIENTS:

Egg whites	8 ounces	1 pound
Sugar, granulated	1 pound	2 pounds

METHOD OF PREPARATION:

1. Gather the equipment and ingredients.
2. Place the egg whites in bowl, and begin to whip.
3. Slowly add the granulated sugar while whipping the whites.
4. When all of the sugar has been added, whip to the desired consistency.
5. Use immediately.

Italian Meringue

PASTRY TECHNIQUES:
Boiling, Whipping

Boiling:
1. Bring the cooking liquid to a rapid boil.
2. Stir the contents.

Whipping
1. Hold the whip at a 55-degree angle.
2. Create circles, using a circular motion.
3. The circular motion needs to be perpendicular to the bowl.

HAZARDOUS FOOD:
Egg whites

YIELD:	1 pound, 12 ounces.	3 pounds, 8 ounces.

INGREDIENTS:

Sugar, granulated	1 pound	2 pounds
Water	4 ounces	8 ounces
Egg whites	8 ounces	1 pound

METHOD OF PREPARATION:

1. Gather the equipment and ingredients.
2. Place the sugar and water in a pot.
3. Cook to 250° F.
4. Place the egg whites in a bowl, and whip.
5. When the sugar has reached the correct temperature, slowly add the hot sugar in a slow, steady stream into the egg whites.
6. Whip to the desired consistency.

CAKES: BASES · ICINGS · CAKES: FINISHED · CREAMS · FILLINGS · PIES · SLOW BAKING · BATTER · DOUGHS · SAUCES

PASTRY TECHNIQUES:
Heating, Whipping, Folding

Heating:
1. Prepare the food product according to the formula's instructions.
2. Choose the appropriate method of heating (on the range or stove top, in the oven, etc.)
3. Apply the product to the heat.

Whipping:
1. Hold the whip at a 55-degree angle.
2. Create circles, using a circular motion.
3. The circular motion needs to be perpendicular to the bowl.

Folding:
Do steps 1, 2, and 3 in one continuous motion.
1. Run a bowl scraper under the mixture, across the bottom of the bowl.
2. Turn the bowl counterclockwise.
3. Bring the bottom mixture to the top.

HACCP:
Store at 60° F to 65° F.

HAZARDOUS FOODS:
Egg whites

Japonaise

Almond Nut Meringue

YIELD:		3 pounds, 9 ounces. 8, 9-inch Layers	14 pounds, 4 ounces 32, 9-inch Layers

INGREDIENTS:

Egg whites		1 pound	4 pounds
Sugar, granulated		1 pound, 11 ounces	6 pounds, 12 ounces
Almonds, blanched, toasted, and finely ground		12 ounces	3 pounds
Flour, bread		2 ounces	8 ounces

METHOD OF PREPARATION:

1. Gather the equipment and ingredients.
2. Place the egg whites and sugar in a bowl.
3. Heat over a double boiler to 120° F while stirring.
4. Remove from the heat, and place on a mixer; whip the egg whites and sugar at high speed to a stiff peak.
5. Remove from the mixer.
6. Fold in the combined almonds and flour by hand.
7. Spread 9-inch disks, ½-inch thick, on lightly greased parchment paper; transfer to a sheet pan. (Or use a large, round tube; pipe the Japonaise in a circular motion; move outward in a 9-inch circle.)
8. Bake at 200° F to 220° F for at least 2½ hours until dry and airy-light, or leave in a pilot-lit oven overnight with a starting temperature of 200° F to 220° F.

Pots de Crème

CAKES: BASES
ICINGS
CAKES: FINISHED
CREAMS
FILLINGS
PIES
SLOW BAKING
BATTER
DOUGHS
SAUCES

PASTRY TECHNIQUES:
Combining, Scalding, Tempering,
Slow Baking

Combining:
Bringing together two or more components.
1. Prepare the components to be combined.
2. Add one to the other, using the appropriate mixing method (if needed).

Scalding:
1. Heat the liquid on high heat.
2. Do not boil the liquid.

Tempering:
1. Whisk the eggs vigorously while ladling hot liquid.

Slow Baking:
1. Use an appropriate baking dish.
2. Use hot water in the pan.
3. Replenish the water when needed.

HACCP:
Store at 40° F.

HAZARDOUS FOOD:
Egg yolks
Heavy cream

YIELD:	3 pounds, 8½ ounces.	7 pounds, 1 ounce.
INGREDIENTS:		
Egg yolks	6 ounces	12 ounces
Sugar, granulated	3 ounces	6 ounces
Cream, heavy	2 pounds	4 pounds
Chocolate, dark, bittersweet, finely chopped	13 ounces	1 pound, 10 ounces
Grand Marnier	2½ ounces	5 ounces
Extract, vanilla	To taste	To taste

METHOD OF PREPARATION:

1. Gather the equipment and ingredients.
2. Whisk the egg yolks and sugar together.
3. Scald the heavy cream.
4. Temper the egg yolk–sugar mixture with the scalded cream.
5. Pour over the finely chopped chocolate, Grand Marnier, and vanilla extract; stir gently to avoid creating air bubbles, until chocolate melts.
6. Fill the custard molds.
7. Place the molds in a hot-water bath.
8. Bake at 325° F until firm.
9. Chill.

PASTRY TECHNIQUES:
Heating, Whipping

Heating:
1. Prepare the food product according to the formula's instructions.
2. Choose the appropriate method of heating (on the range or stove top, in the oven, etc.)
3. Apply the product to the heat.

Whipping:
1. Hold the whip at a 55-degree angle.
2. Create circles, using a circular motion.
3. The circular motion needs to be perpendicular to the bowl.

HAZARDOUS FOOD:
Egg whites

Swiss Meringue

YIELD: 1 pound, 8 ounces.   3 pounds.

INGREDIENTS:

Egg whites	8 ounces	1 pound
Sugar, granulated	1 pound	2 pounds

METHOD OF PREPARATION:

1. Gather the equipment and ingredients.
2. Place the egg whites and sugar in a bowl.
3. Place over a double boiler; whip constantly until the mixture is warmed to 120° F.
4. Remove from the double boiler, and place on a mixer.
5. Whip at high speed until stiff peaks form.
6. Ready for use.

Batters and
Pâté à Choux

Batters and Pâté à Choux

PASTRY TECHNIQUES:
Combining, Boiling, Piping, Freezing

Combining:
Bringing together two or more components.
1. Prepare the components to be combined.
2. Add one to the other, using the appropriate mixing method (if needed).

Boiling:
1. Bring the cooking liquid to a rapid boil.
2. Stir the contents.

Piping:
With bag:
1. Use a bag with a disposable tip; cut the bag at 45-degree angle.
2. Fill to no more than half full.
3. Burp the bag.
With cone:
1. Cut and fold the piping cone to the appropriate size.
2. Fill the cone with a small amount.
3. Fold the ends to form a triangle.
4. Pipe the desired designs.

Freezing:
1. Prepare the product.
2. Place the product in the freezing cabinet for the appropriate length of time.

HAZARDOUS FOODS:
Milk
Eggs

Beignet Batter

YIELD:	2 pounds, 11 ounces.	5 pounds, 6 ounces.

INGREDIENTS:

Flour, pastry	13 ounces	1 pound, 10 ounces
Sugar, granulated	2 ounces	4 ounces
Milk, whole	1 pound	2 pounds
Butter, unsalted, chopped	4 ounces	8 ounces
Eggs, whole	8 ounces	1 pound
Oil, vegetable (for frying)	As needed	As needed
Cinnamon and sugar mixture	As needed	As needed

METHOD OF PREPARATION:

1. Gather the equipment and ingredients.
2. Combine the flour and sugar.
3. Place the milk and butter in a pot; bring to a boil.
4. Add the flour mixture all at once to the boiling milk; stir until well mixed and a skin begins to form on the bottom of the pan.
5. Remove from the heat, and place in a bowl with a paddle; mix on low speed until cool.
6. Add in the eggs gradually, and incorporate well.
7. Pipe the mixture into beignets or cruellers; use a pastry bag or scoop with a metal spoon, and place them into the hot oil.
8. Fry in 360° F hot oil, on each side, until a nice golden brown.
9. Remove, and drain on paper towels.
10. Dredge in cinnamon and sugar.
11. Serve.

CAKES: BASES
ICINGS
CAKES: FINISHED
CREAMS
FILLINGS
PIES
SLOW BAKING
BATTER
DOUGHS
SAUCES

Fritter Batter

PASTRY TECHNIQUES:
Combining, Whipping, Folding,
  Frying

Combining:
Bringing together two or more components.
1. Prepare the components to be combined.
2. Add one to the other, using the appropriate mixing method (if needed).

Whipping:
1. Hold the whip at a 55-degree angle.
2. Create circles, using a circular motion.
3. The circular motion needs to be perpendicular to the bowl.

Folding:
Do steps 1, 2, and 3 in one continuous motion.
1. Run a bowl scraper under the mixture, across the bottom of the bowl.
2. Turn the bowl counterclockwise.
3. Bring the bottom mixture to the top.

Frying:
1. Heat the frying liquid to the appropriate temperature.
2. Place the food product into the hot liquid.
3. Cook the product, turning frequently, until golden brown and tender.

HAZARDOUS FOODS:
Egg yolks
Egg whites

YIELD:	2 pounds, 2⅛ ounces.	4 pounds, 4¼ ounces.
INGREDIENTS:		
Egg yolks	2⅝ ounces	5¼ ounces
Oil, vegetable	2 ounces	4 ounces
Flour, pastry	11¼ ounces	1 pound, 6½ ounces
Wine, white	12 ounces	1 pound, 8 ounces
Salt	Pinch	Pinch
Egg whites	4 ounces	8 ounces
Sugar, granulated	2¼ ounces	4½ ounces
Oil, vegetable (for frying)	As needed	As needed

METHOD OF PREPARATION:

1. Gather the equipment and ingredients.
2. Beat the egg yolks slightly, and combine with the oil.
3. Add the pastry flour, white wine, and salt to the yolk-oil mixture.
4. Let this mixture stand for 20 to 30 minutes.
5. Place the egg whites in a bowl, and whip to a soft peak; gradually add the granulated sugar to make a meringue.
6. Fold this meringue mixture carefully into the yolk mixture.

To Use:

1. Dredge the item in the fritter batter.
2. Fry immediately in hot oil for approximately 4 to 6 minutes, turning halfway through, or until completely golden brown.
3. Remove, and drain.

CAKES: BASES
ICINGS
CAKES: FINISHED
CREAMS
FILLINGS
PIES
SLOW BAKING
BATTER
DOUGHS
SAUCES

PASTRY TECHNIQUES:
Boiling, Combining, Piping

Boiling:
1. Bring the cooking liquid to a rapid boil.
2. Stir the contents.

Combining:
Bringing together two or more components.
1. Prepare the components to be combined.
2. Add one to the other, using the appropriate mixing method (if needed).

Piping:
With bag:
1. Use a bag with a disposable tip; cut the bag at 45-degree angle.
2. Fill to no more than half full.
3. Burp the bag.

With cone:
1. Cut and fold the piping cone to the appropriate size.
2. Fill the cone with a small amount.
3. Fold the ends to form a triangle.
4. Pipe the desired designs.

HAZARDOUS FOODS:
Milk
Eggs

Pâté à Choux No. 1
Solid Fat-Based

YIELD:	3 pounds, 3 ounces.	6 pounds, 6 ounces.

INGREDIENTS:

Butter (unsalted) or shortening (all-purpose)	8 ounces	1 pound
Salt	¼ ounce	½ ounce
Sugar, granulated (optional)	¼ ounce	½ ounce
Water or milk (whole)	1 pound	2 pounds
Flour, bread, sifted	10½ ounces	1 pound, 5 ounces
Eggs, whole	1 pound	2 pounds

METHOD OF PREPARATION:

1. Gather the equipment and ingredients.
2. Place the butter, salt, granulated sugar, and water or milk in a pot.
3. Bring to a boil.
4. Add all of the sifted flour at once.
5. Stir with a wooden spoon for approximately 5 minutes or until the mixture forms a ball that does not stick to the inside of the pot.
6. Cook at this point for an additional 3 minutes.
7. Remove from the heat, and place the mixture in a mixing bowl.
8. Mix on low speed until cooled slightly.
9. Add the eggs gradually; mix at low speed; make sure the eggs are fully incorporated before the next addition.
10. When the eggs are fully incorporated, pipe into the desired shapes on parchment-lined sheet pans.
11. Bake at 400° F to 425° F until brown and dry on the inside.

Variations:
1. Éclairs
2. Swans
3. Profiteroles
4. Paris-Brest
5. Gâteau St. Honore
6. Croquembouche
7. Beignets Soufflé

PASTRY TECHNIQUES:
Boiling, Combining, Piping

Boiling:
1. Bring the cooking liquid to a rapid boil.
2. Stir the contents.

Combining:
Bringing together two or more components.
1. Prepare the components to be combined.
2. Add one to the other, using the appropriate mixing method (if needed).

Piping:
With bag:
1. Use a bag with a disposable tip; cut the bag at 45-degree angle.
2. Fill to no more than half full.
3. Burp the bag.
With cone:
1. Cut and fold the piping cone to the appropriate size.
2. Fill the cone with a small amount.
3. Fold the ends to form a triangle.
4. Pipe the desired designs.

HAZARDOUS FOODS:
Eggs
Egg whites

Pâté à Choux No. 2

Oil-Based

YIELD:	2 pounds, 9½ ounces.	5 pounds, 3¼ ounces.

INGREDIENTS:

Water	12 ounces	1 pound, 8 ounces
Salt	To taste	To taste
Oil, vegetable	6 ounces	12 ounces
Flour, bread	8½ ounces	1 pound, 1¼ ounces
Eggs, whole	12 ounces	1 pound, 8 ounces
Egg whites	3 ounces	6 ounces

METHOD OF PREPARATION:

1. Gather the equipment and ingredients.
2. Place the water, salt, and oil in a pot.
3. Bring to a boil.
4. Add all of the flour at once.
5. Stir with a wooden spoon for approximately 5 minutes or until the mixture forms a ball that does not stick to the inside of the pot.
6. Remove from the heat, and place in a mixer; cool slightly.
7. Add the whole eggs and egg whites gradually; make sure the eggs are fully incorporated before the next addition.
8. Pipe into the desired shapes on parchment-lined sheet pans.
9. Bake at 400° F to 425° F until golden brown and dry in appearance.

Variations:

1. Éclairs
2. Swans
3. Profiteroles
4. Paris-Brest
5. Gâteau St. Honore
6. Croquembouche
7. Beignets Soufflé

9

Doughs

Doughs

Linzer Dough

CAKES: BASES

ICINGS

CAKES: FINISHED

CREAMS

FILLINGS

PIES

SLOW BAKING

BATTER

DOUGHS

SAUCES

PASTRY TECHNIQUES:
Creaming, Combining

Creaming:
1. Soften the fats on low speed.
2. Add the sugar(s) and cream; increase the speed slowly.
3. Add the eggs one at a time; scrape the bowl frequently.
4. Add the dry ingredients in stages.

Combining:
Bringing together two or more components.
1. Prepare the components to be combined.
2. Add one to the other, using the appropriate mixing method (if needed).

HACCP:
Store at 40° F.

HAZARDOUS FOODS:
Eggs
Milk

YIELD: 6 pounds, 10 ounces.   13 pounds, 4 ounces.

INGREDIENTS:

Hazelnuts, toasted	10½ ounces	1 pound, 5 ounces
Butter, unsalted, chopped	1 pound, 1 ounce	2 pounds, 2 ounces
Sugar, granulated	1 pound, 1 ounce	2 pounds, 2 ounces
Eggs, whole	5 ounces	10 ounces
Flour, pastry	2 pounds	4 pounds
Flour, bread	1 ounce	2 ounces
Cinnamon, ground	½ ounce	1 ounce
Cloves, ground	¼ ounce	½ ounce
Lemon or orange zest	¼ ounce	½ ounce
Crumbs, cake or bread	8 ounces	1 pound
Glucose	14½ ounces	9 ounces
Milk, whole	As needed	As needed

METHOD OF PREPARATION:

1. Gather the equipment and ingredients.
2. Ground the hazelnuts fine in robo-coupe or food processor.
3. Cream the butter and the sugar together in a bowl until smooth and creamy; use a paddle.
4. Add the eggs, a little at a time, scraping the bowl down after each addition.
5. Sift the flours, cinnamon, and cloves together, and add to the creamed mixture in two stages.
6. Add the zest and cake crumbs; combine.
7. Add the ground hazelnuts.
8. Mix until incorporated.
9. Add the glucose and milk (if the mixture seems to be too dry). Mix just enough to incorporate; *do not overmix*.
10. Allow the dough to rest for 20 minutes before using.

Pâté Sable

(Sand Dough) Table Mix

YIELD: 2 pounds, 8½ ounces. 5 pounds, 1 ounce.

PASTRY TECHNIQUE:
Combining

Combining:
Bringing together two or more components.
1. Prepare the components to be combined.
2. Add one to the other, using the appropriate mixing method (if needed).

HACCP:
Store at 40° F.

HAZARDOUS FOOD:
Eggs

INGREDIENTS:

Flour, pastry	1 pound, 2 ounces	2 pounds, 4 ounces
Salt	Pinch	Pinch
Baking powder	½ ounce	1 ounce
Butter, unsalted, cubed	9 ounces	1 pound, 2 ounces
Sugar, granulated	9 ounces	1 pound, 2 ounces
Eggs, whole	4 ounces	8 ounces

METHOD OF PREPARATION:

1. Gather the equipment and ingredients.
2. Place the pastry flour, salt, and baking powder in a mound on the table.
3. Cut the butter into cubes.
4. Place the butter cubes on top of the flour mound, and cut the cubes into the flour; use a bench scraper. Stop when the butter is about the size of small peas; mix in the sugar.
5. Whisk the eggs together.
6. Make a well in the flour-butter-sugar mixture, and pour the eggs into the well.
7. Starting with the flour on the inside of the well, work your way around, and slowly start to mix the flour into the water mixture.
8. Continue to mix until all of the water is absorbed into the flour.
9. Chill the dough for at least 20 minutes before using.

Short Dough

1-2-3 Cookie Dough

CAKES: BASES
ICINGS
CAKES: FINISHED
CREAMS
FILLINGS
PIES
SLOW BAKING
BATTER
DOUGHS
SAUCES

PASTRY TECHNIQUES:

Creaming, Combining

Creaming:

1. Soften the fats on low speed.
2. Add the sugar(s) and cream; increase the speed slowly.
3. Add the eggs one at a time; scrape the bowl frequently.
4. Add the dry ingredients in stages.

Combining:

Bringing together two or more components.
1. Prepare the components to be combined.
2. Add one to the other, using the appropriate mixing method (if needed).

HACCP:

Store at 40° F.

HAZARDOUS FOOD:

Eggs

YIELD: 6 pounds, 6 ounces. 12 pounds, 12 ounces.

INGREDIENTS:

Ingredient		
Sugar, granulated	1 pound	2 pounds
Butter, unsalted, room temperature	2 pounds	4 pounds
Eggs, whole	6 ounces	12 ounces
Flour, cake	3 pounds	6 pounds

METHOD OF PREPARATION:

1. Gather the equipment and ingredients.
2. Place the sugar and butter in a bowl; combine, using a paddle.
3. Add the eggs, and blend well.
4. Add the flour, and mix on the lowest speed until well blended.
5. Chill to firm the dough before use.

Sour Cream Pastry Dough

PASTRY TECHNIQUE:
Blending

Blending:
1. Combine the dry ingredients on low speed.
2. Add the softened fat(s) and liquid(s).
3. Mix the ingredients on low speed.
4. Increase the speed gradually.

HACCP:
Store at 40° F.

HAZARDOUS FOOD:
Sour cream

YIELD:	4 pounds.	8 ounces.

INGREDIENTS:		
Flour, pastry	1 pound, 8 ounces	3 pounds
Butter (unsalted) or margarine, room temperature	1 pound, 8 ounces	3 pounds
Sour cream	1 pound	2 pounds

METHOD OF PREPARATION:

1. Gather the equipment and ingredients.
2. Place all of the ingredients in a bowl, and mix together on low speed. *Do not overmix.*
3. Remove the dough from the mixer, and place on a lightly floured sheet pan.
4. Prior to use, refrigerate the dough to chill completely.

CHEF NOTE:
Sour cream pastry dough may be used for all types of desserts, including individual pieces, tart shells, and pie shells.

Steps to Laminated Yeast Dough Preparation

1. Mix according to the straight dough mixing method; mix by hand or machine. Develop until incorporated only.
2. Rest dough covered for 1 to 1½ hours.
3. While dough rests, soften roll-in-fat until smooth.
4. After dough has rested, roll out dough ½-inch to ¾-inch thick to form a rectangle shape.
5. Spot the roll-in-fat over ⅔ of the length of the dough.
6. Fold the third of dough without fat over the center third.
7. Fold the remaining third of dough on top.
8. Rest the dough for 20 to 30 minutes in the refrigerator.
9. Place the dough on bench and turn 90 degrees; roll out the dough again as previously done. Repeat the folding in procedure again until *three* 3-folds have been achieved. Be sure to brush off excess dusting flour from between the folds.
10. After the third fold, cover with plastic wrap to prevent a crust from forming. Rest the dough for several hours or overnight.
11. Make up and bake, as demonstrated by instructor.

CHEF NOTE:
Before baking, the dough should rest the same amount of time as between folding.

CAKES: BASES
ICINGS
CAKES: FINISHED
CREAMS
FILLINGS
PIES
SLOW BAKING
BATTER
DOUGHS
SAUCES

PASTRY TECHNIQUE:
Steps of Laminated Yeast Dough
    Preparation (see page 185)

HAZARDOUS FOOD:
Eggs

American Danish Dough

YIELD:	11 pounds, 4½ ounces.	Baker's Percentage.

INGREDIENTS:

Dough (unlaminated):	9 pounds, 15½ ounces	
Flour, patent	5 pounds	100
Dry milk solids (DMS)	5 ounces	6
Salt	1½ ounces	1.75
Cardamom, ground	½ ounce	0.60
Water	1 pound, 4 ounces	25
Yeast, compressed	5 ounces	6
Extract, vanilla	1½ ounces	2
Sugar, granulated	1 pound	20
Shortening, all-purpose	10 ounces	14
Eggs, whole	1 pound, 4 ounces	25
Roll-in Fat:		13
Margarine	1 pound, 5 ounces	100

METHOD OF PREPARATION:

1. Gather the equipment and ingredients.
2. Follow the steps of laminated yeast dough preparation (see page 185).

CAKES: BASES
ICINGS
CAKES: FINISHED
CREAMS
FILLINGS
PIES
SLOW BAKING
BATTER
DOUGHS
SAUCES

PASTRY TECHNIQUE:
Steps of Laminated Yeast Dough
Preparation (see page 185)

Croissant Dough No. 1

YIELD:		11 pounds, 13 ounces.	Baker's Percentage.

INGREDIENTS:

Dough:

Water, cold	3 pounds	60
Yeast, compressed	3 ounces	4
Flour, bread	4 pounds	80
Flour, pastry	1 pound	20
Salt	2 ounces	2
Sugar, granulated	8 ounces	10

Roll-in Fat:

Butter, unsalted	3 pounds	60

METHOD OF PREPARATION:

1. Gather the equipment and ingredients.
2. Follow the steps of laminated yeast dough preparation (page 185).

Variations:

1. Mini-croissant
2. Regular croissant

PASTRY TECHNIQUE:
Steps of Laminated Yeast Dough Preparation (see page 185)

Croissant Dough No. 2

YIELD:	12 pounds, ½ ounce.	Baker's Percentage.

INGREDIENTS:

Dough (unlaminated):	9 pounds, ½ ounce	
Flour, bread	5 pounds	100
Dry milk solids (DMS)	5 ounces	6
Salt	1 ounce	1
Sugar, granulated	3 ounces	4
Water, cold	2 pounds, 13½ ounces	57
Yeast, compressed	5 ounces	6
Shortening, all-purpose	5 ounces	6
Roll-in Fat:		33
Butter, unsalted (60° F)	2 pounds, 13½ ounces	95
Flour, bread, sifted	2½ ounces	5

METHOD OF PREPARATION:

1. Gather the equipment and ingredients.
2. Follow the steps of laminated yeast dough preparation (page 185).

Variations:

1. Mini-croissant
2. Regular croissant

CAKES: BASES
ICINGS
CAKES: FINISHED
CREAMS
FILLINGS
PIES
SLOW BAKING
BATTER
DOUGHS
SAUCES

Danish Dough No. 1

PASTRY·TECHNIQUE:
Steps of Laminated Yeast Dough
 Preparation (see page 185)

HAZARDOUS FOOD:
Eggs

YIELD: 12 pounds, 1 ounce. Baker's Percentage.

INGREDIENTS:

Dough:

Water, cold	2 pounds	40
Eggs, whole	1 pound	20
Yeast, compressed	3 ounces	4
Flour, bread	4 pounds	80
Flour, pastry	1 pound	20
Salt	2 ounces	2
Sugar, granulated	8 ounces	10
Dried milk solids (DMS)	4 ounces	5

Roll-in Fat:

Butter, unsalted	3 pounds	60

METHOD OF PREPARATION:

1. Follow the steps of laminated yeast dough preparation (see page 185).

Danish Dough No. 2

PASTRY TECHNIQUE:
Steps of Laminated Yeast Dough
Preparation (see page 185)

HAZARDOUS FOOD:

Eggs

YIELD: 19 pounds, 5⅞ ounces. Baker's Percentage.

INGREDIENTS:

Dough (unlaminated):	18 pounds, 15⅞ ounces	
Yeast, compressed	8 ounces	5.30
Water	3 pounds, 8 ounces	37
Shortening, high-ratio	1 pound, 2 ounces	12
Dried milk solids (DMS)	6 ounces	4
Sugar, granulated	1 pound, 14 ounces	20
Salt	2¼ ounces	1.50
Eggs, whole	2 pounds	21.30
Extract, vanilla	1 ounce	0.70
Nutmeg, ground	⅛ ounce	0.08
Cardamom, ground	¼ ounce	0.16
Cinnamon, ground	¼ ounce	0.16
Flour, bread	7 pounds, 8 ounces	80
Flour, cake	1 pound, 14 ounces	20
Roll-in Fat:		
Butter, unsalted	6 pounds	32

METHOD OF PREPARATION:

1. Gather the equipment and ingredients.
2. Follow the steps of laminated yeast dough preparation (see page 185).

CAKES: BASES
ICINGS
CAKES: FINISHED
CREAMS
FILLINGS
PIES
SLOW BAKING
BATTER
DOUGHS
SAUCES

PASTRY TECHNIQUES:
Laminating, Rolling

Laminating:
1. Allow a proper time to rest dough.
2. Roll the dough out to a ½-inch to ¾-inch thickness.
3. Evenly spread the fat.
4. Allow a proper time for the dough to rest.
5. Refrigerate for several hours.

Rolling:
1. Prepare the rolling surface by dusting with the appropriate medium (flour, cornstarch, etc.).
2. Use the appropriate style pin (stick pin or ball bearing pin) to roll the dough to desired thickness; rotate the dough during rolling to prevent sticking.

HAZARDOUS FOOD:
Eggs

Puff Pastry Dough No. 1

YIELD:	7 pounds, 8¾ ounces.	15 pounds, 1¼ ounces.

INGREDIENTS:

Flour, bread	2 pounds, 8 ounces	5 pounds
Salt	½ ounce	1 ounce
Butter, unsalted (55° F)	8 ounces	1 pound
Water, ice cold	1 pound, 4¼ ounces	2 pounds, 8½ ounces
Eggs, whole	2 ounces	4 ounces

Roll-in Fat:

Butter (unsalted) or puff pastry shortening	2 pounds, 12 ounces	5 pounds, 9 ounces
Flour, bread	2¾ ounces	5½ ounces
Flour, cake	2¾ ounces	5½ ounces

METHOD OF PREPARATION:

1. Gather the equipment and ingredients.

Methods for Mixing Dough Portion of Puff Pastry:

Sable Method (Bench Method):

1. Place the bread flour and salt in a mound on the table.
2. Cut the butter (which is at 55° F) into cubes.
3. Place the butter cubes on top of the flour, and cut the cubes into the flour using a bench scraper. Stop when the flour resembles sand.
4. Whisk together the water and whole eggs.
5. Make a well in the flour-butter mixture, and pour the water-egg mixture into the well.
6. Starting with the flour on the inside of the well, work your way around, and slowly start to mix the flour into the water mixture.
7. Continue to mix until all of the water is absorbed into the flour.
8. Knead the dough by hand for 3 minutes.
9. Cover with plastic, and let the dough relax for 20 to 30 minutes.

Machine Method:

1. Place the flour and salt in the appropriate-size bowl.
2. Cut the butter (which is at 55° F.) into 1-inch cubes.
3. Mix the cubes into the flour.

4. Using the paddle attachment, cut the butter into the flour until it resembles sand.
5. Replace the paddle with a dough hook.
6. Make a well in the center of the flour.
7. Whisk together the water and eggs.
8. Add the egg-water mixture to the flour.
9. Mix the dough on second speed for 3 to 5 minutes, or until it comes together.
10. Remove the dough from the mixer.
11. Wrap the dough, and let it rest for 20 to 30 minutes.

Roll-in Fat:

1. Place the butter or puff pastry shortening and the flours in the appropriate-sized bowl.
2. Using the paddle attachment, mix the ingredients together on medium speed; incorporate thoroughly.
3. Scrape the bowl well during this process.
4. Shape into a block form, or leave in the bowl.
5. Allow to chill, if needed.

To Assemble the Dough (Spot Method):

1. On a well-floured surface or on a canvas, roll the dough portion into a rectangular shape that is ¾-inch to 1-inch thick.
2. Place the fat over two thirds of the dough, leaving a small border all around the fat.
3. Fold one third of the dough over the portion of dough covered with butter.
4. Fold the remaining third on top. (The dough is laminated.)
5. Roll out the dough, again to a rectangular shape.
6. Mark the dough into thirds.
7. Fold one third of the dough on top of another third.
8. Fold the remaining third on top (complete a 3-fold).
9. Make a vertical mark in the center of the dough, indicating the center.
10. Fold both ends to this mark.
11. Then fold the ends on top of each (complete a 4-fold).
12. Rest all of the dough for approximately 30 minutes.
13. Roll out the dough, again to a rectangular shape.
14. Complete another 3-fold; allow the dough to rest for 30 minutes.
15. Roll out the dough, again to a rectangular shape.
16. Complete another 4-fold; allow the dough to rest for 45 minutes.
17. The dough is ready for use.

To Assemble the Dough (Block Method):

1. On a well-floured surface or on a canvas, roll out the dough into a square shape that is approximately ¾-inch to 1-inch thick. The square should be slightly larger than the block of butter.

2. Place the butter on the square diagonally so that there are four dough triangles showing.
3. Fold each of the dough triangles over the butter so they will meet in the center.
4. Pinch the edges together to seal in the butter.
5. Roll out the dough to a rectangular shape.
6. Mark the dough into thirds.
7. Fold one third of the dough over another third of the dough.
8. Fold the remaining third of the dough (complete a 3-fold).
9. Allow the dough to rest for 30 minutes.
10. Roll out the dough into a rectangular shape.
11. Indicate the middle of the rectangle.
12. Fold each end of the dough over to meet the center of the dough.
13. Fold each side on top of each other (complete a 4-fold).
14. Allow the dough to rest for 30 minutes.
15. Roll out the dough, and repeat the 3-fold procedure.
16. Allow the dough to rest for 30 minutes.
17. Roll out the dough, again into a rectangular shape; repeat the 4-fold procedure.
18. Allow the dough to rest for 45 minutes.
19. The dough is ready for use.

Variations:

1. Patty shells
2. Vol-au-vent
3. Cream horns
4. Cheese sticks
5. Cream slices
6. Turnovers
7. Napoleons
8. Butterflies
9. Palm leaves
10. Millefeuilles
11. Pithiviers

CAKES: BASES
ICINGS
CAKES: FINISHED
CREAMS
FILLINGS
PIES
SLOW BAKING
BATTER
DOUGHS
SAUCES

PASTRY TECHNIQUES:
Combining, Laminating

Combining:
Bringing together two or more components.
1. Prepare the components to be combined.
2. Add one to the other, using the appropriate mixing method (if needed).

Laminating:
1. Allow a proper time to rest dough.
2. Roll the dough out to a ½-inch to ¾-inch thickness.
3. Evenly spread the fat.
4. Allow a proper time for the dough to rest.
5. Refrigerate for several hours.

Puff Pastry Dough: Blitz Method

YIELD:	15 pounds, 1¾ ounces.	30 pounds, 3½ ounces.

INGREDIENTS:

Water, cold	4 pounds	8 pounds
Flour, bread, sifted	4 pounds, 8 ounces	9 pounds
Flour, pastry, sifted	1 pound, 8 ounces	3 pounds
Salt	¾ ounce	1½ ounces
Cream of tartar	1 ounce	2 ounces
Shortening, puff pastry	5 pounds	10 pounds
Flour, bread or pastry	As needed	As needed

METHOD OF PREPARATION:

1. Gather the equipment and ingredients.
2. Place the cold water in a mixing bowl.
3. Add the bread flour, pastry flour, salt, and cream of tartar to the water.
4. Using a paddle attachment, begin to mix slowly.
5. Break the puff pastry shortening into small pieces, and add slowly to the flour mixture.
6. Mix together until just incorporated. *Do not overmix.*
7. Remove the dough from the mixer, and place it onto flour-dusted sheet pans.
8. Place in a refrigerator to chill and relax for 30 minutes.
9. Remove the pan from the refrigerator, and lay out the dough on a lightly flour-dusted bench.
10. Roll out the dough to approximately the size of a sheet pan or into a rectangle (1-inch thickness).
11. Brush the flour from the dough, and fold one side two thirds of the way to the opposite end.
12. Fold the remaining third over the top of the dough (a 3-fold).
13. Refrigerate the dough again for 20 minutes to relax.
14. Repeat the steps of rolling, folding, and resting three more times.
15. The dough should be ready for use.

10

Sauces

Sauces

CAKES: BASES

ICINGS

CAKES: FINISHED

CREAMS

FILLINGS

PIES

SLOW BAKING

BATTER

DOUGHS

SAUCES

PASTRY TECHNIQUES:
Puréeing, Boiling, Combining

Puréeing:
1. Do not overfill the food processor.
2. First pulse the food processor.
3. Turn food processor to maximum to purée food.

Boiling:
1. Bring the cooking liquid to a rapid boil.
2. Stir the contents.

Combining:
Bringing together two or more components.
1. Prepare the components to be combined.
2. Add one to the other, using the appropriate mixing method (if needed).

HACCP:
Store at 40° F.

Apricot Sauce No. 1
Canned Apricots

YIELD:	1 pound.	2 pounds.

INGREDIENTS:

Apricot, halves, canned, drained	12¼ ounces	1 pound, 8½ ounces
Sugar, granulated	3 ounces	6 ounces
Water	¼ ounce	½ ounce
Brandy, apricot	½ ounce	1 ounce

METHOD OF PREPARATION:

1. Gather the equipment and ingredients.
2. Purée the apricots.
3. Boil the sugar with the water, and cook to a syrup.
4. Add the puréed apricots to the syrup.
5. Add the apricot brandy, to taste.

CHEF NOTE:
Can be served hot or cold.

Apricot Sauce No. 2

Apricot Preserves

PASTRY TECHNIQUES:
Boiling, Thickening, Combining

Boiling:
1. Bring the cooking liquid to a rapid boil.
2. Stir the contents.

Thickening:
1. Mix a small amount of sugar with the starches.
2. Create a slurry.
3. Whisk vigorously until thickened and translucent.

Combining:
Bringing together two or more components.
1. Prepare the components to be combined.
2. Add one to the other, using the appropriate mixing method (if needed).

HACCP:
Store at 40° F.

YIELD:	1 pound, 2 ounces.	2 pounds, 3 ounces.

INGREDIENTS:

Preserves, apricot	12 ounces	1 pound, 8 ounces
Water	2 ounces	3 ounces
Sugar, granulated	3 ounces	6 ounces
Rum	1 ounce	2 ounces

METHOD OF PREPARATION:

1. Gather the equipment and ingredients.
2. Bring the preserves, water, and sugar to a boil.
3. Purée the mixture.
4. Strain the mixture.
5. Add the rum to the sauce.

CHEF NOTE:
Can be served hot or cold.

CAKES: BASES

ICINGS

CAKES: FINISHED

CREAMS

FILLINGS

PIES

SLOW BAKING

BATTER

DOUGHS

SAUCES

Apricot Sauce No. 3
Starch-Thickened

PASTRY TECHNIQUES:
Puréeing, Boiling, Thickening

Puréeing:
1. Do not overfill the food processor.
2. First pulse the food processor.
3. Turn food processor to maximum to purée food.

Boiling:
1. Bring the cooking liquid to a rapid boil.
2. Stir the contents.

Thickening:
1. Mix a small amount of sugar with the starches.
2. Create a slurry.
3. Whisk vigorously until thickened and translucent.

HACCP:
Store at 40° F.

YIELD:	1 pound, 8 ounces.	3 pounds.

INGREDIENTS:

Apricots or apricot pulp, canned	13½ ounces	1 pound, 11 ounces
Water	8 ounces	1 pound
Sugar, granulated	8 ounces	1 pound
Lemon juice	¼ ounce	½ ounce
Cornstarch	¼ ounce	1½ ounce
Water	2 ounces	4 ounces

METHOD OF PREPARATION:
1. Gather the equipment and ingredients.
2. Purée the apricots and water together.
3. Place the puréed fruit and water in a pot with the sugar and lemon juice.
4. Bring to a boil.
5. Place the cornstarch in a dry bowl, and slowly add a small amount of water to dissolve it; stir well.
6. Add the cornstarch mixture to the boiling apricots.
7. Simmer for 3 minutes; stir continuously.
8. Remove from the heat, and strain.

CHEF NOTE:
Can be served hot or cold.

Blueberry Sauce

PASTRY TECHNIQUES:

Puréeing, Boiling, Thickening

Puréeing:

1. Do not overfill the food processor.
2. First pulse the food processor.
3. Turn food processor to maximum to purée food.

Boiling:

1. Bring the cooking liquid to a rapid boil.
2. Stir the contents.

Thickening:

1. Mix a small amount of sugar with the starches.
2. Create a slurry.
3. Whisk vigorously until thickened and translucent.

HACCP:

Store at 40° F.

YIELD:	1 pound, 6¼ ounces.	2 pounds, 12½ ounces.

INGREDIENTS:

Blueberries, whole, fresh	1 pound	2 pounds
Water	2 ounces	4 ounces
Sugar, granulated	4 ounces	8 ounces
Arrowroot	¼ ounce	½ ounce

METHOD OF PREPARATION:

1. Gather the equipment and ingredients.
2. Place the blueberries, water, and sugar in a bowl together. Let them stand for 2 hours.
3. Purée the blueberries.
4. Strain.
5. Place the arrowroot in a bowl; slowly add 2 ounces of strained purée; stir well.
6. Place the remaining purée in a pot and bring it to a boil.
7. Allow the purée to reduce by 25%.
8. Add the arrowroot mixture to the purée.
9. Return to a boil; cook to a desired consistency.

CHEF NOTE:

Can be served hot or cold.

Butterscotch Sauce

PASTRY TECHNIQUES:
Combining, Boiling

Combining:
Bringing together two or more components.
1. Prepare the components to be combined.
2. Add one to the other, using the appropriate mixing method (if needed).

Boiling:
1. Bring the cooking liquid to a rapid boil.
2. Stir the contents.

HACCP:
Store at 40° F.

YIELD:	1 pound, ½ ounce.	2 pounds, 1 ounce.
INGREDIENTS:		
Sugar, light brown	10½ ounces	1 pound, 5 ounces
Milk, evaporated	5 ounces	10 ounces
Butter, unsalted	1 ounce	2 ounces
Extract, vanilla	To taste	To taste

METHOD OF PREPARATION:
1. Gather the equipment and ingredients.
2. Place the sugar, evaporated milk, and butter in a pot.
3. Bring to a boil; boil for 2 minutes, stirring constantly.
4. Add the vanilla extract.

CHEF NOTE:
Can be served hot or cold.

Butterscotch Sauce with Pecans

YIELD:	1 pound, 5¾ ounces.	2 pounds, 11½ ounces.

INGREDIENTS:

Butter, unsalted	2 ounces	4 ounces
Water	4 ounces	8 ounces
Sugar, granulated, light brown	8 ounces	1 pound
Flour, bread	½ ounce	1 ounce
Eggs, whole	2 ounces	4 ounces
Extract, vanilla	To taste	To taste
Pecan pieces	6 ounces	12 ounces

METHOD OF PREPARATION:

1. Gather the equipment and ingredients.
2. Place the butter and half of the amount of water in a pot; heat.
3. Combine the sugar and flour.
4. Add the sugar and flour to the butter mixture.
5. Continue to cook; stir constantly with a wire whisk.
6. Combine the eggs and remaining water.
7. Slowly pour the eggs and water into the mixture, stirring constantly; allow the mixture to thicken. Heat to at least 140° F. *Do not boil.*
8. Remove from the heat, and allow to cool to room temperature.
9. Stir in the vanilla extract and pecans.
10. Store in a refrigerator.

Pastry Technniques:
Combining, Thickening

Combining:
Bringing together two or more components.
1. Prepare the components to be combined.
2. Add one to the other, using the appropriate mixing method (if needed).

Thickening:
1. Mix a small amount of sugar with the starches.
2. Create a slurry.
3. Whisk vigorously until thickened and translucent.

HACCP:
Store at 40° F.

HAZARDOUS FOOD:
Eggs

CHEF NOTE:
Can be served hot or cold.

CAKES: BASES
ICINGS
CAKES: FINISHED
CREAMS
FILLINGS
PIES
SLOW BAKING
BATTER
DOUGHS
SAUCES

Caramel Sauce

YIELD:	1 pound, 4¼ ounces.	2 pounds, 8½ ounces.

INGREDIENTS:

Sugar, granulated	12 ounces	1 pound, 8 ounces
Butter, unsalted	1½ ounces	3 ounces
Cream, heavy	6¾ ounces	13½ ounces

METHOD OF PREPARATION:

1. Gather the equipment and ingredients.
2. Melt the sugar in a heavy-bottomed saucepan, a small amount at a time, until it becomes caramelized.
3. Stir constantly; add the butter.
4. Add the cream; stir.
5. Store in a refrigerator.

PASTRY TECHNIQUES:
Melting, Combining

Melting:
1. Prepare the food product to be melted.
2. Place the food product in an appropriate sized pot over direct heat or over a double boiler.
3. Stir frequently or occasionally, depending on the delicacy of the product, until melted.

Combining:
Bringing together two or more components.
1. Prepare the components to be combined.
2. Add one to the other, using the appropriate mixing method (if needed).

HACCP:
Store at 40° F.

HAZARDOUS FOOD:
Heavy cream

CHEF NOTE:
Can be served hot or cold.

Chocolate Orange Sauce with Coconut

PASTRY TECHNIQUES:

Chopping, Melting, Boiling, Combining

Chopping:

1. Use a sharp knife.
2. Hold the food product properly.
3. Cut with a quick downward motion.

Melting:

1. Prepare the food product to be melted.
2. Place the food product in an appropriately-sized pot over direct heat or over a double boiler.
3. Stir frequently or occasionally, depending on the delicacy of the product, until melted.

OR

1. Place the product on a sheet pan or in a bowl, and place in a low-temperature oven until melted.

Boiling:

1. Bring the cooking liquid to a rapid boil.
2. Stir the contents.

Combining:

Bringing together two or more components.
1. Prepare the components to be combined.
2. Add one to the other, using the appropriate mixing method (if needed).

HACCP:

Store at 40° F.

YIELD:		1 pound, 3¾ ounces.	2 pounds, 7½ ounces.
INGREDIENTS:			
Chocolate, dark, bittersweet		2¼ ounces	4½ ounces
Chocolate, dark, semi-sweet		4 ounces	8 ounces
Sugar, granulated		6½ ounces	13 ounces
Corn syrup		2½ ounces	5 ounces
Water		4 ounces	8 ounces
Orange rind, grated		¼ orange	½ orange
Coconut, sweet, flakes		⅜ ounce	¾ ounce

METHOD OF PREPARATION:

1. Gather the equipment and ingredients.
2. Chop and melt the chocolates together over a double boiler.
3. Place the granulated sugar, corn syrup, water, and orange rind in a sauce pan.
4. Bring the mixture to a boil; boil for 1 minute.
5. Remove from the heat.
6. Add the coconut and chocolates; stir well.
7. Cool before using.

PASTRY TECHNIQUES:
Chopping, Melting, Combining

Chopping:
1. Use a sharp knife.
2. Hold the food product properly.
3. Cut with a quick downward motion.

Melting:
1. Prepare the food product to be melted.
2. Place the food product in an appropriate sized pot over direct heat or over a double boiler.
3. Stir frequently or occasionally, depending on the delicacy of the product, until melted.

OR
1. Place the product on a sheet pan or in a bowl, and place in a low-temperature oven until melted.

Combining:
Bringing together two or more components.
1. Prepare the components to be combined.
2. Add one to the other, using the appropriate mixing method (if needed).

HACCP:
Store at 40° F.

Chocolate Rum Sauce

YIELD:	15½ ounces.	1 pound, 15 ounces.
INGREDIENTS:		
Chocolate, dark, unsweetened	2 ounces	4 ounces
Sugar, granulated	7½ ounces	15 ounces
Cream of tartar	Pinch	Pinch
Milk, evaporated	3 ounces	6 ounces
Rum, dark	3 ounces	6 ounces
Extract, vanilla	To taste	To taste
Salt	Pinch	Pinch

METHOD OF PREPARATION:
1. Gather the equipment and ingredients.
2. Chop the chocolate, and melt over a double boiler.
3. Add the sugar and cream of tartar to the chocolate; stir.
4. Add the milk and dark rum to the chocolate; stir.
5. Add the vanilla extract and salt to the mixture; stir.

CHEF NOTE:
Can be served hot or cold.

Chocolate Sauce

PASTRY TECHNIQUES:
Combining, Chopping

Combining:
Bringing together two or more components.
1. Prepare the components to be combined.
2. Add one to the other, using the appropriate mixing method (if needed).

Chopping:
1. Use a sharp knife.
2. Hold the food product properly.
3. Cut with a quick downward motion.

HACCP:
Store at 40° F.

YIELD:	1 pound, 6 ounces.	2 pounds, 12 ounces.
INGREDIENTS:		
Cocoa powder	4 ounces	8 ounces
Water	8 ounces	1 pound
Sugar, granulated	8 ounces	1 pound
Couverture, dark, semi-sweet	2 ounces	4 ounces

METHOD OF PREPARATION:

1. Gather the equipment and ingredients.
2. Place the cocoa powder in a dry bowl, and slowly add a small amount of water to make a smooth paste.
3. Chop the couverture.
4. Place the sugar and remaining water in a pot; heat over low heat.
5. Stir in the cocoa paste mixture.
6. Bring to a boil; stir constantly.
7. Remove from the heat, and add the chopped couverture; stir constantly until blended.
8. Pass the sauce through a fine sieve.

CHEF NOTE:
Can be served hot or cold.

PASTRY TECHNIQUE:
Chopping, Melting, Combining

Chopping:
1. Use a sharp knife.
2. Hold the food product properly.
3. Cut with a quick downward motion.

Melting:
1. Prepare the food product to be melted.
2. Place the food product in an appropriate sized pot over direct heat or over a double boiler.
3. Stir frequently or occasionally, depending on the delicacy of the product, until melted.

OR

1. Place the product on a sheet pan or in a bowl, and place in a low-temperature oven until melted.

Combining:
Bringing together two or more components.
1. Prepare the components to be combined.
2. Add one to the other, using the appropriate mixing method (if needed).

HACCP:
Store at 40° F.

Chocolate Sauce: Quick Method

YIELD:	1 pound.	2 pounds.

INGREDIENTS:		
Chocolate, dark, semi-sweet	11 ounces	1 pound, 6 ounces
Water	5 ounces	10 ounces

METHOD OF PREPARATION:
1. Gather the equipment and ingredients.
2. Chop the chocolate.
3. Melt over a double boiler.
4. Add the water slowly to the melted chocolate.

CHEF NOTE:
Can be served hot or cold.

CAKES: BASES
ICINGS
CAKES: FINISHED
CREAMS
FILLINGS
PIES
SLOW BAKING
BATTER
DOUGHS
SAUCES

Clear Fruit Sauce

PASTRY TECHNIQUES:
Combining, Thickening, Boiling

Combining:
Bringing together two or more components.
1. Prepare the components to be combined.
2. Add one to the other, using the appropriate mixing method (if needed).

Thickening:
1. Mix a small amount of sugar with the starches.
2. Create a slurry.
3. Whisk vigorously until thickened and translucent.

Boiling:
1. Bring the cooking liquid to a rapid boil.
2. Stir the contents.

HACCP:
Store at 40° F.

YIELD:	1 pound, ¾ ounce.	2 pounds, 1½ ounces.

INGREDIENTS:

Cornstarch	½ ounce	1 ounce
Fruit juice, sweetened	8 ounces	1 pound
Water	6 ounces	12 ounces
Wine, red	2 ounces	4 ounces
Lemon juice	¼ ounce	½ ounce

METHOD OF PREPARATION:

1. Gather the equipment and ingredients.
2. Place the cornstarch in a dry bowl, and slowly add a small amount of water to dissolve it.
3. Place the fruit juice, water, wine, and lemon juice in a pot; heat.
4. Simmer for approximately 3 minutes; stir occasionally.
5. Stir the cornstarch into the simmering fruit juice mixture; whip constantly to prevent burning and lumps.
6. Bring to a boil.
7. Let cool.

CHEF NOTES:
1. Cherry juice, raspberry juice, or strawberry juice may be used.
2. Can be served hot or cold.

CAKES: BASES

ICINGS

CAKES: FINISHED

CREAMS

FILLINGS

PIES

SLOW BAKING

BATTER

DOUGHS

SAUCES

Coulis

Fruit Sauce, Uncooked

YIELD:	1 pound.	1 pound, 8 ounces.

INGREDIENTS:

Fruit, fresh, frozen, or canned	12 ounces	1 pound, 8 ounces
Lemon juice	½ lemon	1 lemon
Simple syrup (see page 415)	4 ounces	8 ounces

METHOD OF PREPARATION:

1. Gather the equipment and ingredients.
2. Prepare the fruit; clean and hull; thaw or drain, as needed.
3. Purée the fruit with lemon juice.
4. Add enough simple syrup to thin to the desired consistency.
5. Strain, if necessary.
6. Store in a refrigerator.

Variations:

1. Kiwi
2. Mango
3. Peach
4. Pineapple
5. Raspberry
6. Strawberry

PASTRY TECHNIQUE:
Combining

Combining:

Bringing together two or more components.
1. Prepare the components to be combined.
2. Add one to the other, using the appropriate mixing method (if needed).

HACCP:

Store at 40° F.

PASTRY TECHNIQUES:
Combining, Boiling, Reducing

Combining:
Bringing together two or more components.
1. Prepare the components to be combined.
2. Add one to the other, using the appropriate mixing method (if needed).

Boiling:
1. Bring the cooking liquid to a rapid boil.
2. Stir the contents.

Reducing:
1. Bring the sauce to a boil; then reduce to a simmer.
2. Stir often; reduce to the desired consistency.

HACCP:
Store at 40° F.

HAZARDOUS FOOD:
Heavy cream

Cream Sauce

YIELD:		1 pound, 5½ ounces.	2 pounds, 11 ounces.
INGREDIENTS:			
Sugar, granulated	10½ ounces	1 pound, 5 ounces
Salt	To taste	To taste
Cream, heavy	8 ounces	1 pound
Butter, unsalted, chopped	3 ounces	6 ounces
Flavorings/compounds, zest	To taste	To taste

METHOD OF PREPARATION:

1. Gather the equipment and ingredients.
2. Place all of ingredients in a sauce pan; heat on medium-high.
3. Bring the mixture to a boil; reduce the heat.
4. Continue cooking until the sauce is reduced to a desired consistency, approximately 5 minutes. (The sauce should be slightly thick.)
5. Remove from the heat.
6. Add the compounds or other flavorings, if desired.
7. Store in a refrigerator.

CHEF NOTE:
Can be served hot or cold.

English Sauce
(Sauce Anglaise)

CAKES: BASES

ICINGS

CAKES: FINISHED

CREAMS

FILLINGS

PIES

SLOW BAKING

BATTER

DOUGHS

SAUCES

PASTRY TECHNIQUES:

Combining, Boiling, Tempering, Thickening

Combining:

Bringing together two or more components.
1. Prepare the components to be combined.
2. Add one to the other, using the appropriate mixing method (if needed).

Boiling:
1. Bring the cooking liquid to a rapid boil.
2. Stir the contents.

Tempering:
1. Whisk the eggs vigorously while ladling hot liquid.

Thickening:
1. Mix a small amount of sugar with the starches.
2. Create a slurry.
3. Whisk vigorously until thickened and translucent.

HACCP:

Store at 40° F.

HAZARDOUS FOODS:

Milk
Heavy cream
Egg yolks

YIELD:	12¼ ounces.	1 pound, 8½ ounces.

INGREDIENTS:

Milk, whole	4 ounces	8 ounces
Cream, heavy	4 ounces	8 ounces
Sugar, granulated	2 ounces	4 ounces
Salt	Pinch	Pinch
Egg yolks	2¼ ounces	4½ ounces
Extract, vanilla	To taste	To taste

METHOD OF PREPARATION:

1. Gather the equipment and ingredients.
2. Place the milk, heavy cream, granulated sugar, and salt in a pot; bring to a boil.
3. Place the egg yolks and vanilla extract in a bowl; whip slightly.
4. Temper the egg yolk mixture with the boiling milk.
5. Cook the mixture to 175° F, and stir constantly. The mixture should be able to coat the back of a spoon.
7. When the mixture thickens, remove it from the heat, and put it in an ice bath to stop the cooking process. Continue to stir frequently to avoid skin creation.
8. Strain, if desired.
9. Refrigerate until use.

Hard Sauce

PASTRY TECHNIQUE:
Creaming

Creaming:

1. Soften the fats on low speed.
2. Add the sugar(s) and cream; increase the speed slowly.
3. Add the eggs one at a time; scrape the bowl frequently.
4. Add the dry ingredients in stages.

HACCP:
Store at 40° F.

YIELD:	10 ounces.	1 pound, 4 ounces.
INGREDIENTS:		
Butter, unsalted, softened	5 ounces	10 ounces
Sugar, confectionery	3 ounces	6 ounces
Rum or brandy	1 ounce	2 ounces
Lemon juice	1 ounce	2 ounces

METHOD OF PREPARATION:

1. Gather the equipment and ingredients.
2. Cream the butter until soft and light.
3. Add the confectionery sugar to the butter.
4. Add the liquor and lemon juice to incorporate thoroughly.
5. Store in a refrigerator.

CHEF NOTE:
Hard sauce is generally served as an accompaniment to bread pudding.

Lemon Custard Sauce

CAKES: BASES

ICINGS

CAKES: FINISHED

CREAMS

FILLINGS

PIES

SLOW BAKING

BATTER

DOUGHS

SAUCES

PASTRY TECHNIQUES:
Combining, Boiling, Tempering, Thickening

Combining:
Bringing together two or more components.
1. Prepare the components to be combined.
2. Add one to the other, using the appropriate mixing method (if needed).

Boiling:
1. Bring the cooking liquid to a rapid boil.
2. Stir the contents.

Tempering:
1. Whisk the eggs vigorously while ladling hot liquid.

Thickening:
1. Mix a small amount of sugar with the starches.
2. Create a slurry.
3. Whisk vigorously until thickened and translucent.

HACCP:
Store at 40° F.

HAZARDOUS FOOD:
Egg yolks

YIELD:	15¼ ounces.	1 pound, 15½ ounces.

INGREDIENTS:

Cornstarch	½ ounce	1 ounce
Water	8 ounces	1 pound
Sugar, granulated	4 ounces	8 ounces
Lemon juice	¾ ounce	1½ ounces
Egg yolks	2 ounces	4 ounces
Lemon rind	1 lemon	2 lemons

METHOD OF PREPARATION:
1. Gather the equipment and ingredients.
2. Place the cornstarch in a dry bowl, and slowly add a small amount of water to dissolve.
3. Add half of the sugar, the lemon juice, and the egg yolks into the cornstarch mixture; combine well, and set aside.
4. Place the remaining water, sugar, and lemon rind in a pot; bring to a boil.
5. Temper the cornstarch mixture; add to the boiling liquid.
6. Boil the liquid for approximately 1 minute; stir constantly.
7. Remove from the heat.
8. Cool.
9. Store in a refrigerator.

Maple Walnut Sauce

PASTRY TECHNIQUES:
Combining, Thickening

Combining:
Bringing together two or more components.
1. Prepare the components to be combined.
2. Add one to the other, using the appropriate mixing method (if needed).

Thickening:
1. Mix a small amount of sugar with the starches.
2. Create a slurry.
3. Whisk vigorously until thickened and translucent.

HACCP:
Store at 40° F.

HAZARDOUS FOOD:
Heavy cream

YIELD:	9⅞ ounces.	1 pound, 3¾ ounces.

INGREDIENTS:		
Cornstarch	⅛ ounce	¼ ounce
Cream, heavy	2 ounces	4 ounces
Butter, unsalted	1⅛ ounces	2¼ ounces
Maple syrup, pure	¾ ounce	1½ ounces
Sugar, granulated, light brown	5¼ ounces	10½ ounces
Salt	Pinch	Pinch
Walnuts, chopped	⅝ ounce	1¼ ounces

METHOD OF PREPARATION:

1. Gather the equipment and ingredients.
2. Place the cornstarch in a dry bowl, and add a small amount of heavy cream to dissolve the cornstarch.
3. Place the remaining cream, butter, maple syrup, sugar, and salt in a pot; heat on low. Stir only to combine the ingredients.
4. Add the cornstarch mixture, and cook the mixture on high heat for 2½ minutes.
5. Remove from the heat.
6. Stir the walnuts into the sauce.
7. Cool.
8. Store in a refrigerator.

CAKES: BASES

ICINGS

CAKES: FINISHED

CREAMS

FILLINGS

PIES

SLOW BAKING

BATTER

DOUGHS

SAUCES

Melba Sauce

PASTRY TECHNIQUES:

Combining, Boiling

Combining:

Bringing together two or more components.
1. Prepare the components to be combined.
2. Add one to the other, using the appropriate mixing method (if needed).

Boiling:

1. Bring the cooking liquid to a rapid boil.
2. Stir the contents.

HACCP:

Store at 40° F.

YIELD:	12¼ ounces.	1 pound, 8½ ounces.
INGREDIENTS:		
Preserves, raspberry	8 ounces	1 pound
Simple syrup (see page 415)	4 ounces	8 ounces
Salt	Pinch	Pinch
Extract, vanilla	To taste	To taste
Lemon juice	¼ ounce	½ ounce

METHOD OF PREPARATION:

1. Gather the equipment and ingredients.
2. Place the raspberry preserves, simple syrup, and salt in a pot.
3. Bring to a boil; boil for approximately 1 minute.
4. Remove from the heat, and strain.
5. Add the vanilla extract and lemon juice.
6. Cool.
7. Store in a refrigerator.

PASTRY TECHNIQUES:
Boiling, Tempering, Thickening

Boiling:
1. Bring the cooking liquid to a rapid boil.
2. Stir the contents.

Tempering:
1. Whisk the eggs vigorously while ladling hot liquid.

Thickening:
1. Mix a small amount of sugar with the starches.
2. Create a slurry.
3. Whisk vigorously until thickened and translucent.

HACCP:
Store at 40° F.

HAZARDOUS FOOD:
Egg yolks

Orange Custard Sauce

YIELD:	15½ ounces.	1 pound, 15 ounces.
INGREDIENTS:		
Water	8 ounces	1 pound
Sugar, granulated	4 ounces	8 ounces
Orange rind	1 each	2 each
Cornstarch	½ ounce	1 ounce
Orange juice	1 ounce	2 ounces
Egg yolks	2 ounces	4 ounces

METHOD OF PREPARATION:

1. Gather the equipment and ingredients.
2. Place the water, half of the granulated sugar, and orange rind in a pot; bring to a boil.
3. Place the cornstarch in a dry bowl, and slowly add a small amount of the orange juice to dissolve it.
4. Add in the remaining orange juice, sugar, and egg yolks to the cornstarch mixture; combine well.
5. Temper the cornstarch mixture, and add to the boiling liquid.
6. Boil the liquid for approximately 1 minute; stir constantly.
7. Remove from the heat.
8. Cool.
9. Store in a refrigerator.

Orange Sauce

PASTRY TECHNIQUES:
Combining, Boiling, Thickening

Combining:
Bringing together two or more components.
1. Prepare the components to be combined.
2. Add one to the other, using the appropriate mixing method (if needed).

Boiling:
1. Bring the cooking liquid to a rapid boil.
2. Stir the contents.

Thickening:
1. Mix a small amount of sugar with the starches.
2. Create a slurry.
3. Whisk vigorously until thickened and translucent.

HACCP:
Store at 40° F.

YIELD:

INGREDIENTS:	1 pound, 7 ounces.	2 pounds, 14 ounces.
Cornstarch or arrowroot	½ ounce	1 ounce
Orange juice	1 pound, 3 ounces	2 pounds, 6 ounces
Sugar, granulated	1½ ounces	3 ounces
Grand Marnier	2 ounces	4 ounces

METHOD OF PREPARATION:

1. Gather the equipment and ingredients.
2. Place the cornstarch or arrowroot in a dry bowl, and add a small amount of orange juice to dissolve it.
3. Place the remaining orange juice and sugar in a pot; place over medium heat.
4. Bring the mixture to a boil.
5. Add the cornstarch or arrowroot to the boiling orange juice; stir gently.
6. Bring the orange juice back to a boil; continue to cook for 1 minute.
7. Remove from the heat.
8. Allow the sauce to cool.
9. Strain the sauce through a fine sieve.
10. Add the Grand Marnier.
11. Store in a refrigerator.

Raisin Rum Sauce

PASTRY TECHNIQUES:
Combining, Simmering

Combining:
Bringing together two or more components.
1. Prepare the components to be combined.
2. Add one to the other, using the appropriate mixing method (if needed).

Simmering:
1. Place the prepared product in an appropriate-sized pot.
3. Bring the product to a boil, then reduce the heat to allow the product to barely boil.
4. Cook until desired doneness is achieved.

HACCP:
Store at 40° F.

YIELD:	1 pound, 2 ounces.	2 pounds, 4 ounces.

INGREDIENTS:

Water	4 ounces	8 ounces
Sugar, granulated	7 ounces	14 ounces
Orange juice	⅛ ounce	¼ ounce
Cloves, whole	2 each	2 each
Raisins, seedless	3 ounces	6 ounces
Rum	4 ounces	8 ounces

METHOD OF PREPARATION:

1. Gather the equipment and ingredients.
2. Place the water, sugar, orange juice, and cloves in a pot; bring to a boil.
3. Simmer for 10 minutes.
4. Remove the cloves, and add the raisins.
5. Simmer for an additional 5 minutes.
6. Remove the sauce from the heat.
7. Add the rum.
8. Store in a refrigerator.

CHEF NOTE:
Can be served hot or cold.

CAKES: BASES

ICINGS

CAKES: FINISHED

CREAMS

FILLINGS

PIES

SLOW BAKING

BATTER

DOUGHS

SAUCES

Raspberry Sauce

YIELD:	9 ounces.	1 pound, 2 ounces.

INGREDIENTS:		
Raspberries, whole, fresh, or frozen	8 ounces	1 pound
Water	1 ounce	2 ounces
Sugar, granulated	2 ounces	4 ounces
Arrowroot	⅛ ounce	¼ ounce

METHOD OF PREPARATION:

1. Gather the equipment and ingredients.
2. Place the raspberries, water, and sugar in a bowl. Let stand for 2 hours.
3. Purée all of the ingredients.
4. Strain.
5. Place the arrowroot in a bowl, and slowly add 2 ounces of strained purée; stir well.
6. Place the remaining purée in a pot, and bring to a boil.
7. The purée will reduce by 25%.
8. Add the arrowroot mixture to the purée.
9. Return to a boil; cook to a desired consistency.
10. Store in a refrigerator.

PASTRY TECHNIQUES:
Puréeing, Boiling, Thickening

Puréeing:
1. Do not overfill the food processor.
2. First pulse the food processor.
3. Turn food processor to maximum to purée food.

Boiling:
1. Bring the cooking liquid to a rapid boil.
2. Stir the contents.

Thickening:
1. Mix a small amount of sugar with the starches.
2. Create a slurry.
3. Whisk vigorously until thickened and translucent.

HACCP:
Store at 40° F.

CHEF NOTE:
Serve cold.

Sabayon à l'Marsala

YIELD:	10 ounces.	1 pound, 4 ounces.

INGREDIENTS:

Egg yolks	4½ ounces	9 ounces
Sugar, granulated	1 ounce	2 ounces
Wine, Marsala	4½ ounces	9 ounces

METHOD OF PREPARATION:

1. Gather the equipment and ingredients.
2. Place the egg yolks and sugar in a bowl; place over a double boiler.
3. Whip constantly until at least 140° F to form a thick, fluffy mixture.
4. When some volume is reached, add the Marsala slowly; continue to whip. Be careful to keep the sides clean so that the egg yolks will not cook along the sides of the bowl.
5. When the mixture has reached a ribbon-like texture, remove from the heat.
6. Serve warm.
7. Store in a refrigerator.

Serving Suggestions:

1. Pour sabayon over fruit.
2. Serve with lady fingers or cubed sponge cake.

Variations:

Supplement or substitute Marsala with a sweet white wine, Grand Marnier, or Kirschwasser.

PASTRY TECHNIQUE:
Whipping

Whipping:
1. Hold the whip at a 55-degree angle.
2. Create circles, using a circular motion.
3. The circular motion needs to be perpendicular to the bowl.

HACCP:
Store at 40° F.

HAZARDOUS FOOD:
Egg yolks

CHEF NOTE:
The name will change according to the flavoring liquid used.

Sabayon à l'Orange

CAKES: BASES

ICINGS

CAKES: FINISHED

CREAMS

FILLINGS

PIES

SLOW BAKING

BATTER

DOUGHS

SAUCES

PASTRY TECHNIQUE:
Whipping

Whipping:
1. Hold the whip at a 55-degree angle.
2. Create circles, using a circular motion.
3. The circular motion needs to be perpendicular to the bowl.

HACCP:
Store at 40° F.

HAZARDOUS FOOD:
Egg yolks

YIELD:	14¾ ounces.	1 pound, 13½ ounces.

INGREDIENTS:

Ingredient		
Egg yolks	3¾ ounces	7½ ounces
Sugar, granulated	3 ounces	6 ounces
Wine, sweet	4 ounces	8 ounces
Lemon juice	2 ounces	4 ounces
Orange juice	2 ounces	4 ounces

METHOD OF PREPARATION:

1. Gather the equipment and ingredients.
2. Place all of the ingredients in a bowl.
3. Place over a double boiler; whip constantly until it reaches at least 140° F, to form a thick fluffy mixture.
4. Serve warm.
5. Store in a refrigerator.

Cookies

11

Cookies

COOKIES

BREADS

SOUFFLES

CREPES

ICE CREAM

SORBETS

CHOCOLATE

OTHERS: FINISHED

MISCELLANEOUS

PASTRY TECHNIQUES:
Combining, Rolling

Combining:
Bringing together two or more components.
1. Prepare the components to be combined.
2. Add one to the other, using the appropriate mixing method (if needed).

Rolling:
1. Prepare the rolling surface by dusting with the appropriate medium (flour, cornstarch, etc.).
2. Use the appropriate style pin (stick pin or ball bearing pin) to roll the dough to desired thickness; rotate the dough during rolling to prevent sticking.

HACCP:
Store unbaked dough at 40° F.

Almond Lace Cookies

(Florentines)

YIELD: 2 pounds, 14¼ ounces. 5 pounds, 12½ ounces.

INGREDIENTS:

Flour, pastry	9 ounces	1 pound, 2 ounces
Sugar, granulated	9 ounces	1 pound, 2 ounces
Butter, unsalted, softened	9 ounces	1 pound, 2 ounces
Corn syrup	10¼ ounces	1 pound, 4½ ounces
Almonds, blanched, sliced, and crushed	9 ounces	1 pound, 2 ounces

METHOD OF PREPARATION:

1. Gather the equipment and ingredients.
2. Place the flour, sugar, and slightly softened butter in a bowl, and place on a mixer.
3. Using a paddle, blend together.
4. Add the corn syrup; mix until creamy.
5. Add the crushed almonds, and mix until the nuts are evenly dispersed.
6. Remove from the mixer.
7. Place 1 pound of dough on parchment paper lengthwise, and roll into a log shape.
8. Refrigerate or freeze until firm.
9. When the dough is firm, slice the log into ⅛-inch slices; place on a greased sheet pan.
10. Bake at 350° F for approximately 5 to 7 minutes, or until golden brown.
11. Remove from the oven, and shape as desired.

225

Almond Macaroons

Whipping:
1. Hold the whip at a 55-degree angle.
2. Create circles, using a circular motion.
3. The circular motion needs to be perpendicular to the bowl.

Combining:

Bringing together two or more components.
1. Prepare the components to be combined.
2. Add one to the other, using the appropriate mixing method (if needed).

Piping:

With bag:
1. Use a bag with a disposable tip; cut the bag at 45-degree angle.
2. Fill to no more than half full.
3. Burp the bag.
With cone:
1. Cut and fold the piping cone to the appropriate size.
2. Fill the cone with a small amount.
3. Fold the ends to form a triangle.
4. Pipe the desired designs.

HAZARDOUS FOOD:

Egg whites

YIELD:	2 pounds, 7½ ounces.	4 pounds, 15 ounces.

INGREDIENTS:

Ingredient		
Almond meal	11½ ounces	1 pound, 7 ounces
Sugar, confectionery	1 pound, 2½ ounces	2 pounds, 5 ounces
Egg whites	9 ounces	1 pound, 2 ounces
Sugar, granulated	½ ounce	1 ounce

METHOD OF PREPARATION:

1. Gather the equipment and ingredients.
2. Sift together the almond meal and confectionery sugar.
3. Place the egg whites in a bowl; whip to a medium peak; slowly add the granulated sugar to create a meringue.
4. Fold the dry ingredients into the meringue.
5. Pipe into desired shapes and sizes on parchment-lined sheet pans.
6. Bake at 400° F on double sheet pans for approximately 12 to 15 minutes, or until the edges are golden brown.

PASTRY TECHNIQUES:
Rolling, Piping, Filling

Rolling:
1. Prepare the rolling surface by dusting with the appropriate medium (flour, cornstarch, etc.).
2. Use the appropriate style pin (stick pin or ball bearing pin) to roll the dough to desired thickness; rotate the dough during rolling to prevent sticking.

Piping:
With bag:
1. Use a bag with a disposable tip; cut the bag at 45-degree angle.
2. Fill to no more than half full.
3. Burp the bag.
With cone:
1. Cut and fold the piping cone to the appropriate size.
2. Fill the cone with a small amount.
3. Fold the ends to form a triangle.
4. Pipe the desired designs.

Filling:
1. Cut open the food product.
2. Carefully spread the filling using an icing spatula, or
3. Carefully pipe the filling using a pastry bag.

Almond Ring Cookies

YIELD:	1 pound, 14 ounces.	3 pounds, 12 ounces.
	25 Cookies	50 Cookies

INGREDIENTS:

Short dough, (see page 183)	12 ounces	1 pound, 8 ounces
Macaroons, (see pages 235, 236)	1 pound, 2 ounces	2 pounds, 4 ounces
Preserves, raspberry	As needed	As needed

METHOD OF PREPARATION:

1. Gather the equipment and ingredients.
2. Roll out the short dough to 1/8-inch thickness.
3. Cut out small, round discs from the short dough; place on a sheet pan.
4. Place the macaroon mix in a pastry bag; use a medium-star tip.
5. Pipe the macaroon mix around the edge of the cookie.
6. Fill the center with raspberry preserves.
7. Bake at 350° F for approximately 15 minutes, or until golden brown.
8. Cool.

CHEF NOTE:
To add a shiny finish to these cookies, brush the macaroon portion of the cooled cookies with heated apricot glaze.

BREADS

SOUFFLES

CREPES

ICE CREAM

SORBETS

CHOCOLATE

OTHERS: FINISHED

MISCELLANEOUS

Brownies, Cake

PASTRY TECHNIQUES:

Combining, Spreading

Combining:

Bringing together two or more components.
1. Prepare the components to be combined.
2. Add one to the other, using the appropriate mixing method (if needed).

Spreading:

1. Using an icing spatula or off-set spatula, smooth the icing or other spreading medium over the surface area.

HAZARDOUS FOOD:

Eggs

YIELD:	4 pounds.	8 pounds.
	½ Sheet Pan	1 Sheet Pan

INGREDIENTS:

Batter:

Cocoa powder, sifted	3¾ ounces	7½ ounces
Flour, cake, sifted	7½ ounces	15 ounces
Flour, pastry, sifted	4 ounces	8 ounces
Salt	¼ ounce	½ ounce
Baking soda, sifted	⅛ ounce	¼ ounce
Shortening, high-ratio	11½ ounces	1 pound, 7 ounces
Sugar, granulated	7½ ounces	15 ounces
Sugar, brown	7½ ounces	15 ounces
Corn syrup	4½ ounces	9 ounces
Eggs, whole	9 ounces	1 pound, 2 ounces
Water	1½ ounces	3 ounces
Walnuts, pieces, toasted (optional)	7½ ounces	15 ounces

Garnish:

Simple syrup (see page 415)	4 ounces	8 ounces
Chocolate fudge icing (see page 46)	2 pounds, 3¾ ounces	4 pounds, 7½ ounces

METHOD OF PREPARATION:

1. Gather the equipment and ingredients.
2. Sift all of the dry ingredients together: cocoa powder, cake flour, pastry flour, salt, and baking soda.
3. Place all of the ingredients in a bowl.
4. Blend well on low speed to combine.
5. Mix for 2 minutes on medium speed.
6. Scale the batter, and pour onto greased, paper-lined sheet pans.
7. Spread the batter evenly with a spatula. Clean the pan edge.
8. Bake at 375° F for approximately 25 to 30 minutes, or until firm but not dry. *Do not overbake.*
9. Remove from the oven; cool completely.
10. Coat the top of the brownies with simple syrup.
11. Cover with fudge icing.
12. Cut a sheet pan of brownies with a sharp knife into the desired sizes.

COOKIES

BREADS

SOUFFLES

CREPES

ICE CREAM

SORBETS

CHOCOLATE

OTHERS: FINISHED

MISCELLANEOUS

PASTRY TECHNIQUES:

Creaming, Combining, Spreading

Creaming:

1. Soften the fats on low speed.
2. Add the sugar(s) and cream; increase the speed slowly.
3. Add the eggs one at a time; scrape the bowl frequently.
4. Add the dry ingredients in stages.

Combining:

Bringing together two or more components.
1. Prepare the components to be combined.
2. Add one to the other, using the appropriate mixing method (if needed).

Spreading:

1. Using an icing spatula or off-set spatula, smooth the icing or other spreading medium over the surface area.

HAZARDOUS FOOD:

Eggs

Brownies, Chocolate Fudge

YIELD:	5 pounds.	10 pounds.
	½ Sheet Pan	1 Sheet Pan

INGREDIENTS:

Batter:

Sugar, granulated	1 pound, 8 ounces	3 pounds
Shortening, all-purpose	12 ounces	1 pound, 8 ounces
Corn syrup	4 ounces	8 ounces
Cocoa powder, sifted	4 ounces	8 ounces
Extract, vanilla	¼ ounce	½ ounce
Eggs, whole	12 ounces	1 pound, 8 ounces
Flour, pastry	1 pound	2 pounds
Walnuts, pieces, toasted (optional)	8 ounces	1 pound

Garnish:

Chocolate fudge icing (see page 46)	2 pounds, 3¾ ounces	4 pounds, 7½ ounces

METHOD OF PREPARATION:

1. Gather the equipment and ingredients.
2. Place the sugar, shortening, corn syrup, cocoa powder, and vanilla extract in a bowl.
3. Cream well on low speed.
4. Add the whole eggs slowly; scrape the bowl.
5. Add the pastry flour, and blend.
6. Add the walnuts, and incorporate.
7. Scrape the bowl; mix until blended.
8. Scale the batter, and pour into greased, paper-lined sheet pans.
9. Spread the batter evenly with spatula. Clean the pan edge.
10. Bake at 375° F for approximately 25 to 30 minutes, or until firm but not dry. *Do not overbake.*
11. Remove from the oven; cool completely.
12. Cover with fudge icing.
13. Cut a sheet pan of brownies with a sharp knife into the desired sizes.

Butter Cookies

PASTRY TECHNIQUES:

Creaming, Combining, Piping

Creaming:

1. Soften the fats on low speed.
2. Add the sugar(s) and cream; increase the speed slowly.
3. Add the eggs one at a time; scrape the bowl frequently.
4. Add the dry ingredients in stages.

Combining:

Bringing together two or more components.
1. Prepare the components to be combined.
2. Add one to the other, using the appropriate mixing method (if needed).

Piping:

With bag:
1. Use a bag with a disposable tip; cut the bag at 45-degree angle.
2. Fill to no more than half full.
3. Burp the bag.
With cone:
1. Cut and fold the piping cone to the appropriate size.
2. Fill the cone with a small amount.
3. Fold the ends to form a triangle.
4. Pipe the desired designs.

HAZARDOUS FOOD:

Egg whites

YIELD:	1 pound, 6½ ounces.	7 pounds, 4 ounces.
	3 Dozen	12 Dozen

INGREDIENTS:

Sugar, granulated	3¾ ounces	1 pound, 4 ounces
Butter, unsalted (70° F)	7½ ounces	2 pounds, 8 ounces
Egg whites	1½ ounces	8 ounces
Flour, bread, sifted	9¾ ounces	3 pounds

METHOD OF PREPARATION:

1. Gather the equipment and ingredients.
2. Place the granulated sugar and butter in a bowl; cream until light and fluffy.
3. Add the egg whites slowly; continue to cream the mixture.
4. Scrape the bowl; continue mixing.
5. Add the sifted bread flour, and blend; scrape the bowl; continue mixing until smooth.
6. Place the mixture into a pastry bag; use a medium-star tip.
7. Pipe out the desired shapes on a parchment-lined sheet pan.
8. Bake at 375° F for approximately 10 to 12 minutes, or until light golden brown.

CHEF NOTE:

The batter may be colored, if desired.

PASTRY TECHNIQUES:
Creaming, Combining, Piping

Creaming:
1. Soften the fats on low speed.
2. Add the sugar(s) and cream; increase the speed slowly.
3. Add the eggs one at a time; scrape the bowl frequently.
4. Add the dry ingredients in stages.

Combining:
Bringing together two or more components.
1. Prepare the components to be combined.
2. Add one to the other, using the appropriate mixing method (if needed).

Piping:
With bag:
1. Use a bag with a disposable tip; cut the bag at 45-degree angle.
2. Fill to no more than half full.
3. Burp the bag.
With cone:
1. Cut and fold the piping cone to the appropriate size.
2. Fill the cone with a small amount.
3. Fold the ends to form a triangle.
4. Pipe the desired designs.

HAZARDOUS FOOD:
Eggs

Cat's Tongues

(Langue de Chat)

YIELD:	1 pound, 3 ounces.	2 pounds, 6 ounces.

INGREDIENTS:

Almond paste	3½ ounces	7 ounces
Eggs, whole	2 ounces	4 ounces
Butter, unsalted, softened	3½ ounces	7 ounces
Sugar, confectionery	4 ounces	8 ounces
Salt	Pinch	Pinch
Lemon rind	½ lemon	1 lemon
Flour, bread	6 ounces	12 ounces

METHOD OF PREPARATION:

1. Gather the equipment and ingredients.
2. Place the almond paste in a bowl with one third of the eggs; paddle until soft, smooth, and lump-free.
3. In a separate bowl, cream the butter, sugar, salt, and lemon rind; cream well.
4. Add the creamed almond mixture to the butter mixture; combine.
5. Add the remaining two thirds of the eggs, and blend well.
6. While mixing on slow speed, add the bread flour all at once; mix together.
7. Place the mixture in a pastry bag with a medium-straight tube, and pipe into 2-inch sticks on parchment-lined sheet pans.
8. Bake at 325° F for approximately 8 to 10 minutes, or until golden brown.

COOKIES

BREADS

SOUFFLES

CREPES

ICE CREAM

SORBETS

CHOCOLATE

OTHERS: FINISHED

MISCELLANEOUS

PASTRY TECHNIQUES:
Combining, Melting, Rolling, Cutting

Combining:
Bringing together two or more components.
1. Prepare the components to be combined.
2. Add one to the other, using the appropriate mixing method (if needed).

Melting:
1. Prepare the food product to be melted.
2. Place the food product in an appropriately-sized pot over direct heat or over a double boiler.
3. Stir frequently or occasionally, depending on the delicacy of the product, until melted.
OR
1. Place the product on a sheet pan or in a bowl, and place in a low-temperature oven until melted.

Rolling:
1. Prepare the rolling surface by dusting with the appropriate medium (flour, cornstarch, etc.).
2. Use the appropriate style pin (stick pin or ball bearing pin) to roll the dough to desired thickness; rotate the dough during rolling to prevent sticking.

Cutting:
Using a sharp knife to cut to the directed size.

HAZARDOUS FOOD:
Egg whites

Chocolate Almond Cookies

(Basler Brunsli)

YIELD:	1 pound, 2¼ ounces.	2 pounds, 4½ ounces.

INGREDIENTS:

Flour, almond (very fine, ground almond)	9 ounces	1 pound, 2 ounces
Sugar, granulated	3½ ounces	7 ounces
Liqueur, Kirschwasser	Drop	¼ ounce
Cloves, ground	Pinch	Pinch
Cinnamon, ground	Pinch	Pinch
Extract, vanilla	To taste	To taste
Egg whites	1½ ounces	3 ounces
Chocolate, dark, semi-sweet	4¼ ounces	8½ ounces
Sugar, granulated, additional	As needed	As needed

METHOD OF PREPARATION:

1. Gather the equipment and ingredients.
2. Place the almond flour, sugar, Kirschwasser, cloves, cinnamon, vanilla extract, and egg whites in a bowl; combine well.
3. Chop and melt the chocolate.
4. Add the melted chocolate to the mixture; mix well.
5. Let the dough rest overnight in a refrigerator.
6. Roll out the dough on a surface sprinkled with granulated sugar to ⅓-inch thick.
7. Cut the dough into 1½-inch by 1-inch rectangles.
8. Bake at 450° F for 5 to 7 minutes. *Do not overbake.*

CHEF NOTE:
These cookies can be dipped in chocolate, decorated with chocolate, or served as is.

Chocolate Chip Cookies No. 1

PASTRY TECHNIQUES:
Creaming, Combining, Portioning

Creaming:
1. Soften the fats on low speed.
2. Add the sugar(s) and cream; increase the speed slowly.
3. Add the eggs one at a time; scrape the bowl frequently.
4. Add the dry ingredients in stages.

Combining:
Bringing together two or more components.
1. Prepare the components to be combined.
2. Add one to the other, using the appropriate mixing method (if needed).

Portioning:
1. Mark the product for portioning, using a ruler, if necessary.
3. Cut, spoon, or scoop the product with the appropriate-sized utensil.

HAZARDOUS FOOD:

Eggs

YIELD:	2 pounds.	10 pounds.
	2 Dozen	10 Dozen

INGREDIENTS:

Ingredient		
Butter, unsalted	2¾ ounces	13¾ ounces
Margarine	2¾ ounces	13¾ ounces
Sugar, granulated	4 ounces	1 pound, 4 ounces
Sugar, brown	3 ounces	15 ounces
Salt	⅛ ounce	⅝ ounce
Baking soda	⅛ ounce	⅝ ounce
Flour, pastry	7½ ounces	2 pounds, 5½ ounces
Eggs, whole	2¼ ounces	11¼ ounces
Extract, vanilla	To taste	To taste
Chips, dark or white	9 ounces	2 pounds, 13 ounces
Pecans or walnuts, chopped (optional)	½ ounce	2½ ounces

METHOD OF PREPARATION:

1. Gather the equipment and ingredients.
2. Place the butter, margarine, granulated sugar, and brown sugar in a bowl with a paddle; cream.
3. Sift the dry ingredients together: salt, baking soda, and pastry flour.
4. Add the eggs and vanilla extract into the butter mixture.
5. Add the sifted dry ingredients; scrape well.
6. Add the chocolate chips and nuts; combine.
7. Portion the dough into 1½-ounce pieces; place on a parchment-lined sheet pan.
8. Bake at 375° F for 8 to 10 minutes, or until the cookies are golden brown.

BREADS
SOUFFLES
CREPES
ICE CREAM
SORBETS
CHOCOLATE
OTHERS: FINISHED
MISCELLANEOUS

PASTRY TECHNIQUES:
Creaming, Combining, Portioning

Creaming:
1. Soften the fats on low speed.
2. Add the sugar(s) and cream; increase the speed slowly.
3. Add the eggs one at a time; scrape the bowl frequently.
4. Add the dry ingredients in stages.

Combining:
Bringing together two or more components.
1. Prepare the components to be combined.
2. Add one to the other, using the appropriate mixing method (if needed).

Portioning:
1. Mark the product for portioning, using a ruler, if necessary.
2. Cut, spoon, or scoop the product with the appropriate-sized utensil.

HAZARDOUS FOOD:
Eggs

Chocolate Chip Cookies No. 2

YIELD:	6 pounds, 3¼ ounces. 7 Dozen	12 pounds, 6½ ounces. 14 Dozen

INGREDIENTS:

Shortening, all-purpose	8 ounces	1 pound
Butter, unsalted	8 ounces	1 pound
Sugar, brown	13 ounces	1 pound, 10 ounces
Sugar, granulated	10 ounces	1 pound, 4 ounces
Eggs, whole	10 ounces	1 pound, 4 ounces
Extract, vanilla	To taste	To taste
Flour, cake	1 pound, 10 ounces	3 pounds, 4 ounces
Baking soda	¼ ounce	½ ounce
Chips, dark or white	1 pound, 8 ounces	3 pounds

METHOD OF PREPARATION:

1. Gather the equipment and ingredients.
2. Place the shortening, butter, brown sugar, and granulated sugar in a bowl; cream until smooth.
3. Scrape the bowl.
4. Add the eggs, one at a time, until incorporated.
5. Add the vanilla extract.
6. Scrape the bowl.
7. Sift together the flour and baking soda; add to the creamed mixture.
8. Add the chocolate chips; mix until incorporated.
9. Portion the dough into 1½-ounce pieces; place the cookies on a parchment-lined sheet pan.
10. Bake at 350° F for approximately 10 to 12 minutes, or until golden brown.

Cookies **235**

COOKIES
BREADS
SOUFFLES
CREPES
ICE CREAM
SORBETS
CHOCOLATE
OTHERS: FINISHED
MISCELLANEOUS

PASTRY TECHNIQUES:

Heating, Whipping, Folding, Piping

Heating:
1. Prepare the food product according to the formula's instructions.
2. Choose the appropriate method of heating (on the range or stove top, in the oven, etc.)
3. Apply the product to the heat.

Whipping:
1. Hold the whip at a 55-degree angle.
2. Create circles, using a circular motion.
3. The circular motion needs to be perpendicular to the bowl.

Folding:

Do steps 1, 2, and 3 in one continuous motion.
1. Run a bowl scraper under the mixture, across the bottom of the bowl.
2. Turn the bowl counterclockwise.
3. Bring the bottom mixture to the top.

Piping:

With bag:
1. Use a bag with a disposable tip; cut the bag at 45-degree angle.
2. Fill to no more than half full.
3. Burp the bag.
With cone:
1. Cut and fold the piping cone to the appropriate size.
2. Fill the cone with a small amount.
3. Fold the ends to form a triangle.
4. Pipe the desired designs.

HAZARDOUS FOOD:

Egg whites

Coconut Macaroons No. 1

YIELD:	2 pounds, 13 ounces.	5 pounds, 10 ounces.

INGREDIENTS:

Egg whites	8 ounces	1 pound
Almond meal	4½ ounces	9 ounces
Sugar, granulated	1 pound, 4 ounces	2 pounds, 8 ounces
Macaroon coconut	10 ounces	1 pound, 4 ounces
Flour, pastry	2½ ounces	5 ounces

METHOD OF PREPARATION:

1. Gather the equipment and ingredients.
2. Place the egg whites in a bowl over a double boiler; heat until they reach 120° F, whipping constantly.
3. Remove from the heat.
4. Combine the almond meal, granulated sugar, macaroon coconut, and pastry flour.
5. Combine the dry ingredients into the heated egg whites.
6. Return the mixture back to heat. Heat until the mixture reaches 120° F.
7. Rest covered for 5 minutes.
8. Pipe into 1-inch rounds, using no tubes.
9. Bake on double pans at 375° F for approximately 12 to 15 minutes, or until golden brown.

PASTRY TECHNIQUES:
Boiling, Combining

Boiling:
1. Bring the cooking liquid to a rapid boil.
2. Stir the contents.

Combining:
Bringing together two or more components.
1. Prepare the components to be combined.
2. Add one to the other, using the appropriate mixing method (if needed).

HAZARDOUS FOOD:

Egg whites

Coconut Macaroons No. 2

YIELD:	1 pound, 5½ ounces.	10 pounds, 13½ ounces.

INGREDIENTS:		
Sugar, granulated	8 ounces	4 pounds
Salt	To taste	½ ounce
Glucose or corn syrup	1 ounce	8 ounces
Egg whites	4 ounces	2 pounds
Macaroon coconut	8 ounces	4 pounds
Extract, vanilla	⅛ ounce	1 ounce
Flour, cake	½ ounce	4 ounces

METHOD OF PREPARATION:

1. Gather the equipment and ingredients.
2. Place the sugar, salt, glucose, and egg whites in a bowl; place on top of a double boiler; heat to 110° F.
3. Fold in the coconut.
4. Add the vanilla extract.
5. Cook the mixture to 135° F to 140° F. Stir the mixture constantly.
6. Remove the mixture from the heat; incorporate the cake flour.
7. Pipe, as demonstrated.
8. Bake the cookies at 350° F for approximately 12 to 15 minutes, or until golden brown.

Cookies **237**

COOKIES
BREADS
SOUFFLES
CREPES
ICE CREAM
SORBETS
CHOCOLATE
OTHERS: FINISHED
MISCELLANEOUS

Florentines

Traditional

PASTRY TECHNIQUES:
Boiling, Combining, Portioning

Boiling:
1. Bring the cooking liquid to a rapid boil.
2. Stir the contents.

Combining:
Bringing together two or more components.
1. Prepare the components to be combined.
2. Add one to the other, using the appropriate mixing method (if needed).

Portioning:
1. Mark the product for portioning, using a ruler, if necessary.
3. Cut, spoon, or scoop the product with the appropriate-sized utensil.

HACCP:
Store unbaked dough at 40° F.

HAZARDOUS FOOD:
Heavy cream

YIELD: 2 pounds, 2 ounces. 4 pounds, 4 ounces.

INGREDIENTS:

Couverture, dark, semisweet	As needed	As needed

Dough:

Butter, unsalted	8 ounces	1 pound
Sugar, granulated	8 ounces	1 pound
Honey	3 ounces	6 ounces
Cream, heavy	3 ounces	6 ounces
Almonds, blanched, sliced, and toasted	3 ounces	6 ounces
Almonds, blanched, chopped, and toasted	2 ounces	4 ounces
Walnut pieces	2 ounces	4 ounces
Fruit, candied	5 ounces	10 ounces

METHOD OF PREPARATION:

1. Gather the equipment and ingredients.
2. Place the butter, sugar, honey, and heavy cream in a pot; bring to a boil, and heat to 240° F.
3. Add the sliced almonds, chopped almonds, walnut pieces, and candied fruit; return to a boil.
4. Cool.
5. Portion ½-ounce pieces.
6. Flatten the pieces on greased, 3-inch florentine pan, or place the dough on parchment-lined sheet pans.
7. Bake at 350° F for approximately 8 minutes, or until golden brown.
8. Cool.
9. Coat the underside of the florentine with melted couverture, and mark with a decorating comb.

CHEF NOTE:
Honey can be replaced with a honey-glucose mixture.

French Macaroons

Whipping, Folding, Piping

Whipping:
1. Hold the whip at a 55-degree angle.
2. Create circles, using a circular motion.
3. The circular motion needs to be perpendicular to the bowl.

Folding:
Do steps 1, 2, and 3 in one continuous motion.
1. Run a bowl scraper under the mixture, across the bottom of the bowl.
2. Turn the bowl counterclockwise.
3. Bring the bottom mixture to the top.

Piping:
With bag:
1. Use a bag with a disposable tip; cut the bag at 45-degree angle.
2. Fill to no more than half full.
3. Burp the bag.
With cone:
1. Cut and fold the piping cone to the appropriate size.
2. Fill the cone with a small amount.
3. Fold the ends to form a triangle.
4. Pipe the desired designs.

HAZARDOUS FOOD:
Egg whites

YIELD:		2 pounds, 10½ ounces.	5 pounds, 5 ounces.
INGREDIENTS:			
Egg whites		9 ounces	1 pound, 2 ounces
Sugar, granulated		1½ ounces	3 ounces
Cream of tartar		Pinch	Pinch
Almond meal		13½ ounces	1 pound, 11 ounces
Sugar, confectionery		1 pound, 2½ ounces	2 pounds, 5 ounces

METHOD OF PREPARATION:

1. Gather the equipment and ingredients.
2. Place the egg whites in a bowl with a whip. Whip to a soft peak, slowly adding the granulated sugar and cream of tartar to make a meringue.
3. Sift together the almond meal and confectionery sugar.
4. Fold the sifted ingredients carefully into the meringue.
5. Using a no. 3 plain tube, pipe immediately into ¾-inch rounds.
6. Bake on double pans at 400° F for approximately 10 to 12 minutes, or until golden on the bottom of the macaroon.

Cookies **239**

COOKIES
BREADS
SOUFFLES
CREPES
ICE CREAM
SORBETS
CHOCOLATE
OTHERS: FINISHED
MISCELLANEOUS

Hazelnut Biscotti

PASTRY TECHNIQUES:

Creaming, Combining, Rolling, Baking, Slicing

Creaming:

1. Soften the fats on low speed.
2. Add the sugar(s) and cream; increase the speed slowly.
3. Add the eggs one at a time; scrape the bowl frequently.
4. Add the dry ingredients in stages.

Combining:

Bringing together two or more components.
1. Prepare the components to be combined.
2. Add one to the other, using the appropriate mixing method (if needed).

Rolling:

1. Prepare the rolling surface by dusting with the appropriate medium (flour, cornstarch, etc.).
2. Use the appropriate style pin (stick pin or ball bearing pin) to roll the dough to desired thickness; rotate the dough during rolling to prevent sticking.

Baking:

1. Preheat the oven.
2. Position the item appropriately in the oven.
3. Check for appropriate firmness and/or color.

Slicing:

1. Prepare the product for cutting; clean and clear the work area.
2. Slice the product using the "claw" grasp or the rocking motion.

HAZARDOUS FOOD:

Eggs

YIELD:	2 pounds, 4⅛ ounces. 30 Biscuits	4 pounds, 8¼ ounces. 60 Biscuits
INGREDIENTS:		
Hazelnuts	4 ounces	8 ounces
Butter, unsalted	4 ounces	8 ounces
Sugar, granulated	5 ounces	10 ounces
Lemon zest	½ ounce	1 ounce
Eggs, whole	6 ounces	12 ounces
Extract, vanilla	To taste	To taste
Flour, pastry, sifted	1 pound	2 pounds
Baking powder	½ ounce	1 ounce
Salt	⅛ ounce	¼ ounce

METHOD OF PREPARATION:

1. Gather the equipment and ingredients.
2. Toast the hazelnuts, chop coarsely, and set aside.
3. Place the butter, granulated sugar, and lemon zest in a bowl; cream together until light and fluffy. Scrape the bowl well.
4. Add in the eggs and vanilla extract gradually; incorporate well.
5. Sift together the dry ingredients: pastry flour, baking powder, and salt.
6. Add the sifted dry ingredients to the butter mixture in three stages.
7. Stir in the chopped hazelnuts.
8. Divide the dough into three equal portions.
9. Roll each portion into a 3½-inch-diameter log.
10. Place the logs on parchment-lined sheet pans.
11. Press the dough down to increase the diameter, and create an arch shape.
12. Bake at 350° F for approximately 20 minutes.
13. Remove from the oven, and, with a sharp knife, cut the logs into ¾-inch slices.
14. Place the slices on sheet pans, and continue baking until they are dry and lightly browned on the sides.
15. Remove from the oven, and transfer to sheet pans to cool.

CHEF NOTE:

If preferred, the ends can be dipped into chocolate; make sure the biscotti are cool before dipping.

PASTRY TECHNIQUES:

Creaming, Combining, Piping, Filling, Dipping

Creaming:

1. Soften the fats on low speed.
2. Add the sugar(s) and cream; increase the speed slowly.
3. Add the eggs one at a time; scrape the bowl frequently.
4. Add the dry ingredients in stages.

Combining:

Bringing together two or more components.
1. Prepare the components to be combined.
2. Add one to the other, using the appropriate mixing method (if needed).

Piping:

With bag:
1. Use a bag with a disposable tip; cut the bag at 45-degree angle.
2. Fill to no more than half full.
3. Burp the bag.
With cone:
1. Cut and fold the piping cone to the appropriate size.
2. Fill the cone with a small amount.
3. Fold the ends to form a triangle.
4. Pipe the desired designs.

Filling:

1. Cut open the food product.
2. Carefully spread the filling using an icing spatula, or
3. Carefully pipe the filling using a pastry bag.

Dipping:

1. Prepare the product to the proper dipping temperature.
2. Carefully submerge the product.
3. Dry on parchment paper or a screen.

HAZARDOUS FOODS:

Eggs
Egg yolks

Hazelnut Cookies

(Haselnuss Bogen)

YIELD:		1 pound, 10 ounces.	3 pounds, 4 ounces.

INGREDIENTS:			
Preserves, apricot		1 pound	2 pounds
Chocolate, dark, coating		1 pound	2 pounds
Dough:			
Butter, unsalted		7 ounces	14 ounces
Sugar, granulated		4 ounces	8 ounces
Eggs, whole		2 ounces	4 ounces
Egg yolks		1⅓ ounces	2⅔ ounces
Lemon rind, grated		1 lemon	2 lemons
Extract, vanilla		To taste	To taste
Flour, bread		8½ ounces	1 pound, 1 ounce
Hazelnuts, ground very fine		3 ounces	6 ounces

METHOD OF PREPARATION:

1. Gather the equipment and ingredients.
2. Place the butter and granulated sugar in a bowl, and paddle until light and fluffy.
3. Add the eggs, egg yolks, lemon rind, and vanilla extract; blend well.
4. After combining the flour and hazelnuts, add them to mixture, and mix lightly.
5. Using a medium-straight tube, pipe 1½-inch crescent shapes on parchment-lined sheet pans.
6. Bake at 325° F for 8 to 10 minutes, or until golden brown.
7. Cool the cookies thoroughly.

To Assemble:

1. Soften the apricot preserves, as instructed.
2. Pipe apricot preserves onto the back of a single cookie.
3. Sandwich another cookie flat-side down.
4. Dip the ends in chocolate coating; place on a paper-lined pan to dry.
5. Chill before serving.

Cookies **241**

COOKIES

BREADS

SOUFFLES

CREPES

ICE CREAM

SORBETS

CHOCOLATE

OTHERS: FINISHED

MISCELLANEOUS

PASTRY TECHNIQUES:
Combining, Spreading

Combining:

Bringing together two or more components.
1. Prepare the components to be combined.
2. Add one to the other, using the appropriate mixing method (if needed).

Spreading:

1. Using an icing spatula or off-set spatula, smooth the icing or other spreading medium over the surface area.

HACCP:

Store unbaked paste at 40° F.

HAZARDOUS FOODS:
Egg whites
Milk

Hippen Paste No. 1
Almond Wafer Paste

YIELD:	3 pounds, 14 ounces.	7 pounds, 12 ounces.

INGREDIENTS:

Almond paste	1 pound, 5 ounces	2 pounds, 10 ounces
Sugar, confectionery	14 ounces	1 pound, 12 ounces
Flour, bread	7 ounces	14 ounces
Cinnamon, ground (optional)	To taste	To taste
Egg whites	1 pound, 1 ounce	2 pounds, 2 ounces
Milk, whole	3 ounces	6 ounces
Extract, vanilla	To taste	To taste

METHOD OF PREPARATION:

1. Gather the equipment and ingredients.
2. Place the almond paste, sugar, bread flour, and cinnamon (optional) in a bowl; paddle until crumbly.
3. Combine the egg whites, milk, and vanilla extract.
4. Slowly add to the almond paste mixture. This must be done slowly, or the mixture will become lumpy and will have to be strained.
5. Store in a container.

To Make Cookies:

1. Grease the sheet pan well.
2. Make a pattern form, or use a stencil.
3. Spread the batter evenly over the stencil.
4. Remove the stencil.
5. Bake at 400° F for about 5 to 7 minutes, or until golden brown.
6. Remove from the pan, and shape accordingly while still warm.

PASTRY TECHNIQUES:
Combining, Spreading

Combining:
Bringing together two or more components.
1. Prepare the components to be combined.
2. Add one to the other, using the appropriate mixing method (if needed).

Spreading:
1. Using an icing spatula or off-set spatula, smooth the icing or other spreading medium over the surface area.

HACCP:
Store unbaked paste at 40° F.

HAZARDOUS FOODS:
Egg whites
Milk

Hippen Paste No. 2
Almond Wafer Paste

YIELD:		15 ounces.	3 pounds, 8 ounces.

INGREDIENTS:			
Almond paste	7 ounces		1 pound, 12 ounces
Sugar, granulated	2 ounces		7 ounces
Flour, bread	2 ounces		7 ounces
Egg whites	2 ounces		7 ounces
Milk, whole	2 ounces		7 ounces
Extract, vanilla	To taste		To taste

METHOD OF PREPARATION:

1. Gather the equipment and ingredients.
2. Place the almond paste, sugar, and flour in a bowl, and paddle until crumbly.
3. Combine the egg whites, milk, and vanilla extract.
4. Slowly add the liquid mixture to the almond paste mixture. This must be done slowly to prevent lumps from forming in the batter.
5. Mix well.
6. Store in a container.

To Make Cookies:

1. Grease the sheet pans well.
2. Make a pattern form, or use a stencil.
3. Spread the batter evenly over the stencil.
4. Remove the stencil.
5. Bake at 400° F for 5 to 7 minutes, or until light, golden brown.
6. Remove from the pan.
7. Shape accordingly while still warm.

Cookies **243**

COOKIES
BREADS
SOUFFLES
CREPES
ICE CREAM
SORBETS
CHOCOLATE
OTHERS: FINISHED
MISCELLANEOUS

Ice Box Cookies

YIELD:	Vanilla	3 pounds, 1½ ounces.	6 pounds, 3 ounces.
	Chocolate	3 pounds, 2¾ ounces	6 pounds, 5½ ounces

INGREDIENTS:

Vanilla Portion:

Sugar, confectionery	8 ounces	1 pound
Butter, unsalted, softened	8 ounces	1 pound
Shortening, all-purpose	8 ounces	1 pound
Egg yolks	1½ ounces	3 ounces
Salt	Pinch	Pinch
Lemon rind, grated	1 each	2 each
Flour, cake	12 ounces	1 pound, 8 ounces
Flour, bread	12 ounces	1 pound, 8 ounces

Chocolate Portion:

Sugar, confectionery	10 ounces	1 pound, 4 ounces
Butter, unsalted	5 ounces	10 ounces
Shortening, all-purpose	5 ounces	10 ounces
Eggs, whole	5 ounces	10 ounces
Salt	Pinch	Pinch
Milk, whole	2 ounces	4 ounces
Baking soda	Pinch	Pinch
Flour, cake	10 ounces	1 pound, 4 ounces
Flour, bread	10 ounces	1 pound, 4 ounces
Cocoa powder	3¾ ounces	7½ ounces

METHOD OF PREPARATION:

Gather the equipment and ingredients.

Preparation of Vanilla Portion:

1. Place the sugar, butter, and shortening in a bowl; cream until smooth.
2. Add the eggs, salt, and flavorings; combine well.
3. Sift the dry ingredients; add to the creamed mixture.
4. Mix slowly until a smooth paste, but *do not overmix*.
5. Refrigerate until cold.

PASTRY TECHNIQUES:
Creaming, Rolling

Creaming:
1. Soften the fats on low speed.
2. Add the sugar(s) and cream; increase the speed slowly.
3. Add the eggs one at a time; scrape the bowl frequently.
4. Add the dry ingredients in stages.

Rolling:
1. Prepare the rolling surface by dusting with the appropriate medium (flour, cornstarch, etc.).
2. Use the appropriate style pin (stick pin or ball bearing pin) to roll the dough to desired thickness; rotate the dough during rolling to prevent sticking.

HACCP:
Store unbaked dough at 40° F.

HAZARDOUS FOODS:
Egg yolks
Eggs
Milk

Preparation of Chocolate Portion:

1. Place the sugar, butter, and shortening in a bowl; cream until smooth.
2. Add the eggs, salt, and milk; combine well.
3. Sift the dry ingredients; add to the creamed mixture.
4. Mix slowly until a smooth paste, but *do not overmix.*
5. Refrigerate until cold.

Construction of Cookies:

1. Roll and shape.
2. Place on parchment-lined sheet pans.
3. Bake at 365° F for approximately 10 to 12 minutes, or until golden brown.

PASTRY TECHNIQUES:

Whipping, Folding, Piping

Whipping:

1. Hold the whip at a 55-degree angle.
2. Create circles, using a circular motion.
3. The circular motion needs to be perpendicular to the bowl.

Folding:

Do steps 1, 2, and 3 in one continuous motion.
1. Run a bowl scraper under the mixture, across the bottom of the bowl.
2. Turn the bowl counterclockwise.
3. Bring the bottom mixture to the top.

Piping:

With bag:
1. Use a bag with a disposable tip; cut the bag at 45-degree angle.
2. Fill to no more than half full.
3. Burp the bag.

With cone:
1. Cut and fold the piping cone to the appropriate size.
2. Fill the cone with a small amount.
3. Fold the ends to form a triangle.
4. Pipe the desired designs.

HAZARDOUS FOODS:

Egg yolks
Egg whites

Ladyfingers No. 1

YIELD:	1 pound, 3½ ounces.	2 pounds, 7 ounces.

INGREDIENTS:

Ingredient		
Egg yolks	4 ounces	8 ounces
Sugar, granulated	6 ounces	12 ounces
Egg whites	5 ounces	10 ounces
Cream of tartar	Pinch	Pinch
Lemon juice	½ ounce	1 ounce
Flour, cake, sifted	4 ounces	8 ounces
Sugar, confectionery (optional)	As needed	As needed

METHOD OF PREPARATION:

1. Gather the equipment and ingredients.
2. Place the egg yolks and 3 ounces of granulated sugar in bowl; whip until thick and light in color.
3. In another bowl, place the egg whites; add a pinch of cream of tartar, and whip until firm; gradually add 3 more ounces of granulated sugar.
4. Add the lemon juice to the yolks, and incorporate.
5. Fold the yolks into the whipped egg whites.
6. Fold the sifted cake flour gently into the mixture.
7. Using a plain tube, pipe the batter immediately onto a parchment-lined sheet pan.
8. Bake at 425° F for 8 minutes, or until golden brown.

CHEF NOTE:

If a crispy surface is desired, sift confectionery sugar on the top.

COOKIES
BREADS
SOUFFLES
CREPES
ICE CREAM
SORBETS
CHOCOLATE
OTHERS: FINISHED
MISCELLANEOUS

PASTRY TECHNIQUES:

Whipping, Folding, Piping

Whipping:

1. Hold the whip at a 55-degree angle.
2. Create circles, using a circular motion.
3. The circular motion needs to be perpendicular to the bowl.

Folding:

Do steps 1, 2, and 3 in one continuous motion.
1. Run a bowl scraper under the mixture, across the bottom of the bowl.
2. Turn the bowl counterclockwise.
3. Bring the bottom mixture to the top.

Piping:

With bag:
1. Use a bag with a disposable tip; cut the bag at 45-degree angle.
2. Fill to no more than half full.
3. Burp the bag.
With cone:
1. Cut and fold the piping cone to the appropriate size.
2. Fill the cone with a small amount.
3. Fold the ends to form a triangle.
4. Pipe the desired designs.

HAZARDOUS FOODS:

Egg whites
Egg yolks

Ladyfingers No. 2

YIELD:	1 pound, 9¾ ounces.	3 pounds, 3½ ounces.

INGREDIENTS:

Egg whites	7 ounces	14 ounces
Sugar, granulated	6½ ounces	13 ounces
Egg yolks	4¾ ounces	9½ ounces
Flour, pastry, sifted	5 ounces	10 ounces
Cornstarch, sifted	2½ ounces	5 ounces
Sugar, confectionery	As needed	As needed

METHOD OF PREPARATION:

1. Gather the equipment and ingredients.
2. Place the egg whites in a bowl, and whip to medium-stiff peak; slowly add in the granulated sugar to make a meringue.
3. Place the egg yolks in a bowl, and whip to full volume.
4. Sift together the pastry flour and cornstarch.
5. Gently fold the meringue into the whipped egg yolks.
6. Gently fold the sifted dry ingredients into the egg mixture.
7. Pipe immediately using a medium-straight tip; pipe the mixture into finger-shaped cookies on a parchment-lined sheet pan.
8. Sprinkle the cookies with confectionery sugar.
9. Bake at 350° F for 5 minutes, or until just set.

COOKIES

BREADS

SOUFFLES

CREPES

ICE CREAM

SORBETS

CHOCOLATE

OTHERS: FINISHED

MISCELLANEOUS

Macaroons

PASTRY TECHNIQUES:

Combining, Piping

Combining:

Bringing together two or more components.
1. Prepare the components to be combined.
2. Add one to the other, using the appropriate mixing method (if needed).

Piping:

With bag:
1. Use a bag with a disposable tip; cut the bag at 45-degree angle.
2. Fill to no more than half full.
3. Burp the bag.
With cone:
1. Cut and fold the piping cone to the appropriate size.
2. Fill the cone with a small amount.
3. Fold the ends to form a triangle.
4. Pipe the desired designs.

HAZARDOUS FOOD:

Egg whites

YIELD:	1 pound, 3 ounces.	4 pounds, 12 ounces.

INGREDIENTS:

Almond paste	8 ounces	2 pounds
Sugar, granulated	8 ounces	2 pounds
Egg whites	3 ounces	12 ounces

METHOD OF PREPARATION:

1. Gather the equipment and ingredients.
2. Place the almond paste and granulated sugar in a bowl with a paddle; combine until crumbly in texture.
3. Add the egg whites very slowly to avoid lumps; combine until well blended.
4. Using a pastry bag with a small, round tube, pipe the mixture into desired shapes onto parchment-lined sheet pans.
5. Bake for 10 minutes, or until golden brown, at 325° F for crispy cookies or 375° F for chewy cookies; double the sheet pan when baking.
6. Cool on sheet pans. Do not touch the macaroons prior to cooling, or the cookie will break.

PASTRY TECHNIQUES:

Creaming, Combining, Portioning

Creaming:

1. Soften the fats on low speed.
2. Add the sugar(s) and cream; increase the speed slowly.
3. Add the eggs one at a time; scrape the bowl frequently.
4. Add the dry ingredients in stages.

Combining:

Bringing together two or more components.
1. Prepare the components to be combined.
2. Add one to the other, using the appropriate mixing method (if needed).

Portioning:

1. Mark the product for portioning, using a ruler, if necessary.
3. Cut, spoon, or scoop the product with the appropriate-sized utensil.

HAZARDOUS FOOD:

Eggs

Oatmeal Chocolate Chip Cookies

YIELD:	2 pounds, 1½ ounces.	8 pounds, 6½ ounces.
INGREDIENTS:		
Shortening, all-purpose	2 ounces	8 ounces
Butter, unsalted	2 ounces	8 ounces
Sugar, brown	3½ ounces	14 ounces
Sugar, granulated	3¾ ounces	15 ounces
Eggs, whole	2 ounces	8 ounces
Extract, vanilla	To taste	To taste
Coconut, shredded	2 ounces	8¼ ounces
Flour, pastry	3 ounces	12½ ounces
Salt	Pinch	¼ ounce
Baking soda	Pinch	¼ ounce
Cinnamon, ground	Pinch	¼ ounce
Oats, old-fashioned	6¼ ounces	1 pound, 8 ounces
Raisins (optional)	3 ounces	12 ounces
Nuts (optional)	3 ounces	12 ounces
Chips, chocolate or butterscotch	3 ounces	12 ounces

METHOD OF PREPARATION:

1. Gather the equipment and ingredients.
2. Paddle together the shortening, butter, brown sugar, and granulated sugar until light and fluffy.
3. In two stages, add the eggs and vanilla extract; mix well.
4. Add the shredded coconut.
5. Add the sifted dry ingredients: pastry flour, salt, baking soda, and cinnamon; mix only until blended.
6. Fold in the oats by hand.
7. Add the raisins, nuts, and chips, if desired.
8. Scale 1½-ounce portions, and place on parchment-lined sheet pans.
9. Bake at 360° F for 10 to 12 minutes, or until golden brown.

Cookies **249**

COOKIES

BREADS

SOUFFLES

CREPES

ICE CREAM

SORBETS

CHOCOLATE

OTHERS: FINISHED

MISCELLANEOUS

Oatmeal Cookies

PASTRY TECHNIQUES:
Creaming, Combining, Rolling

Creaming:
1. Soften the fats on low speed.
2. Add the sugar(s) and cream; increase the speed slowly.
3. Add the eggs one at a time; scrape the bowl frequently.
4. Add the dry ingredients in stages.

Combining:
Bringing together two or more components.
1. Prepare the components to be combined.
2. Add one to the other, using the appropriate mixing method (if needed).

Rolling:
1. Prepare the rolling surface by dusting with the appropriate medium (flour, cornstarch, etc.).
2. Use the appropriate style pin (stick pin or ball bearing pin) to roll the dough to desired thickness; rotate the dough during rolling to prevent sticking.

HAZARDOUS FOOD:
Eggs

YIELD:	1 pound, 10 ounces. 3¼ Rolls	1 pound, 10 ounces. 6½ Rolls
INGREDIENTS:		
Sugar, granulated	10 ounces	1 pound, 4 ounces
Sugar, brown	1 pound	2 pounds
Shortening, all-purpose	14 ounces	1 pound, 12 ounces
Nulomoline (invert sugar)	2 ounces	4 ounces
Salt	½ ounce	1 ounce
Baking soda	¼ ounce	½ ounce
Extract, vanilla	To taste	To taste
Eggs, whole	8 ounces	1 pound
Oats, old-fashioned	1 pound, 2 ounces	2 pounds, 4 ounces
Flour, pastry	13 ounces	1 pound, 10 ounces
Nuts, chopped	4 ounces	8 ounces

METHOD OF PREPARATION:

1. Gather the equipment and ingredients.
2. Place the granulated sugar, brown sugar, shortening, nulomoline, salt, and baking soda in a bowl with a paddle. Paddle until well blended.
3. Combine the vanilla extract and eggs.
4. Add the egg mixture slowly to the sugar-shortening mixture; scrape the bowl well.
5. Add the oatmeal, pastry flour, and nuts; mix until blended together.
6. Scale 1 pound, 10-ounce pieces of mixture; roll, and place into even logs.
7. Place the rolls on sheets pans, and refrigerate to chill.
8. To bake, remove the parchment paper from the logs, and cut to a desired thickness.
9. Bake at 375° F for 8 to 10 minutes, or until golden brown.

PASTRY TECHNIQUES:
Creaming, Combining, Rolling

Creaming:
1. Soften the fats on low speed.
2. Add the sugar(s) and cream; increase the speed slowly.
3. Add the eggs one at a time; scrape the bowl frequently.
4. Add the dry ingredients in stages.

Combining:
Bringing together two or more components.
1. Prepare the components to be combined.
2. Add one to the other, using the appropriate mixing method (if needed).

Rolling:
1. Prepare the rolling surface by dusting with the appropriate medium (flour, cornstarch, etc.).
2. Use the appropriate style pin (stick pin or ball bearing pin) to roll the dough to desired thickness; rotate the dough during rolling to prevent sticking.

HAZARDOUS FOODS:
Eggs
Milk

Peanut Butter Cookies

YIELD:		4 pounds, 6⅛ ounces.	8 pounds, 12½ ounces.

INGREDIENTS:

Shortening, all-purpose		7½ ounces	15 ounces
Peanut butter		12 ounces	1 pound, 8 ounces
Sugar, granulated		12 ounces	1 pound, 8 ounces
Salt		⅓ ounce	⅔ ounce
Extract, vanilla		To taste	To taste
Baking soda, sifted		⅛ ounce	¼ ounce
Eggs, whole		3½ ounces	7 ounces
Milk, whole		12 ounces	1 pound, 8 ounces
Flour, pastry		1 pound, 6 ounces	2 pounds, 12 ounces
Baking powder		¾ ounce	1½ ounces

METHOD OF PREPARATION:

1. Gather the equipment and ingredients together.
2. Place the shortening, peanut butter, granulated sugar, salt, vanilla extract, and baking soda in a bowl with a paddle; cream together for about 3 minutes.
3. Add the whole eggs, and mix well; scrape the bowl.
4. Add the milk, and mix well; scrape the bowl.
5. Sift together the pastry flour and baking powder; add to the mixture, and mix well.
6. Scale 1 pound, 2 ounces of dough onto parchment paper; roll into an even log approximately 12 inches in length.
7. Chill until firm.
8. To bake, remove the paper from the log, and cut into the desired thickness.
9. Place on parchment-lined sheet pans.
10. Bake at 375° F for 8 to 10 minutes, or until light golden brown.

BREADS

SOUFFLES

CREPES

ICE CREAM

SORBETS

CHOCOLATE

OTHERS: FINISHED

MISCELLANEOUS

PASTRY TECHNIQUES:
Creaming, Combining, Rolling

Creaming:
1. Soften the fats on low speed.
2. Add the sugar(s) and cream; increase the speed slowly.
3. Add the eggs one at a time; scrape the bowl frequently.
4. Add the dry ingredients in stages.

Combining:
Bringing together two or more components.
1. Prepare the components to be combined.
2. Add one to the other, using the appropriate mixing method (if needed).

Rolling:
1. Prepare the rolling surface by dusting with the appropriate medium (flour, cornstarch, etc.).
2. Use the appropriate style pin (stick pin or ball bearing pin) to roll the dough to desired thickness; rotate the dough during rolling to prevent sticking.

HAZARDOUS FOOD:
Eggs

Peanut Butter and Chocolate Cookies

YIELD:	3 pounds, 14⅛ ounces.	15 pounds, 8½ ounces.
	20 Cookies	80 Cookies

INGREDIENTS:

Ingredient		
Butter, unsalted	8 ounces	2 pounds
Peanut butter	6 ounces	1 pound, 8 ounces
Sugar, brown	10 ounces	2 pounds, 8 ounces
Sugar, granulated	3½ ounces	14 ounces
Salt	Pinch	⅓ ounce
Extract, vanilla	To taste	To taste
Baking soda, sifted	⅛ ounce	¾ ounce
Eggs, whole	4 ounces	1 pound
Flour, pastry	10 ounces	2 pounds, 8 ounces
Peanuts, toasted, chopped	7½ ounces	1 pound, 14 ounces
Chocolate, dark, semi-sweet, chunks	13 ounces	3 pounds, 4 ounces

METHOD OF PREPARATION:

1. Gather the equipment and ingredients.
2. Place the butter, peanut butter, brown sugar, granulated sugar, salt, vanilla extract, and baking soda in a bowl; paddle for 3 minutes.
3. Add the whole eggs, and mix well; scrape the bowl.
4. Sift the pastry flour.
5. Add the sifted flour to the mixture, and mix only until blended.
6. Fold the peanuts and chocolate chunks into the dough.
7. Scale 1 pound, 14 ounces of mixture; roll into a nice even log; place on parchment paper.
8. Refrigerate or freeze.
9. To bake, remove the paper, and cut the dough into a desired thickness.
10. Place on parchment-lined sheet pans.
11. Bake at 350° F for 8 to 10 minutes, or until light golden brown.

Pecan Diamonds

PASTRY TECHNIQUES:
Rolling, Boiling, Combining, Pouring

Rolling:
1. Prepare the rolling surface by dusting with the appropriate medium (flour, cornstarch, etc.).
2. Use the appropriate style pin (stick pin or ball bearing pin) to roll the dough to desired thickness; rotate the dough during rolling to prevent sticking.

Boiling:
1. Bring the cooking liquid to a rapid boil.
2. Stir the contents.

Combining:
Bringing together two or more components.
1. Prepare the components to be combined.
2. Add one to the other, using the appropriate mixing method (if needed).

Pouring:
1. Place the product in an appropriate container for pouring: a pitcher or large ladle.
2. Pour the product into desired containers or over another product.

HAZARDOUS FOOD:
Heavy cream

YIELD:	½ Sheet Pan.	1 Sheet Pan.

INGREDIENTS:

Short dough (see page 183)	1 pound, 12 ounces	
3 pounds, 8 ounces		

Filling:

	½ Sheet Pan	1 Sheet Pan
Butter, unsalted	1 pound	2 pounds
Sugar, granulated	4 ounces	8 ounces
Honey	12 ounces	1 pound, 8 ounces
Sugar, brown	1 pound	2 pounds
Pecan pieces	2 pounds	4 pounds
Cream, heavy	4 ounces	8 ounces

METHOD OF PREPARATION:

Gather the equipment and ingredients.

To Prepare Pan:
1. Roll out the dough, and line the sheet pan with dough.
2. Bake the dough at 425° F for 5 minutes, or until prebaked.

Filling:
1. In a pan, combine the butter, granulated sugar, honey, and brown sugar.
2. Boil for 3 minutes, or to 257° F.
3. Stir in the pecan pieces and heavy cream.
4. Pour into the prepared pan.
5. Bake at 350° F for 20 minutes, or until the mixture bubbles and the top is semi-firm.
6. Cool.
7. Cut into diamond shapes.

Pignoles

COOKIES

BREADS

SOUFFLES

CREPES

ICE CREAM

SORBETS

CHOCOLATE

OTHERS: FINISHED

MISCELLANEOUS

PASTRY TECHNIQUES:

Combining, Creaming, Folding, Piping

Combining:

Bringing together two or more components.
1. Prepare the components to be combined.
2. Add one to the other, using the appropriate mixing method (if needed).

Creaming:

1. Soften the fats on low speed.
2. Add the sugar(s) and cream; increase the speed slowly.
3. Add the eggs one at a time; scrape the bowl frequently.
4. Add the dry ingredients in stages.

Folding:

Do steps 1, 2, and 3 in one continuous motion.
1. Run a bowl scraper under the mixture, across the bottom of the bowl.
2. Turn the bowl counterclockwise.
3. Bring the bottom mixture to the top.

Piping:

With bag:
1. Use a bag with a disposable tip; cut the bag at 45-degree angle.
2. Fill to no more than half full.
3. Burp the bag.
With cone:
1. Cut and fold the piping cone to the appropriate size.
2. Fill the cone with a small amount.
3. Fold the ends to form a triangle.
4. Pipe the desired designs.

HAZARDOUS FOOD:

Egg whites

CHEF NOTE:

Different nuts (ground) can be used in the formula for variety: walnuts, pecans, pine nuts, pistachios, almonds, and so forth.

YIELD:	2 pounds, 6 ounces.	4 pounds, 12 ounces.

INGREDIENTS:

Almond paste	5 ounces	10 ounces
Sugar, granulated	8 ounces	1 pound
Butter, unsalted (70° F)	8 ounces	1 pound
Nuts, ground	8 ounces	1 pound
Egg whites	4 ounces	8 ounces
Flour, pastry	5 ounces	10 ounces

METHOD OF PREPARATION:

1. Gather the equipment and ingredients.
2. Place the almond paste and granulated sugar in a bowl with a paddle, and soften.
3. Cut the butter into small pieces, and add in small amounts to the softened almond paste.
4. When all of the butter is added, cream lightly.
5. Add the ground nuts, and combine.
6. Add the egg whites, and combine.
7. Remove from the mixer; fold in the pastry flour.
8. Pipe ¾-inch rounds, using a no. 3 plain round tube.
9. Bake at 375° F for 8 to 10 minutes, or until very light in color.

Scottish Shortbread

Creaming, Combining, Rolling

Creaming:

1. Soften the fats on low speed.
2. Add the sugar(s) and cream; increase the speed slowly.
3. Add the eggs one at a time; scrape the bowl frequently.
4. Add the dry ingredients in stages.

Combining:

Bringing together two or more components.
1. Prepare the components to be combined.
2. Add one to the other, using the appropriate mixing method (if needed).

Rolling:

1. Prepare the rolling surface by dusting with the appropriate medium (flour, cornstarch, etc.).
2. Use the appropriate style pin (stick pin or ball bearing pin) to roll the dough to desired thickness; rotate the dough during rolling to prevent sticking.

YIELD:		1 pound, 8½ ounces. 1 pound, 1½ ounces biscuits	7 pounds, 2 ounces. 4 pounds, 13½ ounces biscuits

INGREDIENTS:			
Flour, pastry, sifted, divided		12 ounces	4 pounds
Butter, unsalted, softened		8 ounces	2 pounds
Sugar, confectionery, sifted		4 ounces	1 pound
Marzipan (see page 422)	½ ounce		2 ounces

METHOD OF PREPARATION:

1. Gather the equipment and ingredients.
2. In a mixing bowl, cream together half of the pastry flour with the butter, confectionery sugar, and marzipan; use a paddle.
3. Incorporate the second half of the pastry flour, and mix until combined fully with the first mixture.
4. Roll out the dough on a pastry cloth until ¼-inch thick.
5. Cut into circular or rectangular biscuits, and place on parchment-lined sheet pans.
6. Bake at 385° F for 12 to 15 minutes, or until they are a light, yellow-brown.

Cookies **255**

COOKIES

BREADS

SOUFFLES

CREPES

ICE CREAM

SORBETS

CHOCOLATE

OTHERS: FINISHED

MISCELLANEOUS

Tuiles

PASTRY TECHNIQUES:
Combining, Spreading

Combining:
Bringing together two or more components.
1. Prepare the components to be combined.
2. Add one to the other, using the appropriate mixing method (if needed).

Spreading:
1. Using an icing spatula or off-set spatula, smooth the icing or other spreading medium over the surface area.

HACCP:
Store unbaked batter at 40° F.

HAZARDOUS FOODS:
Eggs
Egg whites

YIELD:	1 pound, 3½ ounces.	2 pounds, 7 ounces.
INGREDIENTS:		
Sugar, confectionery	4½ ounces	9 ounces
Flour, pastry	2 ounces	4 ounces
Eggs, whole	4 ounces	8 ounces
Egg whites	2 ounces	4 ounces
Extract, vanilla	To taste	To taste
Butter, unsalted, softened	1½ ounces	3 ounces
Almonds, blanched and sliced	5½ ounces	11 ounces
Butter, unsalted	As needed	As needed

METHOD OF PREPARATION:

1. Gather the equipment and ingredients.
2. Sift together the confectionery sugar and pastry flour.
3. Whisk together the whole eggs, egg whites, and vanilla extract.
4. Place the dry ingredients into a bowl, and slowly whisk in the liquids; be careful to prevent lumps from forming.
5. Add the softened butter.
6. Fold in the sliced almonds.
7. Allow the dough to rest for 1 hour.
8. Butter the bottom of a sheet pan, and freeze.
9. Spoon the rested dough onto the inverted frozen sheet pan, and press out with a fork dipped in water until the dough is 2½ inches in diameter and as thin as a sliced almond.
10. Bake at 375° F for 5 minutes, or until golden brown.
11. Form the warm cookies into a cup shape over the end of a 1½-inch-diameter dowel.

Tulip or Cigarette Paste

PASTRY TECHNIQUES:
Combining, Spreading

Combining:

Bringing together two or more components.
1. Prepare the components to be combined.
2. Add one to the other, using the appropriate mixing method (if needed).

Spreading:

1. Using an icing spatula or off-set spatula, smooth the icing or other spreading medium over the surface area.

Stuffing:

1. Place the stuffing inside the cavity of the food product using a gloved hand or a piping bag.
2. Be sure to fill the cavity completely.

HACCP:

Store unbaked batter at 40° F.

HAZARDOUS FOOD:

Egg whites

YIELD:		1 pound, 2 ounces.	2 pounds, 4 ounces.
INGREDIENTS:			
Butter, unsalted		3½ ounces	7 ounces
Sugar, confectionery		6 ounces	12 ounces
Flour, bread		5 ounces	10 ounces
Egg whites		3½ ounces	7 ounces
Butter, additional, unsalted		As needed	As needed

METHOD OF PREPARATION:

1. Gather the equipment and ingredients.
2. Place the butter, sugar, and bread flour in a bowl; paddle until smooth.
3. Add the egg whites slowly to avoid creating lumps; mix until smooth.
4. Butter a sheet pan, and place in the freezer for 10 minutes.
5. Make a pattern form, or use a stencil.
6. Place the stencil on the cold sheet pan, and spread the batter evenly over the stencil.
7. Bake at 350° F for 5 minutes, or until very light brown around the edges.
8. Remove from the pan immediately; mold into shape while hot, as desired.

12

*Breads,
Quick
Breads, and
Muffins*

12

Breads, Quick Breads, and Muffins

The Ten Steps of Bread Making

There are basically 10 steps in the baking process when using a straight dough method. If a sponge or pre-dough method is used, these 10 steps are usually followed from the mixing stage (step 2) *after* the mixing and fermentation of the sponge. Although formulas vary, if the 10 steps to baking bread are understood, they can be used as a guideline for making any yeast-raised product.

- **Step 1: Scaling the Ingredients**

  The exact scaling of ingredients is an integral part of the baking process. If ingredients have not been scaled properly, an inconsistent and often inferior product will result. The proper use of a baker's scale can ensure that amounts of ingredients conform to a given formula.

  Eggs, oil, liquid shortening, malt, honey, molasses, and other heavy liquids with a viscosity denser than milk or water should be weighed on the baker's scale. Water and milk can be measured with liquid measures: 1 pint equals 1 pound.

- **Step 2: Mixing of Yeast-Raised Dough**

  Mixing accomplishes two major objectives: It evenly and thoroughly distributes ingredients, and it allows for maximum development of the gluten. The procedure for mixing doughs can vary with the type of yeast used. The method that follows uses compressed, fresh yeast. If instant yeast is used, it must be added just after the liquids have absorbed into the flour. For a straight dough, the water and fresh yeast are mixed together.

  Over-mixing will give a let-down, or complete breakdown, of the dough. The dough will be warm and sticky and will come apart easily. There are four stages in the mixing process:

1. **Pick-up**

   A low speed is used to mix the flour and dry ingredients together; then the water and yeast are added. Any other wet ingredients are usually added to the water and yeast just before they are added to the dry ingredients. All of the water should be added before the kneader is accelerated to medium speed. Any solid fats that are used in the formula are added last; oils are usually added at the beginning of the mixing process, just after the water and yeast.

2. **Clean-up**

   During the clean-up stage, the ingredients come together, and the bottom of the bowl can be seen clearly. At this point, the kneader is accelerated to medium speed.

3. **Development**

   This is the longest stage in the mixing process. It is called the development stage because the gluten is being developed. Oxygen is being absorbed into the dough. The starch will come to the surface as gluten is forming, and the dough will be whiter. The dough will tear easily, and the color will be uneven.

4. **Final clear**

   The final clear stage occurs when the proper development of gluten has been obtained; when a small piece of dough is cut from the mass, it is stretched to a thinness that light will shine clearly through. The dough also can be stretched a few times without tearing. Once the dough reaches this stage, it is properly developed and can be removed from the mixing bowl.

   The dough should be lightly coated with oil before floor fermentation to prevent the dough from sticking to its container (usually a bulk proof box or trough) and from developing a skin. If dough improvers, conditioners, or instant yeast are used, bulk fermentation (step 3) is not necessary. If conditioners are used, bulk fermentation is eliminated, and the dough may be divided immediately.

259

- **Step 3: Bulk or Floor Fermentation**

  During the fermentation process, yeast cells act on sugary agents in the dough and produce carbon dioxide (CO_2) gas and alcohol. The gluten structure, formed by mixing, will contain the CO_2 gas produced by the yeast. The gluten is conditioned and mellowed and becomes more elastic as a result of the effect of the alcohol given off by the yeast and the lower acidity in the dough. The important factors for good fermentation are

  - Properly developed dough
  - Proper humidity of between 75% and 85%. The dough should be kept covered and away from drafts. Bulk fermentation is done in a proof box where the humidity can be controlled and observed.
  - A dough temperature between 78° F and 82° F, for optimum fermentation.

  Fermentation must be regulated throughout to ensure proper flavor and conditioning.

SIDEBAR:

In many bake shops, fermentation time is cut considerably with the use of dough conditioners; these chemically conditioned additives eliminate the need for bulk fermentation and save on labor costs. Unfortunately, the rich yeast flavor of bulk-fermented breads is lost in this type of product. In addition, the texture and crumb of a bread or roll made with conditioners is not as high in quality as that of bulk-fermented bread.

- **Step 4: Dividing the Dough and Punch Down**

  When bulk fermentation has caused the dough to rise (in most cases, close to double in volume or 50% fermentation), it is tested for punch down—the fingers are inserted into the dough to the knuckles, and the dough is observed to see if the finger marks leave a slight indentation and then close very slowly—if so, the dough is ready for punch down. Punch down is done by folding the sides of the dough into the middle and turning the dough over. Punching keeps the dough at an even temperature by turning the dough inside out; it also releases some of the carbon dioxide, which, if allowed to stay concentrated, will eventually

restrict fermentation; it introduces fresh oxygen to the dough to help with fermentation, and it helps develop gluten.

Dividing the dough should be done as quickly and accurately as possible. The dough continues to ferment during dividing, and delay will cause over-fermentation of the last unit scaled. The dough is divided using a bench scraper and is weighed to the desired weight, either for a dough press or for individual loaves. Leftover dough from inaccurate scaling should be divided evenly among the number of large pieces and tucked under. Smaller pieces will ferment faster and must be incorporated properly.

- **Step 5: Rounding or Folding Over**

  Rounding or folding the dough over are ways for the newly divided and scaled dough to be shaped into better condition for the further shaping that will come after the second fermentation. Rounding also prevents too much gas loss by providing the dough with a thin skin that entraps the gas. Folding over allows old gases to escape and new gases to be created. When rounding or folding over, the pieces of dough should be kept in order—the first piece rounded or folded should be the first piece shaped after having been bench rested, so that all of the rounded pieces of dough will receive the proper fermentation time.

- **Step 6: Bench Rest/Intermediate Proof**

  This is a short resting period in which the rounded or folded pieces of dough are relaxed. Fermentation continues, and the pieces become gassy; the gluten relaxes in this step to make future handling of the dough easier. The dough must be covered to keep in moisture and prevent crust formation; usually the dough is put back in the proof box, even for this short period, to ensure that the proper humidity and temperature are maintained. Sometimes it is left in the dough troughs; the troughs cover each other as they are stacked and prevent crust formation. It is during this rest period that the dough will begin to feel lighter and softer, and more yeast flavor will develop.

- **Step 7: Shaping**

  This is the step in which the properly rested dough is formed into the desired shape. Shaping should be done quickly, with as little dusting flour as possible, to prevent the dough from drying. If a seam is a part of the finished product, it should be placed on the bottom; a proper seam should be straight and tight, because the seam is the weakest part of any shaped product and could open during baking. Rolls, braids, and other rustic loaves are all shaped at this stage. The first piece of dough that was rounded or folded over is the first piece of dough to be shaped.

- **Step 8: Panning**

At this stage, the proper pan is selected and prepared accordingly, depending on the type of bread being made: pullman loaves, French baguettes, soft rolls, and so on. (Bread formulas will indicate the proper mise en place for panning.) All washes and appropriate garnishes should be applied after panning. Generally, lean doughs are placed on perforated pans with cornmeal and are water-washed; soft or medium doughs are placed on sheet pans with parchment or in lightly greased loaf pans and are egg-washed.

- **Step 9: Final Proof**

This stage should achieve maximum fermentation prior to the baking of the product. Final proofing should occur in a proof box, which produces a warm and humid environment. The proof box should be maintained at a temperature of 90° F to 95° F, with a humidity of 80% to 90%. In most cases, a properly proofed product should be nearly doubled in volume and light and airy to the touch, and will close around a finger indentation slowly without collapsing.

Proofing time is affected by the type of dough and the size and shape of the product. Sweet doughs should be proofed only partially before they are baked to prevent the richness of the dough from exerting extra weight on the gluten strands and compromising the final structure of the item.

Some items, particularly hard or lean doughs, are stippled (cut) either before, during, or after final proof. *Stippling* is the term used for the characteristic and decorative cuts made on the top of certain types of bread. Stippling improves the look of the product by making it more interesting visually; it also lightens the product by allowing the crumb to move upward and

expand during baking. If done correctly, stippling cuts will look like a scar on the surface of the product.

For most breads, stippling is done during the last 20% of the final proof, or when the loaf has three fourths of its maximum volume. The loaf will then expand more by moving up. A razor is better than a serrated knife for stippling, because the knife tends to drag across the dough. If the dough is very wet, using light rye flour will help the knife cut cleanly. In either case, the blade should never be dragged across the dough; a clear, sharp cut is desired. The following describes the method for stippling:

- Hold the blade almost parallel to the length of the dough.
- Cut just under the surface of the dough, not a deep, straight cut.
- The cuts must overlap by one third the length of each cut.
- All cuts must be the same length.
- The cuts must cover the full length of the dough.
- Use both hands, one to steady the product and the other to cut.

- **Step 10: Baking**

Baking changes and transforms the dough into an appetizing, desirable product. Baking times and temperatures are determined by the type of dough, the size of the unit, the richness of the unit, the crust color desired, and, often, the weather. Generally, the leaner the dough, the higher the oven temperature and the shorter the baking time; richer doughs usually require lower oven temperatures and longer baking periods. As the product is baked, the internal temperature rises, and four major changes take place, in the following order:

- **Natural Oven Spring**

This is a sudden rise and expansion due to the last effort of the yeast, reacting to the heat of the oven, to ferment before it is killed at 138° F to 140° F and the rapid expansion of the carbon dioxide created during the proofing process. This process occurs during the first 5 minutes or so of baking. Some reasons for the failure of this reaction include the following: There was too much salt in the dough;

the product was over-proofed; not enough yeast was added during mixing. The dough is very soft at this stage and will collapse if touched.

- **Starch Gelatinization**

  At 130° F., the starch granules will begin to swell from a transfer of moisture from other ingredients; as they swell, they will become fixed in the gluten structure. At 150° F, the starches will gelatinize and become the chief structure of the dough, rather than the gluten, which begins to dry out and coagulate at 165° F and continues to coagulate until the product is finished baking. The structure will begin to finalize in the crumb.

- **Protein Coagulation**

  The crust will be formed at 165° F due to the exposed starch and sugar at the surface of the dough. This finalizes the structure of the product. At this point, the product will begin to appear done, but the taste will still be heavy with alcohol because evaporation of alcohol has not yet taken place.

- **Alcohol Evaporation**

  The alcohol given off by the yeast as a by-product will be burned off from the product at 176° F. The finished bread will have an approximate internal temperature of 220° F.

- **Baking with Steam**

  Some breads, such as French and Italian loaves, require a thin, hard, crispy crust. Most professional bakers accomplish this through the use of steam in the oven during baking. Steam provides a moist environment that prevents a crust from forming too soon; the sugar present in the dough mixes with the moisture on the surface of the product and caramelizes. When the steam is released by the opening of the oven's damper, a crispy crust is formed. All ovens have different steam pressures, and timing must be adjusted to each situation, as well as how many seconds of steam will actually be applied. Older ovens and deck ovens may need to be loaded with steam prior to placing the product in the oven. Steam will produce a few major effects on a product: (1) The moisture helps improve natural oven spring by creating a proof box–type environment. This keeps the product soft and creates a glossy shine. (2) Steam prevents cracking of the crust during baking. (3) Starches and sugars mix with the steam, caramelizing to create crust color. The damper is then opened to let the steam out and prevent over-browning. In older products (old dough), the yeast will have digested a large amount of sugar, and the product will have less color.

COOKIES
BREADS
SOUFFLES
CREPES
ICE CREAM
SORBETS
CHOCOLATE
OTHERS: FINISHED
MISCELLANEOUS

Bagels

PASTRY TECHNIQUE:
The Ten Steps of Bread Making (see page 259)

YIELD: 15 pounds, 15¾ ounces. Baker's Percentage.

INGREDIENTS:

Flour, high-gluten, sifted	10 pounds	100
Water (variable)	5 pounds	50
Yeast, compressed	1 ounce	1
Dough conditioner (optional)	3½ ounces	2
Salt	3¼ ounces	2
Malt, dry diastatic	3½ ounces	2
Sugar, granulated	4½ ounces	3

METHOD OF PREPARATION:

1. Gather the equipment and ingredients.
2. Follow the 10 steps of bread making (see page 259).

Variation: Cinnamon Raisin Bagels

INGREDIENTS (In addition to above):

Cinnamon, ground	1 ounce
Raisins, seedless	1 pound
Yeast, compressed	½ ounce

PREPARATION:

1. Add the cinnamon and raisins during the last 2 minutes of the second mixing cycle.
2. Add extra yeast to the dough mixture.

PASTRY TECHNIQUE:
The Ten Steps of Bread Making (see page 259)

Basic Lean Dough
(Hard)

YIELD: 24 pounds, 15½ ounces.   Baker's Percentage.

INGREDIENTS:

Flour, high-gluten, sifted	15 pounds	100
Water	9 pounds	60
Yeast, compressed	4½ ounces	1.8
Salt	4½ ounces	1.8
Dough conditioner (optional)	6½ ounces	2

METHOD OF PREPARATION:

1. Gather the equipment and ingredients.
2. Follow the 10 steps of bread making (page 259).

Variations (items that can be produced from basic lean dough):

1. French breads: baguettes, batard
2. Italian breads
3. Crusty rolls
4. Pizza shells

COOKIES
BREADS
SOUFFLES
CREPES
ICE CREAM
SORBETS
CHOCOLATE
OTHERS: FINISHED
MISCELLANEOUS

PASTRY TECHNIQUE:
Mixing

Mixing:
1. Follow the proper mixing procedure: creaming, blending, whipping, or combination.

HACCP:
Store for 12 hours at 60° F to 65° F, or refrigerate for up to 7 days.

Biga

(White Starter)

YIELD: 16 pounds, 1¼ ounces. Baker's Percentage.

INGREDIENTS:

Yeast, compressed	1¼ ounces	0.86
Water	7 pounds	77.80
Flour, high-gluten	9 pounds	100

METHOD OF PREPARATION:

1. Gather the equipment and ingredients.
2. Dissolve the yeast in water.
3. Add the flour.
4. Mix for 2 minutes on low speed.
5. Mix for 2 minutes on medium speed.
6. Place in bowl and leave for 12 hours at room temperature or refrigerate for up to 7 days.

Brioche

PASTRY TECHNIQUE:
The Ten Steps of Bread Making (see page 259)

HAZARDOUS FOODS:
Milk
Eggs

YIELD: 10 pounds, 5½ ounces.   Baker's Percentage.

INGREDIENTS:

Yeast, compressed	5 ounces	6.9
Milk, whole	1 pound	21
Eggs, whole	2 pounds	44
Flour, pastry	1 pound, 2 ounces	25
Flour, bread	3 pounds, 6 ounces	75
Sugar, granulated	5 ounces	6.9
Salt	½ ounce	0.7
Butter, unsalted, soft	2 pounds, 4 ounces	50

METHOD OF PREPARATION:

1. Gather the equipment and ingredients.
2. Dissolve the yeast in the milk and eggs.
3. Add all of the dry ingredients; mix on medium speed for 5 minutes.
4. Slice the butter into ½-inch pieces; incorporate into dough on medium speed for 2 minutes.
5. Refrigerate overnight on a floured surface. Cover with a damp cloth, and seal with a plastic bag.
6. On the next day, remove the dough from the refrigerator.
7. Scale.
8. Mold.
9. Proof.
10. Egg-wash.
11. Bake at 375° F for approximately 20 minutes, or until brown on all sides.

Challah

COOKIES

BREADS

SOUFFLES

CREPES

ICE CREAM

SORBETS

CHOCOLATE

OTHERS: FINISHED

MISCELLANEOUS

PASTRY TECHNIQUE:
The Ten Steps of Bread Making (see page 259)

HAZARDOUS FOOD:
Eggs

YIELD: 7 pounds, 11½ ounces.   Baker's Percentage.

INGREDIENTS:

Water	2 pounds	50
Yeast, compressed	4 ounces	6.25
Sugar, granulated	6 ounces	9.38
Salt	1½ ounces	2.30
Oil, vegetable	6 ounces	9.38
Eggs, whole	10 ounces	56
Flour, high-gluten	4 pounds	100

METHOD OF PREPARATION:

1. Gather the equipment and ingredients.
2. Follow the 10 steps of bread making (page 259).

PASTRY TECHNIQUE:
The Ten Steps of Bread Making (see page 259)

HAZARDOUS FOOD:
Eggs

Cinnamon-Raisin Bread

YIELD: 19 pounds, 14 ounces. Baker's Percentage.

INGREDIENTS:

Flour, high-gluten, sifted	10 pounds	100
Sugar, granulated	13 ounces	8
Salt	3 ounces	2
Water	3 pounds, 14 ounces	39
Yeast, compressed	12½ ounces	7.75
Eggs, whole	1 pound	10
Shortening, high-ratio	10 ounces	6
Raisins	2 pounds, 8 ounces	25
Cinnamon, ground	1½ ounces	1
Dough conditioner (optional)	3½ ounces	1–2

METHOD OF PREPARATION:

1. Gather the equipment and ingredients.
2. Follow the 10 steps of bread making (page 259).

Variations:

1. Pullman loaves
2. Rolls

COOKIES
BREADS
SOUFFLES
CREPES
ICE CREAM
SORBETS
CHOCOLATE
OTHERS: FINISHED
MISCELLANEOUS

PASTRY TECHNIQUE:

The Ten Steps of Bread Making (see page 259)

English Muffins

YIELD: 20 pounds, 1½ ounces.   Baker's Percentage.

INGREDIENTS:

Salt	4 ounces	2.5
Dry milk solids (DMS)	1 pound	10
Sugar, granulated	5 ounces	3
Water	5 pounds, 8 ounces	55
Yeast, compressed	8 ounces	5
Water, additional	2 pounds	20
Butter, unsalted	6 ounces	4
Flour, bread	10 pounds	100
Dough conditioner (optional)	2½ ounces	1.5

METHOD OF PREPARATION:

1. Gather the equipment and ingredients.
2. Follow the 10 steps of bread making (see page 259).

CHEF NOTE:

Set the griddle at 375° F. Brush the griddle with a small amount of melted butter, and grill the muffins on both sides until light brown. Finish off the baking process in the oven at 375° F for about 6 to 8 minutes to ensure that the muffins are fully baked in the center.

French Bread

PASTRY TECHNIQUE:
The Ten Steps of Bread Making (see page 259)

YIELD: 30 pounds, 10 ounces. Baker's Percentage.

INGREDIENTS:

Sponge:

Water	6 pounds	31.6
Yeast, compressed	6 ounces	2
Flour, high-gluten	6 pounds	31.6
Malt powder	3 ounces	1

Dough:

Water	4 pounds, 8 ounces	23.7
Flour, high-gluten	13 pounds	68.4
Salt	6 ounces	2
Dough conditioner (optional)	3 ounces	1

METHOD OF PREPARATION:

1. Gather the equipment and ingredients.
2. Follow the 10 steps of bread making (page 259).

Kaiser

PASTRY TECHNIQUE:
The Ten Steps of Bread Making (see page 259)

HAZARDOUS FOOD:
Eggs

YIELD:	16 pounds, 15 ounces.	Baker's Percentage.

INGREDIENTS:

Water	5 pounds	50
Yeast, compressed	8 ounces	5
Flour, high-gluten	10 pounds	100
Salt	3 ounces	1.8
Eggs, whole	10 ounces	6.3
Oil, vegetable	10 ounces	6.3

METHOD OF PREPARATION:

1. Gather the equipment and ingredients.
2. Follow the 10 steps of bread making (see page 259).

COOKIES
BREADS
SOUFFLES
CREPES
ICE CREAM
SORBETS
CHOCOLATE
FINISHED OTHERS: MISCELLANEOUS

Light Rye

YIELD: 17 pounds, 6½ ounces.   Baker's Percentage.

INGREDIENTS:

Flour, first clear, sifted	7 pounds	70
Flour, light rye, sifted	3 pounds	30
Salt	3 ounces	2
Water (variable)	5 pounds, 6 ounces	54
Molasses	8 ounces	5
Yeast, compressed	10 ounces	6
Shortening, all-purpose	10 ounces	6
Seeds, caraway (optional)	1½ ounces	1
Rye sour starter	1 pound	10

METHOD OF PREPARATION:

1. Gather the equipment and ingredients.
2. Follow the 10 steps of bread making (page 259).

Variations:

1. Pullman loaves
2. Rolls
3. Boulé loaves
4. Oblong loaves

COOKIES

BREADS

SOUFFLES

CREPES

ICE CREAM

SORBETS

CHOCOLATE

OTHERS: FINISHED

MISCELLANEOUS

Marbled Rye Bread

PASTRY TECHNIQUE:
The Ten Steps of Bread Making (see page 259)

YIELD:	34 pounds, 3 ounces.	Baker's Percentage.

INGREDIENTS:

Dark Color:	*17 pounds, 7 ounces*	
Flour, rye, white	3 pounds	30
Flour, first clear	7 pounds	70
Water	5 pounds, 8 ounces	55
Color, caramel	8 ounces	5
Molasses	6 ounces	4
Salt	3 ounces	2
Seeds, caraway	1 ounce	0.5
Shortening, all-purpose	10 ounces	6
Yeast, SAF, instant	3 ounces	2
Light Color:	*16 pounds, 12 ounces*	
Flour, rye, white	3 pounds, 8 ounces	35
Flour, first clear	6 pounds, 8 ounces	65
Water	5 pounds, 5 ounces	53
Molasses	6 ounces	4
Salt	3 ounces	2
Seeds, caraway	1 ounce	0.5
Shortening, all-purpose	10 ounces	6
Yeast, SAF, instant	3 ounces	2

METHOD OF PREPARATION:

1. Gather the equipment and ingredients.
2. Follow the 10 steps of bread making (see page 259).

Variations:

1. Rolls
2. Loaves

PASTRY TECHNIQUE:

The Ten Steps of Bread Making (see page 259)

Medium Wheat Dough

YIELD: 17 pounds, 8½ ounces. Baker's Percentage.

INGREDIENTS:

Ingredient	Amount	Baker's %
Flour, first clear, sifted	6 pounds, 11 ounces	67
Flour, whole wheat, *not* sifted	3 pounds, 5 ounces	33
Salt	3 ounces	2
Dry milk solids (DMS)	10 ounces	6.25
Water (variable)	5 pounds, 8 ounces	55
Yeast, compressed	9½ ounces	6
Shortening, all-purpose	10 ounces	6.25

METHOD OF PREPARATION:

1. Gather the equipment and ingredients.
2. Follow the 10 steps of bread making (page 259).

Variations:

1. Pullman bread
2. Rolls

COOKIES

BREADS

SOUFFLES

CREPES

ICE CREAM

SORBETS

CHOCOLATE

OTHERS: FINISHED

MISCELLANEOUS

PASTRY TECHNIQUE:
Combining

Combining:
Bringing together two or more components.
1. Prepare the components to be combined.
2. Add one to the other, using the appropriate mixing method (if needed).

Pecan Roll Smear

(Pan Preparation for Pecan Rolls)

YIELD:	4 pounds.	8 pounds.

INGREDIENTS:

Sugar, brown	2 pounds	4 pounds
Margarine	1 pound, 2 ounces	2 pounds, 4 ounces
Salt	½ ounce	1 ounce
Syrup, corn	12 ounces	1 pound, 8 ounces
Extract, rum	¾ ounce	1½ ounces
Extract, vanilla	¾ ounce	1½ ounces
Pecan, halves	As needed	As needed

METHOD OF PREPARATION:

1. Gather the equipment and ingredients.
2. Place all of the ingredients in a bowl with a paddle, and combine together until a smooth, spreading consistency is achieved. If too dry, moisten with a small amount of water.
3. Using a spoon, deposit 1 ounce in the bottom of each cup of a heavily greased muffin tin.
4. Place three or four pecan halves on top of the mixture in each cup.

CHEF NOTE:
This preparation is an excellent base for pineapple upside-down cake.

Pita Dough

PASTRY TECHNIQUE:
The Ten Steps of Bread Making (see page 259)

YIELD: 21 pounds, 15 ounces.   Baker's Percentage.

INGREDIENTS:

Flour, wheat, bread	13 pounds	100
Water	8 pounds	61.5
Yeast, compressed	4 ounces	2
Sugar, granulated	4 ounces	1.9
Oil, vegetable	4 ounces	1.9
Salt	3 ounces	1.4

METHOD OF PREPARATION:

1. Gather the equipment and ingredients.
2. Follow the 10 steps of bread making (see page 259).

CHEF NOTE:
Bake at 475° F to 500° F for approximately 10 to 15 minutes.

Breads, Quick Breads, and Muffins **277**

COOKIES
BREADS
SOUFFLES
CREPES
ICE CREAM
SORBETS
CHOCOLATE
OTHERS: FINISHED
MISCELLANEOUS

Portuguese Sweet Bread

PASTRY TECHNIQUES:
The Ten Steps of Bread Making (see page 259), Creaming

Creaming:
1. Soften the fats on low speed.
2. Add the sugar(s) and cream; increase the speed slowly.
3. Add the eggs one at a time; scrape the bowl frequently.
4. Add the dry ingredients in stages.

HAZARDOUS FOOD:
Eggs

| YIELD: | 14 pounds, 6 ounces. | Baker's Percentage. |

INGREDIENTS:

Sponge:

Flour, bread	8 ounces	7
Sugar, granulated	4 ounces	3
Yeast, compressed	7 to 8 ounces	6 to 8
Water	1 pound, 6 ounces	20

Dough:

Sugar, granulated	1 pound	15
Salt	1 ounce	1
Butter, unsalted, room temperature	8 ounces	6
Shortening, all-purpose	8 ounces	6
Eggs, whole	1 pound, 6 ounces	20

Dough:

Water	1 pound, 6 ounces	20
Color, egg shade (optional)	As desired	—
Lemons, zest	To taste	—
Oranges, zest	To taste	—
Flour, bread	6 pounds, 8 ounces	93
Dry milk solids (DMS)	8 ounces	6

METHOD OF PREPARATION:

1. Gather the equipment and ingredients.
2. Mix the first four ingredients (sponge), and let this mixture come to a full rise, approximately 1½ to 2 hours.
3. Cream the second five ingredients (dough).
4. When the sponge has fully risen and begins to fall, add it to the creamed mass.
5. Add the water, egg color, and lemon and orange zests.

6. Add the flour and DMS, and mix until developed.
7. Follow the 10 steps of bread making that are remaining (see page 259).

Variations:

1. Rolls
2. Boulé

PASTRY TECHNIQUE:
The Ten Steps of Bread Making (see page 259)

Potato Rosemary Bread

YIELD:	22 pounds, 15¼ ounces.	Baker's Percentage.

INGREDIENTS:		
Flour, high-gluten	10 pounds	100
Water	5 pounds, 5 ounces	53.1
Salt	4 ounces	2.5
Yeast, compressed	2 ounces	1.3
Pre-ferment	4 pounds	40
Potatoes, mashed	3 pounds	30
Oil, olive	3¼ ounces	2
Rosemary, chopped	1 ounce	0.6

METHOD OF PREPARATION:

1. Gather the equipment and ingredients.
2. Follow the 10 steps of bread making (see page 259).

COOKIES
BREADS
SOUFFLES
CREPES
ICE CREAM
SORBETS
CHOCOLATE
OTHERS: FINISHED
MISCELLANEOUS

Pre-ferment

PASTRY TECHNIQUE:
Mixing

Mixing:

1. Follow the proper mixing proce-dure: creaming, blending, whip-ping, or combination.

HACCP:

Ferment for 2 to 5 hours, or up to 7 days in a refrigerator.

YIELD:	5 pounds, 2 ounces.	Baker's Percentage.
INGREDIENTS:		
Flour, high-gluten	3 pounds	100
Water	2 pounds	66
Salt	1 ounce	2
Yeast, compressed	1 ounce	2

METHOD OF PREPARATION:

1. Gather the equipment and ingredients.
2. Use the straight mixing method.
3. Ferment for 2 to 5 hours, or for up to 7 days in a refrigerator.

Pre-ferment Rye

PASTRY TECHNIQUE:
Combining

Combining:
Bringing together two or more components.
1. Prepare the components to be combined.
2. Add one to the other, using the appropriate mixing method (if needed).

HACCP:
Ferment for 2 to 5 hours, or up to 7 days in a refrigerator.

YIELD:	4 pounds, 9 ounces.	Baker's Percentage.

INGREDIENTS:

Water	2 pounds	80
Flour, rye, white or dark	2 pounds, 8 ounces	100
Yeast, compressed	1 ounce	2.5
Onion	1 each	

METHOD OF PREPARATION:

1. Gather the equipment and ingredients.
2. Combine all of the ingredients.
3. After all of the ingredients are combined, bury the onion in the mixture.
4. Let the dough rest for 5 hours.

CHEF NOTE:
If kept for 24 hours before using, the onions must be removed.

Pullman Bread

PASTRY TECHNIQUE:
The Ten Steps of Bread Making (see page 259)

HAZARDOUS FOOD:

Eggs

YIELD: 39 pounds, 12¾ ounces. Baker's Percentage.

INGREDIENTS:

Ingredient	Amount	Baker's %
Flour, bread	20 pounds	100
Water	11 pounds, 6 ounces	56.9
Yeast, compressed	1 ounce	0.5
Dry milk solids (DMS)	1 pound, 6 ounces	6.9
Sugar, granulated	1 pound, 12 ounces	8.8
Shortening, all-purpose	2 pounds, 4 ounces	11.3
Salt	6 ounces	1.9
Eggs, whole	1 pound, 6 ounces	6.9
Dough conditioner (optional)	4¾ ounces	1.5

METHOD OF PREPARATION:

1. Gather the equipment and ingredients.
2. Follow the 10 steps of bread making (see page 259).

Pumpernickel

COOKIES

BREADS

SOUFFLES

CREPES

ICE CREAM

SORBETS

CHOCOLATE

OTHERS: FINISHED

MISCELLANEOUS

PASTRY TECHNIQUE:
The Ten Steps of Bread Making (see page 259)

YIELD: 18 pounds, 14½ ounces.   Baker's Percentage.

INGREDIENTS:

Ingredient	Amount	%
Flour, light rye, sifted	2 pounds	21
Flour, first clear	7 pounds, 8 ounces	79
Rye chops	8 ounces	5
Salt	3 ounces	2
Seeds, caraway	2½ ounces	1.5
Water	5 pounds, 10 ounces	56
Yeast, compressed	13 ounces	8
Molasses	6½ ounces	4
Color, caramel	6½ ounces	4
Shortening, all-purpose	8 ounces	5
Onions, fresh, finely diced	13 ounces	8
Dough conditioner (optional)	2 ounces	1

METHOD OF PREPARATION:

1. Gather the equipment and ingredients.
2. Follow the 10 steps of bread making (see page 259).

Variations:

1. Pullman loaves
2. Rolls

Rustic Wheat Dough

PASTRY TECHNIQUES:
Soaking, The Ten Steps of Bread Making (see page 259)

Soaking:
1. Place the item(s) to be soaked in a large bowl or appropriate container.
2. Pour water or other liquid over the items to be soaked.
3. Allow to sit until desired saturation or softening is achieved.

YIELD: 17 pounds, 12½ ounces. Baker's Percentage.

INGREDIENTS:

Wheat flakes or cracked wheat	3 pounds, 5 ounces	33
Water (variable)	5 pounds	50
Salt	5 ounces	3

Dough:

Flour, first clear, sifted	6 pounds, 11 ounces	67
Water	8 ounces	5
Molasses	11 ounces	7
Yeast, compressed	9½ ounces	6
Shortening, all-purpose	11 ounces	7

METHOD OF PREPARATION:

1. Gather the equipment and ingredients.
2. Place the wheat flakes, water, and salt in a bowl. Allow to soak for 90 minutes to 3 hours (ideally, overnight).
3. Follow the 10 steps of bread making (page 259).

Variations:

1. Pullman loaves
2. Rolls

Soft Rolls

COOKIES

BREADS

SOUFFLES

CREPES

ICE CREAM

SORBETS

CHOCOLATE

OTHERS: FINISHED

MISCELLANEOUS

PASTRY TECHNIQUE:

The Ten Steps of Bread Making (see page 259)

YIELD: 26 pounds, 15 ounces. Baker's Percentage.

INGREDIENTS:

Water	9 pounds	64
Dry milk solids (DMS)	1 pound	7
Sugar, granulated	1 pound	7
Yeast, compressed	8 ounces	3.5
Flour, bread	14 pounds	100
Salt	4½ ounces	2
Shortening, all-purpose	1 pound	7
Dough conditioner (optional)	2½ ounces	1

METHOD OF PREPARATION:

1. Gather the equipment and ingredients.
2. Follow the 10 steps of bread making (page 259).

Variations:

1. Rolls
2. Pecan rolls
3. Cinnamon rolls
4. Coffee cakes

Sour Rye Dough

PASTRY TECHNIQUE:
The Ten Steps of Bread Making (see page 259)

YIELD: 19 pounds, 14½ ounces. Baker's Percentage.

INGREDIENTS:

Ingredient	Weight	Baker's Percentage
Rye sour starter, fermented	3 pounds, 12 ounces	37.5
Flour, light rye, sifted	2 pounds	20
Flour, first clear, sifted	8 pounds	80
Salt	4 ounces	2.5
Water (variable)	4 pounds	40
Yeast, compressed	10 ounces	6
Molasses	10 ounces	6
Seeds, caraway	1¾ ounces	1
Shortening, all-purpose	6¼ ounces	4
Dough conditioner (optional)	2½ ounces	1.5

METHOD OF PREPARATION:

1. Gather the equipment and ingredients.
2. Follow the 10 steps of bread making (see page 259).

Variations:

1. Loaves
2. Rolls

Swedish Rye Bread

COOKIES

BREADS

SOUFFLES

CREPES

ICE CREAM

SORBETS

CHOCOLATE

OTHERS: FINISHED

MISCELLANEOUS

PASTRY TECHNIQUES:

Boiling, The Ten Steps of Bread Making (see page 259)

Boiling:

1. Bring the cooking liquid to a rapid boil.
2. Stir the contents.

YIELD: 29 pounds, 5 ounces.   Baker's Percentage.

INGREDIENTS:

Water	2 pounds	13
Molasses	1 pound, 8 ounces	10
Orange peels, dried	8 ounces	3
Anise, ground	3 ounces	1.25
Fennel, ground	2 ounces	0.80
Water	4 pounds	27
Yeast, compressed	2 ounces	0.80
Flour, rye	2 pounds, 8 ounces	17
Water	2 pounds	13
Yeast, compressed	10 ounces	4
Salt	4 ounces	1.60
Shortening, all-purpose	1 pound	6
Sugar, brown	2 pounds	13
Flour, bread	12 pounds, 8 ounces	83

METHOD OF PREPARATION:

1. *The day before:* Place the water (2 pounds), molasses, dried orange peels, ground anise, and ground fennel in a pot, and bring to a boil. Allow to stand overnight.
2. Gather the equipment and ingredients.
3. Mix additional water (4 pounds), yeast (2 ounces), and rye flour together; allow to rest 1½ hours, or until double in volume.
4. Place the remaining ingredients in a bowl; add the sponge and the boiled mixture.
5. Mix on medium speed for about 6 to 7 minutes, or until the dough clears the bowl.
6. Follow any steps of the 10 steps of bread making that remain (page 259).

Variation:

Round loaves

Sweet Dough

PASTRY TECHNIQUE:
The Ten Steps of Bread Making (see page 259)

HAZARDOUS FOOD:
Eggs

YIELD: 18 pounds, 9½ ounces. Baker's Percentage.

INGREDIENTS:

Ingredient	Amount	Baker's %
Sugar, granulated	1 pound, 8 ounces	17
Dry milk solids (DMS)	8 ounces	5.50
Salt	2½ ounces	1.70
Shortening, all-purpose	1 pound, 8 ounces	17
Eggs, whole	1 pound	11
Water	4 pounds	44.40
Yeast, compressed	14 ounces	1.0
Color, egg shade	5 drops	0.10
Compound or flavor, lemon	1 ounce	0.10
Flour, bread	9 pounds	100

METHOD OF PREPARATION:

1. Gather the equipment and ingredients.
2. Follow the 10 steps of bread making (page 259).

Tuscan

COOKIES

BREADS

SOUFFLES

CREPES

ICE CREAM

SORBETS

CHOCOLATE

OTHERS: FINISHED

MISCELLANEOUS

PASTRY TECHNIQUE:

The Ten Steps of Bread Making (see page 259)

YIELD:	24 pounds, 5½ ounces.	Baker's Percentage.
INGREDIENTS:		
Flour, high-gluten	12 pounds, 8 ounces	100
Biga (see page 265)	2 pounds, 8 ounces	20
Water	8 pounds	64
Oil, olive	8 ounces	4
Yeast, compressed	10 ounces	5
Salt	3½ ounces	1.75

METHOD OF PREPARATION:

1. Gather the equipment and ingredients.
2. Follow the 10 steps of bread making (see page 259).

Vienna Bread

PASTRY TECHNIQUE:

The Ten Steps of Bread Making (see page 259)

HAZARDOUS FOOD:

Eggs

YIELD: 16 pounds, 11¼ ounces.   Baker's Percentage.

INGREDIENTS:

Flour, high-gluten, sifted	10 pounds	100
Water (variable)	5 pounds, 2 ounces	51
Oil, vegetable	4 ounces	2.50
Eggs, whole, or egg whites	4 ounces	2.50
Yeast, compressed	8 ounces	5
Sugar, sifted	6 ounces	3.70
Salt	3¼ ounces	2
Dough conditioner (optional)	2 ounces	1.25
Malt syrup (optional)	2 ounces	1.25

METHOD OF PREPARATION:

1. Gather the equipment and ingredients.
2. Follow the 10 steps of bread making (page 259).

Variations:

1. Braid, three-strand
2. Loaves
3. Rolls

COOKIES

BREADS

SOUFFLES

CREPES

ICE CREAM

SORBETS

CHOCOLATE

OTHERS: FINISHED

MISCELLANEOUS

PASTRY TECHNIQUE:
The Ten Steps of Bread Making (see page 259)

100% Whole Wheat Dough

YIELD:	18 pounds, 6½ ounces.	Baker's Percentage.

INGREDIENTS:

Flour, whole wheat, sifted	10 pounds	100
Sugar, granulated	11 ounces	7
Yeast, compressed	9½ ounces	6
Dried milk solids (DMS)	5 ounces	3
Salt	3 ounces	2
Water (variable)	5 pounds, 13 ounces	58
Malt syrup	5 ounces	3
Shortening, all-purpose	8 ounces	5

METHOD OF PREPARATION:

1. Gather the equipment and ingredients.
2. Follow the 10 steps of bread making (see page 259).

Variations:

1. Pullman loaves
2. Rolls
3. Boulé
4. Baguettes, batards

PASTRY TECHNIQUE:
The Ten Steps of Bread Making (see page 259), Frying

Frying:
1. Heat the frying liquid to the appropriate temperature.
2. Place the food product into the hot liquid.
3. Cook the product, turning frequently, until golden brown and tender.

HAZARDOUS FOOD:

Eggs

Yeast-Raised Doughnuts

YIELD: 7 pounds, 5¼ ounces. Baker's Percentage.

INGREDIENTS:

Eggs, whole	6 ounces	11
Water (variable)	2 pounds	57
Extract, vanilla	1 ounce	2
Flour, bread	3 pounds, 8 ounces	100
Sugar, granulated	8 ounces	14
Salt	1 ounce	2
Dry milk solids (DMS)	3 ounces	5.5
Mace	¼ ounce	0.5
Yeast, compressed	4 ounces	7.5
Shortening, all-purpose	6 ounces	11
Oil, vegetable (for frying)	As needed	—

METHOD OF PREPARATION:

1. Gather the equipment and ingredients.
2. In a separate bowl, mix together all of the liquid ingredients: eggs, water, and vanilla extract.
3. Place all of the liquids in a bowl; then add all of the dry ingredients on top, except the shortening; mix on low speed until slightly incorporated.
4. Add the shortening, and mix until incorporated.
5. Mix on medium speed until fully developed.
6. Proof.
7. Scale.
8. Round up.
9. Let the dough rest for 15 to 20 minutes.
10. Make up, as demonstrated by the instructor.
11. Place on screens.
12. Final proof until three fourths of maximum size.
13. Fry, as demonstrated by the instructor, in fresh oil at 360° F to 370° F (2½ minutes total time).
14. Cool slightly.
15. Garnish or glaze, as demonstrated by the instructor.

Apple Date Muffins

YIELD:	8 pounds, 2⅜ ounces.	16 pounds, 4¾ ounces.

COOKIES
BREADS
SOUFFLES
CREPES
ICE CREAM
SORBETS
CHOCOLATE
OTHERS: FINISHED
MISCELLANEOUS

PASTRY TECHNIQUE:
Creaming

Creaming:
1. Soften the fats on low speed.
2. Add the sugar(s) and cream; increase the speed slowly.
3. Add the eggs one at a time; scrape the bowl frequently.
4. Add the dry ingredients in stages.

HAZARDOUS FOOD:

Eggs

INGREDIENTS:

Ingredient		
Butter, unsalted	1 pound	2 pounds
Sugar, brown	1 pound, 4 ounces	2 pounds, 8 ounces
Eggs, whole	7 ounces	14 ounces
Flour, all-purpose	1 pound, 4 ounces	2 pounds, 8 ounces
Baking powder	⅝ ounce	1¼ ounces
Cinnamon, ground	¼ ounce	½ ounce
Salt	¼ ounce	½ ounce
Applesauce	1 pound, 2 ounces	2 pounds, 4 ounces
Dates, chopped	1 pound, 8 ounces	3 pounds
Oats, rolled, regular	1 pound	2 pounds

METHOD OF PREPARATION:

1. Gather the equipment and ingredients.
2. Place the butter and brown sugar in a bowl with a paddle; cream together.
3. Add the eggs gradually until blended.
4. Sift the dry ingredients together: all-purpose flour, baking powder, cinnamon, and salt.
5. Slowly add the dry ingredients to the sugar-egg mixture alternately with applesauce until blended. *Do not overmix.*
6. Slowly add the dates and oats until blended.
7. Place the batter in well-greased muffin tins.
8. Bake at 375° F for 25 minutes, or until a muffin springs back when lightly touched.

293

PASTRY TECHNIQUE:

Blending

Blending:

1. Combine the dry ingredients on low speed.
2. Add the softened fat(s) and liquid(s).
3. Mix the ingredients on low speed.
4. Increase the speed gradually.

HAZARDOUS FOOD:

Eggs

Apple Walnut Bread

YIELD: 18 pounds, 6½ ounces.   36 pounds, 13 ounces.

INGREDIENTS:

Flour, pastry	5 pounds	10 pounds
Sugar, granulated	3 pounds, 5 ounces	6 pounds, 10 ounces
Baking powder	4 ounces	8 ounces
Salt	1 ounce	2 ounces
Cinnamon, ground	½ ounce	1 ounce
Eggs, whole	1 pound	2 pounds
Applesauce	5 pound, 8 ounces	11 pounds
Butter, unsalted, melted	8 ounces	1 pound
Walnuts, chopped	2 pounds, 12 ounces	5 pounds, 8 ounces

METHOD OF PREPARATION:

1. Gather the equipment and ingredients.
2. Sift together all of the dry ingredients: pastry flour, granulated sugar, baking powder, salt, and cinnamon.
3. Place the dry ingredients in a bowl.
4. Combine the eggs and applesauce.
5. Add the liquid ingredients to the dry ingredients. Using a paddle attachment, mix only enough to incorporate; do not remove.
6. Add the melted butter.
7. Add the walnuts; combine.
8. Scale at 1 pound, 6 ounces for small loaves or 2 pounds, 8 ounces for large loaves. Pans should be well greased.
9. Bake at 350° F for 45 to 55 minutes, or until loaves are golden brown and firm in center.

PASTRY TECHNIQUES:
Rubbing, Combining, Rolling

Rubbing:
1. Use a pastry cutter to keep the fat in large pieces.
2. Add the liquid in stages.

Combining:
Bringing together two or more components.
1. Prepare the components to be combined.
2. Add one to the other, using the appropriate mixing method (if needed).

Rolling:
1. Prepare the rolling surface by dusting with the appropriate medium (flour, cornstarch, etc.).
2. Use the appropriate style pin (stick pin or ball bearing pin) to roll the dough to desired thickness; rotate the dough during rolling to prevent sticking.

HAZARDOUS FOOD:

Eggs

Baking Powder Biscuits

YIELD:	2 pounds, 11¼ ounces.	5 pounds, 6½ ounces.
INGREDIENTS:		
Flour, bread	10 ounces	1 pound, 4 ounces
Flour, cake	10 ounces	1 pound, 4 ounces
Sugar, granulated	1½ ounces	3 ounces
Dry milk solids (DMS)	1½ ounces	3 ounces
Baking powder	1¼ ounces	2½ ounces
Salt	¼ ounce	½ ounce
Shortening, all-purpose	5 ounces	10 ounces
Water, cold	11¾ ounces	1 pound, 7½ ounces
Eggs, whole	2 ounces	4 ounces
Flour, bread, additional	As needed	As needed

METHOD OF PREPARATION:

1. Gather the equipment and ingredients.
2. Sift the dry ingredients together: bread flour, cake flour, granulated sugar, DMS, baking powder, and salt; place in a bowl.
3. Add the shortening. Using your hands, mix the dough until the shortening is broken into pieces about the size of peas.
4. Mix the water and eggs together.
5. Add the liquid to the mixture, and mix lightly. *Do not overmix or overwork* this dough.
6. Place the dough on a bench on a thin layer of bread flour.
7. Using a rolling pin, bench pin, or your hands, roll or press the dough to a 1-inch thickness.
8. With a standard biscuit cutter, cut out biscuits close together to avoid leaving excess scraps.
9. Place the biscuits 1-inch apart on parchment-lined sheet pans. If desired, allow the dough to relax for 10 to 15 minutes before baking.
10. Bake at 425° F for 10 to 15 minutes, or until golden brown.

COOKIES

BREADS

SOUFFLES

CREPES

ICE CREAM

SORBETS

CHOCOLATE

OTHERS: FINISHED

MISCELLANEOUS

PASTRY TECHNIQUES:
Creaming, Combining

Creaming:
1. Soften the fats on low speed.
2. Add the sugar(s) and cream; increase the speed slowly.
3. Add the eggs one at a time; scrape the bowl frequently.
4. Add the dry ingredients in stages.

Combining:
Bringing together two or more components.
1. Prepare the components to be combined.
2. Add one to the other, using the appropriate mixing method (if needed).

HAZARDOUS FOOD:
Eggs

Banana Nut Bread No. 1

YIELD:	6 pounds, 3⅝ ounces.	12 pounds, 7¼ ounces.
INGREDIENTS:		
Sugar, granulated	1 pound, 4 ounces	2 pounds, 8 ounces
Shortening, high-ratio	6 ounces	12 ounces
Baking soda, sifted	½ ounce	1 ounce
Lemon powder	½ ounce	1 ounce
Salt	⅛ ounce	¼ ounce
Bananas, fresh or canned, mashed	8 ounces	1 pound
Eggs, whole	2 ounces	4 ounces
Water, cold	1 pound, 8 ounces	3 pounds
Flour, bread, sifted	1 pound	2 pounds
Flour, cake, sifted	1 pound	2 pounds
Baking powder, sifted	½ ounce	1 ounce
Nuts, finely chopped	4 ounces	8 ounces
Compound, banana	2 ounces	4 ounces

METHOD OF PREPARATION:

1. Gather the equipment and ingredients.
2. Place the granulated sugar, shortening, baking soda, lemon powder, and salt in a bowl; paddle for 2 minutes.
3. Add the bananas and eggs to the mixture in the bowl; cream for an additional 1 minute.
4. Add one third the amount of the water, and mix at low speed.
5. Sift together the flours and baking powder.
6. Add the sifted ingredients to the mixture in two stages. Mix at low speed.
7. Add one third of the water, and mix only until everything is incorporated; *do not overmix.*
8. Scrape the bowl well.
9. Add the chopped nuts and banana compound.
10. Add the remaining third of water; mix until incorporated.
11. Scale at 1 pound, 6 ounces for small loaves or 2 pounds, 8 ounces for large loaf pans.
12. Bake at 375° F until the loaves are light brown overall and firm in the center.
13. Cool.
14. Remove from the pans.

COOKIES

BREADS

SOUFFLES

CREPES

ICE CREAM

SORBETS

CHOCOLATE

OTHERS: FINISHED

MISCELLANEOUS

PASTRY TECHNIQUE:
Blending

Blending:
1. Combine the dry ingredients on low speed.
2. Add the softened fat(s) and liquid(s).
3. Mix the ingredients on low speed.
4. Increase the speed gradually.

HAZARDOUS FOOD:
Eggs

Banana Nut Bread No. 2

YIELD:	17 pounds, 4½ ounces.	34 pounds, 8½ ounces.

INGREDIENTS:		
Flour, bread	1 pound	2 pounds
Flour, pastry	4 pounds	8 pounds
Sugar, granulated	2 pounds	4 pounds
Baking powder	4 ounces	8 ounces
Baking soda	¾ ounce	1½ ounces
Salt	1 ounce	2 ounces
Bananas, fresh or canned, mashed	5 pounds	10 pounds
Eggs, whole	2 pounds	4 pounds
Oil, vegetable	1 pound, 10½ ounces	3 pounds, 5 ounces
Nuts, chopped (optional)	1 pound, 4 ounces	2 pounds, 8 ounces

METHOD OF PREPARATION:

1. Gather the equipment and ingredients.
2. Sift together all the dry ingredients: bread flour, pastry flour, granulated sugar, baking powder, baking soda, and salt.
3. Place the dry ingredients in a bowl with a paddle.
4. Add the bananas, and combine.
5. Combine the eggs, oil, and nuts (optional).
6. Add the liquid ingredients to the mixture; combine. *Do not overmix.*
7. Scale at 1 pound, 6 ounces for small loaves or 2 pounds, 8 ounces for large loaves. Pans should be lightly greased.
8. Bake at 350° F for 35 to 40 minutes, or until golden brown.

Basic Muffins

Oil Mix

PASTRY TECHNIQUE:
Blending

Blending:
1. Combine the dry ingredients on low speed.
2. Add the softened fat(s) and liquid(s).
3. Mix the ingredients on low speed.
4. Increase the speed gradually.

HAZARDOUS FOOD:
Eggs

YIELD:	6 Dozen Muffins.	12 Dozen Muffins.
INGREDIENTS:		
Sugar, granulated	2 pounds, 8 ounces	5 pounds
Salt	¾ ounce	1½ ounces
Eggs, whole	1 pound	2 pounds
Oil, vegetable	1 pound, 8 ounces	3 pounds
Water	2 pounds, 8 ounces	5 pounds
Flour, high-gluten, sifted	4 pounds, 12 ounces	9 pounds, 8 ounces
Baking powder, sifted	3¼ ounces	6½ ounces
Dry milk solids (DMS)	8 ounces	1 pound
Compound, lemon	2 ounces	4 ounces
Compound, orange	2 ounces	4 ounces
Fruit (optional)	See variations 1½ lbs.	See variations 3 lbs.

METHOD OF PREPARATION:

1. Gather the equipment and ingredients.
2. Put the sugar and salt in a bowl.
3. Using the paddle to mix, add the eggs slowly, and blend well.
4. Add the oil on low speed.
5. Add the water on low speed.
6. Sift all of the dry ingredients together.
7. Add the dry ingredients; mix just enough to incorporate; this batter should be rough, with small lumps.
8. If adding fruit to the mix, dredge it first with flour to prevent it from bleeding color into the batter. Fold in the fruit.
9. Drop 3 ounces of batter into greased muffin tins or to three-fourths full.
10. Bake at 400° F for 20 minutes, or until light brown overall and firm in the center.

Variations:

1. *Blueberry Muffins* (with frozen blueberries):
   a. ¾ quart (6 dozen muffins)
   b. 1½ quart (12 dozen muffins)
2. *Cranberry Muffins* (with frozen cranberries):
   a. 1 pound (6 dozen muffins)
   b. 2 pounds (12 dozen muffins)
3. *Spiced Apple Muffins:*
   a. Place an apple slice in each cup.
   b. Sprinkle the tops with cinnamon-sugar mixture.

COOKIES
BREADS
SOUFFLES
CREPES
ICE CREAM
SORBETS
CHOCOLATE
OTHERS: FINISHED
MISCELLANEOUS

Buttermilk Biscuits

PASTRY TECHNIQUES:
Combining, Rolling

Combining:

Bringing together two or more components.
1. Prepare the components to be combined.
2. Add one to the other, using the appropriate mixing method (if needed).

Rolling:

1. Prepare the rolling surface by dusting with the appropriate medium (flour, cornstarch, etc.).
2. Use the appropriate style pin (stick pin or ball bearing pin) to roll the dough to desired thickness; rotate the dough during rolling to prevent sticking.

HAZARDOUS FOODS:
Eggs
Buttermilk

YIELD:

	6 pounds, 14½ ounces. 4 Dozen	13 pounds, 13 ounces. 8 Dozen
INGREDIENTS:		
Sugar, granulated	8 ounces	1 pound
Salt	½ ounce	1 ounce
Dry milk solids (DMS)	4 ounces	8 ounces
Baking powder, sifted	3 ounces	6 ounces
Flour, bread, sifted	1 pound, 10 ounces	3 pounds, 4 ounces
Flour, pastry, sifted	1 pound, 10 ounces	3 pounds, 4 ounces
Shortening, all-purpose	5 ounces	10 ounces
Margarine or butter, unsalted	6 ounces	12 ounces
Eggs, whole	5 ounces	10 ounces
Extract, vanilla	1 ounce	2 ounces
Water	10 ounces	1 pound, 4 ounces
Buttermilk	1 pound	2 pounds
Flour, pastry or flour	As needed	As needed
Egg wash (see page 411)	As needed	As needed

METHOD OF PREPARATION:

1. Gather the equipment and ingredients.
2. Sift all the dry ingredients together: granulated sugar, salt, DMS, baking powder, bread flour, and pastry flour; place in a dry bowl.
3. Add the fats to the dry ingredients, and mix until crumbly in texture.
4. Combine all of the liquid ingredients together: eggs, vanilla extract, water, and buttermilk.
5. Add the liquid ingredients to the mixture, and mix only until blended.
6. Place the dough on a floured surface, and cover with parchment.
7. Allow to relax for 15 to 20 minutes at room temperature.
8. Roll out the dough to a 1-inch thickness.
9. Cut using a standard biscuit cutter.
10. Place on parchment-lined sheet pans.
11. Egg-wash the tops.
12. Bake at 360° F until raised and the tops are golden brown.

Buttermilk Scones

Combining, Rolling

Combining:

Bringing together two or more components.
1. Prepare the components to be combined.
2. Add one to the other, using the appropriate mixing method (if needed).

Rolling:

1. Prepare the rolling surface by dusting with the appropriate medium (flour, cornstarch, etc.).
2. Use the appropriate style pin (stick pin or ball bearing pin) to roll the dough to desired thickness; rotate the dough during rolling to prevent sticking.

HAZARDOUS FOOD:

Buttermilk

YIELD:	5 pounds, 6⅛ ounces.	10 pounds, 12¼ ounces.
INGREDIENTS:		
Flour, bread	1 pound, 14 ounces	3 pounds, 12 ounces
Flour, cake	10 ounces	1 pound, 4 ounces
Salt	¼ ounce	½ ounce
Sugar, granulated	5¼ ounces	10½ ounces
Baking powder	1⅞ ounces	3¾ ounces
Butter, unsalted	10 ounces	1 pound, 4 ounces
Buttermilk	1 pound, 4 ounces	2 pounds, 8 ounces
Currants	8¾ ounces	1 pound, 1½ ounces
Flour, bread or cake	As needed	As needed
Egg wash (see page 411)	As needed	As needed

METHOD OF PREPARATION:

1. Gather the equipment and ingredients.
2. Sift all of the dry ingredients together: bread flour, cake flour, salt, granulated sugar, and baking powder.
3. Place the dry ingredients in a bowl.
4. Add the butter. Using your hands, mix the dough until the butter is broken into pieces about the size of peas.
5. Add the buttermilk to the mixture, and mix lightly.
6. Add the currants; *do not overmix* or *overwork* this dough.
7. Place the dough on a floured surface; allow it to rest for 15 minutes.
8. Using a rolling pin, bench pin, or your hands, roll or press the dough to a 1-inch thickness.
9. With a standard biscuit cutter, cut out biscuits close together to avoid leaving excess scraps.
10. Place the biscuits 1-inch apart on parchment-lined sheet pans.
11. Egg-wash the tops.
12. Bake at 425° F for 10 to 15 minutes, or until golden brown.

COOKIES

BREADS

SOUFFLES

CREPES

ICE CREAM

SORBETS

CHOCOLATE

OTHERS: FINISHED

MISCELLANEOUS

Carrot Apple Muffins

PASTRY TECHNIQUE:
Blending

Blending:
1. Combine the dry ingredients on low speed.
2. Add the softened fat(s) and liquid(s).
3. Mix the ingredients on low speed.
4. Increase the speed gradually.

HAZARDOUS FOOD:
Eggs

YIELD:	6 pounds, 11¾ ounces.	13 pounds, 7½ ounces.
INGREDIENTS:		
Flour, pastry, sifted	12 ounces	1 pound, 8 ounces
Flour, bread, sifted	5 ½ ounces	11 ounces
Sugar, granulated	1 pound, 4 ounces	2 pounds, 8 ounces
Salt	⅜ ounce	¾ ounce
Baking soda	¾ ounce	1½ ounces
Cinnamon, ground	¾ ounce	1½ ounces
Eggs, whole	9 ounces	1 pound, 2 ounces
Oil, vegetable	14 ounces	1 pound, 12 ounces
Extract, vanilla	½ ounce	1 ounce
Raisins, seedless	6 ounces	12 ounces
Coconut, shredded	3 ounces	6 ounces
Apples, shredded	12 ounces	1 pound, 8 ounces
Carrots, shredded	1 pound, 4 ounces	2 pounds, 8 ounces
Walnuts, chopped	4 ounces	8 ounces

METHOD OF PREPARATION:
1. Gather the equipment and ingredients.
2. Sift together all of the dry ingredients: pastry flour, bread flour, granulated sugar, salt, baking soda, and cinnamon.
3. Place the dry ingredients in a bowl.
4. Combine all of the liquid ingredients: eggs, salad oil, and vanilla extract.
5. Add the liquid ingredients to the dry ingredients using a paddle attachment. Mix only enough to incorporate; *do not overmix.*
6. Add the raisins and coconut; mix well.
7. Add the shredded apples, carrots, and walnuts; combine.
8. Drop into greased muffin tins to three-fourths full.
9. Bake at 360° F for 25 to 30 minutes, or until they are golden brown overall and firm in the center.

PASTRY TECHNIQUE:
Blending

Blending:
1. Combine the dry ingredients on low speed.
2. Add the softened fat(s) and liquid(s).
3. Mix the ingredients on low speed.
4. Increase the speed gradually.

HAZARDOUS FOOD:

Eggs

Carrot Pineapple Muffins

YIELD:	7 pounds, 15¼ ounces.	15 pounds, 14⅝ ounces.
INGREDIENTS:		
Butter, unsalted	12 ounces	1 pound, 8 ounces
Sugar, granulated	1 pound, 12 ounces	3 pounds, 8 ounces
Baking powder	1¼ ounces	2½ ounces
Salt	¾ ounce	1½ ounces
Eggs, whole	1 pound	2 pounds
Oil, vegetable	12 ounces	1 pound, 8 ounces
Flour, cake	8 ounces	1 pound
Flour, bread	1 pound	2 pounds
Cinnamon, ground	¼ ounce	½ ounce
Nutmeg, ground	Pinch	⅛ ounce
Carrots, grated	1 pound, 8 ounces	3 pounds
Pineapple, chopped	2 ounces	4 ounces
Walnuts, chopped	2 ounces	4 ounces
Coconut, shredded, sweet	2 ounces	4 ounces
Raisins	3 ounces	6 ounces
Flour, bread	As needed	As needed

METHOD OF PREPARATION:

1. Gather the equipment and ingredients.
2. Place the butter in a bowl, and cream with a paddle until soft.
3. Add the granulated sugar, baking powder, and salt; combine.
4. Add the eggs slowly until combined.
5. Add the oil slowly; mix until incorporated.
6. Sift the dry ingredients together: cake flour, bread flour, cinnamon, and nutmeg.
7. Add the dry ingredients to the cream; combine only until smooth. *Do not overmix.*
8. Add the grated carrots, chopped pineapple, chopped walnuts, shredded sweet coconut, and raisins. (Dredge the raisins in flour to help suspend them in the batter.) Mix only until incorporated. *Do not overmix.*
9. Drop into greased muffin tins to ¾ full.
10. Bake at 400° F for 20 minutes, or until the muffins spring back where lightly touched.

COOKIES
BREADS
SOUFFLES
CREPES
ICE CREAM
SORBETS
CHOCOLATE
OTHERS: FINISHED
MISCELLANEOUS

Corn Bread

PASTRY TECHNIQUE:
Blending

Blending:
1. Combine the dry ingredients on low speed.
2. Add the softened fat(s) and liquid(s).
3. Mix the ingredients on low speed.
4. Increase the speed gradually.

HAZARDOUS FOOD:
Eggs

YIELD:

	4 pounds, 10⅞ ounces. ½ sheet pan	9 pounds, 5¾ ounces. 1 sheet pan

INGREDIENTS:

Flour, bread, sifted	14 ounces	1 pound, 12 ounces
Flour, pastry, sifted	6 ounces	12 ounces
Baking powder	1⅜ ounces	2¾ ounces
Salt	½ ounce	1 ounce
Dry milk solids (DMS)	3 ounces	6 ounces
Cornmeal	8 ounces	1 pound
Sugar, granulated	13 ounces	1 pound, 10 ounces
Water	15 ounces	1 pound, 14 ounces
Eggs, whole	8 ounces	1 pound
Oil, vegetable	6 ounces	12 ounces

METHOD OF PREPARATION:

1. Gather the equipment and ingredients.
2. Sift the dry ingredients together: bread flour, pastry flour, baking powder, salt, DMS, cornmeal, and granulated sugar.
3. Place all of the dry ingredients in bowl.
4. Mix the water and eggs together.
5. Add the water-egg mixture to the dry ingredients only until combined.
6. Add the oil, and mix just enough to mix together.
7. Scale out the batter into lightly greased sheet pans.
8. Bake at 370° F for approximately 22 to 25 minutes.

CHEF NOTE:
This batter also can be used to make corn muffins.

Creaming:

1. Soften the fats on low speed.
2. Add the sugar(s) and cream; increase the speed slowly.
3. Add the eggs one at a time; scrape the bowl frequently.
4. Add the dry ingredients in stages.

Combining:

Bringing together two or more components.
1. Prepare the components to be combined.
2. Add one to the other, using the appropriate mixing method (if needed).

HAZARDOUS FOOD:

Eggs

Cranberry Bread

YIELD:		4, 1-pound Loaves.	8, 1-pound Loaves.
INGREDIENTS:			
Sugar, granulated		11½ ounces	1 pound, 7 ounces
Shortening, high-ratio		3 ounces	6 ounces
Baking soda, sifted		¼ ounce	½ ounce
Salt		¼ ounce	½ ounce
Cinnamon, ground		¼ ounce	½ ounce
Eggs, whole		3½ ounces	7 ounces
Flour, bread		15 ounces	1 pound, 14 ounces
Flour, cake		4½ ounces	9 ounces
Baking powder		½ ounce	1 ounces
Water		13½ ounces	1 pound, 11 ounces
Cranberries		8 ounces	1 pound
Oranges, peeled, rind and juice		1½ each	3 each
Pecans, chopped		3 ounces	6 ounces
Compound, orange		1 ounce	2 ounces
Compound, lemon		1 ounce	2 ounces

METHOD OF PREPARATION:

1. Gather the equipment and ingredients.
2. Place the granulated sugar, shortening, baking soda, salt, and cinnamon in a bowl; cream with a paddle for 3 minutes on medium speed.
3. Add the whole eggs gradually; mix for 3 minutes at medium speed.
4. Sift together the bread flour, cake flour, and baking powder.
5. Alternately add the dry ingredients and water into the cream mixture.
6. Mix on slow speed for 3 minutes, and scrape the bowl well.
7. Coarsely grind the cranberries, and drain the juice.
8. Grate the orange rind, and extract the juice; reserve.
9. Add the cranberries, orange rind, orange juice, nuts, orange compound, and lemon compound to the mixture; mix only until incorporated.
10. Scale 1 pound of batter into greased loaf pans.
11. Place the pans on sheet pans, and bake at 380° F until light brown overall and firm in the center.
12. Cool, and remove from the loaf pans.

CHEF NOTE:

Other types of fruit, such as dates, raisins, blueberries, or raspberries, can be used in place of cranberries and oranges.

Irish Soda Bread

COOKIES

BREADS

SOUFFLES

CREPES

ICE CREAM

SORBETS

CHOCOLATE

OTHERS: FINISHED

MISCELLANEOUS

PASTRY TECHNIQUE:
Combining, Shaping

Combining:
Bringing together two or more components.
1. Prepare the components to be combined.
2. Add one to the other, using the appropriate mixing method (if needed).

Shaping:
1. Prepare the medium to be shaped.
2. Prepare the surface area for shaping.
3. Mold medium into desired shapes according to the instructor's directions.

HAZARDOUS FOOD:
Buttermilk

YIELD: 24 pounds, 11 ounces. Baker's Percentage.

INGREDIENTS:

Flour, bread	7 pounds	70
Flour, whole wheat	3 pounds	30
Salt	4 ounces	2.50
Caraway	4 ounces	2.50
Baking powder	2 ounces	1.25
Baking soda	1 ounce	0.62
Butter, unsalted	1 pound	10
Buttermilk	8 pounds	80
Currants	5 pounds	50
Flour, white rye	As needed	

METHOD OF PREPARATION:

1. Gather the equipment and ingredients.
2. Place all of the dry ingredients on a surface, and cut butter into the flour until a mealy consistency is achieved.
3. Add the buttermilk until incorporated.
4. Add the currants, and blend slightly.
5. Scale, as instructed. Dust with white rye flour; score a deep X into the top of each loaf.
6. Bake at 425° F until lightly browned.

PASTRY TECHNIQUE:
Creaming

Creaming:
1. Soften the fats on low speed.
2. Add the sugar(s) and cream; increase the speed slowly.
3. Add the eggs one at a time; scrape the bowl frequently.
4. Add the dry ingredients in stages.

HAZARDOUS FOODS:

Eggs
Milk

Lemon–Poppy Seed Muffins

YIELD:	9 pounds, 3⅞ ounces.	18 pounds, 6¾ ounces.
INGREDIENTS:		
Sugar, granulated	1 pound, 13 ounces	3 pounds, 10 ounces
Butter, unsalted, softened	11½ ounces	1 pound, 7 ounces
Shortening, high-ratio	7 ounces	14 ounces
Salt	⅝ ounce	1¼ ounces
Eggs, whole	1 pound, 2 ounces	2 pounds, 4 ounces
Seeds, poppy	2 ounces	4 ounces
Flour, bread	1 pound, 8 ounces	3 pounds
Flour, pastry	1 pound	2 pounds
Baking powder	2 ounces	4 ounces
Milk, whole	1 pound, 15 ounces	3 pounds, 14 ounces
Lemon juice	2¼ ounces	4½ ounces
Lemon rind	4½ ounces	9 ounces

METHOD OF PREPARATION:

1. Gather the equipment and ingredients.
2. Place the granulated sugar, softened butter, shortening, and salt in bowl with a paddle, and cream together.
3. Add the eggs gradually until blended.
4. Add the poppy seeds to the mixture; combine.
5. Sift the dry ingredients together: bread flour, pastry flour, and baking powder.
6. Combine the milk, lemon juice, and lemon rind.
7. Slowly add the dry ingredients to the sugar-egg mixture alternately with the milk mixture until blended. *Do not overmix.*
8. Drop into greased muffin tins to ¾ full.
9. Bake at 375° F for about 20 minutes, or until the muffins spring back when lightly touched.

Quick Coffee Cake

COOKIES

BREADS

SOUFFLES

CREPES

ICE CREAM

SORBETS

CHOCOLATE

OTHERS: FINISHED

MISCELLANEOUS

PASTRY TECHNIQUE:

Blending

Blending:

1. Combine the dry ingredients on low speed.
2. Add the softened fat(s) and liquid(s).
3. Mix the ingredients on low speed.
4. Increase the speed gradually.

HAZARDOUS FOOD:

Eggs

YIELD:	6 pounds. 1 Sheet Pan	12 pounds. 2 Sheet Pans
INGREDIENTS:		
Eggs, whole	10 ounces	1 pound, 4 ounces
Oil, vegetable	12 ounces	1 pound, 8 ounces
Extract, vanilla	To taste	To taste
Water	1 pound, 8 ounces	3 pounds
Flour, pastry, sifted	1 pound, 12 ounces	3 pounds, 8 ounces
Baking powder	1¼ ounces	2½ ounces
Dry milk solids (DMS)	3 ounces	6 ounces
Salt	½ ounce	1 ounce
Sugar, granulated	1 pound, 8 ounces	3 pounds

METHOD OF PREPARATION:

1. Gather the equipment and ingredients.
2. Place the whole eggs, oil, vanilla extract, and water in a bowl; combine well.
3. Sift together the pastry flour, baking powder, DMS, salt, and sugar.
4. Add the sifted dry ingredients to the liquids, and mix lightly.
5. Scale into parchment-lined sheet pans.
6. Spread evenly.
7. Bake at 375° F until light golden brown.

Variations:

1. *Streusel Topping:*
   a. If used, sprinkle on the top of the cake.
   b. Bake.
2. *Fruit Topping:*
   a. Remove the finished cake from the oven, and allow it to cool before topping.
   b. Top with desired fruit, and add a layer of streusel.
   c. Return to the oven to brown the streusel.
   d. Use double sheet pans when browning the streusel to prevent excessive browning of the bottom of the cake.

Pumpkin Muffins

PASTRY TECHNIQUE:
Blending

Blending:
1. Combine the dry ingredients on low speed.
2. Add the softened fat(s) and liquid(s).
3. Mix the ingredients on low speed.
4. Increase the speed gradually.

HAZARDOUS FOOD:
Eggs

YIELD:	4 pounds, ¾ ounce.	8 pounds, 1½ ounces.
INGREDIENTS:		
Purée, pumpkin	14ounces	1 pound, 12 ounces
Sugar, granulated	1 pound, 2 ounces	2 pounds, 4 ounces
Flour, bread	14 ounces	1 pound, 12 ounces
Flour, pastry	2 ounces	4 ounces
Baking soda	⅛ ounce	⅜ ounce
Baking powder	¼ ounce	⅝ ounce
Salt	¼ ounce	½ ounce
Cinnamon, ground	⅛ ounce	¼ ounce
Eggs, whole	6 ounces	12 ounces
Oil, vegetable	6 ounces	12 ounces
Water	4 ounces	8 ounces

METHOD OF PREPARATION:

1. Gather the equipment and ingredients.
2. Place the pumpkin purée, granulated sugar, bread flour, pastry flour, baking soda, baking powder, salt, and cinnamon in a bowl; blend well using a paddle implement.
3. Scrape the bowl well.
4. Combine the eggs, oil, and water.
5. Add the liquid mixture to the pumpkin mixture in three stages, scraping the bowl after each addition.
6. Drop into greased muffin tins to ¾ full.
7. Bake at 360° F for 25 to 30 minutes, or until golden brown and firm in the center.

Scones

COOKIES

BREADS

SOUFFLES

CREPES

ICE CREAM

SORBETS

CHOCOLATE

OTHERS: FINISHED

MISCELLANEOUS

PASTRY TECHNIQUES:

Combining, Rolling

Combining:

Bringing together two or more components.
1. Prepare the components to be combined.
2. Add one to the other, using the appropriate mixing method (if needed).

Rolling:

1. Prepare the rolling surface by dusting with the appropriate medium (flour, cornstarch, etc.).
2. Use the appropriate style pin (stick pin or ball bearing pin) to roll the dough to desired thickness; rotate the dough during rolling to prevent sticking.

HAZARDOUS FOODS:

Heavy cream
Eggs
Egg yolks

YIELD:	6 pounds, 13½ ounces.	13 pounds, 11 ounces.
INGREDIENTS:		
Flour, bread	2 pounds, 8 ounces	5 pounds
Salt	⅝ ounce	1⅜ ounces
Sugar, granulated	2 ounces	4 ounces
Baking powder	1⅜ ounces	2¾ ounces
Butter, unsalted	8½ ounces	1 pound, 1 ounce
Cream, heavy	1 pound, 2½ ounces	2 pounds, 5 ounces
Eggs, whole	14½ ounces	1 pound, 13 ounces
Egg yolks	2¾ ounces	5½ ounces
Currants, conditioned	1 pound, 3¼ ounces	2 pounds, 6½ ounces
Flour, bread	As needed	As needed
Egg wash (see page 411)	As needed	As needed

METHOD OF PREPARATION:

1. Gather the equipment and ingredients.
2. Sift all of the dry ingredients: bread flour, salt, granulated sugar, and baking powder; place in a bowl.
3. Add the butter; using your hands, mix the dough until the butter is broken into pieces about the size of peas.
4. Combine the heavy cream, whole eggs, and egg yolks.
5. Add the liquid ingredients to the dry mixture; mix lightly.
6. Add the currants; *do not overmix* or overwork this dough.
7. Place the dough on a lightly floured surface.
8. Then let it rest in refrigerator for 15 minutes.
9. Using a rolling pin, bench pin, or your hands, roll or press the dough to a 1-inch thickness.
10. With a standard biscuit cutter, cut out biscuits close together to avoid excess scraps.
11. Place 1-inch apart on parchment-lined sheet pans.
12. Egg-wash the tops.
13. Bake at 425° F for 10 to 15 minutes, or until golden brown.

PASTRY TECHNIQUE:
Creaming, Blending

Creaming:
1. Soften the fats on low speed.
2. Add the sugar(s) and cream; increase the speed slowly.
3. Add the eggs one at a time; scrape the bowl frequently.
4. Add the dry ingredients in stages.

Blending:
1. Combine the dry ingredients on low speed.
2. Add the softened fat(s) and liquid(s).
3. Mix the ingredients on low speed.
4. Increase the speed gradually.

HAZARDOUS FOODS:
Eggs
Sour cream

Sour Cream Muffins

YIELD:	4 pounds, 7⅝ ounces.	8 pounds, 15¼ ounces.

INGREDIENTS:

Butter, unsalted	3 ounces	6 ounces
Margarine	3 ounces	6 ounces
Sugar, granulated	1 pound, 1 ounce	2 pounds, 2 ounces
Salt	Pinch	⅛ ounce
Baking soda	⅝ ounce	1¼ ounces
Eggs, whole	8 ounces	1 pound
Flour, bread	1 pound, 4 ounces	2 pounds, 8 ounces
Sour cream	1 pound, 4 ounces	2 pounds, 8 ounces

METHOD OF PREPARATION:

1. Gather the equipment and ingredients.
2. Place the butter, margarine, granulated sugar, salt, and baking soda in a bowl; cream for 3 minutes.
3. Add the eggs to the ingredients in the bowl; cream for an additional 2 minutes.
4. Add the bread flour, and mix only until incorporated.
5. Blend in the sour cream, mixing for 1 minute.
6. Drop into greased muffin tins to three fourths of the way full.
7. Bake at 360° F for 25 to 30 minutes, or until golden brown and firm in the center.

COOKIES

BREADS

SOUFFLES

CREPES

ICE CREAM

SORBETS

CHOCOLATE

OTHERS: FINISHED

MISCELLANEOUS

PASTRY TECHNIQUE:
Blending

Blending:
1. Combine the dry ingredients on low speed.
2. Add the softened fat(s) and liquid(s).
3. Mix the ingredients on low speed.
4. Increase the speed gradually.

HAZARDOUS FOOD:
Eggs

Zucchini-Raisin-Walnut Quick Bread

YIELD:	14 pounds, 8 ounces.	29 pounds.

INGREDIENTS:

Zucchini	4 pounds	8 pounds
Sugar, granulated	2 pounds	4 pounds
Sugar, brown	1 pound, 4 ounces	2 pounds, 8 ounces
Oil, vegetable	1 pound, 4 ounces	2 pounds, 8 ounces
Eggs, whole	1 pound, 4 ounces	2 pounds, 8 ounces
Salt	½ ounce	1 ounce
Dry milk solids (DMS)	1½ ounces	3 ounces
Baking soda	½ ounce	1 ounce
Baking powder	1 ounce	2 ounces
Cinnamon, ground	¼ ounce	½ ounce
Nutmeg, ground	¼ ounce	½ ounce
Flour, bread	2 pounds, 6 ounces	4 pounds, 12 ounces
Flour, cake	8 ounces	1 pound
Walnuts, ground	14 ounces	1 pound, 12 ounces
Raisins	12 ounces	1 pound, 8 ounces

METHOD OF PREPARATION:

1. Gather the equipment and ingredients.
2. Wash and split zucchini in lengths, deseed, grate, and keep as dry as possible.
3. Place the granulated sugar, brown sugar, vegetable oil, and eggs in a bowl with a paddle, and combine.
4. Add the grated zucchini.
5. Sift all of the dry ingredients: salt, DMS, baking soda, baking powder, cinnamon, nutmeg, bread flour, and cake flour. Blend into the zucchini mixture just until moist.
6. Add the walnuts and raisins just until combined; *do not overmix.*
7. Place in pans, and run a trowel down the center before baking.
8. Bake at 375° F to 400° F for approximately 30 minutes, or until the bread springs back when lightly touched.

CHEF NOTE:
Zucchini should be washed and patted dry. Cut off ends and split in the length.

13

Soufflés

Soufflés

Apricot Soufflé

COOKIES
BREADS
SOUFFLES
CREPES
ICE CREAM
SORBETS
CHOCOLATE
MISCELLANEOUS | OTHERS: FINISHED

PASTRY TECHNIQUES:

Puréeing, Boiling, Combining, Whipping

Puréeing:

1. Do not overfill the food processor.
2. First pulse the food processor.
3. Turn food processor to maximum to purée food.

Boiling:

1. Bring the cooking liquid to a rapid boil.
2. Stir the contents.

Combining:

Bringing together two or more components.
1. Prepare the components to be combined.
2. Add one to the other, using the appropriate mixing method (if needed).

Whipping:

1. Hold the whip at a 55-degree angle.
2. Create circles, using a circular motion.
3. The circular motion needs to be perpendicular to the bowl.

HAZARDOUS FOOD:

Egg whites

YIELD:	2 pounds, 2 ounces.	4 pounds, 4 ounces.
INGREDIENTS:		
Apricots, large, dried	8 ounces	1 pound
Sugar, granulated	12 ounces	1 pound, 8 ounces
Water	2 ounces	4 ounces
Brandy, apricot	2 ounces	4 ounces
Egg whites	8 ounces	1 pound
Sugar, granulated, additional	2 ounces	4 ounces
Sugar, confectionery	As needed	As needed
Cocoa powder	As needed	As needed

METHOD OF PREPARATION:

1. Soak the apricots in cold water overnight.
2. Gather the equipment and ingredients.
3. Butter soufflé dishes, sprinkle with granulated sugar, and set aside.
4. Cook the apricots until tender.
5. Strain the apricots completely; it may be necessary to dry them slightly. Purée them completely; keep the purée warm.
6. Place the granulated sugar and water in a pot; boil them until they reach 250° F, to make a sugar syrup.
7. Combine the sugar syrup and puréed apricots; cook for a few minutes.
8. Add the apricot brandy to the mixture.
9. Place the egg whites in a bowl, and whip to a medium-stiff peak; slowly add the additional, granulated sugar to make a meringue.
10. Fold the meringue carefully into the apricot base.
11. Pour the mixture into prepared soufflé molds.
12. Bake at 400° F for 10 to 12 minutes, or until light golden brown and slightly firm. The soufflé should rise above the mold and have a rough appearance.
13. Dust with confectionery sugar and/or cocoa.
14. Serve immediately.

CHEF NOTE:

To prevent soufflé from collapsing, open the oven door for a minute before removing the soufflé to avoid a sudden temperature change.

Chocolate Soufflé

PASTRY TECHNIQUES:
Melting, Folding, Whipping,
  Ribboning

Melting:
1. Prepare the food product to be melted.
2. Place the food product in an appropriate sized pot over direct heat or over a double boiler.
3. Stir frequently or occasionally, depending on the delicacy of the product, until melted.

OR

1. Place the product on a sheet pan or in a bowl, and place in a low-temperature oven until melted.

Folding:
Do steps 1, 2, and 3 in one continuous motion.
1. Run a bowl scraper under the mixture, across the bottom of the bowl.
2. Turn the bowl counterclockwise.
3. Bring the bottom mixture to the top.

Whipping:
1. Hold the whip at a 55-degree angle.
2. Create circles, using a circular motion.
3. The circular motion needs to be perpendicular to the bowl.

Ribboning:
1. Use a high speed on the mixer.
2. Do not overwhip the egg yolks.

HAZARDOUS FOODS:
Egg yolks
Heavy cream
Egg whites

INGREDIENTS:

Ingredient	Amount
Butter, unsalted	As needed
Sugar, granulated	As needed
Egg yolks	5 ounces
Sugar, granulated	5 ounces
Salt	Pinch
Chocolate, dark, bittersweet, or semi-sweet	8 ounces
Chocolate, dark, unsweetened	2 ounces
Cream, heavy	2 ounces
Espresso, instant	¼ ounce
Rum or brandy	1½ ounces
Egg whites	10 ounces

METHOD OF PREPARATION:

1. Gather the equipment and ingredients.
2. Butter the soufflé dishes, sprinkle with granulated sugar, as needed, and set aside.
3. Ribbon the egg yolks, sugar, and salt.
4. Melt both chocolates together slowly over a double boiler.
5. Stir the melted chocolates into the egg yolk–sugar mixture.
6. Stir in the heavy cream, instant espresso, and liquor.
7. Whip the egg whites to a medium peak.
8. Carefully fold the egg whites into the chocolate mixture.
9. Pour the batter into prepared soufflé dishes immediately.
10. Bake at 400° F in a deck oven for 30 minutes, or until done. (*Do not bake this soufflé in a convection oven.*)
11. Serve immediately.

CHEF NOTE:
The 2 ounces of unsweetened chocolate can be replaced with 1¾ ounces of cocoa powder and 1 ounce of oil.

Frozen Soufflé No. 1

(Soufflé Glacé)

PASTRY TECHNIQUES:

Heating, Whipping, Folding, Piping

Heating:

1. Prepare the food product according to the formula's instructions.
2. Choose the appropriate method of heating (on the range or stove top, in the oven, etc.)
3. Apply the product to the heat.

Whipping:

1. Hold the whip at a 55-degree angle.
2. Create circles, using a circular motion.
3. The circular motion needs to be perpendicular to the bowl.

Folding:

Do steps 1, 2, and 3 in one continuous motion.
1. Run a bowl scraper under the mixture, across the bottom of the bowl.
2. Turn the bowl counterclockwise.
3. Bring the bottom mixture to the top.

Piping:

With bag:
1. Use a bag with a disposable tip; cut the bag at 45-degree angle.
2. Fill to no more than half full.
3. Burp the bag.
With cone:
1. Cut and fold the piping cone to the appropriate size.
2. Fill the cone with a small amount.
3. Fold the ends to form a triangle.
4. Pipe the desired designs.

HACCP:

Store at 0° F

HAZARDOUS FOODS:

Egg yolks
Eggs
Heavy cream

YIELD:	1 pound, 8 ounces.	3 pounds.

INGREDIENTS:

Egg yolks	2 ounces	4 ounces
Eggs, whole	2 ounces	4 ounces
Sugar, granulated	4 ounces	8 ounces
Cream, heavy	1 pound	2 pounds
Flavorings	To taste	To taste

METHOD OF PREPARATION:

1. Gather the equipment and ingredients.
2. Place the egg yolks, whole eggs, and granulated sugar in a bowl, and place over a double boiler; heat to 145° F, whipping constantly.
3. Remove from the heat, and whip to a medium peak; cool.
4. Whip the heavy cream to a soft peak.
5. Fold the cooled egg mixture into the whipped cream.
6. Flavor, as desired.
7. Pipe into desired containers.
8. Freeze.

CHEF NOTES:

1. Flavorings may be added according to the name of the frozen soufflé (e.g., Soufflé Glacé Grand Marnier.)
2. Soufflé cups can be used; prior to piping in the mixture, place a paper collar around the cups.

COOKIES

BREADS

SOUFFLES

CREPES

ICE CREAM

SORBETS

CHOCOLATE

MISCELLANEOUS | OTHERS: FINISHED

PASTRY TECHNIQUES:

Whipping, Cooking, Folding

Whipping:
1. Hold the whip at a 55-degree angle.
2. Create circles, using a circular motion.
3. The circular motion needs to be perpendicular to the bowl.

Cooking:

Preparing food through the use of various sources of heating.
1. Choose the appropriate heat application: baking, boiling, simmering, etc.
2. Prepare the formula according to instructions.
3. Cook according to instructions.

Folding:

Do steps 1, 2, and 3 in one continuous motion.
1. Run a bowl scraper under the mixture, across the bottom of the bowl.
2. Turn the bowl counterclockwise.
3. Bring the bottom mixture to the top.

HACCP:

Store at 0° F.

HAZARDOUS FOODS:

Egg yolks
Heavy cream

Frozen Soufflé No. 2

(Pâté à Bombe Method)

YIELD:	2 pounds, 5½ ounces.	4 pounds, 11 ounces.

INGREDIENTS:

Egg yolks	7 ounces	14 ounces
Sugar, granulated	7½ ounces	15 ounces
Water	3 ounces	6 ounces
Cream, heavy, whipped	1 pound, 4 ounces	2 pounds, 8 ounces
Flavorings	To taste	To taste

METHOD OF PREPARATION:

1. Gather the equipment and ingredients.
2. Place the egg yolks in a bowl, and whip to full volume.
3. Place the sugar and water in a pot, and cook to 238° F.
4. Add the cooked sugar to the whipped egg yolks; mix on medium speed.
5. Whip the heavy cream to a soft peak.
6. Fold the whipped cream into the egg yolk–sugar mixture.
7. Flavor, as desired.
8. Pipe into soufflé cups. Prior to piping in the mixture, place a paper collar around each cup.
9. Freeze.

Hazelnut Soufflé

COOKIES

BREADS

SOUFFLES

CREPES

ICE CREAM

SORBETS

CHOCOLATE

OTHERS: FINISHED

MISCELLANEOUS

PASTRY TECHNIQUES:

Boiling, Whipping, Folding, Combining

Boiling:

1. Bring the cooking liquid to a rapid boil.
2. Stir the contents.

Whipping:

1. Hold the whip at a 55-degree angle.
2. Create circles, using a circular motion.
3. The circular motion needs to be perpendicular to the bowl.

Folding:

Do steps 1, 2, and 3 in one continuous motion.
1. Run a bowl scraper under the mixture, across the bottom of the bowl.
2. Turn the bowl counterclockwise.
3. Bring the bottom mixture to the top.

Combining:

Bringing together two or more components.
1. Prepare the components to be combined.
2. Add one to the other, using the appropriate mixing method (if needed).

HAZARDOUS FOODS:

Milk
Egg yolks
Egg whites

CHEF NOTE:

This is a basic recipe for soufflé. Any other type of flavorings can be substituted for the hazelnuts. *Do not* use a convection oven to prepare this soufflé, and *do not* slam the oven door.

YIELD:	2 pounds, 13½ ounces.	5 pounds, 11 ounces.
INGREDIENTS:		
Butter, unsalted	As needed	As needed
Sugar, granulated	As needed	As needed
Butter, unsalted, additional	3½ ounces	7 ounces
Flour, pastry	3½ ounces	7 ounces
Milk, whole	1 pound	2 pounds
Extract, vanilla	To taste	To taste
Frangelico	1½ ounces	3 ounces
Egg yolks	3½ ounces	7 ounces
Hazelnuts, roasted, ground	4 ounces	8 ounces
Egg whites	10 ounces	1 pound, 4 ounces
Sugar, granulated, additional	3½ ounces	7 ounces
Sugar, confectionery	As needed	As needed

METHOD OF PREPARATION:

1. Gather the equipment and ingredients.
2. Butter the soufflé cups, and sprinkle with granulated sugar.
3. *Preparation of Roux:*
   a. Place the butter in a saucepan, and melt.
   b. Add the flour, and stir with a wooden spoon.
   c. Cook the mixture until it smells like toasted nuts (3 to 6 minutes).
4. Place the milk in another pot; add the vanilla extract and Frangelico. Bring to a boil.
5. Add the boiling milk mixture to the roux, and cook for 5 to 7 minutes.
6. Remove from the heat, and cool slightly.
7. Add the egg yolks and hazelnuts to the cooked flour mixture; mix well.
8. Heat the egg whites and sugar to 110° F over a double boiler, whipping constantly.
9. Remove the egg whites from the heat, and whip to a medium-stiff peak.
10. Fold the whipped egg whites very carefully into the flour mixture.
11. Fill the soufflé cups almost to the top with the mixture.
12. Place the cups in a hotel pan.
13. Bake at 400° F for 15 minutes without opening the oven door. The soufflés are ready when they bake out of the cup and are firm to the touch.
14. Remove from the pan, and sprinkle with confectionery sugar; serve immediately.

Raspberry Soufflé

PASTRY TECHNIQUES:

Reducing, Whipping, Folding,
Slow Baking

Reducing:

1. Bring the sauce to a boil; then reduce to a simmer.
2. Stir often; reduce to the desired consistency.

Whipping:

1. Hold the whip at a 55-degree angle.
2. Create circles, using a circular motion.
3. The circular motion needs to be perpendicular to the bowl.

Folding:

Do steps 1, 2, and 3 in one continuous motion.
1. Run a bowl scraper under the mixture, across the bottom of the bowl.
2. Turn the bowl counterclockwise.
3. Bring the bottom mixture to the top.

Slow Baking:

1. Use an appropriate baking dish.
2. Use hot water in the pan.
3. Replenish the water when needed.

HAZARDOUS FOOD:

Egg whites

YIELD: 1 pound, 6 ounces.

INGREDIENTS:

Butter, unsalted	As needed
Sugar, granulated	As needed
Raspberries, puréed	1 pound
Kirschwasser or Framboise	1 ounce
Egg whites	4 ounces
Sugar, granulated, additional	1 ounce
Sugar, confectionery or cocoa powder	As needed

METHOD OF PREPARATION:

1. Gather the equipment and ingredients.
2. Butter the soufflé cups, and sprinkle with granulated sugar.
3. Place the raspberry purée in a pot, and reduce to half the original amount. Remove from the heat, and cool.
4. When the purée has cooled, add the Kirschwasser or Framboise.
5. Place the egg whites in a bowl, and whip to a medium-stiff peak; slowly add the additional granulated sugar to make a meringue.
6. Fold the meringue carefully into the raspberry purée.
7. Fill the soufflé cups almost to the top with the mixture.
8. Bake at 400° F for about 12 to 15 minutes, or until light golden brown and slightly firm.
9. Dust with confectionery sugar and/or cocoa powder, and serve immediately.

Soufflé

COOKIES
BREADS
SOUFFLES
CREPES
ICE CREAM
SORBETS
CHOCOLATE
OTHERS: FINISHED
MISCELLANEOUS

PASTRY TECHNIQUES:
Combining, Whipping, Folding

Combining:
Bringing together two or more components.
1. Prepare the components to be combined.
2. Add one to the other, using the appropriate mixing method (if needed).

Whipping:
1. Hold the whip at a 55-degree angle.
2. Create circles, using a circular motion.
3. The circular motion needs to be perpendicular to the bowl.

Folding:
Do steps 1, 2, and 3 in one continuous motion.
1. Run a bowl scraper under the mixture, across the bottom of the bowl.
2. Turn the bowl counterclockwise.
3. Bring the bottom mixture to the top.

HACCP:
Store at 40° F.

HAZARDOUS FOODS:
Milk
Egg yolks
Egg whites

YIELD:	1 pound, 6¾ ounces.	2 pounds, 13½ ounces.
INGREDIENTS:		
Butter, unsalted	As needed	As needed
Sugar, granulated	As needed	As needed
Milk, whole	4¼ ounces	8½ ounces
Sugar, granulated	2 ounces	4 ounces
Milk, whole	4¼ ounces	8½ ounces
Flour, cake	1¾ ounces	3½ ounces
Egg yolks	1½ ounces	3 ounces
Liqueur (see chef note 1)	1¾ ounces	3½ ounces
Egg whites	6¾ ounces	13½ ounces
Sugar, granulated	½ ounce	1 ounce
Cream of tartar	Pinch	Pinch

METHOD OF PREPARATION:
1. Gather the equipment and ingredients.
2. Butter and sugar the soufflé cups; be sure the top edge is clean to get maximum rise.
3. Combine the milk and sugar; bring to a simmer.
4. Make a paste of the milk and cake flour.
5. Combine the paste with the simmering milk, and cook for 2 minutes, or until the mixture thickens.
6. Remove from the heat, and cool.
7. Whisk the egg yolks and liqueur together.
8. Add the egg yolk mixture to the milk mixture.
9. Place the egg whites in a bowl, and whip to a medium-soft peak; gradually add the granulated sugar and cream of tartar to make a meringue.
10. Combine the meringue and the milk-egg mixture carefully.
11. Place in prepared soufflé cups about three fourths of the way full.
12. Bake at 375° F for 8 to 10 minutes, or until the soufflé is firm but not dry.

CHEF NOTES:
1. Suggestions for liqueur include Grand Marnier, Kahlua, or Triple Sec.
2. This mixture can be prepared in advance; however, the meringue can be whipped up at the last moment before baking and folded into mixture.

14

Crêpes

14

Crêpes

COOKIES
BREADS
SOUFFLES
CREPES
ICE CREAM
SORBETS
CHOCOLATE
OTHERS: FINISHED
MISCELLANEOUS

PASTRY TECHNIQUE:
Combining

Combining:
Bringing together two or more components.
1. Prepare the components to be combined.
2. Add one to the other, using the appropriate mixing method (if needed).

HACCP:
Store at 40° F.

HAZARDOUS FOODS:
Milk
Eggs

Crêpe Batter No. 1

YIELD:	2 pounds, 4 ounces.	4 pounds, 8 ounces.

INGREDIENTS:

Butter, unsalted	¾ ounce	1½ ounces
Milk, whole	1 pound, 2 ounces	2 pounds, 4 ounces
Eggs, whole	6 ounces	12 ounces
Rum	½ ounce	1 ounce
Oil, vegetable	1¾ ounces	3½ ounces
Sugar, granulated	1¾ ounces	3½ ounces
Salt	Pinch	⅛ ounce
Flour, bread	7 ounces	14 ounces
Orange, zest only	1 each	2 each

METHOD OF PREPARATION:

1. Gather the equipment and ingredients.
2. Melt the butter, and set aside.
3. Combine the milk, eggs, rum, and oil.
4. Add the melted butter into the milk mixture.
5. Place all of the dry ingredients into a bowl: sugar, salt, flour.
6. Using a whip, slowly add the liquid mixture into the dry mixture. Add zest.
7. Let the mixture rest for 30 minutes.
8. To prepare crêpes, use a non-stick crepe pan.

Crêpe Batter No. 2

PASTRY TECHNIQUE:

Combining

Combining:

Bringing together two or more components.
1. Prepare the components to be combined.
2. Add one to the other, using the appropriate mixing method (if needed).

HACCP:

Store at 40° F.

HAZARDOUS FOODS:

Eggs
Milk

YIELD:		1 pound, 6 ounces.	2 pounds, 12 ounces.
INGREDIENTS:			
Eggs, whole		4 ounces	8 ounces
Sugar, confectionery		¾ ounce	1½ ounces
Salt		To taste	To taste
Milk, whole		10½ ounces	1 pound, 5 ounces
Oil, vegetable		½ ounce	1 ounce
Flour, pastry		6 ounces	12 ounces
Extract, vanilla		To taste	To taste
Lemon, rind only		½ each	1 each
Orange, rind only		½ each	1 each

METHOD OF PREPARATION:

1. Gather the equipment and ingredients.
2. Combine the eggs, sugar, salt, milk, and oil. Mix until the liquid is smooth.
3. Place the pastry flour in a dry bowl, and slowly add the liquid ingredients to it. (Strain the mixture.)
4. Add the vanilla extract, lemon rind, and orange rind.
5. Let the mixture rest for 30 minutes.
6. To prepare crêpes, use a non-stick crepe pan.

CHEF NOTES:
1. If a thicker batter is desired, add more flour.
2. If a thinner batter is desired, add more liquid.
3. Milk can be partially replaced with club soda in a 1:1 ratio, which will result in a lighter product.

COOKIES
BREADS
SOUFFLES
CREPES
ICE CREAM
SORBETS
CHOCOLATE
OTHERS: FINISHED
MISCELLANEOUS

Crêpe Batter No. 3

PASTRY TECHNIQUE:

Combining

Combining:

Bringing together two or more components.
1. Prepare the components to be combined.
2. Add one to the other, using the appropriate mixing method (if needed).

HACCP:

Store at 40° F

HAZARDOUS FOODS:

Milk
Eggs

YIELD: 1 pound, 4½ ounces. 2 pounds, 9 ounces.

INGREDIENTS:

Flour, pastry	3½ ounces	7 ounces
Sugar, granulated	⅞ ounce	1¾ ounces
Salt	Pinch	¼ ounce
Milk, whole	9 ounces	1 pound, 2 ounces
Eggs, whole	6 ounces	12 ounces
Oil, vegetable	1 ounce	2 ounces
Extract, vanilla	To taste	To taste

METHOD OF PREPARATION:

1. Gather the equipment and ingredients.
2. Place the pastry flour, granulated sugar, and salt in a bowl.
3. Slowly add the milk into the dry ingredients. (Strain the mixture.)
4. Add the eggs, oil, and vanilla extract.
5. Combine well.
6. Let the mixture rest for 1 hour.
7. To prepare crêpes, use a non-stick omelette pan.

Crêpes Georgette

Combining:

Bringing together two or more components.
1. Prepare the components to be combined.
2. Add one to the other, using the appropriate mixing method (if needed).

YIELD:	12 Servings.	24 Servings.
INGREDIENTS:		
Crêpes (see pages 325–327)	24 each	48 each
English sauce (see page 211)	As needed	As needed
Melba sauce (see page 215)	As needed	As needed
Filling:		
Walnuts, finely chopped and toasted	10 ounces	1 pound, 4 ounces
Sugar, granulated	6 ounces	12 ounces
Cinnamon, ground	¼ ounce	½ ounce

METHOD OF PREPARATION:

1. Gather the equipment and ingredients.
2. Combine the walnuts, sugar, and cinnamon.
3. Place a small spoonful of the walnut mixture in the center of each crêpe.
4. Roll or bundle the crêpe.
5. Place the crêpe on a dessert plate, and garnish with English sauce and melba sauce.

COOKIES
BREADS
SOUFFLES
CREPES
ICE CREAM
SORBETS
CHOCOLATE
OTHERS: FINISHED
MISCELLANEOUS

Crêpes Suzette

PASTRY TECHNIQUES:
Combining, Folding

Combining:

Bringing together two or more components.
1. Prepare the components to be combined.
2. Add one to the other, using the appropriate mixing method (if needed).

Folding:

Do steps 1, 2, and 3 in one continuous motion.
1. Run a bowl scraper under the mixture, across the bottom of the bowl.
2. Turn the bowl counterclockwise.
3. Bring the bottom mixture to the top.

YIELD:	6 Servings.	12 Servings.
INGREDIENTS:		
Oranges, zest only	3 each	6 each
Lemons, zest only	3 each	6 each
Sugar, granulated	2⅓ ounces	5¼ ounces
Butter, unsalted	3 ounces	6 ounces
Orange juice	12 ounces	1 pound, 8 ounces
Grand Marnier	6 ounces	12 ounces
Crêpes (see pages 325–327)	12 each	24 each
Cognac	3 ounces	6 ounces

METHOD OF PREPARATION:

1. Gather the equipment and ingredients.
2. Zest all of the oranges and lemons.
3. Heat a suzette pan, sprinkle sugar over the pan, add the butter, and mix until all of the sugar is dissolved.
4. While the sugar is dissolving, add the zest from the oranges and lemons.
5. Add the orange juice.
6. Remove the pan from the flame, and add the Grand Marnier; *do not flame.*
7. Return the pan to the heat and dip the crêpes into the sauce one at a time. Fold the crêpes into quarters.
8. Move the crêpes to the side of the pan.
9. When all crêpes are folded, remove the pan from the flame, and add the cognac.
10. Return to flame, and ignite.
11. Remove the crêpes from the pan; place on a heated platter.
12. Reduce the sauce, and serve; spoon the sauce over the crêpes.

CHEF NOTES:

The following are variations that can be used:
1. For a more syrupy sauce, caramelize the sugar before adding the butter.
2. If no fresh oranges are available, orange preserves or orange marmalade can be used as a substitute.
3. If marmalade is used, use less sugar.

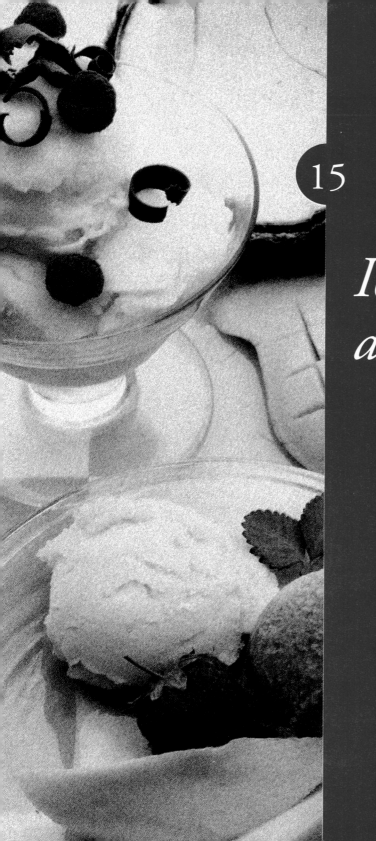

15

Ice Creams
and Sorbets

Ice Creams and Sorbets

American Ice Cream

Vanilla

YIELD:		2 pounds, 10 ounces.	5 pounds, 4 ounces.

INGREDIENTS:

Cream, heavy		10½ ounces	1 pound, 5 ounces
Milk, whole		1 pound, 5 ounces	2 pounds, 10 ounces
Sugar, granulated		10½ ounces	1 pound, 5 ounces
Extract, vanilla		To taste	To taste
Salt		Pinch	Pinch

METHOD OF PREPARATION:

1. Gather the equipment and ingredients.
2. Combine all of the ingredients.
3. Heat to 180° F.
4. Cool immediately.
5. Freeze in an ice cream machine.

PASTRY TECHNIQUES:

Combining, Heating, Freezing

Combining:

Bringing together two or more components.
1. Prepare the components to be combined.
2. Add one to the other, using the appropriate mixing method (if needed).

Heating:

1. Prepare the food product according to the formula's instructions.
2. Choose the appropriate method of heating (on the range or stove top, in the oven, etc.)
3. Apply the product to the heat.

Freezing:

1. Prepare the product.
2. Place the product in the freezing cabinet for the appropriate length of time.

HACCP:

Store at 0° F.

HAZARDOUS FOODS:

Heavy cream
Milk

COOKIES
BREADS
SOUFFLES
CREPES
ICE CREAM
SORBETS
CHOCOLATE
OTHERS: FINISHED
MISCELLANEOUS

French Vanilla Ice Cream

PASTRY TECHNIQUES:

Combining, Boiling, Tempering,
  Freezing

Combining:

Bringing together two or more components.
1. Prepare the components to be combined.
2. Add one to the other, using the appropriate mixing method (if needed).

Boiling:

1. Bring the cooking liquid to a rapid boil.
2. Stir the contents.

Tempering:

1. Whisk the eggs vigorously while ladling hot liquid.

Freezing:

1. Prepare the product.
2. Place the product in the freezing cabinet for the appropriate length of time.

HACCP:

Store at 0° F.

HAZARDOUS FOODS:

Milk
Heavy cream
Egg yolks

YIELD:		3 pounds, 1½ ounces.	6 pounds, 3 ounces.
INGREDIENTS:			
Milk, whole		1 pound	2 pounds
Cream, heavy		1 pound	2 pounds
Salt		Pinch	Pinch
Sugar, granulated		9 ounces	1 pound, 2 ounces
Egg yolks		8 ounces	1 pound
Vanilla bean, *or*		½ each	1 each
Vanilla extract		½ ounce	1 ounce

METHOD OF PREPARATION:

1. Gather the equipment and ingredients.
2. Place the milk, heavy cream, salt, and granulated sugar in a pot, and bring to a boil.
3. Place the egg yolks and vanilla in a bowl; whisk together.
4. Temper the egg yolk mixture, and add to the boiling milk.
5. Place over the double boiler, and heat to 175° F, or until the mixture coats the back of a spoon.
6. Cool immediately over an ice bath.
7. Freeze in an ice cream machine.

CHEF NOTE:

This mixture is best if left to sit in the refrigerator overnight for freezing the next day.

Frozen Yogurt

YIELD:	2 pounds, 6 ounces.	4 pounds, 12 ounces.

INGREDIENTS:

Yogurt, plain	8 ounces	1 pound
Milk, whole	1 pound, 8 ounces	3 pounds
Sugar, granulated	6 ounces	12 ounces
Extract, vanilla	To taste	To taste
Egg shade, liquid color (optional)	As needed	As needed

METHOD OF PREPARATION:

1. Gather the equipment and ingredients.
2. Combine all of the ingredients.
3. Strain the mixture.
4. Freeze in an ice cream machine.

IF USING CORNSTARCH:

Yield:

2 *ounces* of cornstarch for 2 pounds, 6 ounces of batter.
4 *ounces* of cornstarch for 4 pounds, 12 ounces of batter.

Method of Preparation:

1. Place the cornstarch in a bowl, and add one third of the milk to the cornstarch; slowly stir with a whip until smooth and well mixed.
2. Cook the milk-starch mixture over medium heat; stir constantly with a whip until the mixture comes to a rolling boil and no starch taste remains.
3. Add all of the remaining ingredients, including the cooked milk-starch mixture. Stir to remove any lumps.
4. Strain.
5. Freeze in an ice cream machine.

PASTRY TECHNIQUES:
Combining, Freezing

Combining:
Bringing together two or more components.
1. Prepare the components to be combined.
2. Add one to the other, using the appropriate mixing method (if needed).

Freezing:
1. Prepare the product.
2. Place the product in the freezing cabinet for the appropriate length of time.

HACCP:
Store at 0° F.

HAZARDOUS FOODS:
Yogurt
Milk

CHEF NOTES:
Cornstarch can be used to prevent this product from becoming icy, if stored in the freezer overnight. If available, an instant starch or modified starch could be substituted and will produce a more stable frozen yogurt than when using cornstarch.

COOKIES
BREADS
SOUFFLES
CREPES
ICE CREAM
SORBETS
CHOCOLATE
OTHERS: FINISHED
MISCELLANEOUS

Fruit with Cassis

PASTRY TECHNIQUES:
Combining, Boiling, Freezing

Combining:
Bringing together two or more components.
1. Prepare the components to be combined.
2. Add one to the other, using the appropriate mixing method (if needed).

Boiling:
1. Bring the cooking liquid to a rapid boil.
2. Stir the contents.

Freezing:
1. Prepare the product.
2. Place the product in the freezing cabinet for the appropriate length of time.

HACCP:
Store at 0° F.

YIELD: 3 pounds, 6½ ounces. 6 pounds, 13 ounces.

INGREDIENTS:

Ingredient		
Water	1 pound	2 pounds
Sugar, granulated	10 ounces	1 pound, 4 ounces
Strawberries or raspberries, puréed	1 pound	2 pounds
Lemon juice	½ ounce	1 ounce
Syrup, cassis	12 ounces	1 pound, 8 ounces

METHOD OF PREPARATION:

1. Gather the equipment and ingredients.
2. Place the water and sugar in a pot, and bring to a boil. Simmer for 5 minutes.
3. Cool completely.
4. Add the fruit purée, lemon juice, and cassis syrup to the cooled sugar mixture; mix thoroughly.
5. Freeze in an ice cream machine.

COOKIES
BREADS
SOUFFLES
CREPES
ICE CREAM
SORBETS
CHOCOLATE
OTHERS: FINISHED
MISCELLANEOUS

Ice Cream Flavors

PASTRY TECHNIQUES:
Combining, Boiling, Freezing

Combining:
Bringing together two or more components.
1. Prepare the components to be combined.
2. Add one to the other, using the appropriate mixing method (if needed).

Boiling:
1. Bring the cooking liquid to a rapid boil.
2. Stir the contents.

Freezing:
1. Prepare the product.
2. Place the product in the freezing cabinet for the appropriate length of time.

HACCP:
Store at 0° F.

INGREDIENTS:

	YIELD:
Ice cream, American or French (see pages 333, 334)	1 quart

Flavorings:

Chocolate:

Chocolate, dark, semi-sweet, melted	6 ounces

Banana:

Banana purée	1 pound
Lemon juice	½ each

Strawberry:

Strawberries, chopped and cleaned	3 pounds
Strawberry compound	1 ounce

Rum and Raisin:

Rum	To taste
Raisins, macerated in rum	3 ounces

Chocolate Chip:

Chocolate chips	3 ounces

Praline:

Praline paste	5 ounces

Nougat:

Praline paste	2 ounces
Nougat, ground	5 ounces

Eggnog:

Nutmeg, ground	⅛ ounce
Rum or brandy	To taste

Mocha/Coffee:

Instant coffee, *or*	1 ounce
Coffee paste	2 ounces

Almond:

Almond paste	3 ounces
Almonds, ground, toasted	2 ounces

METHOD OF PREPARATION:

1. Gather the equipment and ingredients.
2. Prepare the ice cream, and freeze as instructed.

Lime Ice

PASTRY TECHNIQUES:
Combining, Boiling, Freezing

Combining:
Bringing together two or more components.
1. Prepare the components to be combined.
2. Add one to the other, using the appropriate mixing method (if needed).

Boiling:
1. Bring the cooking liquid to a rapid boil.
2. Stir the contents.

Freezing:
1. Prepare the product.
2. Place the product in the freezing cabinet for the appropriate length of time.

HACCP:
Store at 0° F.

YIELD:		3 pounds, ½ ounce.	6 pounds, 1 ounce.
INGREDIENTS:			
Sugar, granulated	1 pound		2 pounds
Water	1 pound		2 pounds
Lime, rind, grated	½ ounce		1 ounce
Lime juice, freshly squeezed	1 pound		2 pounds

METHOD OF PREPARATION:

1. Gather the equipment and ingredients.
2. Combine the sugar and water in a pot, and bring to a boil; simmer for 5 minutes.
3. Cool the sugar mixture.
4. Add the lime rind and lime juice to the sugar mixture.
5. Freeze in an ice cream machine.

Variations (the following substitutions make grapefruit ice):
1. Replace the lime rind with grapefruit rind.
2. Substitute fresh, unsweetened grapefruit juice for half of the lime juice.

CHEF NOTE:
This is a rather tart ice. For a less tart ice, increase the water to 1½ times the amount indicated, but *do not* alter the quantities of any other ingredients.

COOKIES
BREADS
SOUFFLES
CREPES
ICE CREAM
SORBETS
CHOCOLATE
OTHERS: FINISHED
MISCELLANEOUS

Parfait Glacé

PASTRY TECHNIQUES:
Heating, Whipping, Folding, Piping

Heating:
1. Prepare the food product according to the formula's instructions.
2. Choose the appropriate method of heating (on the range or stove top, in the oven, etc.)
3. Apply the product to the heat.

Whipping:
1. Hold the whip at a 55-degree angle.
2. Create circles, using a circular motion.
3. The circular motion needs to be perpendicular to the bowl.

Folding:
Do steps 1, 2, and 3 in one continuous motion.
1. Run a bowl scraper under the mixture, across the bottom of the bowl.
2. Turn the bowl counterclockwise.
3. Bring the bottom mixture to the top.

Piping:
With bag:
1. Use a bag with a disposable tip; cut the bag at 45-degree angle.
2. Fill to no more than half full.
3. Burp the bag.
With cone:
1. Cut and fold the piping cone to the appropriate size.
2. Fill the cone with a small amount.
3. Fold the ends to form a triangle.
4. Pipe the desired designs.

HACCP:
Store at 0° F.

HAZARDOUS FOODS:
Egg yolks
Heavy cream

YIELD:		2 pounds, 2½ ounces.	4 pounds, 5 ounces.

INGREDIENTS:

Egg yolks		8 ounces	1 pound
Sugar, granulated		5½ ounces	11 ounces
Extract, vanilla		To taste	To taste
Liqueur, brandy or Grand Marnier		To taste	To taste
Cream, heavy		1 pound, 5 ounces	2 pounds, 10 ounces

METHOD OF PREPARATION:

1. Gather the equipment and ingredients.
2. Place the egg yolks and sugar in a bowl over a double boiler; heat to 145° F while whisking constantly.
3. Remove from the heat, and continue whipping to full volume; cool.
4. Add the vanilla extract and liqueurs.
5. Whip the cream to a soft peak.
6. Fold the whipped cream into the whipped egg yolks.
7. Pipe or pour into parfait glasses or other molds.
8. Freeze until firm.

CHEF NOTE:
Parfait can be prepared in different flavors; e.g., fruits and chocolates.

COOKIES

BREADS

SOUFFLES

CREPES

ICE CREAM

SORBETS

CHOCOLATE

OTHERS: FINISHED

MISCELLANEOUS

PASTRY TECHNIQUES:
Reducing, Combining, Poaching, Puréeing, Freezing

Reducing:
1. Bring the sauce to a boil; then reduce to a simmer.
2. Stir often; reduce to the desired consistency.

Combining:
Bringing together two or more components.
1. Prepare the components to be combined.
2. Add one to the other, using the appropriate mixing method (if needed).

Poaching:
1. Bring the liquid to a boil; then reduce to a simmer.
2. Submerge and anchor the product.
3. Do not overcook the product.

Puréeing:
1. Do not overfill the food processor.
2. First pulse the food processor.
3. Turn food processor to maximum to purée food.

Freezing:
1. Prepare the product.
2. Place the product in the freezing cabinet for the appropriate length of time.

HACCP:
Store at 0° F.

Apple and Cinnamon Sorbet

YIELD: 32 ounces.

INGREDIENTS:

Apples, Granny Smith, Wine Sap, or Fuji	1 pound

Sugar Syrup:

Lemon	1 each
Water	8 ounces
Sugar, granulated	8 ounces

Poaching Liquid:

Wine, white zinfandel	1 bottle (28 to 32 ounces)
Sugar, granulated	4 ounces
Ginger, fresh	2, ¼-inch slices
Cinnamon, sticks	2 each
Thyme, fresh, crushed	3 sprigs
Peppercorns, crushed	3 to 5 pink

METHOD OF PREPARATION:

1. Gather the equipment and ingredients.
2. *Preparation of Sugar Syrup:*
   a. Zest and juice the lemon.
   b. Place the zest, lemon juice, water, and sugar in a pot, and bring to a boil.
   c. Let the mixture reduce for approximately 8 minutes.
   d. Remove from the heat, and set aside to cool.
3. *Preparation of Poaching Liquid:*
   a. Place all of the ingredients in a large sauce pot, and bring to a boil.
   b. Turn down the heat, and allow to simmer.
4. Peel, core, and chop the apples.
5. Place the apples in the simmering poaching liquid, and cook until soft.
6. Strain the poaching liquid from the apples, and purée them in a food processor.
7. Cool the puréed apples.
8. Add the puréed apples to the sugar syrup, and mix thoroughly.
9. Freeze in an ice machine until fully frozen.

341

Lemon Sorbet

PASTRY TECHNIQUES:
Combining, Whipping, Freezing

Combining:
Bringing together two or more components.
1. Prepare the components to be combined.
2. Add one to the other, using the appropriate mixing method (if needed).

Whipping:
1. Hold the whip at a 55-degree angle.
2. Create circles, using a circular motion.
3. The circular motion needs to be perpendicular to the bowl.

Freezing:
1. Prepare the product.
2. Place the product in the freezing cabinet for the appropriate length of time.

HACCP:
Store at 0° F.

HAZARDOUS FOOD:
Egg whites

YIELD:	3 pounds, 1½ ounces.	6 pounds, 3 ounces.

INGREDIENTS:		
Sugar, granulated	1 pound	2 pounds
Water	1 pound, 10½ ounces	3 pounds, 5 ounces
Lemon juice	5 ounces	10 ounces
Salt	Pinch	Pinch
Lemons, rind, freshly grated	1½ each	3 each
Egg whites	2 ounces	4 ounces

METHOD OF PREPARATION:

1. Gather the equipment and ingredients.
2. Place the sugar, water, lemon juice, salt, and grated lemon rind in a container.
3. Let the mixture stand for 1 hour, or until all of the sugar has dissolved.
4. Strain through a very fine sieve.
5. Beat the egg whites to the froth stage.
6. Add the egg whites to the sugar mixture; combine.
7. Freeze in an ice cream machine.

COOKIES
BREADS
SOUFFLES
CREPES
ICE CREAM
SORBETS
CHOCOLATE
OTHERS: FINISHED
MISCELLANEOUS

Sorbet

PASTRY TECHNIQUES:
Combining, Reducing, Freezing

Combining:
Bringing together two or more components.
1. Prepare the components to be combined.
2. Add one to the other, using the appropriate mixing method (if needed).

Reducing:
1. Bring the sauce to a boil; then reduce to a simmer.
2. Stir often; reduce to the desired consistency.

Freezing:
1. Prepare the product.
2. Place the product in the freezing cabinet for the appropriate length of time.

HACCP:
Store at 0° F.

YIELD:	2 pounds.	4 pounds.
INGREDIENTS:		
Lemon, rind, juice	1 each	2 each
Simple syrup (see page 415)	1 pound	2 pounds
Purée, fruit	1 pound	2 pounds

METHOD OF PREPARATION:
1. Gather the equipment and ingredients.
2. Add the lemon rind to the simple syrup when preparing it.
3. Reduce the simple syrup so it will read 18° on the Baumé scale.
4. Combine the simple syrup, lemon juice, and fruit purée.
5. Strain, if necessary.
6. Freeze in an ice cream machine.

Variations:
The following purées can be used:
1. Raspberry purée
2. Apricot purée
3. Peach purée
4. Strawberry purée
5. Pineapple purée

Wine Sorbet

PASTRY TECHNIQUES:
Combining, Boiling, Freezing,
Whipping

Combining:
Bringing together two or more components.
1. Prepare the components to be combined.
2. Add one to the other, using the appropriate mixing method (if needed).

Boiling:
1. Bring the cooking liquid to a rapid boil.
2. Stir the contents.

Freezing:
1. Prepare the product.
2. Place the product in the freezing cabinet for the appropriate length of time.

Whipping:
1. Hold the whip at a 55-degree angle.
2. Create circles, using a circular motion.
3. The circular motion needs to be perpendicular to the bowl.

HACCP:
Store at 0° F.

HAZARDOUS FOODS:
Egg whites

YIELD:		2 pounds, 9 ounces.	5 pounds, 2 ounces.
INGREDIENTS:			
Water		1 pound	2 pounds
Sugar, granulated		6 ounces	12 ounces
Honey or glucose		2 ounces	4 ounces
Orange, zest and juice		½ each	1 each
Lemon, zest and juice		½ each	1 each
Wine, red, white, rosé, champagne, or apple		1 pound	2 pounds
Egg whites, beaten		1 ounce	2 ounces

METHOD OF PREPARATION:

1. Gather the equipment and ingredients.
2. Place the water, sugar, and honey or glucose in a pot; bring to a boil. Remove from heat after the sugar has been dissolved totally.
3. Add the orange and lemon zests and juices into the hot syrup.
4. Cool the syrup.
5. Strain the syrup, and add the wine.
6. Freeze the sorbet in an ice cream machine until two-thirds frozen.
7. Whip the egg whites to a soft peak.
8. Add the whipped egg whites to the sorbet.
9. Continue to freeze.

CHEF NOTE:
When served, additional wine or champagne can be poured over the sorbet. For more intense flavor and/or color, more wine can be substituted for the water.

16

Chocolate

16

Chocolate

Aida Pistachio

YIELD: 2 pounds, 15 ounces.   130 Pralines.

INGREDIENTS:

Couverture, dark, semi-sweet, heated to 113° F	9 ounces
Paste, praline or peanut butter	14 ounces
Marzipan, pistachio-flavored (see page 422)	1 pound, 8 ounces
Simple syrup (see page 415)	As needed
Couverture, dark, semi-sweet, additional, tempered (for brushing)	As needed

METHOD OF PREPARATION:

1. Gather the equipment and ingredients.
2. Preparation of filling: Stir together the 9 ounces of heated dark couverture and the praline paste.
3. Cool the filling in a cold water bath until it develops a pasty consistency.
4. Using a pastry bag with a large, round tip, pipe the filling into the logs.
5. Let them set.
6. Roll out the pistachio marzipan to a $\frac{1}{12}$-inch (2-mm) thickness.
7. Brush lightly with simple syrup.
8. Place the log on top of the marzipan.
9. Roll the log until it is covered completely with marzipan.
10. Using a clean, dry brush, brush the log with tempered chocolate; use short strokes; brush the top first. Let it set; then brush the remaining surface. (Ensure that the couverture is at the maximum temperature so that it will not cool before the project is complete.)
11. As soon as the chocolate has set, cut the log into ½-inch pieces, using a knife.
12. Leave the cut pralines in the log to retard drying of the filling.

PASTRY TECHNIQUES:
Piping, Tempering, Brushing

Piping:
With bag:
1. Use a bag with a disposable tip; cut the bag at 45-degree angle.
2. Fill to more than half full.
3. Burp the bag.
With cone:
1. Cut and fold the piping cone to the appropriate size.
2. Fill the cone with a small amount.
3. Fold the ends to form a triangle.
4. Pipe the desired designs.

Tempering:
1. Whisk the eggs vigorously while ladling hot liquid.

Brushing:
1. Use a pastry brush.
2. Lightly apply the glaze.

HACCP:
Store at 60° F to 65° F.

PASTRY TECHNIQUES:
Melting, Folding, Rolling, Cutting,
   Dipping

Melting:
1. Prepare the food product to be
   melted.
2. Place the food product in an appropriately-sized pot over direct
   heat or over a double boiler.
3. Stir frequently or occasionally, depending on the delicacy of the
   product, until melted.
OR
1. Place the product on a sheet pan
   or in a bowl, and place in a low-
   temperature oven until melted.

Folding:
Do steps 1, 2, and 3 in one continuous motion.
1. Run a bowl scraper under the mixture, across the bottom of the
   bowl.
2. Turn the bowl counterclockwise.
3. Bring the bottom mixture to the
   top.

Rolling:
1. Prepare the rolling surface by
   dusting with the appropriate medium (flour, cornstarch, etc.).
2. Use the appropriate style pin
   (stick pin or ball bearing pin) to
   roll the dough to desired thickness; rotate the dough during rolling to prevent sticking.

Cutting:
Using a sharp knife to cut to the directed size.

Dipping:
1. Prepare the product to the proper
   dipping temperature.
2. Carefully submerge the product.
3. Dry on parchment paper or a
   screen.

HACCP:
Store at 60° F to 65° F.

CHEF NOTE:
Work fast when forming this praline,
because it will harden quickly.

Almond Blätterkrokant

YIELD: 2 pounds, 14 ounces.   100 Pralines.

INGREDIENTS:

Nougat, almond, pralinosa	1 pound, 2 ounces
Almonds, slightly toasted, ground very fine	7 ounces
Sugar, granulated	1 pound, 5 ounces
Couverture, dark, semi-sweet, tempered (for dipping)	As needed

METHOD OF PREPARATION:

1. Gather the equipment and ingredients.
2. Melt the nougat, and add the toasted, ground almonds to it.
3. Keep the nougat warm.
4. Melt the sugar until it reaches about 360° F.
5. Heat a sheet pan; lightly oil it.
6. Pour the nougat mixture onto the sheet pan.
7. Pour the sugar in the center on top of the nougat mixture.
8. Immediately start folding the mixture together with two oiled metal scrapers until a stiff mixture is formed.
9. Transfer the mixture between metal bars; roll it out to a ½-inch thickness
   with parchment paper on the top and bottom.
10. Remove the bars; cut into ¾-inch by 1-inch pieces.
11. Cool; then dip in dark couverture; decorate immediately with fork lines.

PASTRY TECHNIQUES:
Mixing, Portioning

Mixing:
1. Follow the proper mixing procedure: creaming, blending, whipping, or combination.

Portioning:
1. Mark the product for portioning,
   using a ruler, if necessary.
2. Cut, spoon, or scoop the product
   with the appropriate-sized utensil.

HACCP:
Store at 60° F to 65° F.

Almond Chocolate Pralines

YIELD: 6 pounds.   150 Pralines.

INGREDIENTS:

Sugar, granulated	10½ ounces
Water	3½ ounces
Almonds, toasted, slivered	3 pounds, 5 ounces
Couverture, milk, tempered	1 pound, 8 ounces
Cocoa butter	5 ounces

METHOD OF PREPARATION:

1. Gather the equipment and ingredients.
2. Cook the sugar and water to 235° F, and pour over the toasted, slivered almonds.
3. Stir with a wooden spoon until the sugar begins to crystallize and the almonds separate.
4. Cool to about 80° F.
5. Combine the tempered milk couverture and the cocoa butter.
6. Pour the couverture mixture over the almond mixture, and stir until all of the almonds are coated.
7. Portion ½-ounce clusters on the parchment paper. (A 1-ounce ice cream scoop may be used.)
8. Let the clusters set.

PASTRY TECHNIQUES:
Creaming, Piping, Coating

Creaming:
1. Soften the fats on low speed.
2. Add the sugar(s) and cream; increase the speed slowly.
3. Add the eggs one at a time; scrape the bowl frequently.
4. Add the dry ingredients in stages.

Piping:
With bag:
1. Use a bag with a disposable tip; cut the bag at 45-degree angle.
2. Fill to no more than half full.
3. Burp the bag.
With cone:
1. Cut and fold the piping cone to the appropriate size.
2. Fill the cone with a small amount.
3. Fold the ends to form a triangle.
4. Pipe the desired designs.

Coating:
1. Use a coating screen, with a sheet pan underneath.
2. Ensure that the product is the correct temperature.
3. Coat the product; use an appropriately-sized utensil.

HACCP:
Store at 40° F to 65° F.

Almond Liqueur Butter Pralines

YIELD: 1 pound, 8 ounces.   110 Pralines.

INGREDIENTS:

Almond paste	1 pound, 2 ounces
Butter, unsalted, soft	4 ounces
Liqueur, Kirschwasser	2 ounces
Couverture, dark, semi-sweet, stencils	220 each
Marmalade, apricot	3 ounces
Couverture, dark, semi-sweet, tempered (for coating)	As needed
Couverture, milk, tempered (for decorating)	As needed

METHOD OF PREPARATION:

1. Gather the equipment and ingredients.
2. Cream the almond paste.
3. Add the butter, and mix to form a smooth paste.
4. Slowly add the liqueur.
5. Using a round tube, pipe the mixture in a dome shape approximately ¼-inch to ½-inch high onto a couverture stencil.
6. Place a dot of apricot marmalade on the top; place another couverture stencil on top, and press down lightly.
7. Coat with tempered dark couverture; decorate with tempered milk couverture.

CHEF NOTE:
Kirschwasser can be substituted for another liqueur.

COOKIES
BREADS
SOUFFLES
CREPES
ICE CREAM
SORBETS
CHOCOLATE
OTHERS: FINISHED
MISCELLANEOUS

PASTRY TECHNIQUES:

Melting, Folding, Rolling, Cutting, Spreading, Coating

Melting:

1. Prepare the food product to be melted.
2. Place the food product in an appropriately-sized pot over direct heat or over a double boiler.
3. Stir frequently or occasionally, depending on the delicacy of the product, until melted.

OR

1. Place the product on a sheet pan or in a bowl, and place in a low-temperature oven until melted.

Folding:

Do steps 1, 2, and 3 in one continuous motion.
1. Run a bowl scraper under the mixture, across the bottom of the bowl.
2. Turn the bowl counterclockwise.
3. Bring the bottom mixture to the top.

Rolling:

1. Prepare the rolling surface by dusting with the appropriate medium (flour, cornstarch, etc.).
2. Use the appropriate style pin (stick pin or ball bearing pin) to roll the dough to desired thickness; rotate the dough during rolling to prevent sticking.

Cutting:

Using a sharp knife to cut to the directed size.

Spreading:

1. Using an icing spatula or off-set spatula, smooth the icing or other spreading medium over the surface area.

Coating:

1. Use a coating screen, with a sheet pan underneath.
2. Ensure that the product is the correct temperature.
3. Coat the product; use an appropriately-sized utensil.

HACCP:

Store at 60° F to 65° F.

Almond Nougat Pralines

(Sheet Nougat/Almond Blätterkrokant)

YIELD: 2 pounds, 14 ounces.   160 Pralines.

INGREDIENTS

Nougat, almond, pralinosa	1 pound, 2 ounces
Almonds, toasted, ground very fine	7 ounces
Cocoa butter	As needed
Sugar, granulated	1 pound, 5 ounces
Couverture, dark, semi-sweet, tempered (for spreading and coating)	As needed

METHOD OF PREPARATION:

1. Gather the equipment and ingredients.
2. Melt the nougat.
3. Add the ground (very fine), toasted almonds to the nougat.
4. Pour onto a sheet pan, oiled with cocoa butter.
5. Melt the sugar.
6. Pour the sugar over the nougat, and fold.
7. Roll out, between two metal bars, to a ⅓-inch thickness.
8. Remove the bars, mark, and cut immediately into 1-inch by ¾-inch pieces.
9. Cool, and spread with a thin layer of tempered dark couverture on both sides.
10. Coat with tempered couverture.
11. Finish with a fork decoration, as desired.

PASTRY TECHNIQUES:

Creaming, Piping, Coating

Creaming:

1. Soften the fats on low speed.
2. Add the sugar(s) and cream; increase the speed slowly.
3. Add the eggs one at a time; scrape the bowl frequently.
4. Add the dry ingredients in stages.

Piping:

With bag:
1. Use a bag with a disposable tip; cut the bag at 45-degree angle.
2. Fill to no more than half full.
3. Burp the bag.

With cone:
1. Cut and fold the piping cone to the appropriate size.
2. Fill the cone with a small amount.
3. Fold the ends to form a triangle.
4. Pipe the desired designs.

Coating:

1. Use a coating screen, with a sheet pan underneath.
2. Ensure that the product is the correct temperature.
3. Coat the product; use an appropriately sized utensil.

HACCP:

Store at 60° F to 65° F.

Apricot Butter Truffles

YIELD: 3 pounds, 1 ounce.   160 Truffles.

INGREDIENTS:

Butter, unsalted, softened	10 ounces
Fondant	10 ounces
Brandy, apricot	5 ounces
Compound, apricot	To taste
Couverture, milk, melted	14 ounces
Couverture, dark, semi-sweet, melted	10 ounces
Couverture, milk, stencils	160 each
Couverture, milk, tempered (for coating)	As needed
Couverture, dark, semi-sweet, tempered (for decorating)	As needed

METHOD OF PREPARATION:

1. Gather the equipment and ingredients.
2. Cream the butter and fondant to a smooth paste.
3. Add the brandy and compound.
4. Incorporate the melted couvertures, but do not exceed 92° F (or tempered).
5. Pipe, with a star tip, onto the couverture stencils.
6. Coat with tempered milk couverture; decorate with a dot of tempered dark couverture.

Apricot Slices

YIELD: 2 pounds, 9 ounces.   150 Pralines.

INGREDIENTS

Apricots, dried	3 ounces
Brandy, apricot	As needed
Cream, heavy	8 ounces
Couverture, white, chopped	1 pound
Couverture, milk, chopped	8 ounces
Pistachios, ground	3 ounces
Brandy, apricot	1½ ounces
Compound, apricot	½ ounce
Butter, unsalted, softened	1 ounce
Couverture, milk, tempered (for dipping)	As needed
Pistachios, ground, additional (for decorating)	As needed

METHOD OF PREPARATION:

1. Gather the equipment and ingredients.
2. Soak the apricots in brandy (preferably overnight).
3. Drain the apricots, and save the apricot brandy for future soaking.
4. Chop the apricots finely and add to the heavy cream.
5. Bring the heavy cream and chopped apricots to a boil.
6. Add the chopped white and milk couvertures to the cream mixture; stir until smooth to create ganache.
7. Add the pistachios, apricot brandy, and coumpound; combine well.
8. Let the ganache set until it begins to firm up.
9. Add the soft butter; lightly beat it, using a rubber spatula.
10. Spread the ganache, between metal bars, about ⅓-inch thick to form a rectangular sheet.
11. Using a small knife, remove the bars; let the ganache set until firm.
12. Spread a very thin layer of tempered milk couverture on both sides of the sheet.
13. Cut the ganache into 1¹¹⁄₁₆-inch by 1-inch rectangles.
14. Using a three-prong fork, dip in the tempered milk couverture.
15. Decorate with three fork lines and ground pistachios.

PASTRY TECHNIQUES:

Mixing, Spreading, Cutting, Tempering, Dipping

Mixing:

1. Follow the proper mixing procedure: creaming, blending, whipping, or combination.

Spreading:

1. Using an icing spatula or off-set spatula, smooth the icing or other spreading medium over the surface area.

Cutting:

Using a sharp knife to cut to the directed size.

Tempering:

1. Whisk the eggs vigorously while ladling hot liquid.

Dipping:

1. Prepare the product to the proper dipping temperature.
2. Carefully submerge the product.
3. Dry on parchment paper or a screen.

HACCP:

Store at 60° F to 65° F.

HAZARDOUS FOOD:

Heavy cream

COOKIES
BREADS
SOUFFLES
CREPES
ICE CREAM
SORBETS
CHOCOLATE
OTHERS: FINISHED
MISCELLANEOUS

Chocolate Fondant Liqueurs

YIELD: 2 pounds, 10 ounces.   180 Pralines.

INGREDIENTS:

Couverture, dark, semi-sweet, tempered (for molding)	As needed
Fruit, soaked in liqueur	10 ounces
Fondant, warm, flavored with liqueur	2 pounds

METHOD OF PREPARATION:

1. Gather the equipment and ingredients.
2. Fill the chocolate molds with tempered couverture.
3. Tap the molds to release air bubbles.
4. Pour out excess couverture, and place the molds, upside down, on a dipping screen until the chocolate begins to set.
5. Turn the open cavity up and, using a clean bench scraper, scrape off excess couverture.
6. When the chocolate shells are set, place a piece of fruit in each shell.
7. Warm the fondant to 105° F, and reduce the temperature to 80° F to 85° F.
8. Pipe enough warm fondant into the chocolate shells to cover the fruit, but do not fill more than seven eighths full.
9. Fill the remainder of the mold with dark couverture.
10. Clean the surface of the mold with a spatula.
11. Cool in a refrigerator until the chocolate releases from the mold.
12. Tap the mold on a table to release the pralines.

PASTRY TECHNIQUES:

Molding, Filling

Molding:

1. Wash your hands.
2. Clear the work area.
3. Carefully shape the substance.

Filling:

1. Cut open the food product.
2. Carefully spread the filling using an icing spatula.
3. Carefully pipe the filling using a pastry bag.

HACCP:

Store at 60° F to 65° F.

CHEF NOTE:

Any fruit liqueur that complements the fruit may be used. Liquors, brandy, or rum offer a suitable alternative for soaking the fruit.

COOKIES
BREADS
SOUFFLES
CREPES
ICE CREAM
SORBETS
CHOCOLATE
MISCELLANEOUS | OTHERS: FINISHED

PASTRY TECHNIQUES:

Whipping, Mixing, Piping, Dipping

Whipping:

1. Hold the whip at a 55-degree angle.
2. Create circles, using a circular motion.
3. The circular motion needs to be perpendicular to the bowl.

Mixing:

1. Follow the proper mixing procedure: creaming, blending, whipping, or combination.

Piping:

With bag:
1. Use a bag with a disposable tip; cut the bag at 45-degree angle.
2. Fill to no more than half full.
3. Burp the bag.

With cone:
1. Cut and fold the piping cone to the appropriate size.
2. Fill the cone with a small amount.
3. Fold the ends to form a triangle.
4. Pipe the desired designs.

Dipping:

1. Prepare the product to the proper dipping temperature.
2. Carefully submerge the product.
3. Dry on parchment paper or a screen.

HACCP:

Store at 60° F to 65° F.

Cognac Truffles

YIELD: 2 pounds.   140 Truffles.

INGREDIENTS:

Couverture, milk, tempered (for stencils)	220 each
Butter, unsalted (70° F)	8 ounces
Honey	5 ounces
Cognac	3 ounces
Couverture, milk, additional, tempered	1 pound
Couverture, milk, additional, tempered (for dipping)	As needed
Couverture, dark, semi-sweet, tempered (for decorating)	As needed

METHOD OF PREPARATION:

1. Gather the equipment and ingredients.
2. Prepare small disks of tempered milk couverture; use the 220 stencils.
3. Whip the butter and honey until light.
4. Add the cognac, and whip lightly.
5. Using a rubber spatula, quickly mix in the tempered milk couverture.
6. Using a medium-straight tip, pipe the filling onto 110 of the couverture stencils; form little mounts.
7. Quickly place a second couverture stencil on top of the filling, and press gently; leave no empty spaces between the couverture stencils.
8. Using a three-prong fork, dip them in tempered milk couverture.
9. Decorate on top with the letter "C" piped out in tempered dark couverture.

PASTRY TECHNIQUES:

Mixing, Piping, Coating, Dipping, Tempering, Spiking

Mixing:

1. Follow the proper mixing procedure: creaming, blending, whipping, or combination.

Piping:

With bag:
1. Use a bag with a disposable tip; cut the bag at 45-degree angle.
2. Fill to no more than half full.
3. Burp the bag.

With cone:
1. Cut and fold the piping cone to the appropriate size.
2. Fill the cone with a small amount.
3. Fold the ends to form a triangle.
4. Pipe the desired designs.

Coating:

1. Use a coating screen, with a sheet pan underneath.
2. Ensure that the product is the correct temperature.
3. Coat the product; use an appropriately-sized utensil.

Dipping:

1. Prepare the product to the proper dipping temperature.
2. Carefully submerge the product.
3. Dry on parchment paper or a screen.

Tempering:

1. Whisk the eggs vigorously while ladling hot liquid.

Spiking:

1. Use chocolate that is appropriately tempered.
2. Drag the truffles across a screen.
3. Use three to four clean swift strokes.

Dark Truffles

YIELD: 3 pounds, 3 ounces.   200 Truffles.

INGREDIENTS:

Couverture, dark, semi-sweet	2 pounds
Cream, heavy	1 pound
Butter, unsalted	3 ounces
Sugar, confectionery (rolling)	As needed
Couverture, additional dark, semi-sweet, tempered (for dipping)	As needed

METHOD OF PREPARATION:

1. Gather the equipment and ingredients.
2. Chop the couverture into small pieces.
3. Scald the heavy cream, and remove from the heat.
4. Add the chopped couverture and butter into the scalded cream.
5. Whisk until smooth.
6. Wrap well, and allow to cool to room temperature.
7. As soon as the ganache mixture is cooled and set, transfer to a mixing bowl; mix, using a rubber spatula, until light in color and texture.
8. Using a pastry bag and a round tip, immediately pipe out ¾-inch round dots of ganache mixture onto parchment-lined sheet pans.
9. When the piping is complete, place the truffles in the refrigerator; allow them to set to marzipan consistency (not fully hardened).
10. Powder your hands with confectionery sugar to reduce sticking; roll each truffle in your hand until rounded.
11. Return the truffles to the parchment-lined sheet pan, and return to the refrigerator; allow them to set.
12. Melt the dark couverture, and temper.
13. Remove the truffles from the refrigerator when fully set.
14. Place a small amount of tempered couverture in one hand, pick up a truffle with the other hand, and roll the truffle gently between the palms of your hands to coat evenly.

(continued)

COOKIES
BREADS
SOUFFLES
CREPES
ICE CREAM
SORBETS
CHOCOLATE
OTHERS: FINISHED
MISCELLANEOUS

HACCP:

Store at 60° F to 65° F.

HAZARDOUS FOOD:

Heavy cream

15. Return the truffles to the sheet pans, and allow to set at room temperature.
16. Use a dipping fork to dip each truffle in tempered dark couverture.
17. Immediately place the truffle on a wire rack.
18. Using two forks, roll the truffle three to four times on the screen; allow the chocolate to develop a spiked texture.
19. Using two dipping forks, place the truffles back on parchment paper. (Do *not* allow the truffles to set on the screen.)

CHEF NOTES:

1. After piping the ganache, do *not* leave the truffles in the refrigerator too long, or they will be too hard to roll.
2. Do *not* overspike, or the chocolate will appear dull.
3. Do *not* spike the truffles too soon, or the texture will melt.
4. Use gloves (latex) to roll the truffle in your hands.

PASTRY TECHNIQUES:

Melting, Cutting

Melting:

1. Prepare the food product to be melted.
2. Place the food product in an appropriate-sized pot over direct heat or over a double boiler.
3. Stir frequently or occasionally, depending on the delicacy of the product, until melted.

OR

1. Place the product on a sheet pan or in a bowl, and place in a low-temperature oven until melted.

Cutting:

Using a sharp knife to cut to the directed size.

HACCP:

Store at 60° F to 65° F.

HAZARDOUS FOODS:

Heavy cream
Egg yolks

Egg-Milk Ganache Pralines

YIELD: 2 pounds, 6 ounces.   120 Pralines.

INGREDIENTS:

Sugar, granulated	3½ ounces
Cream, heavy	9 ounces
Egg yolks	1¾ ounces
Couverture, milk	1 pound, 7¾ ounces
Couverture, dark, semi-sweet, tempered (for coating and decorating)	As needed
Couverture, milk, tempered (for coating)	As needed

METHOD OF PREPARATION:

1. Gather the equipment and ingredients.
2. Melt the sugar in a copper pot over medium heat; continue to cook until golden brown.
3. Remove the sugar from the heat; add the heavy cream, and mix to thoroughly incorporate.
4. Add the egg yolks, and heat the mixture over a double boiler to the stage of nappé, approximately 165° F to 175° F.
5. Chop the milk couverture finely.
6. Add the chopped couverture to the warm mixture, and stir until melted.
7. Pour the mixture, between metal bars, to a ⅓-inch thickness on parchment paper.
8. Chill until set.
9. Coat the bottom with a thin layer of semi-sweet couverture.
10. Turn again, and cut into ¾-inch by 1-inch pieces.
11. Coat with milk couverture.
12. Pipe an "N" on top; use dark couverture.

COOKIES
BREADS
SOUFFLES
CREPES
ICE CREAM
SORBETS
CHOCOLATE
OTHERS: FINISHED
MISCELLANEOUS

PASTRY TECHNIQUES:
Nappér, Mixing, Piping, Dipping

Nappér:
1. Stir the sauce frequently.
2. Frequently check the consistency of the sauce.

Mixing:
1. Follow the proper mixing procedure: creaming, blending, whipping, or combination.

Piping:
With bag:
1. Use a bag with a disposable tip; cut the bag at 45-degree angle.
2. Fill to no more than half full.
3. Burp the bag.
With cone:
1. Cut and fold the piping cone to the appropriate size.
2. Fill the cone with a small amount.
3. Fold the ends to form a triangle.
4. Pipe the desired designs.

Dipping:
1. Prepare the product to the proper dipping temperature.
2. Carefully submerge the product.
3. Dry on parchment paper or a screen.

HACCP:
Store at 60° F to 65° F.

HAZARDOUS FOOD:
Heavy cream
Egg yolks

Egg Yolk–Heavy Cream Truffles

YIELD: 2 pounds, 4½ ounces.   140 Truffles.

INGREDIENTS:

Cream, heavy	9 ounces
Egg yolks	2½ ounces
Couverture, dark, semi-sweet	1 pound, 5½ ounces
Butter, unsalted, soft	3½ ounces
Couverture, milk, stencils	280 each
Couverture, milk, tempered (for dipping)	As needed
Couverture, dark, semi-sweet, tempered (for decorating)	As needed

METHOD OF PREPARATION:

1. Gather the equipment and ingredients.
2. Combine the heavy cream and egg yolks.
3. Heat over a double boiler to the stage of nappé, approximately 165° F to 175° F.
4. Chop the semi-sweet couverture, and add to the cream mixture.
5. Incorporate until the couverture is completely melted.
6. Let the mixture cool to room temperature.
7. Add the butter to the cooled mixture, and whip.
8. Pipe the mixture onto 140 couverture stencils, approximately ¼ ounce each.
9. Top each praline with a second couverture stencil; press lightly.
10. Dip in milk couverture.
11. Decorate with an "S" line, using tempered dark couverture.

PASTRY TECHNIQUES:

Nappér, Mixing, Pouring, Coating, Cutting

Nappér:

1. Stir the sauce frequently.
2. Frequently check the consistency of the sauce.

Mixing:

1. Follow the proper mixing procedure: creaming, blending, whipping, or combination.

Pouring:

1. Place the product in an appropriate container for pouring: a pitcher or large ladle.
2. Pour the product into desired containers or over another product.

Coating:

1. Use a coating screen, with a sheet pan underneath.
2. Ensure that the product is the correct temperature.
3. Coat the product; use an appropriately-sized utensil.

Cutting:

Using a sharp knife to cut to the directed size.

HACCP:

Store at 60° F to 65° F.

HAZARDOUS FOODS:

Heavy cream
Egg yolks

Egg Yolk Mocha Truffles

YIELD: 1 pound, 9 ounces.   100 Truffles.

INGREDIENTS:

Coffee, instant	⅛ ounce
Cream, heavy	6 ounces
Egg yolks	1¼ ounces
Sugar, confectionery, sifted	2½ ounces
Couverture, milk	12 ounces
Couverture, dark, semi-sweet	3 ounces
Couverture, dark, semi-sweet, tempered (for coating)	As needed
Couverture, milk, tempered (for decorating)	As needed

METHOD OF PREPARATION:

1. Gather the equipment and ingredients.
2. Dissolve the instant coffee in a portion of the heavy cream; set aside.
3. Combine the egg yolks, confectionery sugar, and remaining heavy cream; heat over a double boiler to the stage of nappé, approximately 165° F to 175° F.
4. Chop the milk couverture and dark couverture into fine pieces.
5. Place the chopped couverture into the heated cream mixture, and stir until completely melted.
6. Cool the mixture to room temperature.
7. Add the dissolved instant coffee, and stir to combine.
8. Pour, between metal bars, on parchment paper, and spread out to a ½-inch thickness.
9. Chill until set.
10. Turn upside down; coat the bottom thinly with semi-sweet couverture; allow the couverture to set up.
11. Turn again, and cut into ¾-inch by 1-inch pieces.
12. Coat with tempered dark couverture; decorate with one diagonal line and two dots; use tempered milk couverture.

Fruitkrokant

PASTRY TECHNIQUES:

Melting, Pouring, Cutting, Dipping

Melting:

1. Prepare the food product to be melted.
2. Place the food product in an appropriately-sized pot over direct heat or over a double boiler.
3. Stir frequently or occasionally, depending on the delicacy of the product, until melted.

OR

1. Place the product on a sheet pan or in a bowl, and place in a low-temperature oven until melted.

Pouring:

1. Place the product in an appropriate container for pouring: a pitcher or large ladle.
2. Pour the product into desired containers or over another product.

Cutting:

Using a sharp knife to cut to the directed size.

Dipping:

1. Prepare the product to the proper dipping temperature.
2. Carefully submerge the product.
3. Dry on parchment paper or a screen.

HACCP:

Store at 60° F to 65° F.

YIELD: 1 pound, 11 ounces.   80 Pralines.

INGREDIENTS:

Sugar, granulated	6 ounces
Butter, unsalted	2½ ounces
Honey	1 ounce
Almonds, toasted, slivered	5½ ounces
Almonds, toasted, sliced	4½ ounces
Pistachios, ground	1 ounce
Walnuts, chopped	3½ ounces
Compound, banana-flavored	3 ounces
Couverture, dark, semi-sweet, tempered (for dipping)	As needed

METHOD OF PREPARATION:

1. Gather the equipment and ingredients.
2. Melt the sugar gradually in small stages.
3. Cook until golden brown.
4. Remove from the heat.
5. Add the butter, and stir.
6. Add the honey, and stir.
7. Combine all of the nuts, and incorporate into the sugar mixture.
8. Add the compound to the mixture.
9. Pour the mixture, between metal bars, onto slightly oiled parchment paper; cover with parchment paper, and roll to a ⅓-inch thickness.
10. Let the mixture cool at room temperature.
11. Spread a thin layer of tempered dark couverture on the bottom.
12. Turn over, and cut into ¾-inch by ¾-inch pieces.
13. Dip the sides and bottom in tempered dark couverture.

CHEF NOTE:

Banana compound may be substituted with pear compound or apple compound.

Ganache No. 1

PASTRY TECHNIQUES:
Chopping, Scalding, Combining

Chopping:
1. Use a sharp knife.
2. Hold the food product properly.
3. Cut with a quick downward motion.

Scalding:
1. Heat the liquid on high heat.
2. Do not boil the liquid.

Combining:
Bringing together two or more components.
1. Prepare the components to be combined.
2. Add one to the other, using the appropriate mixing method (if needed).

HACCP:
Store at 40° F.

HAZARDOUS FOOD:
Heavy cream

YIELD:	SOFT 2 pounds, 12 ounces.	SEMI-HARD 2 pounds.	HARD 1 pound, 12 ounces.
INGREDIENTS:			
Cream, heavy	1 pound, 12 ounces	1 pound	8 ounces
Butter, unsalted	As needed	As needed	4 ounces
Couverture, dark, semi-sweet	1 pound	1 pound	1 pound

METHOD OF PREPARATION:

1. Gather the equipment and ingredients.
2. Place the heavy cream and butter, if necessary, in a saucepan and scald.
3. Chop the dark couverture very fine.
4. Add the couverture to the scalded cream.
5. Stir until smooth and the consistency is uniform.
6. Cool to room temperature.

CHEF NOTE:
For best results, let the ganache sit for at least 24 hours before use. Butter also may be added to either soft or semi-hard ganache to enhance its texture.

Ganache No. 2

COOKIES

BREADS

SOUFFLES

CREPES

ICE CREAM

SORBETS

CHOCOLATE

OTHERS: FINISHED

MISCELLANEOUS

PASTRY TECHNIQUES:
Chopping, Scalding, Combining

Chopping:
1. Use a sharp knife.
2. Hold the food product properly.
3. Cut with a quick downward motion.

Scalding:
1. Heat the liquid on high heat.
2. Do not boil the liquid.

Combining:
Bringing together two or more components.
1. Prepare the components to be combined.
2. Add one to the other, using the appropriate mixing method (if needed).

HACCP:
Store at 40° F.

HAZARDOUS FOOD:
Heavy cream

YIELD:	1 pound, 14 ounces.	3 pounds, 12 ounces.
INGREDIENTS:		
Couverture, dark, semi-sweet	1 pound, 2 ounces	2 pounds, 4 ounces
Cream, heavy	8 ounces	1 pound
Butter, unsalted	4 ounces	8 ounces

METHOD OF PREPARATION:

1. Gather the equipment and ingredients.
2. Place the heavy cream and butter in a saucepan, and scald.
3. Chop the dark couverture very fine.
4. Add couverture to scalded cream.
5. Stir until smooth and uniform in consistency.
6. Cool to room temperature.

CHEF NOTE:
For best results, let the ganache sit for at least 24 hours before use.

PASTRY TECHNIQUES:

Mixing, Molding

Mixing:

1. Follow the proper mixing procedure: creaming, blending, whipping, or combination.

Molding:

1. Wash your hands.
2. Clear the work area.
3. Carefully shape the substance.

HAZARDOUS FOOD:

Heavy cream

Ganache Cordials

YIELD: 3 pounds, 9 ounces.   200 Pralines.

INGREDIENTS:

Cream, heavy	14 ounces
Glucose	3 ounces
Orange zest, very fine (optional)	1 orange
Couverture, milk	1 pound
Couverture, dark, semi-sweet	1 pound
Butter, unsalted	3 ounces
Liqueur, orange	5 ounces
Couverture, dark, semi-sweet, tempered (for molding)	As needed

METHOD OF PREPARATION:

1. Gather the equipment and ingredients.
2. Bring the heavy cream, glucose, and (optional) orange zest to a boil.
3. Strain this mixture.
4. Chop the milk couverture and dark couverture into fine pieces.
5. Add the milk couverture, dark couverture, and butter to the heated cream mixture.
6. Stir well until everything is melted.
7. Add the liqueur, and stir well.
8. Set aside.

Molding and Assembling Pralines:

1. Fill the chocolate molds with tempered couverture.
2. Tap the molds to release air bubbles.
3. Pour out excess couverture, and place the molds, upside down, on a dipping screen until the chocolate begins to set.
4. Turn the open cavity up, and, using a clean bench scraper, scrape off excess couverture.
5. When the chocolate shells are set, pipe the soft ganache mixture into the shells; fill the shells nine tenths full.
6. Fill the remainder of the mold with tempered couverture.
7. Remove excess couverture with a spatula; scrape hard to ensure a clean shell.
8. Cool in a refrigerator until the praline releases from the mold. (Do not freeze.)
9. Tap the mold on a table to release the praline.

CHEF NOTE:

Suitable liqueurs for ganache cordials include Kirschwasser, Cointreau, Grand Marnier, or brandy or rum can also be used.

Gianduja No. 1

COOKIES
BREADS
SOUFFLES
CREPES
ICE CREAM
SORBETS
CHOCOLATE
OTHERS: FINISHED
MISCELLANEOUS

PASTRY TECHNIQUES:

Mixing

Mixing:

1. Follow the proper mixing procedure: creaming, blending, whipping, or combination.

HACCP:

Store at 60° F to 65° F.

YIELD: 4 pounds.

INGREDIENTS:

Couverture, dark, semi-sweet	1 pound, 8 ounces
Paste, praline or peanut butter	2 pounds, 8 ounces

METHOD OF PREPARATION:

1. Gather the equipment and ingredients.
2. Chop the dark couverture into fine pieces.
3. Melt the finely chopped dark couverture to 113° F, and remove from the heat.
4. Smooth the praline paste with a spoon, or, if necessary, warm it slightly over a double boiler.
5. Add the smooth praline paste to the melted dark couverture; combine well.
6. Before using, temper the mixture to a paste-like consistency over a cold water bath.

Gianduja No. 2

YIELD: 4 pounds.

PASTRY TECHNIQUES:
Mixing

Mixing:
1. Follow the proper mixing procedure: creaming, blending, whipping, or combination.

HACCP:
Store at 60° F to 65° F.

INGREDIENTS:

Couverture, dark, semi-sweet	1 pound, 8 ounces
Paste, praline or peanut butter	2 pounds, 8 ounces

METHOD OF PREPARATION:

1. Gather the equipment and ingredients.
2. Temper the dark couverture properly.
3. Smooth the praline paste with a spoon, or, if necessary, warm it slightly over a double boiler.
4. Add the smooth praline paste to the dark couverture; combine well.

Chocolate **367**

COOKIES

BREADS

SOUFFLES

CREPES

ICE CREAM

SORBETS

CHOCOLATE

FINISHED

MISCELLANEOUS | OTHERS: FINISHED

PASTRY TECHNIQUES:
Melting, Whipping, Piping, Dipping

Melting:
1. Prepare the food product to be melted.
2. Place the food product in an appropriately-sized pot over direct heat or over a double boiler.
3. Stir frequently or occasionally, depending on the delicacy of the product, until melted.
OR
1. Place the product on a sheet pan or in a bowl, and place in a low oven until melted.

Whipping:
1. Hold the whip at a 55-degree angle.
2. Create circles, using a circular motion.
3. The circular motion needs to be perpendicular to the bowl.

Piping:
With bag:
1. Use a bag with a disposable tip; cut the bag at 45-degree angle.
2. Fill to no more than half full.
3. Burp the bag.
With cone:
1. Cut and fold the piping cone to the appropriate size.
2. Fill the cone with a small amount.
3. Fold the ends to form a triangle.
4. Pipe the desired designs.

Dipping:
1. Prepare the product to the proper dipping temperature.
2. Carefully submerge the product.
3. Dry on parchment paper or a screen.

HACCP:
Store at 60° F 65 to ° F.

Grand Marnier Butter Truffles

YIELD: 1 pound, 9¼ ounces.   80 Truffles.

INGREDIENTS:

Butter, unsalted, room temperature	5¼ ounces
Fondant	5¼ ounces
Couverture, milk	7 ounces
Couverture, dark, semi-sweet	5¼ ounces
Liqueur, Grand Marnier	2½ ounces
Couverture, milk, stencils	80 each
Couverture, milk, tempered (for dipping)	As needed

METHOD OF PREPARATION:
1. Gather the equipment and ingredients.
2. Combine the butter and fondant until smooth.
3. Melt the milk couverture and dark couverture, but do not exceed 90° F.
4. Fold the couvertures into the butter and fondant mixture.
5. Add the Grand Marnier into the mixture, and combine well.
6. Cool the mixture at room temperature.
7. Whip the mixture slightly.
8. With a star tip, pipe the mixture onto stencils.
9. Cool in a refrigerator until set.
10. Dip in milk couverture.

Grenoble No. 1

Rolling:

1. Prepare the rolling surface by dusting with the appropriate medium (flour, cornstarch, etc.).
2. Use the appropriate style pin (stick pin or ball bearing pin) to roll the dough to desired thickness; rotate the dough during rolling to prevent sticking.

Cutting:

Using a sharp knife to cut to the directed size.

Dipping:

1. Prepare the product to the proper dipping temperature.
2. Carefully submerge the product.
3. Dry on parchment paper or a screen.

HACCP:

Store at 60° F to 65° F.

YIELD: 2 pounds, 10 ounces.   150 Pralines.

INGREDIENTS:

Marzipan (see page 422)	2 pounds
Walnuts, ground	7 ounces
Glucose	1 ounce
Kirschwasser	2 ounces
Sugar, confectionery	As needed
Fondant, Kirschwasser-flavored	As needed
Walnuts or pecans	130 halves
Couverture, dark, semi-sweet, tempered (for dipping)	As needed

METHOD OF PREPARATION:

1. Gather the equipment and ingredients.
2. Mix the marzipan, ground walnuts, glucose, and Kirschwasser by hand until well combined.
3. Roll out the marzipan ⅓-inch thick on a surface dusted lightly with confectionery sugar.
4. Using a 1-inch round cutter, cut the marzipan.
5. Place the marzipan rounds on parchment-lined sheet pans, and allow to dry slightly.
6. Melt the fondant to 120° F.
7. Using a two-prong dipping fork, dip the bottom and sides of the marzipan disks into the fondant.
8. Return the rounds to the sheet pans, fondant side up. Place a nut half on each fondant disk, and allow to set.
9. Temper the dark couverture.
10. Using the dipping fork or holding the nut with the fingertips, dip the bottom and sides of the marzipan round into dark couverture. (The top surface of the praline should be clear of couverture.)

COOKIES

BREADS

SOUFFLES

CREPES

ICE CREAM

SORBETS

CHOCOLATE

OTHERS: FINISHED

MISCELLANEOUS

PASTRY TECHNIQUES:
Mixing, Rolling, Cutting, Coating

Mixing:
1. Follow the proper mixing procedure: creaming, blending, whipping, or combination.

Rolling:
1. Prepare the rolling surface by dusting with the appropriate medium (flour, cornstarch, etc.).
2. Use the appropriate style pin (stick pin or ball bearing pin) to roll the dough to desired thickness; rotate the dough during rolling to prevent sticking.

Cutting:
Using a sharp knife to cut to the directed size.

Coating:
1. Use a coating screen, with a sheet pan underneath.
2. Ensure that the product is the correct temperature.
3. Coat the product; use an appropriately-sized utensil.

HACCP:
Store at 60° F to 65° F.

Grenoble No. 2

YIELD: 1 pound, 6½ ounces.   80 Pralines.

INGREDIENTS:

Almond paste	18 ounces
Arrak (rice brandy) or brandy	1 ounce
Walnuts, finely chopped	3½ ounces
Couverture, white, tempered (for coating)	As needed
Walnut pieces	80 each
Couverture, dark, semi-sweet, tempered (for coating)	As needed

METHOD OF PREPARATION:

1. Gather the equipment and ingredients.
2. Mix the almond paste and brandy to a smooth, lump-free paste.
3. Add the chopped walnuts to the mixture.
4. Roll out, between metal bars, to a ½-inch thickness, and cut out with a round ⅞-inch cutter.
5. Coat the top with tempered white couverture; immediately place a walnut piece on top.
6. Coat the sides and bottom with dark couverture.

PASTRY TECHNIQUES:
Whipping, Mixing, Piping, Dipping

Whipping:
1. Hold the whip at a 55-degree angle.
2. Create circles, using a circular motion.
3. The circular motion needs to be perpendicular to the bowl.

Mixing:
1. Follow the proper mixing procedure: creaming, blending, whipping, or combination.

Piping:
With bag:
1. Use a bag with a disposable tip; cut the bag at 45-degree angle.
2. Fill to no more than half full.
3. Burp the bag.
With cone:
1. Cut and fold the piping cone to the appropriate size.
2. Fill the cone with a small amount.
3. Fold the ends to form a triangle.
4. Pipe the desired designs.

Dipping:
1. Prepare the product to the proper dipping temperature.
2. Carefully submerge the product.
3. Dry on parchment paper or a screen.

HACCP:
Store at 60° F to 65° F.

Hawaii

YIELD: 1 pound, 14¾ ounces.   100 Pralines.

INGREDIENTS:

Pineapple, dried, candied	1½ ounces
Rum, dark	As needed
Couverture, milk, stencils	200 each
Butter, unsalted (70° F)	8 ounces
Fondant	3 ounces
Rum, dark, additional	1 ounce
Compound, pineapple	1¼ ounces
Couverture, milk, tempered	1 pound
Couverture, milk or dark (semisweet), tempered (for dipping)	As needed

METHOD OF PREPARATION:

1. Gather the equipment and ingredients.
2. Soak the pineapple in dark rum (preferably overnight).
3. Drain the soaked pineapple and save the dark rum for future soakings. Chop finely.
4. Prepare 200 milk couverture stencils.
5. Whip the butter and fondant until light.
6. Add 1 ounce of dark rum, the pineapple compound, and the soaked dried pineapple; whip together.
7. Using a rubber spatula, quickly mix the tempered milk couverture into the butter mixture.
8. Using a medium-straight tube, pipe the filling onto 100 of the couverture stencils; form little mounts.
9. Quickly place a second dot on the fillings, and press gently; do not leave any empty spaces between the chocolate dots.
10. Let the filling set.
11. Using a three-prong fork, dip the fillings in tempered milk couverture or dark couverture.
12. Decorate with lines of dark (or milk) couverture.

COOKIES
BREADS
SOUFFLES
CREPES
ICE CREAM
SORBETS
CHOCOLATE
OTHERS: FINISHED
MISCELLANEOUS

PASTRY TECHNIQUES:

Mixing, Piping, Dipping, Decorating

Mixing:

1. Follow the proper mixing procedure: creaming, blending, whipping, or combination.

Piping:

With bag:
1. Use a bag with a disposable tip; cut the bag at 45-degree angle.
2. Fill to no more than half full.
3. Burp the bag.

With cone:
1. Cut and fold the piping cone to the appropriate size.
2. Fill the cone with a small amount.
3. Fold the ends to form a triangle.
4. Pipe the desired designs.

Dipping:

1. Prepare the product to the proper dipping temperature.
2. Carefully submerge the product.
3. Dry on parchment paper or a screen.

Decorating:

1. Follow the formula's instructions or the instructor's guidelines to appropriately decorate each cake or pastry.

HACCP:

Store at 60° F to 65° F.

HAZARDOUS FOOD:

Heavy cream

Kahlua–Heavy Cream Truffles

YIELD: 1 pound, 1½ ounces.   70 Truffles.

INGREDIENTS:

Coffee, instant	⅛ ounce
Kahlua	1¾ ounces
Cream, heavy	5¼ ounces
Couverture, dark, semi-sweet, chopped	10½ ounces
Paste, mocha	As needed
Couverture, dark, semi-sweet, stencils	70 each
Couverture, dark, semi-sweet, tempered (for dipping)	As needed
Couverture, milk, tempered (for decorating)	As needed
Sugar, granulated	As needed

METHOD OF PREPARATION:

1. Gather the equipment and ingredients.
2. Dissolve the instant coffee in the Kahlua.
3. Bring the heavy cream to a boil.
4. Add the chopped couverture to the boiling cream; stir well.
5. Cool to room temperature.
6. Add the dissolved coffee-Kahlua mixture and mocha paste; combine.
7. Using a medium-large star tip, pipe the mixture onto the couverture stencils.
8. After this sets for 1 hour, dip it in dark couverture.
9. Decorate the pointed top of the praline only, using milk couverture and granulated sugar.

Lemon Ganache

YIELD: 1 pound, 11½ ounces.   110 Pralines.

PASTRY TECHNIQUES:
Mixing, Spreading, Cutting, Dipping

Mixing:
1. Follow the proper mixing procedure: creaming, blending, whipping, or combination.

Spreading:
1. Using an icing spatula or off-set spatula, smooth the icing or other spreading medium over the surface area.

Cutting:
Using a sharp knife to cut to the directed size.

Dipping:
1. Prepare the product to the proper dipping temperature.
2. Carefully submerge the product.
3. Dry on parchment paper or a screen.

HACCP:
Store at 60° F to 65° F.

HAZARDOUS FOOD:
Heavy cream

INGREDIENTS:

Couverture, dark, semi-sweet	1 pound, 2 ounces
Cream, heavy	8 ounces
Lemon rind	1 large lemon
Butter, unsalted, room temperature	1½ ounces
Couverture, dark, semi-sweet, tempered (for dipping)	As needed

METHOD OF PREPARATION:

1. Gather the equipment and ingredients.
2. Chop the dark couverture very fine.
3. Bring the heavy cream to a boil.
4. Grate the lemon rind as fine as possible.
5. Add the grated rind to the heavy cream, and mix well.
6. Place the chopped couverture into the heavy cream mixture, and using a whisk, stir until all of the lumps have been removed.
7. Pour the ganache on parchment paper; place it on a marble slab or in the refrigerator until the ganache begins to set up.
8. Place the ganache in a bowl, and add the butter. Using a rubber spatula, mix until well blended. (The butter should not be firmer than the ganache.)
9. Quickly spread the ganache, between metal bars, until it is ⅓-inch thick, to form a rectangular sheet.
10. Remove the bars with a small knife.
11. Let the sheet become firm in the refrigerator for 5 minutes and then at room temperature for at least 10 minutes until fully set.
12. Spread a very thin layer of tempered dark couverture on both sides of the sheet.
13. Cut the ganache into ¹¹⁄₁₆-inch by 1-inch rectangles.
14. Dip in tempered dark couverture, using a three-prong fork; decorate with one fork line (diagonal).

Malakoff

YIELD: 2 pounds.   110 Pralines.

PASTRY TECHNIQUES:

Mixing, Spreading, Cutting, Pouring, Decorating

Mixing:

1. Follow the proper mixing procedure: creaming, blending, whipping, or combination.

Spreading:

1. Using an icing spatula or off-set spatula, smooth the icing or other spreading medium over the surface area.

Cutting:

Using a sharp knife to cut to the directed size.

Pouring:

1. Place the product in an appropriate container for pouring: a pitcher or large ladle.
2. Pour the product into desired containers or over another product.

Decorating:

1. Follow the formula's instructions or the instructor's guidelines to appropriately decorate each cake or pastry.

HACCP:

Store at 60° F to 65° F.

CHEF NOTES:

1. Do not allow the chocolate to harden too much, or it will crack when it is cut. Two persons should work together. One person should coat the strips while the other person cuts them.
2. Instead of using milk couverture and praline paste or peanut butter, replaced them with pre-made gianduja.
3. Almonds, peanuts, or hazelnuts may be used as the toasted nuts.

INGREDIENTS:

Couverture, milk	10 ounces
Paste, praline or peanut butter	15 ounces
Nuts, toasted, chopped or sliced	5 ounces
Cherries, candied, finely chopped	2 ounces
Couverture, milk, tempered (for pouring)	As needed

METHOD OF PREPARATION:

1. Gather the equipment and ingredients.
2. Melt the milk couverture to 113° F.
3. Using a metal spoon or stiff rubber spatula, add the praline paste or peanut butter to the couverture.
4. Cool the mixture in a cold water bath, stirring constantly, until it begins to firm up.
5. Add the nuts and candied cherries; mix until blended.
6. Spread the paste, between metal bars, ⅓-inch thick, to form a rectangle (about 8 inches wide.)
7. Remove the bars using a small knife.
8. Let the paste set.
9. Spread a small amount of tempered milk couverture on the top of the sheet, and flip it over.
10. Cut the sheet into 1-inch strips.
11. Put two or three strips about 1-inch apart onto a small dipping screen.
12. Place the screen over a bowl of tempered couverture. The screen should rest on the edge of the bowl.
13. Using a ladle, pour couverture over the strips to completely cover them. Knock the screen to remove excess chocolate.
14. Using a four-prong fork, make lines on the surface.
15. Using a spatula, remove the coated strips from the screen while the couverture is still soft. Place them on parchment paper.
16. As soon as the chocolate begins to set, cut into ¾-inch pieces.

COOKIES
BREADS
SOUFFLES
CREPES
ICE CREAM
SORBETS
CHOCOLATE
OTHERS: FINISHED
MISCELLANEOUS

Messina

YIELD: 1 pound, 2 ounces.   80 Pralines.

PASTRY TECHNIQUES:
Mixing, Rolling, Cutting, Dipping, Decorating

Mixing:

1. Follow the proper mixing procedure: creaming, blending, whipping, or combination.

Rolling:

1. Prepare the rolling surface by dusting with the appropriate medium (flour, cornstarch, etc.).
2. Use the appropriate style pin (stick pin or ball bearing pin) to roll the dough to desired thickness; rotate the dough during rolling to prevent sticking.

Cutting:

Using a sharp knife to cut to the directed size.

Dipping:

1. Prepare the product to the proper dipping temperature.
2. Carefully submerge the product.
3. Dry on parchment paper or a screen.

Decorating:

1. Follow the formula's instructions or the instructor's guidelines to appropriately decorate each cake or pastry.

HACCP:

Store at 60° F to 65° F.

INGREDIENTS:

Marzipan (see page 422)	1 pound
Orange rind, grated	1 orange
Powder, citric acid	To taste
Compound, orange	2 ounces
Sugar, confectionery	As needed to stiffen mixture
Couverture, dark, semi-sweet, tempered (for dipping)	As needed

METHOD OF PREPARATION:

1. Gather the equipment and ingredients.
2. Place the marzipan, orange rind, citric acid powder, orange compound, and confectionery sugar in a bowl.
3. Mix until it becomes a smooth, medium-soft paste. (The amount of confectionery sugar to be added depends on the marzipan. The paste should not be sticky.)
4. Roll out to a $\frac{1}{3}$-inch thickness.
5. Cut into small, round pieces.
6. Allow the centers to dry slightly to prevent them from sticking to the dipping fork.
7. Dip them into dark couverture.
8. Decorate with three fork lines on top of each praline.

Milk Truffles

COOKIES
BREADS
SOUFFLES
CREPES
ICE CREAM
SORBETS
CHOCOLATE
OTHERS: FINISHED
MISCELLANEOUS

PASTRY TECHNIQUES:
Mixing, Piping, Coating, Dipping, Tempering, Spiking

Mixing:
1. Follow the proper mixing procedure: creaming, blending, whipping, or combination.

Piping:
With bag:
1. Use a bag with a disposable tip; cut the bag at 45-degree angle.
2. Fill to no more than half full.
3. Burp the bag.
With cone:
1. Cut and fold the piping cone to the appropriate size.
2. Fill the cone with a small amount.
3. Fold the ends to form a triangle.
4. Pipe the desired designs.

Coating:
1. Use a coating screen, with a sheet pan underneath.
2. Ensure that the product is the correct temperature.
3. Coat the product; use an appropriately-sized utensil.

Dipping:
1. Prepare the product to the proper dipping temperature.
2. Carefully submerge the product.
3. Dry on parchment paper or a screen.

Tempering:
1. Whisk the eggs vigorously while ladling hot liquid.

YIELD: 3 pounds, 11 ounces.   230 Truffles

INGREDIENTS:

Couverture, milk	2 pounds, 8 ounces
Cream, heavy	1 pound
Butter, unsalted	3 ounces
Sugar, confectionery (rolling)	As needed
Couverture, additional milk, tempered (for dipping)	As needed

METHOD OF PREPARATION:

1. Gather the equipment and ingredients.
2. Chop the couverture into small pieces.
3. Scald the heavy cream, and remove from the heat.
4. Add the chopped couverture and butter into the scalded cream.
5. Whisk until smooth.
6. Wrap well, and allow to cool to room temperature.
7. As soon as the ganache mixture is cooled and set, transfer to a mixing bowl, and mix, using a rubber spatula, until light in color and texture.
8. Using a pastry bag and a round tip, immediately pipe out ¾-inch round dots of ganache mixture onto parchment-lined sheet pans.
9. When the piping is complete, place the truffles in the refrigerator; allow them to set to marzipan consistency (not fully hardened).
10. Powder your hands with confectionery sugar to reduce sticking, and roll each truffle in your hand until rounded.
11. Return the truffles to the parchment-lined sheet pan, and return to the refrigerator; allow them to set.
12. Melt the milk couverture, and temper.
13. Remove the truffles from the refrigerator when fully set.
14. Place a small amount of tempered couverture in one hand, pick up a truffle with the other hand, and roll the truffle gently between the palms of your hands to coat evenly.

(continued)

Spiking:
1. Use chocolate that is appropriately tempered.
2. Drag the truffles across a screen.
3. Use three to four clean swift strokes.

HACCP:
Store at 60° F to 65° F.

HAZARDOUS FOOD:
Heavy cream

15. Return the truffles to the sheet pans, and allow them to set at room temperature.
16. Using a dipping fork, dip each truffle in tempered milk couverture.
17. Immediately place the truffle on a wire rack.
18. Using two forks, roll the truffle three to four times on the screen; allow the chocolate to develop a spiked texture.
19. Using two dipping forks, place the truffles back on the parchment paper. (Do *not* allow the truffles to set on the screen.)

CHEF NOTES:
1. After piping the ganache, do *not* leave the truffles in the refrigerator too long, or they will be too hard to roll.
2. Do *not* overspike, or the chocolate will appear dull.
3. Do *not* spike the truffles too soon, or the texture will melt.
4. Use gloves (latex) to roll the truffles in your hand.

PASTRY TECHNIQUES:
Mixing, Spreading, Cutting, Dipping, Decorating

Mixing:
1. Follow the proper mixing procedure: creaming, blending, whipping, or combination.

Spreading:
1. Using an icing spatula or off-set spatula, smooth the icing or other spreading medium over the surface area.

Cutting:
Using a sharp knife to cut to the directed size.

Dipping:
1. Prepare the product to the proper dipping temperature.
2. Carefully submerge the product.
3. Dry on parchment paper or a screen.

Decorating:
1. Follow the formula's instructions or the instructor's guidelines to appropriately decorate each cake of pastry.

HACCP:
Store at 60° F to 65° F.

HAZARDOUS FOOD:
Heavy cream

Mocha Squares

YIELD: 2 pounds, 7 ounces.   150 Pralines.

INGREDIENTS:

Coffee, instant	½ ounce
Brandy	½ ounce
Cream, heavy	10 ounces
Couverture, milk, chopped	1 pound, 6 ounces
Couverture, dark, semi-sweet, chopped	3 ounces
Butter, unsalted, soft	3 ounces
Couverture, milk, tempered (for spreading and dipping)	As needed
Chocolate coffee beans	150 each

METHOD OF PREPARATION:

1. Gather the equipment and ingredients.
2. Dissolve the instant coffee in the brandy.
3. Bring the heavy cream to a boil.
4. Add the chopped couvertures; stir until the couvertures have melted; make sure the mixture is free of lumps.
5. Add the dissolved instant coffee, and mix well.
6. Pour the ganache on parchment paper; place it on a marble table or in the refrigerator until the ganache begins to set.
7. After it begins to set, place the ganache in a bowl; add the soft butter. (The butter should not be firmer than the ganache.)
8. Using a rubber spatula, mix until well blended.
9. Quickly spread the ganache, between metal bars, to a ⅓-inch thickness to form a rectangular sheet.
10. Remove the bars with a small knife.
11. Let the ganache firm up completely.
12. When the ganache is firm, spread a very thin layer of tempered milk couverture on both sides of the sheet.
13. Cut the ganache into ¹³/₁₆-inch squares.
14. Using a three-prong fork, dip in tempered milk couverture.
15. Decorate each with a chocolate coffee bean.

Mocha Sticks

YIELD: 2 pounds, 3½ ounces.   130 Pralines.

PASTRY TECHNIQUES:

Mixing, Whipping, Piping, Cutting, Dipping, Decorating

Mixing:

1. Follow the proper mixing procedure: creaming, blending, whipping, or combination.

Whipping:

1. Hold the whip at a 55-degree angle.
2. Create circles, using a circular motion.
3. The circular motion needs to be perpendicular to the bowl.

Piping:

With bag:
1. Use a bag with a disposable tip; cut the bag at 45-degree angle.
2. Fill to no more than half full.
3. Burp the bag.

With cone:
1. Cut and fold the piping cone to the appropriate size.
2. Fill the cone with a small amount.
3. Fold the ends to form a triangle.
4. Pipe the desired designs.

Cutting:

Using a sharp knife to cut to the directed size.

Dipping:

1. Prepare the product to the proper dipping temperature.
2. Carefully submerge the product.
3. Dry on parchment paper or a screen.

Decorating:

1. Follow the formula's instructions or the instructor's guidelines to appropriately decorate each cake or pastry.

HACCP:

Store at 60° F to 65° F.

HAZARDOUS FOOD:

Heavy cream

INGREDIENTS:

Coffee, instant	½ ounce
Brandy	As needed
Cream, heavy	10 ounces
Couverture, milk, chopped	1 pound, 6 ounces
Couverture, dark, semi-sweet, chopped	3 ounces
Couverture, milk, tempered (for dipping)	As needed
Sugar, confectionery, or couverture, dark, semi-sweet, tempered (for decorating)	As needed

METHOD OF PREPARATION:

1. Gather the equipment and ingredients.
2. Dissolve the instant coffee in the brandy.
3. Bring the heavy cream to a boil.
4. Add the chopped couvertures, and stir until completely melted.
5. Add the dissolved instant coffee.
6. Cool the mixture to room temperature.
7. Whip lightly.
8. Using a medium-large round tip, pipe log shapes onto parchment paper.
9. Chill until set.
10. Cut into 1-inch lengths; dip in tempered milk couverture.
11. Sift a thin layer of confectionery sugar over the pralines before they set completely, or pipe lines of tempered dark couverture on the surface.

Mont Blanc

YIELD: 2 pounds, 1 ounce.   120 Pralines.

COOKIES
BREADS
SOUFFLES
CREPES
ICE CREAM
SORBETS
CHOCOLATE
OTHERS: FINISHED
MISCELLANEOUS

PASTRY TECHNIQUES:
Whipping, Folding, Piping, Dipping

Whipping:
1. Hold the whip at a 55-degree angle.
2. Create circles, using a circular motion.
3. The circular motion needs to be perpendicular to the bowl.

Folding:
Do steps 1, 2, and 3 in one continuous motion.
1. Run a bowl scraper under the mixture, across the bottom of the bowl.
2. Turn the bowl counterclockwise.
3. Bring the bottom mixture to the top.

Piping:
With bag:
1. Use a bag with a disposable tip; cut the bag at 45-degree angle.
2. Fill to no more than half full.
3. Burp the bag.
With cone:
1. Cut and fold the piping cone to the appropriate size.
2. Fill the cone with a small amount.
3. Fold the ends to form a triangle.
4. Pipe the desired designs.

Dipping:
1. Prepare the product to the proper dipping temperature.
2. Carefully submerge the product.
3. Dry on parchment paper or a screen.

HACCP:
Store at 60° F to 65° F.

INGREDIENTS:

Couverture, dark, semi-sweet, stencils	120 stencils
Butter, unsalted, room temperature	8 ounces
Fondant	6 ounces
Liqueur, Kirschwasser	3 ounces
Couverture, tempered, dark (semi-sweet) or milk	1 pound
Couverture, dark, semi-sweet, tempered (for dipping)	As needed

METHOD OF PREPARATION:

1. Gather the equipment and ingredients.
2. Prepare the couverture stencils, still adhering to parchment paper.
3. Whip the butter and fondant until light and airy.
4. Slowly incorporate the liqueur.
5. Whip again until the maximum lightness is achieved.
6. Using a rubber spatula, fold in the tempered couverture that is at 90° F.
7. Place this mixture in a pastry bag with a round tube; pipe the mixture immediately onto the couverture stencils. The shape should be comparable to a Hershey kiss or teardrop.
8. Place on rack to set, or refrigerate until they are set.
9. Using a three-prong fork, dip each praline in tempered dark couverture, and let them set.

CHEF NOTES:
1. The liqueur used can be Kirschwasser, brandy, or rum.
2. The classical way of finishing a Mont Blanc is to dip the tip in melted cocoa butter, then in granulated sugar, to resemble a snow-covered mountain, hence the name Mont Blanc.
3. If the tempered couverture is below 90° F when added to the butter mixture, it will begin to set before it is incorporated with the other ingredients. This will result in a lumpy filling that will remain too soft.

PASTRY TECHNIQUES:
Melting, Rolling, Cutting, Coating

Melting:
1. Prepare the food product to be melted.
2. Place the food product in an appropriately-sized pot over direct heat or over a double boiler.
3. Stir frequently or occasionally, depending on the delicacy of the product, until melted.
OR
1. Place the product on a sheet pan or in a bowl, and place in a low oven until melted.

Rolling:
1. Prepare the rolling surface by dusting with the appropriate medium (flour, cornstarch, etc.).
2. Use the appropriate style pin (stick pin or ball bearing pin) to roll the dough to desired thickness; rotate the dough during rolling to prevent sticking.

Cutting:
Using a sharp knife to cut to the directed size.

Coating:
1. Use a coating screen, with a sheet pan underneath.
2. Ensure that the product is the correct temperature.
3. Coat the product; use an appropriately-sized utensil.

HACCP:
Store at 60° F to 65° F.

HAZARDOUS FOOD:
Heavy cream

Nougat with Almond Paste

YIELD: 3 pounds, 3 ounces.   140 Pralines.

INGREDIENTS:

Almond paste	1 pound
Cream, heavy	4 ounces
Extract, vanilla	To taste
Cinnamon, ground	To taste
Sugar, granulated	1 pound, 2 ounces
Glucose	2 ounces
Butter, unsalted	1 ounce
Almonds, lightly toasted, crushed	10 ounces
Couverture, dark, semi-sweet, tempered (for coating)	As needed

METHOD OF PREPARATION:

1. Gather the equipment and ingredients.
2. In a bowl, soften the almond paste with half of the heavy cream.
3. Add the vanilla extract and cinnamon to the almond paste mixture.
4. Melt the sugar, glucose, and butter together until it reaches a golden color.
5. Add the remaining cream; stir well.
6. Add the almond paste mixture to the caramel mixture, and stir to a thick paste. (The mixture will lose shine if overmixed.)
7. Remove from the heat, and incorporate the almonds.
8. Pour the paste, between metal bars, onto oiled parchment paper, and roll out with an oiled rolling pin to a ⅓-inch thickness.
9. Let cool completely, and turn it over.
10. Spread a thin layer of tempered couverture over the bottom; allow it to set.
11. Turn it over again, and cut it into 1-inch by 1-inch squares.
12. Coat half of the top diagonally with tempered dark couverture.
13. Coat the sides and bottom with tempered couverture.

COOKIES
BREADS
SOUFFLES
CREPES
ICE CREAM
SORBETS
CHOCOLATE
OTHERS: FINISHED
MISCELLANEOUS

Whipping, Mixing, Pouring, Cutting, Coating

Whipping:

1. Hold the whip at a 55-degree angle.
2. Create circles, using a circular motion.
3. The circular motion needs to be perpendicular to the bowl.

Mixing:

1. Follow the proper mixing procedure: creaming, blending, whipping, or combination.

Pouring:

1. Place the product in an appropriate container for pouring: a pitcher or large ladle.
2. Pour the product into desired containers or over another product.

Cutting:

Using a sharp knife to cut to the directed size.

Coating:

1. Use a coating screen, with a sheet pan underneath.
2. Ensure that the product is the correct temperature.
3. Coat the product; use an appropriately-sized utensil.

HACCP:

Store at 60° F to 65° F.

HAZARDOUS FOOD:

Egg whites

Nougat Montélimar

YIELD: 2 pounds, 5¾ ounces.   120 Pralines.

INGREDIENTS:

Honey	9 ounces
Water	1¾ ounces
Sugar, granulated	9 ounces
Egg whites	3 ounces
Extract, vanilla	To taste
Almonds, crushed, lightly toasted	10½ ounces
Pistachio pieces	4½ ounces
Compound, lemon	To taste
Cinnamon	To taste
Couverture, dark, semi-sweet, tempered (for coating)	As needed
Glaze, confectionery (optional)	As needed

METHOD OF PREPARATION:

1. Gather the equipment and ingredients.
2. Combine the honey, water, and half of the sugar, and cook to 266° F.
3. In a separate bowl, whip the egg whites with the remaining sugar and vanilla until they reach a medium peak, to create a meringue.
4. Incorporate the liquid sugar slowly into the meringue.
5. Over a boiling water bath, whip the mixture for about 25 to 30 minutes to reduce the moisture.
6. Once the mixture has thickened properly, add the crushed, toasted almonds, pistachios, lemon compound, and cinnamon; combine well.
7. Pour, between metal bars, to a ½-inch thickness on parchment paper.
8. Press another parchment paper on top, roll out evenly, and let cool to room temperature.
9. Remove the parchment paper; coat the bottom with a thin layer of semi-sweet couverture.
10. Cut into ¾-inch by 1-inch pieces.
11. *Optional:* Spray the top with confectionery glaze.
12. Coat the sides and bottom with semi-sweet couverture.

Peanut Squares

YIELD: 2 pounds, 7 ounces.   160 Pralines.

PASTRY TECHNIQUES:
Mixing, Spreading, Cutting, Dipping, Decorating

Mixing:
1. Follow the proper mixing procedure: creaming, blending, whipping, or combination.

Spreading:
1. Using an icing spatula or off-set spatula, smooth the icing or other spreading medium over the surface area.

Cutting:
Using a sharp knife to cut to the directed size.

Dipping:
1. Prepare the product to the proper dipping temperature.
2. Carefully submerge the product.
3. Dry on parchment paper or a screen.

Decorating:
1. Follow the formula's instructions or the instructor's guidelines to appropriately decorate each cake or pastry.

HACCP:
Store at 60° F to 65° F.

INGREDIENTS:

Couverture, milk	1 pound
Peanut butter, natural	1 pound, 3 ounces
Rice-Qrokant	4 ounces
Couverture, milk, tempered (for dipping)	As needed
Couverture, dark, semi-sweet, tempered (for decorating)	As needed

METHOD OF PREPARATION:

1. Gather the equipment and ingredients.
2. Melt the milk couverture to 113° F.
3. Add the peanut butter to the couverture, and mix well; stir in the Rice-Qrokant.
4. Cool down the mixture in a cold water bath until pasty in consistency. (Stir constantly during cooling.)
5. Spread the paste evenly, between metal bars, on parchment paper to a ⅓-inch thickness.
6. Refrigerate until firm.
7. When firm, remove the bars with a small knife.
8. Spread a small amount of tempered milk couverture on both sides of the sheet.
9. Cut the sheet into 13/16-inch by 13/16-inch squares.
10. Dip in tempered milk couverture.
11. Decorate with one fork line and a dot of tempered dark couverture.

COOKIES
BREADS
SOUFFLES
CREPES
ICE CREAM
SORBETS
CHOCOLATE
OTHERS: FINISHED
MISCELLANEOUS

PASTRY TECHNIQUES:
Mixing, Piping, Coating, Decorating

Mixing:
1. Follow the proper mixing procedure: creaming, blending, whipping, or combination.

Piping:
With bag:
1. Use a bag with a disposable tip; cut the bag at 45-degree angle.
2. Fill to no more than half full.
3. Burp the bag.
With cone:
1. Cut and fold the piping cone to the appropriate size.
2. Fill the cone with a small amount.
3. Fold the ends to form a triangle.
4. Pipe the desired designs.

Coating:
1. Use a coating screen, with a sheet pan underneath.
2. Ensure that the product is the correct temperature.
3. Coat the product; use an appropriately-sized utensil.

Decorating:
1. Follow the formula's instructions or the instructor's guidelines to appropriately decorate each cake or pastry.

HACCP:
Store at 60° F to 65° F.

Pistachio Marzipan Pralines

YIELD: 1 pound, 10½ ounces.   100 Pralines.

INGREDIENTS:

Almond paste	18 ounces
Simple syrup (30° Baumé) (see page 415)	3½ ounces
Brandy	3½ ounces
Pistachios, ground fine	1½ ounces
Couverture, dark, semi-sweet, stencils	100 each
Couverture, dark, semi-sweet, tempered (for coating)	As needed
Couverture, white, tempered (for decorating)	As needed

METHOD OF PREPARATION:

1. Gather the equipment and ingredients.
2. Mix the almond paste, simple syrup, and brandy to a smooth, lump-free paste.
3. Incorporate the pistachios.
4. Pipe a dome shape with a medium-large round tip onto a couverture stencil (23 mm or ⅞ inch in diameter).
5. Let it dry at room temperature for 1 hour.
6. Coat with tempered dark couverture; decorate by piping a spiral of tempered white couverture, or as demonstrated.

Praline Marosa

YIELD: 1 pound, 6 ounces.   80 Pralines.

PASTRY TECHNIQUES:

Mixing, Rolling, Cutting, Piping, Dipping

Mixing:

1. Follow the proper mixing procedure: creaming, blending, whipping, or combination.

Rolling:

1. Prepare the rolling surface by dusting with the appropriate medium (flour, cornstarch, etc.).
2. Use the appropriate style pin (stick pin or ball bearing pin) to roll the dough to desired thickness; rotate the dough during rolling to prevent sticking.

Cutting:

Using a sharp knife to cut to the directed size.

Piping:

With bag:
1. Use a bag with a disposable tip; cut the bag at 45-degree angle.
2. Fill to no more than half full.
3. Burp the bag.
With cone:
1. Cut and fold the piping cone to the appropriate size.
2. Fill the cone with a small amount.
3. Fold the ends to form a triangle.
4. Pipe the desired designs.

Dipping:

1. Prepare the product to the proper dipping temperature.
2. Carefully submerge the product.
3. Dry on parchment paper or a screen.

HACCP:

Store at 60° F to 65° F.

CHEF NOTE:

Flavored oils are prepared specifically for use in candy making. Their flavor is intense, so very little is required to obtain the desired flavor and retain the texture of the praline. Strawberry-flavored oil can be used as an alternative to strawberry compound in this formula.

INGREDIENTS:

Marzipan (see page 422)	1 pound
Compound, strawberry	To taste
Coloring (optional)	As needed
Sugar, confectionery	As needed to stiffen mixture
Marmalade, jam or strawberry compound	4 ounces
Couverture, dark, semi-sweet, tempered (for dipping)	As needed
Violets, candied	2 ounces

METHOD OF PREPARATION:

1. Gather the equipment and ingredients.
2. Mix the marzipan, strawberry compound, coloring (if desired), and confectionery sugar, as needed, until it becomes a smooth, medium-soft paste. (The amount of confectionery sugar to be added depends on the marzipan. The paste should not be sticky.)
3. Roll out to a 1/8-inch thickness.
4. Cut out 1-inch round pieces.
5. Cut out 1-inch fluted circles.
6. Pipe a small dab of marmalade or jam in the center of the small, round pieces.
7. Place the fluted circle on top, and slightly press together.
8. Let them dry slightly so they will not stick to the fork while being dipped.
9. Dip marosa into the dark couverture.
10. While the couverture is still wet, place a piece of candied violet on top.

Raspberry Dips

YIELD: 2 pounds, 1 ounce.   130 Pralines.

PASTRY TECHNIQUES:

Mixing, Spreading, Cutting, Dipping, Decorating

Mixing:

1. Follow the proper mixing procedure: creaming, blending, whipping, or combination.

Spreading:

1. Using an icing spatula or off-set spatula, smooth the icing or other spreading medium over the surface area.

Cutting:

Using a sharp knife to cut to the directed size.

Dipping:

1. Prepare the product to the proper dipping temperature.
2. Carefully submerge the product.
3. Dry on parchment paper or a screen.

Decorating:

1. Follow the formula's instructions or the instructor's guidelines to appropriately decorate each cake or pastry.

HACCP:

Store at 60° F to 65° F.

HAZARDOUS FOOD:

Heavy cream

INGREDIENTS:

Cream, heavy	6 ounces
Couverture, dark, semi-sweet, chopped	1 pound, 4 ounces
Compound, raspberry	5 ounces
Butter, unsalted, room temperature	2 ounces
Couverture, dark, semi-sweet, tempered (for dipping)	As needed
Couverture, milk, tempered (for decorating)	As needed

METHOD OF PREPARATION:

1. Gather the equipment and ingredients.
2. Bring the heavy cream to a boil.
3. Remove from the heat, and add the chopped couverture. Stir well, until smooth.
4. Add the compound, and stir until smooth.
5. Allow to cool to room temperature.
6. When the ganache is almost fully set, add the softened butter, and beat slightly until the butter is incorporated.
7. Spread the mixture, between metal bars, on parchment paper to a ⅓-inch thickness.
8. When firm, remove the bars; spread a small amount of tempered dark couverture on the top and bottom of the ganache.
9. Cut into 11⁄16-inch by 1-inch rectangles.
10. Dip each praline in tempered dark couverture.
11. Decorate each praline with a tempered milk couverture ornament.

PASTRY TECHNIQUES:
Mixing, Piping, Filling, Coating, Spiking

Mixing:
1. Follow the proper mixing procedure: creaming, blending, whipping, or combination.

Piping:
With bag:
1. Use a bag with a disposable tip; cut the bag at 45-degree angle.
2. Fill to no more than half full.
3. Burp the bag.
With cone:
1. Cut and fold the piping cone to the appropriate size.
2. Fill the cone with a small amount.
3. Fold the ends to form a triangle.
4. Pipe the desired designs.

Filling:
1. Cut open the food product.
2. Carefully spread the filling using an icing spatula.
3. Carefully pipe the filling using a pastry bag.

Coating:
1. Use a coating screen, with a sheet pan underneath.
2. Ensure that the product is the correct temperature.
3. Coat the product; use an appropriately-sized utensil.

Spiking:
1. Use chocolate that is appropriately tempered.
2. Drag the truffles across a screen.
3. Use three to four clean, swift strokes.

HACCP:
Store at 60° F to 65° F.

HAZARDOUS FOOD:
Heavy cream

Soft Ganache Round Truffles

YIELD: 3 pounds, 12½ ounces.   200 Truffles.

INGREDIENTS:

Butter, unsalted	11½ ounces
Fondant	6 ounces
Glucose	6 ounces
Cream, heavy	14 ounces
Couverture, milk, finely chopped	1 pound, 7 ounces
Shells, milk couverture	200 each
Couverture, milk, tempered (for coating)	As needed

METHOD OF PREPARATION:

1. Gather the equipment and ingredients.
2. Combine the butter, fondant, glucose, and heavy cream in a pot.
3. Bring to a boil, and remove from the heat.
4. Add the finely chopped milk couverture to the boiling mixture.
5. Stir until completely melted.
6. Cool to a runny consistency, with a temperature below 86° F.
7. Pipe into the milk-couverture shells until seven eighths full.
8. Seal with tempered milk couverture.
9. Apply the tempered couverture to the palms of your hands. Coat the truffle completely in your hands.
10. Allow to set.
11. Reapply your palms with tempered milk couverture; coat the truffle again, or the truffles may be spiked by using a rack.

COOKIES
BREADS
SOUFFLES
CREPES
ICE CREAM
SORBETS
CHOCOLATE
OTHERS: FINISHED
MISCELLANEOUS

PASTRY TECHNIQUES:

Caramelizing, Mixing, Kneading, Rolling, Cutting, Dipping, Decorating

Caramelizing:

Wet method:
1. Use an extremely clean pot.
2. Place the sugar and water on high heat.
3. Never stir the mixture once the sugar begins to dissolve.
4. Once caramelized, shock in ice water.

Mixing:

1. Follow the proper mixing procedure: creaming, blending, whipping, or combination.

Kneading:

1. Prepare the kneading surface with the appropriate medium (flour, cornstarch, etc.).
2. Press and form the dough into a mass using soft, determined strokes.
3. Continue kneading until appropriate consistency and/or temperature is achieved.

Rolling:

1. Prepare the rolling surface by dusting with the appropriate medium (flour, cornstarch, etc.).
2. Use the appropriate style pin (stick pin or ball bearing pin) to roll the dough to desired thickness; rotate the dough during rolling to prevent sticking.

Cutting:

Using a sharp knife to cut to the directed size.

Dipping:

1. Prepare the product to the proper dipping temperature.
2. Carefully submerge the product.
3. Dry on parchment paper or a screen.

Decorating:

1. Follow the formula's instructions or the instructor's guidelines to appropriately decorate each cake or pastry.

Soft Honey Nougat

YIELD: 3 pounds.   170 Pralines.

INGREDIENTS:

Cream, heavy	8 ounces
Honey	8 ounces
Sugar, granulated	1 pound
Almonds, lightly toasted, sliced	1 pound
Couverture, dark (semi-sweet) or milk, tempered (for dipping)	As needed

METHOD OF PREPARATION:

1. Gather the equipment and ingredients.
2. Bring the cream and honey to a boil.
3. Caramelize the sugar in a clean copper pot.
4. Add the boiling cream mixture to the caramelized sugar in three stages.
5. Stir well until lump-free.
6. Cook the mixture to 243° F (117° C).
7. Add the toasted almonds, and stir well.
8. Pour the nougat, in between oiled metal bars, onto a lightly oiled, marble table top.
9. When the mixture has cooled enough to be worked by hand, fold it together several times and knead it lightly on the marble, or use metal scrapers to fold the mixture.
10. Roll out the mixture to ⅓-inch thick between oiled metal bars; use a lightly oiled, metal rolling pin on a lightly oiled surface or on parchment paper.
11. Cool to room temperature.
12. Spread a thin layer of tempered couverture on both sides of the sheet.
13. Cut the nougat into ¾-inch by ¾-inch diamond-shaped pieces.
14. Dip the nougats in tempered dark or milk coverture; decorate with one diagonal fork line.

HACCP:
Store at 60° F to 65° F.

HAZARDOUS FOOD:
Heavy cream

CHEF NOTE:
Hazelnuts, peanuts, pecans, walnuts, or sesame seeds can be used in place of the sliced almonds.

White Truffles

YIELD: 4 pounds, 6 ounces.   270 Truffles

Mixing, Piping, Coating, Dipping, Tempering, Spiking

Mixing:

1. Follow the proper mixing procedure: creaming, blending, whipping, or combination.

Piping:

With bag:
1. Use a bag with a disposable tip; cut the bag at 45-degree angle.
2. Fill to no more than half full.
3. Burp the bag.

With cone:
1. Cut and fold the piping cone to the appropriate size.
2. Fill the cone with a small amount.
3. Fold the ends to form a triangle.
4. Pipe the desired designs.

Coating:

1. Use a coating screen, with a sheet pan underneath.
2. Ensure that the product is the correct temperature.
3. Coat the product, use an appropriately sized utensil.

Dipping:

1. Prepare the product to the proper dipping temperature.
2. Carefully submerge the product.
3. Dry on parchment paper or a screen.

Tempering:

1. Whisk the eggs vigorously while ladling hot liquid.

Spiking:

1. Use chocolate that is appropriately tempered.
2. Drag the truffles across a screen.
3. Use three to four clean swift strokes.

HACCP:

Store at 60° F to 65° F.

HAZARDOUS FOOD:

Heavy cream

INGREDIENTS:

Couverture, white	3 pounds, 3 ounces
Cream, heavy	1 pound
Liqueur, Kirschwasser	3 ounces
Sugar, confectionery (rolling)	1 pound
Couverture, additional white (for dipping)	As needed

METHOD OF PREPARATION:

1. Gather the equipment and ingredients.
2. Chop the couverture into small pieces.
3. Scald the heavy cream, and remove from the heat.
4. Add the chopped couverture into the scalded cream.
5. Add the Kirschwasser, and whisk lightly until smooth.
6. Wrap well, and allow to cool at room temperature.
7. As soon as the ganache mixture is cooled and set, transfer to a mixing bowl, and mix, using a rubber spatula, until light in color.
8. Using a pastry bag with a round tip, immediately pipe out ¾-inch round dots of ganache mixture onto parchment-lined sheet pans.
9. When the piping is complete, place the truffles in the refrigerator; allow them to set to marzipan consistency (not fully hardened).
10. Powder your hands with confectionery sugar to reduce sticking, and roll each truffle in your hands until rounded.
11. Return the truffles to the parchment-lined sheet pan, and return to the refrigerator; allow them to set.
12. Melt the white couverture, and temper.
13. Remove the truffles from the refrigerator when fully set.

(continued)

CHEF NOTES:

1. After piping the ganache, do *not* leave the truffles in the refrigerator too long, or they will be too hard to roll.
2. Do *not* overspike, or the chocolate will appear dull.
3. Do *not* spike the truffles too soon, or the texture will melt.
4. Use gloves (latex) to roll the truffle in your hands.

14. Place a small amount of tempered couverture in one hand, pick up a truffle with the other hand, and roll the truffle gently between the palms of your hands to coat evenly.
15. Return the truffles to the sheet pans, and allow them to set at room temperature.
16. Using a dipping fork, dip each truffle in white tempered couverture.
17. Immediately place the truffle on a wire rack.
18. Using two forks, roll the truffle three to four times on the screen, allowing the chocolate to develop a spiked texture.
19. Using two dipping forks, place the truffles back on the parchment paper. (Do *not* allow the truffles to set on the screen.)

COOKIES

BREADS

SOUFFLES

CREPES

ICE CREAM

SORBETS

CHOCOLATE

OTHERS: FINISHED

MISCELLANEOUS

17

Other:
Finished
Items

Other: Finished Items

Apple Strudel

COOKIES
BREADS
SOUFFLES
CREPES
ICE CREAM
SORBETS
CHOCOLATE
OTHERS: FINISHED
MISCELLANEOUS

PASTRY TECHNIQUES:
Combining, Kneading, Filling, Rolling

Combining:
Bringing together two or more components.
1. Prepare the components to be combined.
2. Add one to the other, using the appropriate mixing method (if needed).

Kneading:
1. Prepare the kneeding surface with the appropriate medium (flour, cornstarch, etc.).
2. Press and form the dough into a mass using soft, determined strokes.
3. Continue kneading until appropriate consistency and/or temperature is achieved.

Filling:
1. Cut open the food product.
2. Carefully spread the filling using an icing spatula, or
3. Carefully pipe the filling using a pastry bag.

Rolling:
1. Prepare the rolling surface by dusting with the appropriate medium (flour, cornstarch, etc.).
2. Use the appropriate style pin (stick pin or ball bearing pin) to roll the dough to desired thickness; rotate the dough during rolling to prevent sticking.

HAZARDOUS FOOD:
Eggs

YIELD: 3 pounds, 13¾ ounces.   13 pounds, 11½ ounces.

INGREDIENTS:

Oil	As needed	As needed
Flour, bread	As needed	As needed
Butter, unsalted, melted	3 ounces	12 ounces
Crumbs, cake or bread	4 ounces	1 pound
Sugar, confectionery	As needed	As needed

Dough:

Flour, bread	10 ounces	2 pounds, 8 ounces
Butter, unsalted, melted (or oil)	2 ounces	8 ounces
Salt	Pinch	½ ounce
Eggs, whole	2 ounces	8 ounces
Vinegar, white	Pinch	Pinch
Water, lukewarm	3½ ounces	14 ounces

Filling:

Apples, Granny Smith	1 pound, 8 ounces	6 pounds
Cinnamon, ground	¼ ounce	1 ounce
Sugar, granulated	4 ounces	1 pound
Raisins, seedless	3 ounces	12 ounces
Walnuts, chopped	3 ounces	12 ounces

METHOD OF PREPARATION:

Gather the equipment and ingredients.

Preparation of Dough:
1. Place the bread flour, melted butter or oil, salt, eggs, vinegar, and water in a bowl with a dough hook.
2. Mix on high speed for 7 to 9 minutes.
3. Remove, and brush the dough with oil, as needed; place in a covered bowl in a warm place for 1 hour.

Preparation of Filling:
1. Peel, core, and slice or cube the apples.
2. Combine the apples with the cinnamon, sugar, raisins, and walnuts.

Preparation of Rolling Strudel:

1. Cover a table with a pastry cloth, and dust lightly with flour.
2. Have the melted butter, cake crumbs, and rested dough ready.
3. Stretch the dough evenly into a rectangular shape, and pin out, as much as possible.
4. Pull out the edges, using the back of your hands.
5. Using the floured backs of your hands, stretch the dough uniformly.
6. Continue to stretch toward the opposite corners and the sides until the table is completely covered.
7. Trim the excess dough with a pastry wheel.
8. Sprinkle the dough with butter.
9. Sprinkle the cake crumbs over one edge of the dough to cover an area approximately 1 to 1½ feet wide.
10. Place the fruit filling on top of the crumbs.
11. Roll up, using the table cloth to hold and guide the dough.
12. Transfer to a sheet pan; brush the roll with butter.
13. Bake at 400° F for 20 minutes, or until golden brown.
14. Serve fresh and warm, dusted with confectionery sugar.

Variations:

Use the same dough, but substitute any of the following for filling:
1. Cheese filling
2. Poppy seed filling
3. Walnut filling

COOKIES
BREADS
SOUFFLES
CREPES
ICE CREAM
SORBETS
CHOCOLATE
OTHERS: FINISHED
MISCELLANEOUS

PASTRY TECHNIQUES:
Combining, Kneading, Shaping, Proofing

Combining
Bringing together two or more components.
1. Prepare the components to be combined.
2. Add one to the other, using the appropriate mixing method (if needed).

Kneading:
1. Prepare the kneading surface with the appropriate medium (flour, cornstarch, etc.).
2. Press and form the dough into a mass using soft, determined strokes.
3. Continue kneading until appropriate consistency and/or temperature is achieved.

Shaping:
1. Prepare the medium to be shaped.
2. Prepare the surface area for shaping.
3. Mold medium into desired shapes according to the instructor's directions.

Proofing:
1. Set a proof box to the proper temperature.
2. Do not over- or underproof the dough.

HAZARDOUS FOODS:
Milk
Eggs

Baba No. 1

Savarin (Sponge Method)

YIELD: 2 pounds, 10 ounces. 5 pounds, 4 ounces.

INGREDIENTS:

Flour, bread, sifted	1 pound	2 pounds
Yeast, compressed	1 ounce	2 ounces
Milk, whole, lukewarm	4 ounces	8 ounces
Salt	½ ounce	1 ounce
Eggs, whole	12 ounces	1 pound, 8 ounces
Sugar, granulated	1½ ounces	3 ounces
Butter, unsalted, melted	7 ounces	14 ounces

METHOD OF PREPARATION:

1. Gather the equipment and ingredients.
2. Make a sponge; combine 4 ounces of flour, the yeast, and the milk. Cover, and let it rest for 1 hour.
3. Combine the sponge with the remaining ingredients, except the butter, and mix at high speed for about 10 minutes, or until fully developed.
4. Add the butter, and incorporate.
5. Grease the savarin molds, dust with flour, and fill halfway with the dough.
6. Proof for 30 minutes.
7. Bake at 400° F for 25 to 30 minutes.
8. Allow to cool; then unmold.
9. Soak generously with rum-flavored simple syrup (page 415).

PASTRY TECHNIQUES:
Combining, Kneading, Shaping,
Proofing

Combining:
Bringing together two or more components.
1. Prepare the components to be combined.
2. Add one to the other, using the appropriate mixing method (if needed).

Kneading:
1. Prepare the kneading surface with the appropriate medium (flour, cornstarch, etc.).
2. Press and form the dough into a mass using soft, determined strokes.
3. Continue kneading until appropriate consistency and/or temperature is achieved.

Shaping:
1. Prepare the medium to be shaped.
2. Prepare the surface area for shaping.
3. Mold medium into desired shapes according to the instructor's directions.

Proofing:
1. Set a proof box to the proper temperature.
2. Do not over- or underproof the dough.

HAZARDOUS FOODS:
Milk
Eggs

Baba No. 2

Savarin (Fast Rise)

YIELD:	2 pounds, 15¾ ounces.	5 pounds, 15½ ounces.

INGREDIENTS:

Milk, whole	9 ounces	1 pound, 2 ounces
Yeast, compressed	2½ ounces	5 ounces
Flour, bread	1 pound, 4 ounces	2 pounds, 8 ounces
Sugar, granulated	1¾ ounces	3½ ounces
Butter, unsalted, softened	6 ounces	12 ounces
Eggs, whole	8 ounces	1 pound
Salt	½ ounce	1 ounce

METHOD OF PREPARATION:

1. Gather the equipment and ingredients.
2. Heat the milk to lukewarm (approximately 100° F).
3. In a mixing bowl, dissolve the yeast in the lukewarm milk.
4. Add the flour; then add the remaining ingredients; mix with a hook for 10 minutes on high speed.
5. Cover the dough with a cloth, and let it rest for 15 minutes.
6. Punch down the dough, and let it rest for an additional 15 minutes.
7. Grease the savarin molds, and dust with bread flour; fill halfway with the dough.
8. Cover with a cloth for approximately 10 to 15 minutes, and let it rise to double in size.
9. Bake at 400° F for 25 to 30 minutes.
10. Allow to cool; then unmold.
11. Soak generously with rum-flavored simple syrup (page 415).

Baked Apples

COOKIES

BREADS

SOUFFLES

CREPES

ICE CREAM

SORBETS

CHOCOLATE

OTHERS: FINISHED

MISCELLANEOUS

PASTRY TECHNIQUES:

Combining, Filling

Combining:

Bringing together two or more components.
1. Prepare the components to be combined.
2. Add one to the other, using the appropriate mixing method (if needed).

Filling:

1. Cut open the food product.
2. Carefully spread the filling using an icing spatula, or
3. Carefully pipe the filling using a pastry bag.

YIELD:	5 Portions.	10 Portions.

INGREDIENTS:

Apples	5 each	10 each
Lemon juice	As needed	As needed
Water	As needed	As needed
Sugar, granulated	1 ounce	2 ounces
Walnuts, chopped	1 ounce	2 ounces
Raisins, seedless	2 ounces	4 ounces
Cinnamon, ground	⅛ ounce	¼ ounce
Butter, unsalted	2 ounces	4 ounces

Syrup:

Sugar, granulated	12 ounces	1 pound, 8 ounces
Wine, sweet white	4 ounces	8 ounces
Lemon juice	½ ounce	1 ounce

METHOD OF PREPARATION:

1. Gather the equipment and ingredients.
2. Wash, peel, and core the apples. (Place the apples in lemon water after they have been peeled.)
3. Combine the sugar, walnuts, raisins, and cinnamon.
4. Place apples on a half sheet pan.
5. Place the mixture in the center of the apples.
6. Melt the butter, and pour over the apples.
7. Bake at 375° F until done.
8. Place the granulated sugar, white wine, and lemon juice in a pot; boil to a clear syrup.
9. Place a baked apple on preheated dessert plate, and coat with the syrup. Serve hot.

CHEF NOTE:

Remove apples from lemon water and let drip dry.

Baklava

PASTRY TECHNIQUES:
Combining, Filling

Combining:
Bringing together two or more components.
1. Prepare the components to be combined.
2. Add one to the other, using the appropriate mixing method (if needed).

Filling:
1. Cut open the food product.
2. Carefully spread the filling using an icing spatula, or
3. Carefully pipe the filling using a pastry bag.

HACCP:
Store at 60° F to 65° F.

YIELD:	½ Sheet Pan.	1 Sheet Pan.

INGREDIENTS:		
Butter, unsalted	10 ounces	1 pound, 4 ounces
Dough, phyllo	15 leaves	30 leaves
Walnuts, finely chopped	10 ounces	1 pound, 4 ounces
Nuts, pistachio, chopped	5 ounces	10 ounces
Honey	8 ounces	1 pound
Sugar, granulated	4 ounces	8 ounces
Water	3 ounces	6 ounces
Cinnamon sticks	1 each	2 each

METHOD OF PREPARATION:

1. Gather the equipment and ingredients.
2. Melt the butter, and brush on a half sheet pan, or hotel pan.
3. Place one layer of dough on the bottom of the pan, and drizzle with butter.
4. Repeat the procedure with four additional layers of dough.
5. On the fifth layer, sprinkle half of the nuts to completely cover the surface of the dough.
6. Place another five layers of dough on top of the nuts, drizzling butter between each layer.
7. Sprinkle the remaining nuts over the surface of the dough; cover it completely.
8. Place another five layers of dough on top of the nuts, drizzling butter between each layer.
9. Slice the dough into diamond shapes, using a very sharp knife. Be certain to slice completely through the layers, but do not remove any layers of dough.
10. Bake at 420° F until the pastry is golden brown and crispy.
11. Combine the honey, sugar, water, and cinnamon stick in a saucepan.
12. Bring to a boil, and cook for 1 minute, or until a syrupy consistency is reached.
13. Remove the baklava from the oven and, while it is still hot, pour the hot honey syrup over it.
14. Set aside to cool; then separate the diamond-shaped pieces.

CHEF NOTES:
1. Baklava should sit overnight before serving to allow the honey syrup to soak into the layers and provide better flavor.
2. Do not place in refrigerator.

COOKIES

BREADS

SOUFFLES

CREPES

ICE CREAM

SORBETS

CHOCOLATE

OTHERS: FINISHED

MISCELLANEOUS

PASTRY TECHNIQUES:

Heating

Heating:

1. Prepare the food product according to the formula's instructions.
2. Choose the appropriate method of heating (on the range or stove top, in the oven, etc.)
3. Apply the product to the heat.

Coating:

1. Use a coating screen, with a sheet pan underneath.
2. Ensure that the product is the correct temperature.
3. Coat the product, use an appropriately sized utensil.

Banana Flambé

YIELD: 12 Servings.

INGREDIENTS:

Sugar, granulated	6 ounces
Butter, unsalted	6 ounces
Bananas, peeled and sliced	12 each
Rum, dark	3 ounces
Liqueur, banana	3 ounces
Cinnamom-sugar mixture	As needed
Ice cream, vanilla (see pages 333, 334)	3 pounds

METHOD OF PREPARATION:

1. Gather the equipment and ingredients.
2. Heat a suzette pan, and add the sugar and butter; caramelize.
3. Add the bananas, and coat them with caramel.
4. Remove the pan from the flame; add the dark rum and banana liqueur.
5. Return to the flame, and ignite.
6. While still flaming, sprinkle the cinnamon-sugar mixture over the pan.
7. When the flame subsides, place the sliced bananas and sauce over a 4-ounce scoop of ice cream, and serve immediately.

Variations:

1. Use brown sugar or honey rather than granulated sugar.
2. Supplement the rum with lime juice or lemon juice, if desired.

PASTRY TECHNIQUES:

Rubbing, Combining, Rolling, Shaping, Frying

Rubbing:

1. Use a pastry cutter to keep the fat in large pieces.
2. Add the liquid in stages.

Combining:

Bringing together two or more components.
1. Prepare the components to be combined.
2. Add one to the other, using the appropriate mixing method (if needed).

Rolling:

1. Prepare the rolling surface by dusting with the appropriate medium (flour, cornstarch, etc.).
2. Use the appropriate style pin (stick pin or ball bearing pin) to roll the dough to desired thickness; rotate the dough during rolling to prevent sticking.

Shaping:

1. Prepare the medium to be shaped.
2. Prepare the surface area for shaping.
3. Mold medium into desired shapes according to the instructor's directions.

Frying:

1. Heat the frying liquid to the appropriate temperature.
2. Place the food product into the hot liquid.
3. Cook the product, turning frequently, until golden brown and tender.

HAZARDOUS FOOD:

Pastry cream

Cannoli

YIELD:	1 pound, 9 ounces.	3 pounds, 2 ounces.
INGREDIENTS:		
Flour, bread	14 ounces	1 pound, 12 ounces
Sugar, granulated	½ ounce	1 ounce
Salt	⅛ ounce	¼ ounce
Oil, vegetable	2 ounces	4 ounces
Vinegar, white	½ ounce	1 ounce
Water	8 ounces	1 pound
Pastry cream (see page 97)	As needed	As needed
Nuts, pistachio, ground	As needed	As needed
Sugar, confectionery	As needed	As needed

METHOD OF PREPARATION:

1. Gather the equipment and ingredients.
2. Combine the bread flour, granulated sugar, and salt.
3. Rub in the oil.
4. Mix together the vinegar and water.
5. Combine the flour mixture with the vinegar mixture.
6. Form the dough into a rectangle about ½-inch thick.
7. Wrap in plastic, and allow it to rest on the bench for about 1 hour.
8. After the dough has rested, roll it out to ¼-inch thick.
9. Pass the dough through a pasta machine, which should be set on the widest setting.
10. Fold the dough, and continue to roll and fold it 12 to 15 times until all of the air bubbles have been rolled out and the dough is smooth.
11. Rest the dough for 45 minutes.
12. Cut the dough in half.
13. Wrap half of the dough to prevent it from drying.
14. Starting with the widest setting on the pasta machine, pass the dough through; work your way down to the smallest setting.
15. Lay the dough across the surface of the bench, and, using a 3-inch cutter, cut out circles of dough.
16. Using a rolling pin, roll out each disk into an oval shape.
17. To form the cannoli, place an oval of dough around the cannoli tube.
18. Seal the dough around the tube. (Wrap all cannoli tubes before frying.)
19. Fry in preheated 350° F oil for 3 to 5 minutes, or until golden brown.
20. Drain on a paper towel.
21. When cool, remove the cannoli from the tube.
22. Fill the cannoli with pastry cream.
23. Garnish with pistachios and confectionery sugar.

Cherries Jubilee

COOKIES

BREADS

SOUFFLES

CREPES

ICE CREAM

SORBETS

CHOCOLATE

OTHERS: FINISHED

MISCELLANEOUS

PASTRY TECHNIQUES:

Combining, Thickening, Folding

Combining:

Bringing together two or more components.
1. Prepare the components to be combined.
2. Add one to the other, using the appropriate mixing method (if needed).

Thickening:

1. Mix a small amount of sugar with the starches.
2. Create a slurry.
3. Whisk vigorously until thickened and translucent.

Folding:

Do steps 1, 2, and 3 in one continuous motion.
1. Run a bowl scraper under the mixture, across the bottom of the bowl.
2. Turn the bowl counterclockwise.
3. Bring the bottom mixture to the top.

YIELD: 12 Servings.

INGREDIENTS:

Cornstarch	¼ ounce
Cherry juice	1 pound, 2 ounces
Sugar, granulated	6 ounces
Cherries, dark, sweet, pitted	60 each (2 no. 303 cans)
Lemon	½ each
Liqueur, Kirschwasser	3 ounces
Liqueur, Peter Herring	3 ounces
Ice cream, vanilla (see pages 333, 334)	3 pounds

METHOD OF PREPARATION:

1. Gather the equipment and ingredients.
2. Place the cornstarch in a dry bowl, and slowly add ½ ounce cherry juice and mix well to prevent lumps from forming.
3. Place the rest of the juice in a pan over medium heat, and add the granulated sugar, cornstarch mixture, and cherries. Using half of a lemon on a fork, cut-side down, stir the cherry mixture until hot.
4. Remove the pan from the fire, and add the Kirschwasser; flame.
5. Return to the heat. Move the cherries to the side of the pan; add the Peter Herring liqueur, and stir until thick.
6. For each serving, scoop 4 ounces of ice cream, and spoon five cherries and sauce over the ice cream.

Chestnut Barquette

PASTRY TECHNIQUES:
Rolling, Piping, Dipping

Rolling:
1. Prepare the rolling surface by dusting with the appropriate medium (flour, cornstarch, etc.).
2. Use the appropriate style pin (stick pin or ball bearing pin) to roll the dough to desired thickness; rotate the dough during rolling to prevent sticking.

Piping:
With bag:
1. Use a bag with a disposable tip; cut the bag at 45-degree angle.
2. Fill to no more than half full.
3. Burp the bag.
With cone:
1. Cut and fold the piping cone to the appropriate size.
2. Fill the cone with a small amount.
3. Fold the ends to form a triangle.
4. Pipe the desired designs.

Dipping:
1. Prepare the product to the proper dipping temperature.
2. Carefully submerge the product.
3. Dry on parchment paper or a screen.

YIELD:	24 Each.	48 Each.
INGREDIENTS:		
Short dough (see page 183)	1 pound, 8 ounces	3 pounds
Preserves, raspberry	8 ounces	1 pound
Frangipane (see pages 19, 20)	2 pounds, 2 ounces	4 pounds, 4 ounces
Simple syrup, brandy-flavored (see page 415)	1 pound	2 pounds
Buttercream, chestnut-flavored	3 pounds, 6 ounces	6 pounds, 12 ounces
Chocolate, dark, semi-sweet, coating	1 pound, 8 ounces	3 pounds
Couverture, white	2 ounces	4 ounces

METHOD OF PREPARATION:

1. Gather the equipment and ingredients.
2. Roll out the short dough to a ⅛-inch thickness, and place it in barquette molds.
3. Blind-bake at 350° F for 10 minutes, or until prebaked.
4. Place a small dot of raspberry preserves into each barquette.
5. Pipe the frangipane to the height of the shell, but do not pipe over.
6. Bake at 350° F for 15 minutes, or until done.
7. Cool thoroughly.
8. When cool, sprinkle with brandy-flavored simple syrup.
9. With a spatula, mound chestnut-flavored buttercream on the shells. Bring it to a point at the center from two long sides.
10. When set, dip the buttercream end into the warm chocolate coating.
11. Stripe the finished barquette with the white couverture, and allow to set.
12. Refrigerate until served.

Locksmith's Lads

(Stuffed Prunes)

COOKIES
BREADS
SOUFFLES
CREPES
ICE CREAM
SORBETS
CHOCOLATE
OTHERS: FINISHED
MISCELLANEOUS

PASTRY TECHNIQUES:

Stuffing, Dredging, Frying

Stuffing:

1. Place the stuffing inside the cavity of the food product using a gloved hand or a piping bag.
2. Be sure to fill the cavity completely.

Dredging:

1. Coat the food product.
2. Sprinkle or toss the product in an appropriate dredging application.

Frying:

1. Heat the frying liquid to the appropriate temperature.
2. Place the food product into the hot liquid.
3. Cook the product, turning frequently, until golden brown and tender.

YIELD: 16 Each.   32 Each.

INGREDIENTS:

Prunes, whole	16 each	32 each
Almonds, whole, blanched	16 each	32 each
Oil, vegetable (for frying)	As needed	As needed
Fritter batter (see page 176)	As needed	As needed
Chocolate shavings	As needed	As needed
Sugar, powdered	As needed	As needed

METHOD OF PREPARATION:

1. Gather the equipment and ingredients.
2. Stuff the prunes with the whole almonds; set aside.
3. Prepare the oil for frying; heat it to 360° F.
4. Prepare the fritter batter.
5. Dredge the stuffed prunes into the fritter batter to coat completely.
6. Fry immediately in hot oil on both sides until golden brown.
7. Remove the prunes from oil, and drain on paper towels until cool.
8. Once the fritters are cool, dredge them in the chocolate shavings until a chocolate "crust" is formed.
9. Sprinkle with powdered sugar.

Petit Four Glacé

YIELD: 150 Each.

PASTRY TECHNIQUES:
Heating, Coating

Heating:
1. Prepare the food product according to the formula's instructions.
2. Choose the appropriate method of heating (on the range or stove top, in the oven, etc.)
3. Apply the product to the heat.

Coating:
1. Use a coating screen, with a sheet pan underneath.
2. Ensure that the product is the correct temperature.
3. Coat the product; use an appropriately-sized utensil.

INGREDIENTS:

Apricot, coating	10 ounces
Frangipane (see pages 19, 20)	½ sheet
Sugar, granulated	As needed
Marzipan (see page 422)	2 pounds
Fondant	7 pounds, 8 ounces
Simple syrup (see page 415)	As needed

METHOD OF PREPARATION:

Gather the equipment and ingredients.

Building:

1. Bring to a boil the apricot coating, and set aside; keep warm.
2. Sprinkle a half sheet of frangipane (18 inches by 12 inches, 1-inch thick) with sugar. Place a piece of sheet paper on top, and cover with a cardboard sheet. Flip upside down to unmold.
3. Trim the edges to square up.
4. Mark and divide into five 3¼-inch rectangles.
5. Place each on a 3¾-inch by 11½-inch piece of cardboard.
6. Level each piece.
7. Brush the surface of the frangipane with approximately 2 ounces of the apricot coating that was previously brought to a boil.
8. Roll out the marzipan to ⅛-inch thick and slightly wider and longer than the cake.
9. Roll up on the pin, unroll onto the top of the cake, and pin-level.
10. Place a cardboard on the marzipan, and flip over.
11. Carefully trim excess marzipan from the edge of the cake, using a French knife; avoid dragging the knife. (Reserve clean marzipan for reuse.)
12. Measure a 1-inch bar along the length of the cake, and cut, using the French knife. Keep the blade straight; avoid dragging. Cut 1-inch squares from the bar.
13. You should end up with thirty 1-inch by 1-inch pieces.
14. Place the pieces on a glazing screen, leaving 1½ inches of space around each piece; keep in neat rows.

Preparing Fondant:

1. Remove 1 pound, 8 ounces of fondant from the pail of prepared fondant (30 petit fours).
2. Warm to 98° F to 100° F. Either use a water bath and stir, testing often to

determine the temperature, or use a saucepan over low heat; stir with hand, on and off the fire.

3. Flavor and color as desired; use compounds, liqueurs, nuts, butters, and so forth.
4. Adjust the consistency, using 100° F simple syrup until the fondant evenly coats a test piece.
5. The fondant should coat a piece thinly over the entire surface and leave no "foot" at the base.

Glazing (Spoon Method):
1. Place a screen on a clean plastic sheet pan.
2. Using a solid stainless spoon, pour the glaze over an individual piece to coat.
3. Pour from the side of the spoon, slowly and very close to the top of the piece.
4. When you reach the back, stop; allow the fondant to fall down and cover the back side.
5. Twist the spoon to catch drips, and remove.
Note: If necessary, additional methods can be added.

Finishing:
1. Decorate by using the traditional decoration, as instructed.
2. Loosen the petit fours from the screen by using a paring knife dipped in hot water.
3. Dip your fingers in cold water before lifting each piece, to avoid sticking.
Note: Fondant that flows through the screen onto the plastic sheet should be reused, as needed. Pick out any cake crumbs that may have fallen in. Fondant can be warmed and strained, if necessary.

PASTRY TECHNIQUES:
Rolling, Combining, Slicing

Rolling:
1. Prepare the rolling surface by dusting with the appropriate medium (flour, cornstarch, etc.).
2. Use the appropriate style pin (stick pin or ball bearing pin) to roll the dough to desired thickness; rotate the dough during rolling to prevent sticking.

Combining:
Bringing together two or more components.
1. Prepare the components to be combined.
2. Add one to the other, using the appropriate mixing method (if needed).

Slicing:
1. Prepare the product for cutting; clean and clear the work area.
2. Slice the product using the "claw" grasp or the rocking motion.

HACCP:
Store at 40° F.

HAZARDOUS FOODS:
Eggs
Heavy cream

Swiss Apple Flan

YIELD: 3, 9-inch Flans.

INGREDIENTS:

Short dough (see page 183)	2 pounds
Apples, tart	6 to 8 each
Sugar, granulated	6 ounces
Cinnamon, ground	1/8 ounce
Crumbs, cake	9 ounces
Almonds, ground, toasted	6 ounces
Apricot glaze (see pages 197–199)	As needed
Almonds, additional, toasted, crushed	As needed
Custard:	
Eggs, whole	10 ounces
Cream, heavy	1 pound, 8 ounces
Sugar, granulated	4 ounces
Liqueur, brandy or Grand Marnier	To taste

METHOD OF PREPARATION:

1. Gather the equipment and ingredients.
2. Prepare three, 9-inch short-dough tart shells.
3. Peel and core the apples.
4. Slice the apples in thin, shingle-style, 1/4-inch slices. (You may place them in a lemon juice/water solution to prevent their browning.)
5. Combine the granulated sugar, cinnamon, cake crumbs, and ground almonds. Set aside.
6. *Preparation of Custard:*
   a. Combine the eggs and heavy cream.
   b. Add the sugar and liqueur to the egg mixture.
   c. Set aside.
7. Sprinkle the cake crumb mixture over the tart shells.
8. Arrange the sliced apples in a spiral decoration on top of the crumb mixture.
9. Place the tart in 350° F oven, and bake until the apples are semi-tender (approximately 20 minutes).
10. Remove the tarts from the oven, and pour the custard over them until just under the rim.
11. Place them back in the oven, and bake in waterbath until the custard is done (approximately 20 to 30 minutes).
12. Remove the tarts from the tart shell.
13. Glaze with apricot glaze.
14. Place crushed, toasted almonds along the sides of the tart.

Tart Tatin

COOKIES

BREADS

SOUFFLES

CREPES

ICE CREAM

SORBETS

CHOCOLATE

OTHERS: FINISHED

MISCELLANEOUS

PASTRY TECHNIQUES:

Rolling, Peeling, Caramelizing

Rolling:

1. Prepare the rolling surface by dusting with the appropriate medium (flour, cornstarch, etc.).
2. Use the appropriate style pin (stick pin or ball bearing pin) to roll the dough to desired thickness; rotate the dough during rolling to prevent sticking.

Peeling:

1. Use a clean paring knife or peeler.
2. Do not peel over an unsanitary surface.

Caramelizing:

Wet method:
1. Use an extremely clean pot.
2. Place the sugar and water on high heat.
3. Never stir the mixture once the sugar begins to dissolve.
4. Once caramelized, shock in ice water.

YIELD: 1, 8-inch Tart.

INGREDIENTS:

Apples, Granny Smith	2 to 3 each
Butter, unsalted, softened	1 ounce
Sugar, granulated	2 ounces
Puff pastry (see pages 191–194)	1, 8-inch circle, ¼-inch thick

METHOD OF PREPARATION:

1. Gather the equipment and ingredients.
2. Preheat the oven to 425° F.
3. Peel, core, and cut the apples into quarters.
4. In an 8-inch teflon-coated sauté pan, spread the softened butter on the bottom.
5. Sprinkle the granulated sugar over the softened butter.
6. Place each apple quarter on its side in the pan, the thinner portion of the apple being placed toward the center of pan.
7. Place the pan over medium heat, and cook the sugar, butter, and apples until the sugar begins to caramelize and the apples to soften.
8. When the sugar has caramelized, remove the pan from the heat, and lay the puff pastry circle over the top of the apples.
9. Turn the oven temperature to 400° F. Immediately place the pan into the oven, and bake for approximately 15 to 20 minutes; remove from the oven when the puff pastry is baked completely.
10. After removing the tart from the oven, invert it immediately onto a preheated serving plate.

CHEF NOTE:

1. Pears and mangos are great substitutes for the apples.
2. Use a sauté pan with a heat-resistant handle.

18

Miscellaneous

Miscellaneous

COOKIES
BREADS
SOUFFLES
CREPES
ICE CREAM
SORBETS
CHOCOLATE
OTHERS: FINISHED
MISCELLANEOUS

Egg Wash

PASTRY TECHNIQUE:

Combining

Combining:

Bringing together two or more components.
1. Prepare the components to be combined.
2. Add one to the other, using the appropriate mixing method (if needed).

HACCP:

Store at 40° F.

HAZARDOUS FOODS:

Eggs
Milk

YIELD: 6 ounces.   12 ounces.

INGREDIENTS:

Eggs, whole	3 ounces	6 ounces
Milk, whole or water	3 ounces	6 ounces

METHOD OF PREPARATION:

1. Gather the equipment and ingredients.
2. Combine the ingredients; use a whisk to make a smooth mixture.
3. When using an egg wash, apply it with a pastry brush.

CHEF NOTES:

1. If additional browning is required, milk can be used instead of water.
2. If additional browning is required, sugar can be added.
3. If used for savory items, salt may be added.

Poached Fruit

YIELD:

PASTRY TECHNIQUE:
Poaching

Poaching:
1. Bring the liquid to a boil; then reduce to a simmer.
2. Submerge and anchor the product.
3. Do not overcook the product.

INGREDIENTS:

Fruit, desired	As needed
Liquid, basic (for poaching) (see page 414)	To cover fruit

METHOD OF PREPARATION:

1. Gather the equipment and ingredients.
2. Peel and core the desired fruit.
3. Place the poaching liquid in a saucepan, deep enough to cover the fruit.
4. Place the fruit in the liquid, and weigh it down so it does not rise to the surface.
5. Simmer, *do not boil,* over a low flame until the fruit is tender but firm enough to hold its shape and size.

CHEF NOTES:
1. The liquid should be at about 190° F and should not move; it, however, should have steam rising from the surface.
2. For variation, fruit can be poached in the oven at 325° F to 350° F.

COOKIES
BREADS
SOUFFLES
CREPES
ICE CREAM
SORBETS
CHOCOLATE
OTHERS: FINISHED
MISCELLANEOUS

Poached Pear Williams in Wine

PASTRY TECHNIQUE:

Poaching

Poaching:

1. Bring the liquid to a boil; then reduce to a simmer.
2. Submerge and anchor the product.
3. Do not overcook the product.

YIELD: 16 Servings.

INGREDIENTS:

Pears	16 each
Water, cold	As needed
Lemon juice	As needed
Sugar, granulated	4 pounds
Wine, white	2 pounds
Liqueur, Pear Williams	2 pounds
Lemon, sliced	½ each
Orange, sliced	½ each
Cinnamon, stick	1 each

METHOD OF PREPARATION:

1. Gather the equipment and ingredients.
2. Peel and core the pears; place in cold water and lemon juice.
3. Combine the sugar, wine, Pear Williams, lemons, oranges, and cinnamon stick; place in a hotel pan.
4. Add the pears to the liquid, and cover with aluminum foil.
5. Bake in a moderate oven at 380° F for approximately 1½ hours, or until the pears are tender.
6. When cool, plate and serve with an appropriate sauce.

CHEF NOTE:

1. Keep the poaching syrup for preparing a sauce or for other uses.
2. If a sweet wine is used, reduce the amount of sugar.

PASTRY TECHNIQUES:
Combining

Combining:
Bringing together two or more components.
1. Prepare the components to be combined.
2. Add one to the other, using the appropriate mixing method (if needed).

Poaching Liquid, Basic

YIELD:		2 pounds, 8 ounces.	5 pounds.

INGREDIENTS:			
Wine, red or white	1 pound		2 pounds
Water	1 pound		2 pounds
Sugar, granulated	8 ounces		1 pound
Cinnamon	½ stick		1 stick
Cloves	1 to 2 each		2 to 4 each

METHOD OF PREPARATION:

1. Gather the equipment and ingredients.
2. Place all of the ingredients in a pot.
3. Bring to a simmer, and poach the fruit, as desired.

Simple Syrup

PASTRY TECHNIQUES:
Combining, Boiling

Combining:
Bringing together two or more components.
1. Prepare the components to be combined.
2. Add one to the other, using the appropriate mixing method (if needed).

Boiling:
1. Bring the cooking liquid to a rapid boil.
2. Stir the contents.

HACCP:
Store at 40° F.

YIELD: 16 pounds.

INGREDIENTS:

Sugar, granulated	8 pounds
Water	8 pounds
Lemon, sliced	1 each

METHOD OF PREPARATION:

1. Gather the equipment and ingredients.
2. Place the sugar and water in a pot, and bring to a boil.
3. Remove from the heat, and add the lemon slices. (Another form of acid may be substituted for the sliced lemons.)
4. Cool.
5. Store in a refrigerator.

Variations:

Combine all of the ingredients for each flavored simple syrup.

Kahlua: 1 torte

Kahlua	½ ounce
Simple syrup	2½ ounces

Raspberry/chocolate: 1 torte

Raspberry compound	¼ ounce
Simple syrup	2½ ounces

Mandarin orange: 1 torte

Orange compound	¼ ounce
Simple syrup	2½ ounces

Pistachio: 1 torte

Pistachio compound	¼ ounce
Simple syrup	2½ ounces
Lemon juice	¼ ounce

Kirschwasser:	1 torte
Kirschwasser	½ ounce
Simple syrup	1½ ounces
Cherry syrup	1 ounce

Coconut:	1 torte
Coconut liqueur	½ ounce
Simple syrup	2½ ounces

Rum or brandy:	1 torte
Rum or brandy	½ ounce
Simple syrup	2½ ounces

Items for Show Pieces

Items for Show Pieces

Chocolate Boxes

PASTRY TECHNIQUES:
Spreading, Cutting, Assembling

Spreading:
1. Using an icing spatula or off-set spatula, smooth the icing or other spreading medium over the surface area.

Cutting:
Using a sharp knife to cut to the directed size.

Collecting and Assembling:
1. Prepare all of the ingredients to the formula.
2. Clear the area for assembly.
3. Fit the pieces together according to formula instructions or instructor's guidelines.

HAACP:
Store at 60° F to 65° F.

YIELD: 50 Boxes.

INGREDIENTS:

Chocolate, tempered (white, dark, or milk)	4 pounds

METHOD OF PREPARATION:

1. Gather the equipment and ingredients.
2. Spread the tempered chocolate on parchment paper, and allow to almost set.
3. Cut the chocolate into 2-inch squares.
4. Assemble five squares with tempered chocolate to create a box shape with a bottom.

COOKIES

BREADS

SOUFFLES

CREPES

ICE CREAM

SORBETS

CHOCOLATE

OTHERS: FINISHED

MISCELLANEOUS

PASTRY TECHNIQUES:
Chopping, Melting, Mixing

Chopping:
1. Use a sharp knife.
2. Hold the food product properly.
3. Cut with a quick downward motion.

Melting:
1. Prepare the food product to be melted.
2. Place the food product in an appropriately sized pot over direct heat or over a double boiler.
3. Stir frequently or occasionally, depending on the delicacy of the product, until melted.
OR
1. Place the product on a sheet pan or in a bowl, and place in a low-temperature oven until melted.

Mixing:
1. Follow the proper mixing procedure: creaming, blending, whipping, or combination.

HAACP:
Store at 60° F to 65° F.

Chocolate Paste No. 1

Modeling Chocolate

INGREDIENTS:

For Dark Paste:

Dark chocolate	2 parts
Glucose	1 part

For Milk Paste:

Milk chocolate	2½ parts
Glucose	1 part

For White Paste:

White chocolate	3 parts
Glucose	1 part

METHOD OF PREPARATION:

1. Gather the equipment and ingredients.
2. Chop the chocolate into fine pieces.
3. Melt the chocolate in a double boiler to 100° F.
4. In a separate pan, heat the glucose to 100° F.
5. Combine the chocolate and glucose well.
6. Spread the mixture 1-inch to 1½-inches thick on parchment paper.
7. Cover tightly with plastic wrap; make sure no moisture collects on the surface; otherwise, modeling chocolate will not dry.
8. Before using, let the modeling chocolate rest in the refrigerator overnight.

Chocolate Paste No. 2

Modeling Chocolate, Stronger

YIELD: 1 pound, 8 ounces.

INGREDIENTS:

Simple syrup (1:1 ratio) (see page 415)	3 ounces
Glucose	5 ounces
Dark chocolate, tempered	1 pound

METHOD OF PREPARATION:

1. Gather the equipment and ingredients.
2. Bring the simple syrup to a boil.
3. Add the glucose to the simple syrup.
4. Cool the mixture to 95° F.
5. Add the cooled mixture to the tempered chocolate, and mix until well blended; use a metal or wooden spoon.
6. Spread the mixture 1-inch to 1½-inches thick on parchment paper.
7. Cover tightly with plastic wrap; make sure no moisture collects on the surface of chocolate; otherwise, modeling chocolate will not dry.
8. Before using, let the modeling chocolate rest in the refrigerator overnight.

PASTRY TECHNIQUES:
Boiling, Mixing

Boiling:
1. Bring the cooking liquid to a rapid boil.
2. Stir the contents.

Mixing:
1. Follow the proper mixing procedure: creaming, blending, whipping, or combination.

HACCP:
Store at 60° F to 65° F.

Marzipan

Mixing:

1. Follow the proper mixing procedure: creaming, blending, whipping, or combination.

Kneading:

1. Prepare the kneeding surface with the appropriate medium (flour, cornstarch, etc.).
2. Press and form the dough into a mass using soft, determined strokes.
3. Continue kneading until appropriate consistency and/or temperature is achieved.

HACCP:

Store at 60° F to 65° F.

YIELD:		2 pounds, 8 ounces.	5 pounds.
INGREDIENTS:			
Sugar, confectionery	1 pound		2 pounds
Almond paste	1 pound		2 pounds
Fondant	4 ounces		8 ounces
Glucose	4 ounces		8 ounces

METHOD OF PREPARATION:

1. Gather the equipment and ingredients.
2. Place the ingredients in a mixing bowl in this order: confectionery sugar, almond paste, fondant, and glucose.
3. Mix with a paddle until the mixture is combined.
4. Remove from the mixer.
5. Knead the mixture, working it into one piece.
6. Place it in a plastic bag to avoid its becoming dry.

CHEF NOTES:

1. Instead of using a mixer to combine ingredients, your hands may be used.
2. If an almond paste, which contains a high percentage of glucose, is used, reduce or omit the glucose listed in the formula to obtain the desired consistency.

COOKIES
BREADS
SOUFFLES
CREPES
ICE CREAM
SORBETS
CHOCOLATE
OTHERS: FINISHED
MISCELLANEOUS

Pastillage

YIELD: 4 pounds, 10 ounces.

INGREDIENTS:

Gelatin	¾ ounce
Water, cold	9 ounces
Sugar, confectionery	3 pounds, 8 ounces
Cornstarch	8 ounces
Cream of tartar	¼ ounce

METHOD OF PREPARATION:

1. Gather the equipment and ingredients.
2. Place the gelatin in a dry bowl.
3. Pour half of the water over the gelatin, and let the gelatin bloom.
4. Sift all of the dry ingredients together, and place them in a mixing bowl.
5. Dissolve the gelatin over a double boiler; keep the sides clean to avoid specks of gelatin in the pastillage.
6. Once the gelatin has dissolved completely, add the remaining cold water.
7. Heat the gelatin mixture to 110° F. (This will give you enough time to mix the dry ingredients together before the gelatin sets.)
8. Immediately pour the hot gelatin mixture on top of the dry ingredients in a mixing bowl. (When pouring the gelatin, do not hit the sides of the bowl, or specks will remain in the final product.)
9. Using a paddle, mix on low speed; scrape the bowl and paddle often until the mixture is a pliable, smooth paste.
10. Remove from the mixer.
11. Place the paste on a clean table dusted with sifted cornstarch or confectionery sugar.
12. Knead on the table until the mixture is combined; finish smoothing out the paste by working it between the hands while it is off the table. *Do not overlap* the pastillage as in kneading bread dough, because this will cause large air bubbles to incorporate into the paste.
13. The pastillage is ready for use. (If pastillage is stored, wrap it tightly in plastic so that no air will reach the dough.)

PASTRY TECHNIQUES:
Mixing, Kneading

Mixing:
1. Follow the proper mixing procedure: creaming, blending, whipping, or combination.

Kneading:
1. Prepare the kneading surface with the appropriate medium (flour, cornstarch, etc.).
2. Press and form the dough into a mass using soft, determined strokes.
3. Continue kneading until appropriate consistency and/or temperature is achieved.

HACCP:
Store at 60° F to 65° F.

CHEF NOTES:
1. More or less water may be required to obtain the proper consistency.
2. If the pastillage has been stored, warm it slightly to regain pliability.

Rolled Fondant

(Massa Ticino/Austrian Fondant)

YIELD: 10 pounds, 6 ounces.

INGREDIENTS:

Gelatin	1 ounce
Water, cold	9 ounces
Sugar, confectionery	8 pounds
Glucose	1 pound, 6 ounces
Glycerin	2 ounces
Shortening, all-purpose, melted (120° F)	4 ounces
Sugar, confectionery, additional	As needed
Cornstarch	As needed

METHOD OF PREPARATION:

1. Gather the equipment and ingredients.
2. Bloom the gelatin in cold water.
3. Sift the confectionery sugar, and place it in a mixing bowl; make a well in the center.
4. Heat the gelatin over a double boiler until it is completely dissolved.
5. Add the glucose and glycerin to the melted gelatin.
6. Stir the shortening into this mixture, and heat until it reaches 110° F, stirring constantly.
7. Pour the gelatin mixture immediately into the well in the confectionery sugar without pouring down the sides of the bowl; avoid making the gelatin set, which causes small specks in the final product.
8. Mix with a paddle at low speed; scrape, as needed, until a soft, white, pliable dough forms.
9. Remove from the mixer, and place on a table dusted with a mixture of equal parts of confectionery sugar and cornstarch.
10. Knead by hand until smooth.
11. The rolled fondant can be used immediately or stored, wrapped tightly, in a plastic bag.

PASTRY TECHNIQUES:
Mixing, Kneading

Mixing:
1. Follow the proper mixing procedure: creaming, blending, whipping, or combination.

Kneading:
1. Prepare the kneading surface with the appropriate medium (flour, cornstarch, etc.).
2. Press and form the dough into a mass using soft, determined strokes.
3. Continue kneading until appropriate consistency and/or temperature is achieved.

HACCP:
Store at 60° F to 65° F.

CHEF NOTE:
This fondant is used to cover cakes and to make showpieces. More or less water may be required to obtain the proper consistency.

COOKIES
BREADS
SOUFFLES
CREPES
ICE CREAM
SORBETS
CHOCOLATE
OTHERS: FINISHED
MISCELLANEOUS

Crystal Sugar

YIELD: 8 pounds, 7⅛ ounces.

PASTRY TECHNIQUES:
Boiling, Crystallizing

Boiling:
1. Bring the cooking liquid to a rapid boil.
2. Stir the contents.

Crystallizing:
1. Boil the product for 30 seconds to 2 minutes.
2. Drain the water; cook until tender and translucent.
3. Strain the sugar syrup.
4. Dredge the product; dry on a screen.

INGREDIENTS:

Sugar, granulated	6 pounds, 1 ounce
Water	2 pounds, 6⅞ ounces

METHOD OF PREPARATION:

1. Gather the equipment and ingredients.
2. Combine the sugar and water; bring to a rolling boil; cook to 33° to 35° Baumé.
3. Pour the mixture into a clean plastic container, and let cool.
4. After dipping a skewer in simple syrup, place it in granulated sugar; let it dry. Another option is to put a piece of marzipan at the end of a string.
5. Suspend the skewer in the sugar syrup; do not touch the bottom or the sides; cover air tight, and let set for a few weeks. Large sugar crystals will form around the skewer.

CHEF NOTE:
The sugar crystals can be used as a textured addition in a sugar showpiece.

PASTRY TECHNIQUES:
Caramelizing, Mixing, Rolling,
  Shaping

Caramelizing:
Wet method:
1. Use an extremely clean pot.
2. Place the sugar and water on high
   heat.
3. Never stir the mixture once the
   sugar begins to dissolve.
4. Once caramelized, shock in ice
   water.

Mixing:
1. Follow the proper mixing procedure: creaming, blending, whipping, or combination.

Rolling:
1. Prepare the rolling surface by
   dusting with the appropriate medium (flour, cornstarch, etc.).
2. Use the appropriate style pin
   (stick pin or ball bearing pin) to
   roll the dough to desired thickness; rotate the dough during rolling to prevent sticking.

Shaping:
1. Prepare the medium to be
   shaped.
2. Prepare the surface area for shaping.
3. Mold medium into desired shapes
   according to the instructor's directions.

HACCP:
Store at 60° F to 65° F.

Nougat/Crouquant

YIELD: 3 pounds, 9 ounces.   2, ⅝-inch Bowls.

INGREDIENTS:

Almonds, blanched, sliced	1 pound
Sugar, granulated	2 pounds
Lemon juice	1 ounce
Glucose	8 ounces

METHOD OF PREPARATION:

1. Gather equipment and ingredients.
2. Toast the almonds and keep them warm.
3. In a heavy copper pot, place 8 ounces of the granulated sugar over
   medium heat. Stirring constantly, melt sugar to golden brown.
4. Add another 8 ounces of the sugar and repeat the same procedure.
5. Add the remaining sugar with the lemon juice and glucose.
6. When the mixture has reached a golden brown color, remove from heat;
   add the almonds.
7. Pour mixture onto an oiled marble slab, or place between oiled parchment
   paper; roll out and cut to desired shape.
8. Mold over lightly oiled surface to prevent nougat from sticking.
9. Adhere pieces with caramelized sugar.
10. Store in a dry place.

Poured Sugar

YIELD: 6 pounds, 12 ounces.

COOKIES

BREADS

SOUFFLES

CREPES

ICE CREAM

SORBETS

CHOCOLATE

OTHERS: FINISHED

MISCELLANEOUS

PASTRY TECHNIQUES:

Simmering, Mixing, Boiling,
  Washing, Shocking, Pouring

Simmering:
1. Place the prepared product in an appropriate-sized pot.
3. Bring the product to a boil, then reduce the heat to allow the product to barely boil.
4. Cook until desired doneness is achieved.

Mixing:
1. Follow the proper mixing procedure: creaming, blending, whipping, or combination.

Boiling:
1. Bring the cooking liquid to a rapid boil.
2. Stir the contents.

Washing:
1. Brush or spray the product to the desired saturation.
2. Do not under- or oversaturate.

Shocking:
Dipping the copper pot in an ice water bath to stop the medium from boiling.

Pouring:
1. Place the product in an appropriate container for pouring: a pitcher or large ladle.
2. Pour the product into desired containers or over another product.

HACCP:
Store at 60° F to 65° F.

CHEF NOTE:
Up to 2 drops of tartaric acid can be added to each pound of sugar to decrease the chance of crystallization during the pouring. Add the acid after the sugar has been shocked. It is important to note that acid will make the set sugar more sensitive to moisture (hygroscopic) and shorten its shelf life.

INGREDIENTS:

Sugar, granulated	4 pounds
Water	2 pounds
Glucose	12 ounces
Coloring, food, and/or white-white (optional)	As needed

METHOD OF PREPARATION:

1. Gather the equipment and ingredients.
2. Mix the sugar and water in a copper pot; put it on low heat; stir occasionally.
3. Remove the foam that appears on top of the simmering sugar.
4. When it comes to a boil, add the glucose.
5. Turn up the heat.
6. Boil the sugar solution; occasionally wash down the inner side of the pot with a brush and water.
7. Cook to 309° F (154° C).
8. Once the sugar has been cooked, dip the pot in a bowl of cold water until the sugar stops to boil.
9. Color the sugar, as desired.
10. Reheat the sugar to a nice fluid consistency.
11. Pour the sugar into prepared molds.

PASTRY TECHNIQUES:

Simmering, Mixing, Boiling, Washing, Measuring Temperature, Pouring, Folding, Stretching, Pulling

Simmering:

1. Place the prepared product in an appropriate-sized pot.
3. Bring the product to a boil, then reduce the heat to allow the product to barely boil.
4. Cook until desired doneness is achieved.

Mixing:

1. Follow the proper mixing procedure: creaming, blending, whipping, or combination.

Boiling:

1. Bring the cooking liquid to a rapid boil.
2. Stir the contents.

Washing:

1. Brush or spray the product to the desired saturation.
2. Do not under- or oversaturate.

Pouring:

1. Place the product in an appropriate container for pouring: a pitcher or large ladle.
2. Pour the product into desired containers or over another product.

Folding:

Do steps 1, 2, and 3 in one continuous motion.
1. Run a bowl scraper under the mixture, across the bottom of the bowl.
2. Turn the bowl counterclockwise.
3. Bring the bottom mixture to the top.

Stretching:

1. Cover the surface area with a clean pastry cloth.
2. First roll the dough with pin.
3. Use the back of your hands to stretch the dough.

Pulling:

1. Pay attention; do not get distracted.
2. Sugar must be at an even temperature.
3. Work with clean equipment and hands.

Pulled Sugar

YIELD: 6 pounds, 13 ounces.

INGREDIENTS:

Sugar, granulated	4 pounds
Water	2 pounds
Glucose	13 ounces
Tartaric acid	15 drops
Coloring, food (optional)	As needed

METHOD OF PREPARATION:

1. Gather the equipment and ingredients.
2. Mix the sugar and water in a copper pot; put it on low heat; stir occasionally.
3. Remove the foam that appears on the top of the simmering sugar.
4. When it comes to a boil, add the glucose and 5 drops of tartaric acid.
5. Turn up the heat.
6. Boil the sugar solution; occasionally wash down the inner side of the pot with a brush and water.
7. At 280° F (137° C), add 10 drops of acid, and cook to 315° F to 320° F (157° C to 160° C).
8. Once the sugar has been cooked, pour it onto a very clean, lightly oiled, marble tabletop. (If different colors are to be made from one batch, the sugar can be poured into different sections and each portion tinted with food color, as desired. If only one color is desired, the sugar may be tinted during cooking.)
9. Using a lightly oiled bench scraper, quickly flip the edge of the sugar toward the center. As the sugar flows again, repeat this procedure until the sugar is firm enough to be handled by hand. Fold the sugar with its cold side (the side that was against the marble) inside. Fold it several times, until the sugar stops spreading.
10. Taking the sugar in both hands, stretch and fold it back together.
11. Repeat the stretching-folding technique until the sugar is opaque and silky.
12. Fold the sugar together to a bowl shape, and place it under a heating unit (heat lamp). The sugar should rest, for example, on a piece of PVC, canvas, silk, 100% polyester, or silpat. (Under these conditions, the sugar is kept soft and pliable).
13. It is ready to be shaped into various shapes and forms.

HACCP:

Store at 60° F to 65° F.

CHEF NOTE:

If the sugar is too soft and does not hold its shape well after being cold, decrease the amount of acid (second amount added, step 7) by a few drops.

Index